MAX WEBER

MAX WEBER

Politics and the Spirit of Tragedy

JOHN PATRICK DIGGINS

BASIC
BOOKS
A Member of the Perseus Books Group

Copyright © 1996 by John Patrick Diggins.
Published by Basic Books,
A Member of the Perseus Books Group.

Designed by Elliott Beard

Library of Congress Cataloging-in-Publication Data

Diggins, John P.
    Max Weber : politics and the spirit of tragedy / John Patrick
    Diggins—1st ed.
        p.   cm.
    Includes bibliographical references and index.
    ISBN 0-465-01750-9 (cloth)   0-465-00724-4 (pbk)
        1. Weber, Max 1864–1920.   2. Social scientists—Biography.
    3. Social sciences—Methodology.   4. Social sciences—Philosophy.
    I. Title.
H59.W4D54   1996
301'.092—dc20   96-1616
[B]   CIP

98 99 00 01 ❖/RRD 9 8 7 6 5 4 3 2 1

To Elizabeth

Contents

I am ashamed to think how easily we capitulate to badges and names, to large societies and dead institutions.

Ralph Waldo Emerson, "Self Reliance" (1841)

———

History records more frequent and more spectacular instances of the triumph of imbecile institutions over life and culture . . .

Thorstein Veblen, Instinct of Workmanship *(1914)*

———

When I was over there in 1904, the question American students asked me more than any other was how formal duels are arranged in Germany and how people go about getting their scars. They thought it a chivalrous institution; this was the sport they had to have too.

Max Weber, "Socialism" (1918)

———

I had a remarkable dream last night. We were together at Max Weber's. You, Hannah, arrived late, were warmly welcomed. . . . He had just returned from a world trip, had brought back political documents and artworks, particularly from the Far East. He gave us some of them, you the best ones because you understand more of politics than I.

Shouldn't you perhaps reread Max Weber on the archetypes (and on other things too)? So that, if something of the old "total" underlying view of history should remain in your text even this last trace will disappear? . . . All of us today are still inclined, in the intellectual atmosphere created by Hegel and Marx and still not abandoned by Spengler and Toynbee, to nibble instinctively at the crumbs of the false grandeur that was loaded onto history once that grandeur was stolen from God.

Karl Jaspers to Hannah Arendt, April 20, 1950

———

Prompted by your letter I've read a lot of Max Weber lately. I felt so idiotically flattered by it that I was ashamed of myself. Weber's intellectual sobriety is impossible to match, at least for me. With me there's always something dogmatic left hanging around somewhere. (That's what you get when Jews start writing history.)

Hannah Arendt to Karl Jaspers, June 25, 1950

Preface

Although known primarily as the author of the seminal *The Protestant Ethic and the Spirit of Capitalism*, Max Weber had a far-ranging curiosity: he thought about topics as varied as Russian peasants and Oklahoma Indians; types of authority throughout history and possibilities of freedom in an age of bureaucracy; the mystical animism of nonwestern religions and the despiritualizing mechanisms of western rationalism; a theory of politics that emphasized leadership and ethical responsibility and a theory of scientific inquiry that cautioned against ethical intrusions; ancient Judaism and the Torah and modern women and the erotic. No other social scientist explored so many subjects with a mind so restless and rich, and the teacher of American history cannot help but see his overriding relevance to America's own political culture and economic and social institutions.

By no means is this work a detailed biography, much less a "life and times" narrative of Weber and his world. Such works await scholars more knowledgeable in this area than I. The present text might be described as an appreciative study of a social scientist who knew and

liked America, one whose mind was sustained by what Ralph Waldo
Emerson had earlier discerned in the German intellect—"a controlling
sincerity."[1] Weber became intrigued by America as a prospect, a country whose historical development foreshadowed the fate of modern
industrial society. In Benjamin Franklin Weber saw a key to America's
national character, and it was with "a controlling sincerity" that he
tried to explain the meaning of Franklin in relation to an older Protestant moral sense that had brought forth the world of capitalism.

D. H. Lawrence, a contemporary who knew Weber through the circle that surrounded the notorious von Richthofen sisters, and who
shared some of Weber's mental symptoms and antipatriarchical sentiments, presented Americans with an entirely different portrait of
Franklin shortly after Weber's death in 1920. Franklin, Lawrence wrote
in *Studies in Classic American Literature*, authored all the "shalt-not
moralisms" that left Americans fearful and repressed, driven by the
addictions of a Puritan culture and its cult of production. " 'Work, you
free jewel, WORK!' shouts the liberator, cracking his whip. Benjamin,
I will not work. I do not choose to be a free democrat." Franklin left
an ambitious America in bondage to the "muck-heap" of money and
the siren of success. Lawrence wondered, "What's wrong with Benjamin, that we can't stand him? Or else, what's wrong with us, that we
find fault with such a paragon?"[2]

A study of Weber enables Americans to answer both questions,
although not without ambiguity.

A term many Weberian scholars use to illuminate the tensions in
Weber's mind and thought is "antinomie," the unavoidable opposition between principles that are essential to life yet antagonistic
to one another.[3] Part of Weber's appeal to this conspicuously non-
German author is the way his antinomies resemble many of the
dualisms in America's own divided identity. On the one side, we have
Thomas Jefferson's Declaration of Independence and its proclama-
tions of freedom and equality, values that reach an apotheosis in Walt
Whitman and his poetry of democracy and find modern expression
in John Dewey and the philosophy of pragmatism. On the other side,
we are reminded of Calvinism and the Constitution and the *Federalist* authors with their warnings about sin and uncontrolled power,
apprehensions that reach an apotheosis in Herman Melville and the
dilemmas of authority and find modern expression in Reinhold
Niebuhr and the ironies of history. The New England Transcendentalists characterized these dualisms as dividing America between the
"party of hope" and the "party of memory." Perhaps it is no coinci-

dence that Weber had been nurtured on America's Transcendentalist theology.

Weber's tolerance for ambiguity deriving from his antinomic imagination reveals a rare sensibility. Weber enables us to feel a tragic gulf between the real and the ideal, between adaptation and aspiration, between the common facts of natural existence and the yearnings of spirit. "Man would not have attained the possible," Weber wrote, "unless time and again he had reached out for the impossible."[4] In the nineteenth century many romantic writers, in America and England as well as Germany, found fault with the Enlightenment for inventing elaborate intellectual schemes in order to turn the chaotic and unanalyzable into systems whose coherence proved more confining than liberating. We are hardly surprised that Weber's ability to live with unresolved contradictions invokes what John Keats called "negative capability," which the poet defined as "an ability to remain in mysteries, uncertainties, and doubts, without any irritable reaching after fact or reason."[5] Weber saw that reason and analysis undermines value and meaning, as a consequence of "the fate of an epoch which has eaten of the tree of knowledge," thereby bringing about the "disenchantment of the world."[6] Once we know that our beliefs and values have formed in response to our own needs and interests, that they had been forged rather than derived from something sacred or authoritative, why should we believe them? Many nineteenth-century thinkers, from Nathaniel Hawthorne to Friedrich Nietzsche, understood that a determination to know, probe, and dissect leaves the mind estranged from the universe. The poet's refrain that the "tree of knowledge has killed the tree of life" foreshadowed the modernist fear that the liberated mind can create the conditions for that which is its own negation. "Art is the tree of knowledge," wrote William Blake; "science is the tree of death."[7] Weber would juxtapose charisma to rationalization to dramatize the divided nature of human action that knowledge was helpless to unify. Knowing the limits of knowledge, Weber stoically faced the loss of truth and objectivity, and it was his genius that he could still work out a rational theory of ethics and responsibility.

Today the poststructuralist critic might be tempted to deconstruct Weber's antinomies by demonstrating that they are nothing more than "binary oppositions," rhetorical constructions that have no basis beyond language. Weber would have had little patience with the recent "linguistic turn" in modern thought. For Weber reality was existential, not simply textual, and the dualisms he discerned had less to do with verbal description than with a human condition that must face irreconcilable choices, moral decisions in an immoral world, a world too irrational even for the rational reassurances of rhetoric.

The antinomic tensions in Weber's anguished mind and thought are real, and they resemble the tensions that divide America, especially the tension between nationalism and authority on the one side, and individualism and freedom on the other. There is the Hamiltonian Weber, the thinker who believed in the importance of the nation-state and looked to leadership to find what could not be found in democracy, especially the capacity to think with conviction and act with responsibility; the patriot who resented the domination of a country by reactionary rural elites and thus sought to replace the power of the Prussian Junker class with conscious national purpose; the antiformalist who denied that government could be understood in respect to its ends but instead only in respect to the means used to enforce its will; and the realist who saw revolution in twentieth-century Russia as delusionary, just as Alexander Hamilton had seen revolution in eighteenth-century France. There is also the Emersonian Weber, the thinker who believed in individual autonomy, self-reliance, and resistance to comfortable adaptation and conformity; the moralist who protested government succumbing to the cunning of politics; and the restless humanist who saw passion as the precondition of perception. What threatened passion was a life of quiet regulation in which individuals allow themselves to be submerged into institutions. In the struggle of the individual against institutions, what redeems the world is the rise of the semi-miraculous authority of Weber's "charismatic" figure. Ralph Waldo Emerson called such a figure the "genius" of greatness surpassing understanding. "The world is awed before the great and subdued without knowing why," he wrote. While Weber worried that bureaucratic domination would mean the "castration of charisma," Emerson worried that democratic society would have its revenge upon genius.[8]

The relevance of Weber to contemporary America goes beyond these possible Hamiltonian and Emersonian affinities. Today five issues confront America that Weber had confronted almost a century ago: the future of capitalism in a world no longer moved by "spirit"; the possibility of understanding politics when the rhetoric of democracy is mistaken for the reality of history; the tendency to turn to science and technology with the hope that freedom will survive the coils of organization and rationalization; the temptation to respond to modernity and the crisis of knowledge and authority, specifically the shocks of doubt and disbelief that lead to relativism and the loss of innocence, by believing that a country can return to the values of its past; and the long-held assumption that America is unique and exceptional and thus happily escapes the evils of the old world.

Weber's antinomic imagination deserves to be appreciated in an American political culture almost innocent of irony and tragedy.[9] One consequence of that innocence has been the assumption that democracy, morality, and science are harmonious and reinforce one another, thereby rendering antinomies reconcilable and problems of values soluble. That assumption has little basis in American history. Here democracy proved incapable of solving the problem of slavery, the most morally agonizing reality facing America, and it is worth remembering that Abraham Lincoln could confront the issue effectively because he avoided drawing upon Jefferson's "scientific" approach to the concept of equality. Yet the dilemmas Lincoln faced were essentially Weberian antinomies, and the differences Lincoln had with the abolitionists resembled the differences Weber had with the pacifists, as did their positions on the tension between democracy and morality. The debates Lincoln staged with Stephen Douglas later resonate in Weber's famous address, "Politics as a Vocation."

In those debates Douglas held that the issue of slavery was too important to be left to moralists, abolitionists, and particularly to statesmen like Lincoln; instead it should be left up to the people themselves, resolved democratically by means of "popular sovereignty." When Lincoln responded that the people do not have a right to do wrong, he was on shaky ground democratically. Yet in Weberian terms he was bringing an ethics of conviction (*Gessinnungsethik*) to bear on politics. Later, during the midst of the Civil War, when he acknowledged that he was willing to tolerate slavery confined to the South in order to preserve the Union, he was practicing an ethics of responsibility (*Verantwortungsethik*) that looks to practical consequences regardless of moral intention. The decision to go to war itself can hardly be comprehended in democratic terms. The majority of Northern electors who cast their vote for Lincoln never had in mind a war in 1860, either to liberate the slaves or to save the Union. But with the secession crisis, when Lincoln resorted to calling upon arms and weapons to put down the Confederacy, and thereby resolving once and for all where sovereignty lay, he was dramatizing what would be Weber's dictum that a state proves itself as a sovereign state by demonstrating that it has an overwhelming monopoly on the legitimate use of physical force.

Both Weber and Lincoln looked upon history as ironic and tragic. Weber learned from Jacob Burkhardt what Lincoln had learned from Shakespeare and the Bible: politics cannot rise to spiritual redemption, for it must collaborate with power and its corruptions, and thus there can be "no relish of salvation in it."[10] Yet what Weber called the "diabolical forces" of history must be confronted, and in a democracy that refuses to face evil, power may have to do the work of morality. The slave status of black Americans in the South had been incorporated into state laws constituted by democratic majorities. Lincoln tried to appeal to the Declaration of Independence and the Bible to awaken America to the "sin" of slavery. Ultimately, freeing African Americans required the Union army conquering a section of the country too proud to absorb the "spirit" of capitalism.

"All historical evaluation," instructed Weber, "includes a 'contemplative' element."[11] Not since the *Federalist* has an author enabled Americans to contemplate the meaning of power.

———

I wish to thank Dr. Karl-Ludwig Ay, director of the Weber Archivum in der Bayerischen Akademie der Wissenschaften, for his help in locating research materials; Edith Hanke for similar assistance; Steven Fraser, Ann Klefstad, and Michael Wilde for editorial advice; Kenneth Barkan for some helpful criticisms; Christina von Koehler for help with translations; and the National Endowment for the Humanities for a travel fellowship making possible research in Europe.

———

This book is dedicated to Elizabeth Harlan: fellow writer, thoughtful critic, dearest friend.

MAX WEBER

—

Green Bay

Canandaigua
Niagara Falls
Saginaw
Albany
Boston
Pontiac
Buffalo
Auburn
Newport
Detroit
Hartford
Chicago
New York

Baltimore
Philadelphia
Louisville
Cincinnati
St. Louis
Washington
UNITED STATES

Norfolk
Mt. Airy
Nashville
Memphis

Oklahoma

Montgomery
Tuskegee

ATLANTIC OCEAN

New Orleans

N

Tocqueville and Weber in America

Tocqueville's Route ━━━━━
Weber's Route ┄┄┄┄┄

MILES
0   100   200   300

Cal Sacks

Introduction

AMERICA'S TWO VISITORS:
TOCQUEVILLE AND WEBER

Acommon assumption holds that the best and most reliable guide to an interpretation of America is the Frenchman Alexis de Tocqueville and his great classic, *Democracy in America*. Max Weber never wrote a book on America; in fact, all his writings first appeared as articles in scholarly journals and were only later collected as books. But many of his thoughts on America, some based on his trip to the United States in 1904, can be culled from his various writings, wartime journalism, and correspondence, most of which is being published with such commendable Germanic editorial and annotational thoroughness that his oeuvre will be unavailable for years to come.

The trips that Tocqueville and Weber took to America are separated by three-quarters of a century, yet they traveled over many of the same routes (see map) and came away with many of the same impressions about this new nation and new people forming across the Atlantic. Toc-

1

queville confronted a rural society that seemed inchoate, lacking any organizing principles; Weber an industrial society integrated and succumbing to systematic procedures of organization and regulation. The chronological distance that separated their observations led each to see a different America. Tocqueville emphasized democracy, individualism, and equality of conditions; Weber bureaucracy, institutions, and hierarchy of status and power. One could say that Tocqueville told us what America was and Weber what America became.

Despite their different perspectives, the French scholar and his later German counterpart both discerned the relationship of religious liberty to political liberty and the importance of religion in the founding of America. "For my part," wrote Tocqueville, "I more easily understand a man animated at the same time both by religious passion and political passion than by political passion and the passion for well-being. The first two can hold together and be embraced in the same soul, but not the second two. . . . It is religious passion that pushed the Puritans to America and led them to want to govern themselves there." Where American historians would emphasize the frontier and the material environment as the key to explaining America's success, Tocqueville recognized, as would Weber, that convictions reshape conditions: "I have said before that I regarded the origins of the Americans, what I have called their point of departure, as the first and most effective of all the elements leading to their present prosperity. . . . When I consider all that has resulted from this first fact, I think I can see the whole destiny of America contained in the first Puritan who landed on those shores, as that of the whole human race in the first man."

Tocqueville is almost Freudian in believing that the fate of a national character is determined at birth and early childhood, or as he put it, "in the cradle." Hence people "always bear some marks of their origin." Religiosity is destiny: "It was religion that gave birth to the English colonies in America. One must never forget that."[1]

In seeing the relationship of religion to economics and self-government, Tocqueville and Weber saw the relationship of ideals and culture to history and society. In American history the roots of freedom establish themselves prior to politics and social development. Both Weber and Tocqueville believed that a politics without culture and moral sensibility would be little more than the private cupidity of capitalism realizing itself through public means.

Weber and Tocqueville knew that it was the conscience-fired Protestant work ethic that explained America's early character and development, and only a country sufficiently fortunate to have skipped the feudal stage of history would have no aristocracy to disdain labor as a way of life. But what explained America's blessed beginnings may prove inadequate in sustaining her through history.

In seizing upon Ben Franklin as the embodiment of a Protestant ethic about to become secularized—a transitional figure symbolizing the shift from austere Calvinism to Yankee capitalism—Weber was recording what would come to represent certain basic aspects of the American character. He was also reinforcing Tocqueville's observation that in America the seat of authority had moved from church and state to lodge itself in society and public opinion—at least temporarily, for Weber would show that authority ultimately finds its home in the impersonal structure of organized institutions.

Franklin was a mutant, a new species of man who expected to live without authority in a new society of liberal individualism. Traditionally, authority came down from either church or state, and both institutions would see to it that people subdued their "passions and interests" for the sake of either God or country. As Weber recognized, Franklin's *Autobiography* undermines all historical authority. Franklin depicts himself as a self-made man, an achiever who needs no one and is on his own economically, politically, and religiously. But Franklin does need society. The *Autobiography* is an exercise in self-presentation, and Weber sees that Franklin works hard to achieve reputation and social status almost the way the older Puritans worked hard to achieve the salvation of their souls. With Franklin the pursuit of material happiness is rationalized by devotion to public affairs and civic responsibility. Had the American character kept Franklin's vision of a model American citizen, where a sense of public virtue could still check the attractions of interests, Tocqueville would have been pleased and Weber astonished to see the survival of the Protestant ethic. Such was not to be, however, as the young American republic began its descent into democracy.

The expression "descent" is used here to counter the conventional story of American democracy as a "rise," an expression familiar to every youth who had to read high school history textbooks along with saying the pledge of allegiance. In college today the student receives a different message: if democracy arose to lift up the "common man," it did not rise sufficiently high to withstand the coming of capitalism, the emerging "market revolution" that eventually led to concentrations of economic power that thwarted democracy and the will of the people.[2] Weber and Tocqueville, one needs to be reminded, saw liberal capitalism as the natural expression of liberal democracy. Rather than resisting a market economy supposedly imposed upon them, the American people demanded it when they elected Andrew Jackson and cheered his smashing the national Bank of the United States in order to offer his schemes for turning the loaning and borrowing of money over to local communities. Capitalism and democracy may have been entirely compatible, but the peculiar nature of mass democracy in America could jeopardize freedom and start modern society on what both Weber and Tocqueville regarded as the new "road to servitude."[3] How could democracy itself pose a threat to freedom?

Tocqueville worried that the excesses of individualism would turn Americans inward toward self-gratification, and the lack of public virtue would lead to political indifference, social conformity, and submission to the "tyranny" of majority opinion, a kind of creeping, quiet docility that could possibly culminate in "democratic despotism." Weber worried about an opposite tendency. As though he had Tocqueville in mind, Weber observed that those who feared too much democracy and saw society as nothing more than a "sandpile" of atomistic individuals were failing to see its more integrating forces. Instead of turning inward to the private sphere of life, people turn to government to demand this and that, asserting rights that require protections and interests that demand to be served, and such popular pressures transform the state into an expanding administrative monstrosity. When people live not for politics but off it, democracy begets bureaucracy.[4]

To be liberated from the past offers no guarantees for the future. Just as Tocqueville was happy to see France rid itself of an antiquated aristocracy, so too would Weber delight in seeing Germany free itself from the rule of the Prussian Junker class. But the specter of egalitarian democracy in America posed new problems in political philosophy as well as historical reality. Democracy may bring about a leveling of class distinctions and an improved equalization of social relations, but would bourgeois democracy make man free? Both Weber and Tocqueville equated freedom with autonomy and the voice of conscience, and thus freedom meant not simply liberty and political rights but dignity and moral responsibility for one's own actions. Democracy could well sap the spirit of independence and lead the country to sacrifice conviction to comfort, thereby producing a "happy mediocrity" in the people and a government without "virility and greatness."[5]

The problem of American history is, in both Tocqueville's bourgeois republic and Weber's bureaucratic society, the problem of consciousness. Americans are depicted as active but unreflective, possessed of energy but frantic with worry as they become preoccupied with material well-being. "Why the Americans Are Often So Restless in the Midst of Their

Prosperity" is the title of one of Tocqueville's chapters. He attributes this unease to a competitive environment of equality and achievement where everyone is always comparing him- or herself with others and where prosperity as a sign of status remains uncertain. Tocqueville worried that a culture of "virtuous materialism" would surrender its dedication to hard work and succumb to "pernicious materialism" as it became "absorbed in downright selfishness."[6] This phenomenon, whereby humanity gives its life over to chasing commodities in a culture that passes from production to consumption, would come to be called "reification" by twentieth-century Marxists (which will be discussed in connection with Weber's differences with his old Heidelberg visitor Georg Lukács). Both Tocqueville and later Marxists gave us gripping descriptions of this state of "alienation"; Weber also gives us an explanation.

Originating in religious angst, in the "inner loneliness" of feeling separate from God the Creator of all things, capitalism has its origins in the Puritan psyche, and it continues as a desperate effort to work and produce in order to wrest spiritual meaning from a world that, because of the Calvinist doctrine of predestination, is essentially meaningless. Eventually material success becomes confused with religious salvation and money takes on the quality of magic. For Weber this state of alienated existence is not simply a matter of "false consciousness." On the contrary, it suggests how the spirit of capitalism evolved from Protestant asceticism; how religious yearning in an irrational, predetermined, and theoretically uncontrollable world resulted in the will to control and determine what could never, in theological terms, be brought under rational mastery; and how a yearning to be at one with God is causally significant, even if God is dead, since it is that yearning that people act upon. Human striving reflects an inherent need to see a transcendent meaning in the world. Yet, ironically, as materialism replaces asceticism and older emotions atrophy, the more a culture strives, the further it is removed from its goals. Thus modern capitalism, which had its origins in moral discipline, ends up being little more than the gratification of interests and the pursuit of happiness. As work gradually becomes a compulsion instead of a "calling," the successor of the spiritualist becomes a sensualist without knowing it, and eventually leisure replaces labor as a sign of success. Weber died five years before F. Scott Fitzgerald published *The Great Gatsby* in 1925. In the novel the romance of money rules life with no immediate reference to work, and Gatsby yearns for a spiritual "Platonic conception" of himself as he sets out to capture love and beauty after having been brought up on Franklin's maxims about ambition and industry.

Can modern society enjoy the fruits of industry without the drives of ambition? What impressed Tocqueville about America was the admiration that labor commanded in the free states, in contrast to those below the Mason-Dixon line where slavery had stigmatized all forms of work. By the time Weber visited the United States the image of labor had lost status and the Protestant work ethic had all but gone to ashes. Yet at the same time a philosophy had been spreading in the western world that preached a new gospel according to Karl Marx. The Marxism that began to pervade the socialist-labor movements at the end of the nineteenth century rested on the assumption that industry and the fruits of labor could flourish without anything as antiquated as "bourgeois" ambition. The prospect of a social revolution made in the name of labor, a revolution "from below," as Weber put it, rested on the fantasy of renewal, on the hope that the future would restore what the movement of history had destroyed. But when Weber pondered the meaning of Russia and America in 1905, shortly after he had returned from the United States, he concluded that the origins of ideals that began in America, both economic and political, cannot be repeated in a Russia trying to break away from czardom and feudalism. The foundations of freedom, Weber lamented, are so contingent upon past circumstances that we may never again see the convergence of such a "constellation" of forces as that which had established human liberty.[7]

Tocqueville, like Weber, also became absorbed in what might be called the prospect of historical duplication, the question whether the revolutionary heritage of one country is applicable to another. At the outbreak of the French Revolution the Marquis de Lafayette assured Thomas Jefferson that the troubling events in Paris would end up emulating the American model, and thus what began in 1789 need not go wrong.[8] Tocqueville's investigations of America aimed at finding out what had indeed gone wrong, for the French Revolution, in placing all sovereignty in the people, the "general will," had gone disastrously wrong. The American framers of the Constitution thought they had eliminated the danger of the general will ("overbearing" popular factions) by dividing sovereignty and hence taming power. But Tocqueville saw that America had no ancien regime to contend with, and he believed that democracy succeeded not so much by confronting power as escaping from it. Significantly, when studying America, Tocqueville, like Weber, pays little attention to the writings and formal texts of political thinkers and focuses instead on differing conditions that set countries apart from one another. Haunted by the shadow of feudalism, Tocqueville sees little trace of it in America but feels its heavy presence elsewhere as he wonders whether America is exemplary or exceptional.

In *Democracy in America* Tocqueville also wonders about the future of Russia and America, as would Weber years later. "There are now two great nations in the world which, starting from different points, seem to be advancing toward the same goal: the Russians and the Anglo-Americans." Without specifying what that "goal" might be, Tocqueville describes both continental land masses as arising from obscurity to be expanding and marching "easily and quickly forward along a path whose end no eye can yet see." Different kinds of struggle are going on in each country: "The American fights against natural obstacles; the Russian is at grips with men. The former combats the wilderness and barbarism; the latter civilization, with all its arms. America's conquests are made with the plowshare, Russia's with the sword." The energy in one country is dispersed in democratic activity; in the other it is concentrated in the sphere of the tzar. Hence the principle of action in one country is freedom and in the other, servitude. "Their point of departure is different and their path so diverse; nevertheless each seems called by some secret design of Providence one day to hold in its hands the destinies of half the world."[9]

Did it hardly matter that America and Russia had profoundly different beginnings and different paths of development? For Weber a country's original "point of departure" all but fixed a country's historical destiny. Tocqueville also insisted on that point when he described religion as giving "birth" to America. But Puritan religion had nothing to do with Russia's remote birth and sluggish development. What did Tocqueville have in mind when he speculated that America and Russia were advancing toward the "same goal"?

Whatever he was thinking, Tocqueville's observation that America would not produce a "proletariat," a class-conscious mass of workers deprived of tools of trade and bereft of political freedoms, derived from his keen perception that America had no fixed class systems because it had bypassed the feudal stage of history. Hence in the new world labor would be valued and property looked upon as an acquisitive possibility in an open, democratic society lacking an aristocracy and ancien regime. This unique culture would render both Karl Marx and Edmund Burke irrelevant to America: the radical who looked to a proletariat to create a revolution and the conservative who looked to an aristocracy to preserve a tradition. America was "born" free and equal without having to endure the class struggles of the old world; it was a country of liberal individualism free of the dominating need to come to "grips with men" and the "arms" of the state.

Tocqueville made it clear why socialism and revolution itself would have little appeal in an America that lacked the oppressive conditions leading to such phenomena, and his analysis suggests why both would have an irresistible appeal in Russia, a country mired in feudal encumbrances, class structures, and autocratic traditions. But Weber, in contrast, analyzes the basic ethical premise of socialism, and he raised the question whether it could be achievable by virtue of being duplicable, whether it was actually capable of realization given the belated historical circumstances in which it was pursued. Arriving on the political scene long after Tocqueville, Weber confronted a revolutionary world driven by Marx's ideas. The Hegelian Marx had tried to change the world with an idea—the labor theory of value and the mystique of "praxis"—that had lost meaning even in attempting to interpret the world.

In Weber's estimate, Marx was trying to preserve the perishable by identifying action with the making of history. It is significant that Weber addresses this problem in his discussion of "natural right" (to be explored later in more detail), where the rights on which human freedoms are based presumably derived from nature—derived, that is, from a source whose values can neither be made nor alienated. Just as Tocqueville was steeped in Catholic Augustinian traditions, Weber had absorbed Calvinist tenets; both thinkers saw some historical connection between religion and labor.[10] But once modernity made the pursuit of self-interest legitimate, the possession of wealth had no necessary relation to work. Herewith the quandary. Could labor as a conscious value system survive the secularization of the world?

If the religion Marx rejected had once endowed labor with value and meaning, the science he advocated converted everything organically natural and genuinely spiritual into everything cultural and mechanical, routine forms of life whose images and representations made them seem natural and inevitable and thus to be accepted as permanent features of the human condition. Marx had looked to science as the means of overcoming alienation, when in reality science itself brings about the "disenchantment of the world." Weber's pondering over Leo Tolstoy's *The Death of Ivan Ilyich* helps us see that Marxists had yet to feel the acids of modernity. If there is no meaning in life without God, could there be any meaning in either labor or capital without spirit?[11]

"It is simply a myth that new dignity was given to labor," Weber observed. Weber deeply admired Marx, but he depicts later Marxists as tenaciously allowing themselves to be enchanted with the extinct. The Marxist, Weber wrote of the futile effort to bring socialism to tzarist Russia in 1905, assumes that the labor theory of value, having its origins in medieval craft society, can continue into the modern industrial age, where all values succumb to market forces. In the Christian conception, work stood for the wage of sin, an act of atonement that suggests necessity, affliction, and misery; and if work had more positive connotations in the earlier handicraft age, modern industrial life endows it with little moral significance. For a brief moment in history Calvinism compelled sin-struck believers into working hard so that economics at one time had an ethic and even a spiritual purpose, however wracked with anguish. But with the decline of religious belief, whose disappearance Marx had hailed, labor once again becomes drudgery since "the fulfillment of the calling cannot directly be related to the highest spiritual and cultural values." The sphere of economics is now related to little more than a "pursuit of wealth stripped of its religious and ethical meaning," Weber wrote in a concluding passage of the *Protestant Ethic*.[12]

The socialist revolution, declared Marx, "cannot draw its poetry from the past but only from the future." "Victorious capitalism," Weber could well have replied, needs no poetry since it rests on "mechanical foundations" lacking the spiritual ethos that once endowed labor with meaning and value, as Tocqueville saw it so valued north of the Ohio River in the 1830s, and as Marx valorized it in his Economic-Philosophic Manuscripts of 1844. But will labor ever again enjoy such significance? As Georges Bataille observed, the very "irrationality" that Weber discerned at the origins of capitalism holds true for the implications of socialism.[13] If work offers no rational way of attaining the salvation of the soul, how can it bring about the redemption of society? How can anything of intrinsic value survive modernity and the ravages of time and change in order that humanity can regain its unalienated nature? In showing us the historicity of Marx's hope, Weber's own tragic sense of history dramatizes the irreversibility of time.

THE TRAGIC VISION OF HISTORY

Although Tocqueville thought that the "equality of conditions" in America set the new world apart from the old, equality itself he regarded as much alienating as energizing. Long before Weber studied Ben Franklin to speculate about a new character in the making, Tocqueville perceived that the "constant strife" in the American people that compels them to desire material success comes from the illusion of equality. The more equal people are, the more they will attempt to prove themselves in the economic realm in order to attain some vague social standing that eludes them:

Among democratic peoples men easily obtain a certain equality, but they will never get the sort of equality they long for. That is a quality which ever retreats before them without quite getting out of sight, and as it retreats it beckons them on to pursue. Every instant they think that they will catch it, and each time it slips through their fingers. They see it close enough to know its charms, but they do not get near enough to enjoy it, and they be dead before they have fully relished its delights.[14]

Tocqueville and Weber derived from America as well as Europe a tragic vision of history. Neither writer could look forward to a future that held out hope of reconciling humanity with the modern conditions of society. Tocqueville saw himself "on the verge of two abysses," one constituting the social order necessary to human development, the other comprising man's sinful, fallen, demonic nature preventing that development. The "whole book," he wrote of *Democracy in America,* "has been written in the impulse of a kind of religious dread." Tocqueville was haunted by Blaise Pascal, whom Nietzsche called "the only logical Christian," a philosopher who felt the disorder and futility of existence and the weakness and corruption of human nature. The Pascalian vision of longing and restlessness permeates *Democracy in America,* whose inhabitants are "constantly circling about in pursuit of the petty and banal pleasure with which they glut their souls."[15] The restless energy of the American people is conducive to political liberty as well as entrepreneurial activity. But democracy itself remains tragic to the extent that the possibilities of political freedom only enhance the possibilities of human corruption. Will Americans use wisely the freedom history has blessed them with or will they abuse it?

Weber's vision of history, religion, society, and politics contains several dimensions of tragedy. He himself appreciated the writings on tragedy by Nietzsche and Georg Simmel, and he knew the edifying themes of Attic tragedy.[16] Weber viewed history as an indeterminate series of events that develop alongside the contingent and chaotic. Essentially history is the movement of power and the succession of forces that seek to take possession of it, an inexorable movement that must be struggled against as freedom vies with fate. As to religion, it is significant that Weber did not adhere to the bland Unitarianism advised by his mother and aunt; instead, he investigated Calvinism, where human alienation is seen as an outcome of man's original sin; hence humankind's estrangement from God in an evil world, and a world where human effort and labor are irrelevant to the state of the soul.[17] Paradoxically, Weber could view society as tragic precisely because its very progressive development increasingly eliminated the tragic sense of life as conflict and collision.

Modern society, overly organized with routine structures, renders irrelevant the possibility of greatness, the old classical hero who must contend with contingency and *fortuna* and the conflicts inherent in ethical decisions. But if confidence in modern technology creates the impression that nature and even fate itself can be brought under control, no such illusions can be allowed to prevail in politics. To Weber politics is inherently tragic since it entails the "diabolical" use of power, and to engage in politics is to give up all pretense to innocence and virtue and to accept the burdens of responsibility and the lurking presence of evil.

Weber's ability to see society and sociology as tragic and ironic has no clear analogue in American social science (although it does in American literary and political thought, as will be pointed out in the Epilogue in a discussion of Herman Melville and Abraham Lincoln). Weber shared with Simmel and Lukács the sense that modern culture, humanity's creation, stands opposed to human needs and aspirations. Society must be seen as something made and formed; yet the forms of social existence become systems and structures with a logic of their own. Thus the progressive growth of reason in social institutions leads not to progress but to "rationalization," the systematic unification of all that is calculable and controllable. In American liberal thought, especially the pragmatic philosophy of John Dewey, there is no sense of the self and society as alienated from one another. A tragic sensibility is scarcely felt since the self is at one with society and naturally responsive to the processes through which personal identity is forged out of social interaction. But with Weber's generation, many of whose members were influenced by the philosophy of Immanuel Kant, the mind has a higher obligation to declare its autonomy over and against the experience of nature and the grip of society. It is precisely because Weber recognized that society has the capacity to forge "social constructions," to influence our thoughts and shape who we come to think we are, that he defied society and the "over-socializing" fixations of sociologists to remain a moralist of individual autonomy.

Both Tocqueville and Weber viewed democracy as an inevitable development of modern history, whether it was a matter of the "providential" nature of God's will or the "fate" of human action.[18] Each author also analyzed the nature of democracy to explain its limitations. But the forces threatening democracy were seen differently, as were the forces that would preserve it. Tocqueville did not believe that the institutional contrivances devised by the framers of the U.S. Constitution would do much to protect and promote liberty; the idea of "checks and balances" presupposed an environment of class conflict, whereas America came to be held together by a shared consensus. Hence Tocqueville lacked Weber's grasp of the growth of institutions that would evolve from human action and come to take on an independent existence. "You say that institutions are only half my subject," Tocqueville wrote to a friend in 1853:

> I go farther than you, and I say that they are not even half. You know my ideas well enough to know that I accord institutions only a secondary influence on the destiny of men. Would to god I believed more in the omnipotence of institutions! I would have more hope for the future, because by chance we might, someday, stumble onto the precious piece of paper that would contain the recipe for all wrongs, or on the man who knew the recipe. But, alas, there is no such thing, and I am quite convinced that political societies are not what their laws make them, but what sentiments, beliefs, ideas, habits of the heart, and the spirit of the men who form them, prepare them in advance to be, as well as what nature and education have made them.[19]

Weber could share Tocqueville's conviction that moral values and habits are essential to any society worthy of its name—although Weber suspected habits that turned into mindless routines, rendering what endures less a celebration of continuity than a suffocation of consciousness. More seriously, Tocqueville's lack of interest in institutions suggests why he cannot offer the last words on the meaning of America or on social theory in general. Perhaps because he associated established institutions with the ancien regime and its social orders, Tocqueville gave little thought to society as an environment of evolving institutions containing the potential to express new forms of domination. Weber, in contrast, saw institutions as the media through which power moves and the organizations through which people adapt means to realize ends. But if institutions arise from human action in order to realize goals, they undergo an irrational reversal as the means become the end itself. At that point an institution becomes independent of human intention and loses its original purpose. Eventually the total institutionalization of the conditions of existence brings about, on its own, the irrational, arbitrary rules of organizations that have escaped their rational aim and design. We are now inside the bowels of bureaucracy.

Weber sought to save freedom and morality from bureaucracy; Tocqueville sought to save those same values from democracy. Tocqueville hoped that the egalitarian suspicions of authority in democratic America that contained despotic tendencies could be mitigated by the presence of religious sentiment, the rule of law, and the *moeurs* of the people. But Weber saw no threat to democracy emanating from democracy itself, no danger of the "tyranny of the majority," since, as he told Robert Michels, popular sovereignty and the will of the people must be seen as more fiction than fact. As Weber saw it, power will always be better organized than freedom, and what threatens freedom is not necessarily democracy but reason itself.[20] Here Weber is not referring to the Enlightenment's version of reason, whereby the dramatic growth of human knowledge promises to be emancipatory to the extent that truth and its uncoerced reasonings would challenge power and its imposing deceptions. On the contrary, modern society would be subject to "instrumental reason," the operations of mind that seek to organize, manage, administer, manipulate, and regulate. Against this "cage" of subordination, Weber sought to develop a morality of choice and judgment so that people could think and act rather than be ordered and acted upon. And it is a measure of Weber's tragic sensibility that he shows us why even the highest ideals we choose and act upon will be in conflict with other ideals.

THE QUESTION OF "AMERICAN EXCEPTIONALISM"

Weber and Tocqueville were modernists convinced that there could be no turning back to the wisdom of the classical ages. That the ancient world could provide a superior guide to present conduct seemed dubious to both authors. The example of America indicated that modern democratic society would be too novel to learn from classical republics, and Weber and Tocqueville devised a new language of political analysis to deal with such modern novelties as mass society and bureaucratic rationalization. Weber in particular even doubted the alleged wisdom of Greek and Roman philosophers, especially those who had allowed themselves to become so enthralled by the language of civic virtue that they seldom acknowledged politics as simply the expression of power and conflict for the purpose of control and domination. That realistic perspective had been characteristic of some of the American Founders as well. Perhaps it is this darker Nietzschean-Calvinist outlook that led Weber, like the framers of the Constitution, to doubt that religion and the rule of law could be counted upon to preserve a Republic that had left Puritanism behind.

Is it possible to judge Weber a better guide than Tocqueville to what America would become? When one considers the standard of prophecy, one hesitates to say for sure. Clearly Tocqueville was accurate in seeing that the voice of the majority would become so overwhelming in mod-

ern society that politics in America would always court a liberal consensus and move to the center; Weber would see the same development
leading to a conflict between democracy and leadership, between the
whims of public opinion and the rectitude of personal conviction. And
neither author, given their aristocratic sensibilities, would be surprised by
the way in which mass society allows popular culture to dominate in a
democracy under the sway of surveys and opinion polls. But aside from
the conservative, centralizing, and standardizing tendencies of democracy,
neither Weber nor Tocqueville anticipated today's political culture, which
in some ways represents a return to aristocracy and the privileges of
heredity at the expense of equality.

Tocqueville believed that social leveling would continue as a consequence of egalitarian democracy. More and more people would demand
the elimination of privileges and chartered monopolies in order to open
up opportunity, while social pressures would result in conformity and the
disappearance of individuality. Weber, in turn, saw equality expanding as
a result of bureaucratic rationalization as more and more people made
demands upon government for services and protections. And bureaucracy, he was certain, would respond objectively and anonymously, treating everyone alike as society becomes homogenized and routinized. In
today's politics of identity, the visions of both Tocqueville and Weber
have been so qualified that history seems to be moving backwards. The
contemporary cult of multiculturalism offers the shibboleth of "diversity"
as an answer to alleged victimization at the hands of conformity, and government responds by treating ethnic and status groups as different and
special, each deserving of preferential treatment and entitled to programs
that affirm differences rather than eliminate them.

It should be remembered that Tocqueville believed that the tendency
of democracy was to obliterate differences, while Weber believed that
bureaucracy would reduce diversity to monotony. The current spectacle
of politics in America would have astounded Marx as well as Weber and
Tocqueville. Today's politics features neither a class-conscious worker, a
charismatic leader, nor a democratic majoritarian will. With diversity
replacing equality in the public sphere, one sees a politics of institutional
infiltration on the part of minorities who have nothing to lose but their
grievances. Such grievances imply that Tocqueville's "equality of conditions," based on an older Protestant morality of work and achievement,
has failed to fulfill its promise. America must now deal with inherited
preconditions. In the new identity politics of entitlement, who one is
now turns on claims of categories and descriptions based upon ancestry.
This return to a pseudo-aristocratic politics of privilege based on inher-

ited rights by reason of birth defies all past political thought. But Weber, with his sense of ironic outcomes, would at least see that the politics of multiculturalism could hardly be possible without the bureaucratic state and its administrative fiats and court-ordered mandates. He alone among political thinkers recognized that the new tyranny of modern industrial society would not be democracy but the oligarchy of a rule-imposing "officialdom."

It would be no insult to Tocqueville's genius to suggest that he missed seeing the very developments that haunted Weber's observations and that remain to plague American society today. Why? Tocqueville saw America as different, unique, and having enjoyed a revolution so peculiarly conservative that the young republic emerging in the new world would be exempt from the problems facing the old world:

> The Revolution in the United States was caused by a mature and thoughtful taste for freedom, not by some vague, undefined instinct for independence. No disorderly passions drove it on; on the contrary, it proceeded hand in hand with a love for order and legality.
>
> No one in the United States has pretended that, in a free country, a man has the right to do everything; on the contrary, more varied social obligations have been imposed on him than elsewhere; no one thought to attack the very basis of social power or contest its rights, the object was only to divide up the right to exercise it. By this means it was hoped that authority would be made great, but officials small, so that the state could still be well regulated and remain free.
>
> In no country in the world are the pronouncements of the law more categorical than in America, and in no other country is the right to enforce it divided among so many hands.
>
> There is nothing centralized or hierarchic in the constitution of American administrative power, and that is the reason why one is not at all conscious of it. The authority exists, but one does not know where to find its representative.[21]

Tocqueville's dismissal of the importance of "institutions" helps explain his failure to see that authority would be embodied in the inexorable growth of bureaucratization and his tendency to see the sphere of officials as "small." Why did Tocqueville remain "not at all conscious" of the centralizing tendencies of power in America and the hierarchical nature of authority? The obvious explanation is that government had a limited scope in Tocqueville's era and big business had yet to appear, like the skyscrapers Weber would see on his visit to the United States. But the real reason lies elsewhere. What separates the perspectives of Tocqueville from those of Weber is less a matter of time than of direction. Where was America heading?

The more optimistic Tocqueville saw America as a wholesome, if restless, young Republic that had the good fortune to leave behind the old world and all its decadent institutions. Seeing America as heading away from Europe, he believed this new democratic society would rarely have to deal with the harsh realities that had oppressed the rest of the world throughout history. Weber, studying the same country much later, reminds us that America would have to face what Tocqueville thought America had escaped: political corruption, class systems and status formations, the trials of being a world power, self-interest unenlightened by virtue, party bosses hungering for electoral victory and completely indifferent to public responsibility, the concentration of wealth and centralization of authority, work reduced to a compulsion without a conviction, and capitalism as all splurge and no spirit. Tocqueville believed in what came to be called "American exceptionalism"; Weber believed that no modernizing country can escape the fate that awaits industrial society in its inevitable rendezvous with rationalization and the "iron cage" of bureaucracy.

Tocqueville has long been regarded as the author who has illuminated the meaning of American democracy. Weber, a more difficult writer and a brilliantly disturbing thinker, departs from democracy as the focus of analysis in order to describe how power silently steals away from the people to become lodged in institutions where it exercises surveillance and demands compliance. Weber has much to teach America, not the least of which is a new perspective on the meaning of freedom and the cunning of power. Freedom may have as much to do with character and responsibility as with commerce and property, and power may quietly transform itself from a spirit of deliverance into a structure of domination, a process that can take place without conscious human consent even in a liberal democracy. To be sure, both the French and the German perspective are essential to America. But beyond the more familiar wisdom of Tocqueville's thoughts, Weber offers us extraordinarily arresting ideas and, on some topics, deeper insights.

ONE

The Last Puritan

ARRIVAL AND RECOVERY

The crossing did what no doctor could do. Sailing into New York harbor on a September morning in 1904, Max Weber stood on the deck of the ocean liner, observing the towering heights of the approaching skyscrapers, accepting the greeting of the Statue of Liberty, pondering the meaning of her outstretched torch with its message to millions of Europeans. The voyage seemed to be further evidence that his long period of mental breakdown, which began in 1897, had ended at last. The nocturnal "demons" had disappeared, though they would on occasion return to haunt him, sometimes so severely that only a dose of morphine could overcome the resultant insomnia. But at the moment his wife, Marianne, delighted in seeing him brimming with energy, chatting with other passengers in the smoking room, so at peace with himself. The nightly rolling of the waves rocked him to sleep, as though the struggle with sleeplessness found relief deep in the rhythms of nature; the salt air restored an appetite that had turned listless in the sanitarium. On the high seas Weber could hope to be recovered from a nameless illness that had neither a satisfactory diagnosis nor a successful prescription. But he felt confident enough to accept an invitation to deliver a paper in the United States at an international scholars' conference. It would be the first lecture he allowed himself to give in six and a half years. He knew, going down the gangplank, that life as he wanted it—the life of the mind in its search for meaning and value—had returned. Rarely had his curiosity been so intense.[1]

The Webers headed for a twenty-story hotel in mid-Manhattan and took an elevator to their room, which featured a telephone and two high spittoons. Looking down at the streets below made the couple recoil nervously; looking straight out the window the taller commercial buildings seemed to mock their small dwelling. The soaring heights and metallic coldness and impersonality of New York City chilled many of Weber's fellow visitors, used to a village-bred Gemütlichkeit and preferring the old to the new. The presumption of German culture set against American crudeness rankled Weber: "No one can say I am especially 'enthusiastic'; I am merely annoyed at my German fellow travelers who groan about America after a day and a half in New York."[2]

Weber was hardly the first German to ask his countrymen to take America seriously. A century earlier the Revolution of '76 stirred German intellectuals to pen odes to liberty arising from a new environment free of monarchy, aristocracy, and ecclesiastical tyranny. Yet some conservative thinkers saw the American colonists as hypocrites and ingrates who, instead of coughing up taxes and acknowledging parliament's sovereignty, invoked the doctrine of natural right to escape authority and responsibility. What did Weber think of the American Founding?[3]

Weber's gazing at the Statue of Liberty did not move him to head to the Library of Congress to read documents pertaining to the Revolution and Constitution. He would stop at various university libraries to read about religious ideas and institutions in America, but like Tocqueville, Weber paid little attention to the Revolution and its purported ideological origins. Apparently all talk of liberty and virtue and the debate over the locus of sovereignty were not as important as the Puritan's earlier idea that resistance to the abuses of secular authority was obedience to God. But Weber's interest in religion cannot be the only reason for his indifference to the political ideas that supposedly went to make America what it became. He arrived in America with an entirely different perspective about power and authority.

Americans who had learned about their Revolution were taught that power always poses a threat to liberty and the colonists were rebelling against the excesses of arbitrary power by a British government determined to revoke their liberties and rights as Englishmen. Weber saw power as essential to liberty in its need for efficacy, and power was less arbitrary than normal to the extent that it becomes institutionalized and expresses itself in the systematic application of rules and regulations. Power reigns not necessarily when it is abusive but when it conceals itself in everyday routines where conventional behavior is regarded as an inviolable norm of conduct. Moreover, the few times Weber wrote about revolution as a phenomenon he depicted it as a conflict between the forces of resistance upholding an old regime and the forces of movement demanding change, innovation, reform, and a new order. Such a scenario could hardly apply to the American Revolution, which began in deliberate resistance to the changes the British demanded in order to reform and modernize the colonial system.

Weber's way of looking at history and politics, it should be noted at the outset, had no basis in familiar forms of liberalism that made up America's political culture. A people brought up on the principles of Jeffersonian democracy were taught that political struggle always meant a conflict of the many against the few. Weber believed that the struggle of freedom against power was an eternal expression of human existence, and while believing in the Anglo-American tradition of political rights, he was not altogether convinced that the theater of democracy was the stage on which that struggle took place.

Previous German thinkers looked upon America as both a burden and a blessing. The country was seen as either a primitive continent of "noble savages" and a paradise for adventurers and ne'er do wells (*Taugenichtse*, J. G. Herder) or as a land fortunate to have escaped the "cobwebs and castles" of feudalism (Goethe), a Republic in which the ancient ideal of the *polis* is realized in the liberating activity of work (Arnold Ruge). To these thinkers America was a country that released the "moral potency" of time (J. G. Droysen) in a Jeffersonian ethos of "perfect individuality" (Wilhelm von Humboldt), but also a country rushing into a modernity that threatened the world with *Amerikanisierung*—the specter of materialism and the mechanization of mass society (Oswald Spengler). America was seen as an environment of abundance and promise, yet too inchoate to have a truly sovereign state and a citizenry too migratory to reach historical consciousness; it was thus "a land of desire for all those who are weary of the historical lumber-room of old Europe" (Hegel). To a German mind accustomed to assuming that freedom depended on the exercise of the authority of the state, America rather possessed a political mentality whereby freedom depended on flight from authority.[4]

America also confounded Karl Marx and Friedrich Engels. The "existence of classes," wrote Marx about America in 1852, "is bound up with particular historical phases in the development of production." But after the Civil War when America leaped into industrialization, Marx heard reports that denied not only the rise of class struggle but the existence of classes and the possibility of class consciousness. In 1877, Engels thought he saw genuine class conflict suddenly emerging out of strikes taking place in the coal mines of Pennsylvania, and he marveled that miners were moving to establish a political working-class party. "On the more favored soil of America, where no medieval ruins bar the way, where history begins with the elements of the modern bourgeois society as evolved in the seventeenth century, the working class passes through these two stages of its development in ten months."

That the American working class had no remnants of feudalism to struggle against, that America would produce no "proletariat" because, as Tocqueville had observed and Engels came close to seeing, workers enjoyed the political freedoms of the middle class, indicated that Marxism would be almost useless for understanding the United States. Hence after the turn of the century, Weber's colleague Werner Sombardt raised a now well-known question: Why is there no socialism in the United States? In eating habits, dress styles, wages, and profit sharing, the life of the American worker only demonstrated that "all socialist utopians have run aground on the shoals of roast beef and apple pie."[5]

Intellectually America offered no united, single, coherent voice. A culture that produced Ralph W. Emerson, whose "cheerful transcendency" discouraged all despair (Friedrich Nietzsche), also produced Thorstein Veblen, whose "reverence for the historically given" discouraged all hope (T. W. Adorno). German thinkers remained profoundly ambivalent about America, a country whose complex image evoked both political ideals and vulgar realities:

> There are times I'd like to think
> that America's for me
> (Freedom's stable filled with herds
> seeking mob equality),
>
> But I'm fearful of a land
> Where tobacco leaves they chew,
> Where they bowl without a king,
> Where without spittoon they spew.[6]

Heinrich Heine

The one writer who had much to teach Germans about America, and who may have influenced Weber, was Georg Gottfried Gervinus, an influential historian in the mid-nineteenth century. Weber's uncle Herbert Baumgarrten studied under Gervinus and absorbed his admiration of Anglo-American political values and institutions. "The exact copy of the states of ancient Greece and Rome has become . . . impossible in the sight of the new idea of a state that has been realized in America," Gervinus observed, emphasizing that classical categories no longer apply to the new world. But older religious principles still pertain, particularly what was "preached by the first Calvinist teacher of political doctrine—that there may be states without princes, but never without a people."[7]

In America in 1904, the year of Weber's visit, the term "Calvinism" could barely be mentioned in intellectual circles. The disdain for America's Puritan past pervaded American culture (as will be further discussed), which makes one wonder what might have been the response to Weber's Protestant Ethic thesis had American intellectuals been aware of it, the first part of which was published the year he arrived in the country. Whatever the case, the anti-Puritan animus continued through the years of the Greenwich Village rebellion of the pre–World War I period, and in the aftermath of the war, with American intellectuals bitterly disillusioned with themselves for having supported the war that promised to end all future wars, the German writer who captivated America was Oswald Spengler.

Spengler's *The Decline of the West* (1918), which purported to trace the morphological ascendancy of life over reason and of money and the machine over culture and the individual, appealed to intellectuals in revolt against America as a puritanical "business civilization." In the thirties Spengler's text was chosen as one of ten "Books That Changed Our Minds."[8] To the extent that readers of Spengler had no knowledge of Weber, and hence saw institutions as lifeless forms and liberalism as moribund, America read an author who had no capacity to foresee the coming of totalitarianism and to value American democracy as a response to it.

In coming to America to study Puritanism, Weber himself was departing from the three towering figures of nineteenth-century German intellectual history. Marx, Nietzsche, and Ludwig Feurbach had depicted religion as a barrier to humanity's fulfillment, particularly a Christianity that burdened the human race with the fear of evil and the doctrine of original sin. What intellectuals in America as well as Europe saw as a burden Weber saw as an ironic blessing, endowing modern capitalism with an "ethos" or "spirit" (*Geist*) at its very birth. But contemporary America, Weber reflected while exploring New York City, had little resemblance to its humble spiritual beginnings.

Strolling the Brooklyn Bridge, Weber was struck by its multipurpose uses: its pedestrian footpaths, elevated trains, and trams jammed with people hanging from the sides. From the bridge Weber saw "the magnificent view of the fortresses of capital at the southern tip of the island," likening the structures of Wall Street to "towers such as may be seen in the old pictures of Bologna and Florence, surrounded everywhere by the light vapor clouds of the freight elevators." Weber's thoughts took everything in: the colors, smells, and sounds, the dazzling arc lamps, the dried horse manure on the streets, the roaring and hissing of traffic and the rumpetybump beat of trains. Everywhere Weber saw the bustle and energy of the "spirit of capitalism."[9]

Yet Weber's first impressions recorded a thought that would have unsettled exponents of capitalism, especially those who had assumed that a free market economy laid the basis for a free society of self-reliant individuals. The sprawling, throbbing vitality of New York City seemed to diminish human stature. "How great are the works of men, but how small the men themselves appear! When toward evening the fantastic stream surged from the business districts toward the bridge, it was enough to make one shudder; belief in the infinite worth of the individual soul and in immortality seemed absurd." Tocqueville's earlier vision that America's "equality of condition" would release the energies of individualism no longer had relevance in a congested urban society. Weber noted the contrast between the commanding citadels of the business world and the quiet modesty of middle-class life, where economic restrictions precluded the freedom to be different and imposed on metropolitan masses a cramped conformity. "Among this mass agglomeration any stirring of individualism is expensive, be it in housing or in eating," Weber noted as he described the meager domestic conditions of German-American professors at Columbia University. Already Weber sensed that the assumptions of his fellow social scientists had to be reconsidered, especially the assumption that democratic society leads to atomization and capitalist economy to alienation, with the result that modern industrial life would disintegrate into "a dust of individuals" (Durkheim) and American society itself would have no more cohesion than a "sandpile" (Weber). New York City, so shapeless, jostling, and incoherent, yet so structured and syncopated, challenged the assumptions of contemporary sociologists.[10]

The Webers left the steaming asphalt streets of New York and traveled westward along the green banks of the Hudson to Niagara Falls. Having seen the mighty waterfall, Marianne noted that even Max, more interested in human society than nature, could not help being moved by the crashing roar that silenced all spectators. "The natural beauty is so wonderful," Marianne wrote to her mother-in-law, "despite all the shameful spoliation."[11]

After the natural splendor of Niagara, the Webers arrived in Chicago and found themselves jolted by an urban wilderness of glaring contrasts, from stately architecture to comfortable residential districts to more frequent miserable working-class neighborhoods reeking of filth, an "endless human desert" of motley immigrant populations, with Germans waiting on tables, Italians digging ditches, Jews putting on their own plays, and Irish taking care of their own politics. Prostitutes stood in store windows and advertised their price in electric lights. The city of Chicago "is like a man whose skin has been peeled off and whose intestines are seen at work." In the belly of the beast Weber scanned the anatomy of violence:

> All hell had broken loose in the "stockyards": an unsuccessful strike, masses of Italians and Negroes as strikebreakers; daily shootings and dozens of dead on both sides; a streetcar was overturned and a dozen women were squashed because a "non-union man" had sat in it; dynamite threats against the "Elevated Railway," and one of its cars was actually derailed and plunged into the river. Right near our hotel a cigar dealer was murdered in broad daylight; a few streets away three Negroes attacked and robbed a streetcar at dusk, etc.—all in all, a strange flowering of culture.

The stockyards themselves displayed modern economy at its most efficient, an "ocean of blood" that begins with a blow to the head and ends in the butchershop:

> From the moment when the unsuspecting bovine enters the slaughtering area, is hit by a hammer and collapses, whereupon it is immediately gripped by an iron clamp, is hoisted up, and starts on its journey, it is in constant motion—past ever-new workers who eviscerate and skin it, etc., but are always (in the rhythm of work) tied to the machine that pulls the animals past them. One sees an absolutely incredible output in this atmosphere of steam, muck, blood, and hides . . .

Food production stood at the highest stage of rationalization in America, where one "can follow a pig from the sty to the sausage and the can."[12]

The Webers, feeling the shocks of this "monster" city in all its brutal callousness, also felt its more "gentle features that bespoke a capacity for love as well as kindness, justice, and a tenacious desire for beauty and spirituality." On billboards they saw posters proclaiming "Christ in Chicago," suggesting not blatant mockery but the presence of humane souls, such as Jane Addams and her famous Hull House tenement shelter. The religious ethos was especially vital at the University of Chicago, where chapel services were part of the required curriculum. Weber could only wonder whether such mandatory attendance led to religious indifference, particularly when services often concluded with an announcement of a forthcoming football game. "But the power of the Church communities is still tremendous as compared to our Protestantism," he noted, struck by the thought that in America religion is more voluntaristic than ritualistic, a matter of personal conviction rather than the dull habit of tradition.[13]

From Chicago the Webers made the long trip to St. Louis to take part in the International Exposition devoted to science and art. At the conclusion of the scholars' conference the Webers took leave of their German colleagues, many of whom hurried to return to their homeland, and headed to the Southern states, a terra incognita to many Europeans. Weber wanted to learn about American Indians and the transformation of their tribal property into private possessions. He visited the Muskogee Indian Territory in Oklahoma to study the conditions of the reservation. He watched "whole troops of Indians arrive to get their money; the full-blooded ones have peculiar tired facial features and are surely doomed to destruction, but among others one sees intelligent faces. Their clothes are almost invariably European. I learned many other interesting things from all sorts of people, and I think my host, the Cherokee, will attack the latest Indian policy of the United States in the *Archiv*," Weber wrote in reference to his journal; "his eyes sparkled when he spoke about it."[14]

In Oklahoma Weber felt the "boom" mentality everywhere, and he was accosted by real estate agents, an asphalt contractor, and two traveling salesmen. Above the acrid smell of petroleum and fumes stood the oil wells, "Eiffel Tower–like structures" that signaled the beginning of a town. But Weber's stay in Oklahoma ended abruptly. Weber intended to call on the editor of a newspaper in the town of Guthrie, only to discover that the journalist had previously pulled a gun on another newspaperman. Weber, who had delighted in sword-dueling as a youth, exclaimed: "I cannot see how a man who carries a gun can be a 'shentlemans,' and therefore I will not meet him." Guthrie town officials tried to persuade "Professor von Webber" to change his mind, but he took the first train out of town.[15]

After the enervating tropical heat of New Orleans, the Webers arrived in the little city of Tuskegee to see Booker T. Washington's famous college for black Americans. Marianne recalled that "what they found moved them more than anything else on the trip." The dilemma of America could be grasped immediately: "The tragedy of the pariahdom of that ever-increasing mixed race of all shades from dark brown to ivory, people who by virtue of their descent and talents belonged to the master race (*Herrenrasse*) but were excluded from the community as though they bore a stigma." The pariah status of the mulatto applied to both "the slaves' children and children's children." As both a strategy and a psychology, black leaders attempted to instill pride in students and teach them culture as well as practical skills. To gain the white man's respect, blacks practiced "the gospel of the toothbrush." Washington's accommodationist strategy had been challenged by the black historian W. E. B. Du Bois, a scholar trained at both Harvard and Heidelberg. Upon his return to Germany Weber solicited from Du Bois a comprehensive article for his *Archiv,* a more Marxist, class-oriented interpretation of the "Negro Question" (*Negerfrage*) in the United States. But like Washington, Du Bois also emphasized *Bildung,* character formation as well as civic education. The "irremediable discord" of the race issue in America led Weber to consider questions of nationality, separatism, ethnicity, and status.[16]

The Webers were anxious to see relatives on Max's side of the family, the stepcousins of his grandfather, George F. Fallenstein, who as an adolescent had escaped the "despotic" environment of his household to head out for the New World. His descendants settled in Mount Airy, North Carolina. Weber, who had been observing America almost as an anthropologist on a field trip, found himself the object of curiosity. "He had on knicker-type knee pants that blossomed out over heavy socks up to his knees," recalled one relative years later. "We thought that was so funny. His wearing bloomers. All grown men wore long pants."[17]

What Weber observed in North Carolina was serious as well as humorous. The church practices of Southern Baptists left an indelible impression and reinforced his conviction that religion and economics may have some connection, something that ties the psychological phenomenon of believing to the economic need of borrowing, of credo to credit. Weber later recalled:

> This was made particularly clear to me personally when, on a cold Sunday morning in October, I attended a Baptist baptism in the forelands of the Blue Ridge Mountains of North Carolina. Approximately ten people of both sexes in their Sunday-best entered the icy water of a mountain stream one after another and after voluminous declarations of allegiance bent their knees, leaned back into the arms of a black-clothed reverend (who stood waist-deep in the water during the entire

procedure) until their faces disappeared under the water, climbed out sneezing and shivering, were congratulated by the farmers who had come in large numbers by horse and wagon, and quickly made for home (which in some cases was hours away). Faith protects one from catching cold, the saying goes. One of my cousins . . . who scorned the procedure by spitting irreverently . . . showed a certain interest as an intelligent-looking young man submerged himself. "Oh see, Mr. X. I told you so!" Pressed to explain, he responded at first only that Mr. X intended to open a bank in Mt. Airy and needed significant credit. From further discussion I learned that admittance into the Baptist congregation was primarily of decisive importance not on account of his Baptist customers but much more for the non-Baptist ones, because the *on-going inquiries* about moral and business conduct which precede acceptance are considered by far the strongest and most reliable. . . . Unpunctuality in payment of a debt, wanton spending, visits to the tavern, in short, anything that casts a doubtful light on the social qualifications of the person in question, mean rejection by the congregation.[18]

From the "simple people" of rural America Weber would develop a theory of capitalism seen as a sociological phenomenon springing originally from religious convictions, which would eventually give way to secularization as the entrepreneur continued to demonstrate his qualifications as a Christian by his business integrity. In the Blue Ridge mountains of North Carolina Weber found some of the deepest human truths embedded in scarcely noticed customs and rituals.

"SO MARVELLOUS A PHANTASM":
THE ST. LOUIS EXPOSITION

The Webers arrived in St. Louis in sweltering September. The World Congress of Arts and Sciences was part of the 1904 Louisiana Purchase Exposition, a world's fair that had opened in May. The historian Henry Adams attended the fair together with Secretary of State John Hay, whom President Theodore Roosevelt had asked to deliver a paper. Adams enjoyed the beaux arts architecture and electrical illumination that announced a new age of energy. He also took note of the different nationalities that had flocked to this American outpost. "The German is on top. He is not graceful, but useful. The French and the Americans are little evident. The English not at all." Adams worried that the St. Louis Exposition expressed an immature excess. "The pathetic part," he wrote to a friend, "is to see that poor, little, German, half-baked city, staggering under a load that would have broke London." The expenditure was extravagant, the attendance disappointing, "but it is beautifully *Schwärmerisch*"—fanciful. Adams wondered whether the extravagance indicated that Americans would throw away power and money as soon as they had the technological means to do so. The Exposition meant to celebrate progress; Adams saw hubris. Like Weber, Adams saw that the spirit of capitalism, having withered away in modern times, even if lingering on as a gesture in the hills of North Carolina, would issue in a society of sport and spectacle:

> One saw here a third-rate town of half a million people without history, education, unity or art, and with little capital;—without even an element of natural interest except the river which it studiously ignored;—but doing what London, Paris or New York would have shrunk from attempting. This new social conglomerate, with no tie but its steam power and not much of that, threw away thirty or forty million dollars on a pageant as ephemeral as a stage flat. The world had never witnessed so marvellous a phantasm; by night Arabia's crimson sands had never returned a glow half so astonishing, as one wandered among long lines of white palaces, exquisitely lighted by thousands of thousands of electric candles, soft, rich, shadowy, palpable in their sensuous depths; all in deep silence, profound solitude, listening for a voice or a foot-fall or the splash of an oar, as though the Emir Mirza were displaying the beauties of his City of Brass, which could show nothing half so beautiful as this illumination, with its vast, white monumental solitude, bathed in the pure light of setting suns.[19]

Such spectacles of palatial sumptuousness would trouble Weber as much as Adams. During the World War I years he would, remembering his 1904 visit, criticize America's pretentious aristocratic status tendencies lurking beneath supposedly simple democratic virtues, and he had read enough of Thorstein Veblen to understand how modern capitalism could make the transition from honest production to wasteful consumption while worshipping at the new altar of power. Everything happening in America concerned Weber, who, like Tocqueville, believed that the New World would determine the future as matter overtakes spirit and capitalism proceeds free of older religious scruples. Adams depicted the St. Louis Exposition as a stage spectacle of eye-riveting objects, a debauchery of regal dwellings that left no trace of America's modest Puritan beginnings. What had disappeared from American life, and was scarcely mentioned at the Exposition, was praise for work and a "calling" dedicated to productive activity as a discipline and duty—whereas Weber's address, as we shall see, would be all about land and labor and the fading significance of agricultural life. Adams is struck by glimpses of the future brought on by a new age of electricity illuminating an assemblage of glittering images shining on the mud flats of Missouri. Weber would call this "victorious capitalism," an economic system now resting on materialist values and mechanical operations, devoid of all religious meaning and transcendental sanctions, a society with the "character of sport" driven by the display of dazzling objects of desire.

Could science succeed where religion had failed? East of the Mississippi, Adams recounted, the St. Louis Exposition met a conspiracy of silence. The event had been boycotted by a number of prominent American intellectuals who had many things in common with Weber. The misunderstanding resulted from the insistence of the conference organizer, the Harvard psychologist Hugo Münsterberg, that the Exposition have as its theme the unification of all branches of knowledge as an answer to the fragmentation and specialization of the disciplines. That the event took place in St. Louis, the center of German-American Hegelianism, also aroused some suspicion among other American philosophers. The conference, declared Münsterberg, "must strive for unity of thought" in keeping with "the American nation, with its instinctive desire for organization and efficiency." The philosopher John Dewey saw Münsterberg offering up a ready-made, a priori "logic of knowledge" on which to organize the sessions, unaware that epistemology and knowledge of logic had passed into disarray. William James also saw the proposal as alien to pragmatic methods of inquiry. "To me the whole Münsterbergian circus seems a case of the pure love of schematization running mad," he confided to a friend; it is "sheer humbug . . . for the sake of making the authority of professors inalienable . . . as if the bureaucratic mind were the full flavor of nature's revelation."[20]

Münsterberg, a longtime friend of Weber, had invited him to the conference. At the end of the trip the Webers stayed with the Münsterbergs at their home in Boston. On intellectual matters, however, Weber was closer to American thinkers in sensing both the limits of totalizing schemes of knowledge and the dangerous connection between pretensions to authority and the bureaucratic mentality. It was unfortunate, then, that eminent American thinkers lost the opportunity to hear Weber; all the more so in light of the hype that accompanied the Congress's opening. The Congress, "a perfect assemblance of human excellencies," wrote the *St. Louis Post Dispatch,* aimed to "show the interdependence of the sciences, the harmony of thought and act. . . . By studying both we shall know what has been thought and done in the world since man discovered his divine powers." The *World Fair Bulletin* reported American scholars exclaiming that the "world owes to Germany its present high development along philosophical lines, for the reason that in Germany the great universities first liberated themselves from the tyranny of courts and government and the thrall of ecclesiasticism."[21]

Weber's own sensibilities would have dashed such conceits. As he saw it, science, rather than harmonizing branches of knowledge, further fragments them; philosophy, rather than comprehending the truth of things, senses the limits of knowing; and the German university, rather than carrying on the spirit of inquiry, cowers before the conservative state. Weber's vision of things was out of step with much of American thought as well. While the pragmatic philosophers were celebrating the promises of will and intelligence and turning their backs on history, Weber was pondering the past, exploring the circumstances and "constellations" of forces that provide freedom with the conditions of possibility for making an entrance into history.

When Weber went before a sparse audience to deliver his obligatory address, Marianne was thrilled to see her husband appearing in public for the first time in six years. "He spoke excellently, very calmly and yet vigorously; in form and substance the lecture was brilliant, and there were many political points that interested Americans."[22] Weber's paper, delivered in English, dealt with German agrarian conditions past and present, particularly the passing of rural society and the advent of new forms of social relations. Implicitly it contained two concerns that had informed previous addresses Weber gave before his breakdown: the nature and history of capitalism and its contemporary transformation, and the emergence of new structures of power and stratification resulting from science and the systems of organization in modern society and politics. While Münsterberg praised America for its "instinctual desire for organization and efficiency," Weber saw the strong possibility that such instincts could be, although inevitable, threatening and perhaps even tragic.

AMERICAN PROGRESSIVISM

The failure of American scholars to cross paths with Weber in the opening years of the twentieth century had the effect of postponing until recent times an accurate portrait of the man. Rather than an archive-burrowing researcher buried in data, or a social scientist absorbed by the logical self-sufficiency of functional structures, Weber was an existential thinker who saw almost no phenomenon free of irony and contradiction, an anguished humanist who saw rationality and regularity everywhere because he wanted even more to see freedom somewhere. Had leading American scholars met Weber at St. Louis, their own thinking might have been enriched and rendered more problematic, more sensitive to paradox and ambiguity, perhaps more appreciative of a concept of freedom that had more to do with character and conscience than with circumstance and conditions. American pragmatic philosophers advised Americans to turn their faces toward the future; to Weber the meaning of America lay in where it came from—a Puritan heritage that had all but vanished, a heritage that had once bequeathed to America what George Santayana called "an agonized conscience."[23]

At the time Weber delivered his paper he had been preoccupied with the contrast between European social conditions and those of America, a topic to which he would return the following year upon the outbreak of the Russian Revolution of 1905. In the St. Louis address Weber discussed the significance of the passing of rural life for Germany and America. Unburdened by a feudal past, America had no peasantry; instead, confident farmers labored, unconcerned with day-to-day subsistence growing as they produced crops for ever-expanding markets. With the Civil War, "one of the bloodiest wars in modern times," having eliminated the Southern plantation aristocracy, the tension between capitalism and tradition was gone with the wind, and power passed to the urban entrepreneur and lost its connection to land ownership, the power base of the Prussian Junkers. In contrast to Germany, America had no problem of "backwardness" and did not need to deal with the tenacious influence of a gradually disappearing rural class. Yet American history could hardly have been the scene of peace and harmony. "Even in America, with its democratic traditions handed down by Puritanism as an everlasting heirloom, the victory over the planters' aristocracy was difficult and was gained with great political and social sacrifices. But in countries with old civilizations, matters are much more complicated. For there the struggle between the power of historical notions and the pressure of capitalist interests summons certain social forces to battle as adversaries of bourgeois capitalism."

Weber then explained at length the embattled social forces in Germany, where the landlords of the western part of the country appropriated the peasants' income in taxes and competed with eastern landlords, who used the peasant as a laboring force while more and more farmhands left the land and became proletarians. Meanwhile the Eastern Junker, who would liked to have been a feudal lord, found that commercial capitalism had penetrated the countryside to take possession of farms.

Speaking of the present situation, Weber speculates that this process could also take place in the United States. Although the burden of historical tradition scarcely "overwhelmed" America, the effects of capitalist hegemony were stronger and could also result in increasing land monopolies. Above all, America's political freedoms, rooted in religion and a fortuitous combination of early historical circumstances, were born only once and probably could not be repeated:

> The United States does not yet know such problems. This nation will probably never encounter some of them. It has no old aristocracy; hence the tensions caused by the contrast between authoritarian tradition and the purely commercial character of modern economic conditions do not exist. Rightly it celebrates the purchase of this immense territory [Louisiana], in whose presence we are here, as the real historical seal imprinted upon its democratic institutions; without this acquisition, with powerful and warlike neighbors at its side, it would be forced to wear the coat of mail like ourselves, who constantly keep in the drawer of our desks the march order in case of war. But on the other hand, the greater part of the problem for whose solution we are now working will approach America within only a few generations. The way in which they will be solved will determine the character of the future culture of this continent. It was perhaps never before in history made so easy for any nation to become a great civilized power as for the American people. Yet, according to human calculation, it is also the last time, as long as the history of mankind shall last, that such conditions for a free and great development will be given; the areas of free soil are now vanishing everywhere in the world.[24]

A decade earlier, at the Chicago World's Fair of 1893, the historian Frederick Jackson Turner delivered his now-famous "The Significance of the Frontier in American History." According to Turner, the existence of free land explained American development, nurturing the institutions of democracy and the ethos of egalitarianism and forging a national character of individualism, mobility, and self-reliance. Ironically, Turner's thesis went against a traditional school of thought that traced America's Anglo-Saxon political institutions back to the German forests. But Turner's emphasis on the environment seemed deterministic, even fatalistic to the extent that the frontier had come to an end with the disappearance of free land, a process in which Americans stood almost as passive objects rather than conscious subjects, more acted upon than acting as free, willful agents. The double irony is that Weber took his original idea of America freedom out of both the German forests and the frontier's material environment and located it in seventeenth-century theology, in the writings of Roger Williams more than those of Thomas Jefferson. Even though Weber discovered, after visiting Brown University in Rhode Island, that Williams's legacy had succumbed to the forces of secularization, he remained convinced that the radical origins of modern political rights had Puritan sources. Thus instead of seeing freedom dependent upon land and property, as did Jefferson and Turner, Weber saw the struggle for human freedom as a once-born spiritual expression of the human condition.[25]

In locating political freedom in historical religion, Weber was explaining America to Americans better than most American scholars could explain America to themselves. Many contemporary social scientists as well as progressive historians saw Protestant religion as either a superstition from the past that modern science was extirpating or as a "false consciousness" that lingered on in political economy in order to rationalize the lust after profits and power. In developing his stance, Weber was closer to English thought than to that of Germany, where religion, in his estimate, functioned more to subdue the political mind than to arouse it. Weber's debt to English thought may result from his ancestral ties to London and Manchester, a connection only recently discovered in scholarship.[26] At times Weber sounds like Lord Acton, the English historian who also saw that a politics without conscience corrupts into power and that freedom is the "logical offspring of religion," or at least a Protestant religion that emancipates the individual and endows one with the potential autonomy to regulate one's own conduct. Both Acton and Weber looked to the dissenters of Rhode Island and the Quakers of Pennsylvania as evidence that religion could be the "mother of freedom."[27]

But if freedom had its origins in religion, it was politics that would sustain it, and Weber wondered, as did Lincoln and Tocqueville, whether an idea born in "passion" can be perpetuated by an institution that settles for administration and regulation. The state of American politics concerned Weber, and what he observed on his visit he would return to in his later writings during the years of World War I.

Two months after the St. Louis Congress had met, America had its 1904 presidential election, with the charismatic incumbent Republican Theodore Roosevelt thundering from the "bully pulpit." Another figure who would occupy Weber's mind was Woodrow Wilson. A Princeton professor who, like Weber, also studied parliamentary government; a scholar-statesman who also felt the guilty angst of Calvinism, Wilson had delivered a paper at the Congress. Although it remains unknown whether Weber heard it, he would listen carefully to what Wilson had to say during World War I, when Wilsonian and Weberian perspectives on world politics vied with each other.

Wilson became president at the peak of the Progressive era in 1912. The year has been termed the crossroads of American liberalism, since the people were then asked to choose between two alternative definitions of the role of the state in American life. Significantly, Germany had been at a similar crossroad a few years earlier. The occasion was a volatile conference in Vienna in 1909, at an annual convention of the Verein für Sozialpolitik. From old veteran socialists came fiery speeches demanding that the state be further empowered to control the economy and bring about a better society. Weber and his brother Alfred dramatically took the floor to denounce such proposals. "No machinery in the world works as precisely as this human machine," Max Weber declared in reference to bureaucracy. But, he warned, "everyone who integrates himself becomes a little cog in the machine. And even though the idea that someday the world might be full of nothing but professors is frightening—one would have to escape to the desert if something like that happened—the idea that the world would be filled with nothing but little cogs is even more frightening, that is, with people who cling to a small position and strive for a bigger one."[28]

At the same time Weber was taking a stand against the strengthening of the state in Germany, American intellectuals and political figures were trying to find its meaning and purpose in America. Herbert Croly's *The Promise of American Life* appeared the same year as the Vienna conference. The dilemma of American political culture, as Croly and Walter Lippmann would see it in the twentieth century and as Alexander Hamilton had prophesied in the eighteenth, is that America had become a nation without a nation-state.[29] To fill the need for political authority at the federal level, Roosevelt established various bureaus and agencies to enable government to supervise the economy and to take responsibility for a certain measure of social welfare. Roosevelt's program would come to be called the "New Nationalism." In the 1912 election Wilson answered it with the "New Freedom," which called for a return to laissez faire in order to release the forces of competition. Weber's observation of this election is one instance when his perceptions failed him, for he saw Roosevelt's third-party "Bull Moose" movement as an example of the spontaneity of charisma challenging the inertia of bureaucracy:

Since all emotional mass appeals have certain charismatic features, the bureaucratization of the parties and of the electioneering may at its very height suddenly be forced into the service of charismatic hero worship. In this case a conflict arises between charismatic heroism and the mundane power of the party organization, as Roosevelt's campaign demonstrated.[30]

Weber assumed that the charismatic personality would rise to challenge bureaucracy; in 1912 Roosevelt was attempting to expand the role of the bureaucratic state by dint of his personal charisma. Chapter 3 of this volume will note how Weber misperceived what he regarded as the impermeable institutionalized character of American political parties. But when one juxtaposes the premises of American Progressivism to Weberian skepticism, the German mind may still have some lessons to teach the American.

The Progressive assumption that a government representative of the people stood for political ideals while the business sector responding to market transactions stood merely for "interests" never made much sense to Weber. The dialectic of high ideals and material interests could not be explained simply by institutional identification. Similarly with leadership: some Progressives looked to Otto von Bismarck as an example America could use to unify the national will. Weber would remind Americans that Bismarck had smothered the spark of political freedom in Germany and rendered its people too submissive to political authority when they should be, as with the old Puritans, boldly subversive of it. Many Progressives looked to the devices of initiative, recall, and direct election of senators as means of fostering participatory democracy and endowing politics with moral significance. Weber foresaw that the expansion of democratic activity would be followed by an increase in administrative surveillance and controls as more and more people made more and more demands upon government. The American people never had an abiding theory of what the government should or should not do, and only had asked of it that it be responsive in one way or another to their demands. But a democracy that translates desires into demands faces an awkward irony in the history of liberalism. The historical liberal sought to free society from government domination; the new liberal seeks to secure society from its own disruptions through government regulation. From the Puritans to the Progressives the American mind shifted from a wish to be free to the will to control. In Weber's vision of the future, American democracy has a rendezvous with bureaucracy.

Weber's skepticism about the promises of democracy was matched by his skepticism about the promises of science and the mystique of evolutionary progress. And the American environment served as a kind of laboratory where Weber could observe the erroneous implications of such assumptions. Darwinian ideas of evolution, albeit probably misinterpreted, seemed to validate the moral and intellectual superiority of more "advanced" cultures on the assumption that growth moves from the simple to the complex and that the later stood superior to the earlier as the higher to the lower. The modern ethos of change, adaptation, and transformation also implied that progress arises out of civilizing the brute conditions of existence. But Weber remained convinced that such assumptions were subjective biases parading as objective science. He assumed that there could be no transcendent standard by which cultures can be judged superior and inferior. Around the time Weber attended the St. Louis Congress he was working on the methodological issues of relativism and objectivity, and it is revealing that he returned to an American setting to drive home the point that the social scientist has no business formulating a hierarchy of values. How can one tell whether "adaptation" (*Anpassung*) should be praised as enlightened response to change or disparaged as the loss of identity and character in the face of circumstance?

> The few Indians who lived in the Salt Lake area before the Mormon migration were in the biological sense—as well as in all the other of its many conceivable empirical meanings—just as well or poorly "adapted" as the later populous Mormon settlements. This term adds absolutely nothing to our empirical understanding, although we easily delude ourselves that it does. Only in the case of the two otherwise absolutely identical organizations, can one assert that a particular concrete difference is more conducive to the continued existence of the organization which has that characteristic, and which is therefore "better adapted" to the given conditions. But as regards the evaluation of the above situation, one person may assert that the greater numbers and the material and other accomplishments and characteristics which the Mormons brought there and developed are a proof of the superiority of the Mormons over the Indians, while another person who abominates the means and subsidiary effects involved in the Mormon ethics which are responsible at least in part for those achievements, may prefer the desert and the romantic existence of the Indians. No science of any kind can purport to be able to dissuade these persons from their respective views.[31]

In America both the Social Darwinists and the philosophers of pragmatism had looked to the evolutionary process of nature and to patterns of social development in order to see evidence of progress and to take hope for the future. Weber doubted that evolutionary tendencies would yield truth and value and he remained convinced that the key to America lay not in its scientific future but in its religious past. America's entire culture had always been pushed along by what Santayana called "the dominance of the foreground." Weber looked to the background.

"THE WINE OF THE PURITANS"

Writing from the United States toward the end of his trip, Weber told his colleague Georg Jellinek that the visit was "wonderful and interesting" and already becoming "a more beautiful memory for me." Years later he would pause in the midst of an address to ask the audience to allow him to return his thoughts once again to America, because there matters of theoretical inquiry can be observed "in their most massive shape." Weber thought about America, his nephew Eduard Baumgarten wrote, with "heavy doses of fond sympathy . . . without even a trace of European nostalgia for citizens, castles, tradition and classics." Upon his return to Heidelberg, Weber, together with his wife Marianne and Ernst Troeltsch, held a series of group discussions called "American Evenings" in a town conference room. The trio spoke on living conditions in America and Marianne emphasized the respected status of women.[32]

In his thoughts on a variety of subjects—economics, politics, science, value, and objectivity—America became profoundly important to Weber. On no subject was America more a point of reference than on religion.

Weber had published the first part of "The Protestant Ethic and the Spirit of Capitalism" before leaving for the United States, and he would complete part two upon his return. In a letter to Heinrich Rickert in 1905, Weber described his thesis as a "cultural historical essay (asceticism of Protestantism as the basis of modern *vocational* culture, a sort of 'spiritualist' construction of the modern economy)." The following year he published "Churches and Sects in North America." What impressed Weber about religion in America, in contrast to that in Europe, is that the sects, rather than carrying on older gemeinschaft organic communities, operated voluntarily and hence fostered individualism and democracy. In Weber's thoughts the example of the North Carolina banker remained uppermost: the joiner who enters the sect and accepts certain religious responsibilities in return for obtaining standing in the community along with access to credit. In America religion was free, a matter of choice, what William James would call "a live option."[33]

In explaining the origins of capitalism in Protestantism (dealt with more fully in chapter 4 of this volume), Weber was also explaining the meaning of America with rare un-American insight. Tocqueville, America's leading interpreter, had seen a society of autonomous individuals completely indifferent to tradition and with no reverence for political authority, a society that only recognized the whims of public opinion and often succumbed to the punitive pressures of conformity. Tocqueville also believed that the key to America lay in having skipped the feudal stage of history. Thus America, blessed with having no aristocracy to overthrow or proletarian to fear, was "born free" and had no need to struggle to become so. Weber believed that Europeans, with the burden of feudalism haunting their minds, would miss the meaning of America, which lies in the psychological connection between the new individualism of liberal society and the old moralism of Calvinist theology. Sect-based religions ensure cohesion and mutual trust precisely because they are voluntaristic. Despite the doctrine of predestination, no one can really admire that which is predetermined; hence in daily life the personal qualities and achievements of sect members become "reputable" to the extent that their behavior reflects freely chosen religious convictions as well as commercial practices. Americans displayed a willingness to adopt ethical standards rather than having them instilled from above. Old-world cultures, Weber instructed, would have difficulty understanding America, where values are chosen rather than inherited, achieved rather than ascribed. "The exclusive appraisal of a person purely in terms of the religious qualities evidenced in his conduct necessarily prunes feudal and dynastic romanticism from its roots."[34]

The essence of Calvinist religiosity was an "ascetic" mentality that placed the demands of conscience ahead of all else, and this mentality resulted in a hybrid: heroic individuals who desire to form their own holy communities; men and women whose souls are on "probation"; people who are on their own and responsible for their own conduct yet seek to maintain their position by becoming members of a social group. Weber perceived a phenomenon that would have surprised Tocqueville, as well as Emerson and Thoreau: the compatibility of conscience and community, individual conviction and social conformity:

> Whoever represents "democracy" as a mass of fragmentation into atoms, as our romantics prefer to do, is fundamentally mistaken so far as America is concerned. "Atomization" is usually a consequence of

bureaucratic rationalism and, therefore, it cannot be eliminated through the forced imposition of an "organizational structure" from above. The genuine American society . . . was never such a sand pile.

In America, Weber continues, voluntary associations must be seen as artifacts of societies and not of communities, of gesellschaft and not gemeinschaft. Missing in America "is that undifferentiated peasant vegetative 'geniality' without which (as Germans are accustomed to believe) there can be no community." In America it is "sociation" (*Vergesellschaftung*) that places the individual in the purposive activity of the group, "be it a football team or a political party." Does the prevalence of group activity mean the loss of personal identity? Weber adds,

> This in no way means a lessening of the individual's need to constantly attend to his self-affirmation. On the contrary, the task of "*proving*" himself is present more than ever *within* the group, in the circle of his associates. And thus, the social association to which the individual belongs is for him never something "organic," never a mystical total essence that floats over him and envelops him. Rather he is *always* completely conscious of it as a mechanism for his own material and ideal *ends* [*Zwecke*].[35]

Weber's essay on "Church and Sects" is doubly remarkable. For one thing, its author doubts that fellow Germans would be capable of understanding behavior that is moral without being communal, behavior that is personal and responsible yet lacking the traditional organic ties where members feel some mystical oneness with fellow members of a group. Weber also worries that his efforts to introduce old religion into new social theory "are more likely to strengthen the usual German beliefs concerning Puritanism, that it basically has been and still is idle 'hypocrisy.' " Because Germany's historical development differs from that of America, especially in having a Reformation that led to officialdom rather than to idealism, and because liberalism and modernity have been hostile to religion, Weber wonders how his work will be received. "We modern, religiously 'unattuned' people are hard pressed to conceptualize or even simply to *believe* what a powerful role these religious factors had in those periods when the characters of the modern national cultures were being stamped." In those periods people concerned themselves with the "hereafter" and little else. "It remains the fate of us Germans that due to numerous historical causes, the religious revolution of that time meant a development that favored not the energy of the individual but the prestige of 'office.'" In Germany Protestantism became a state-supported church of methodological clerics serving as clerks responsible only to their office; in America Protestantism was a consciously chosen way of life in which the individual is responsible to the self and its troubled conscience.[36]

The second remarkable feature of Weber's reflections is that the "fate of us Germans" becomes also the fate of us Americans. American intellectuals, too, would have no patience with the thesis that liberalism and individualism had somehow evolved from the moral discipline of Calvinism. To the Progressive generation of Americans, Puritanism stalked the country like a curse from the past, the original sin that left everyone guilty and repressed. H. L. Mencken, the American journalist who, like Weber, had been influenced by Nietzsche, presented to Americans a portrait of Puritanism that smacked of Nietzsche's critique of Christianity as docile and slavish. Mencken accused Puritanism of anti-intellectual philistinism, censorious prying into private affairs, and hostility to beauty. A sarcastic wit, Mencken once defined Puritanism as the suspicion that someone, somewhere, at some time might be happy. Of German ancestry, he resented an American country in the grip of Anglo-Saxon culture.[37]

"To the modern young person who tries to live well there is no type so devastating and harassing as the Puritan." Thus spake Randolph Bourne, a hero of the Greenwich Village rebellion of the World War I years. Bourne comes amazingly close to Weber's description of the Puritan as the willing joiner of social groups who accepts individual responsibility, only to depart from Weber when he concludes that the whole process is crippling and terrifying. How can the Puritan get satisfaction from sternly subjecting himself? Bourne, a Nietzschean, advised America to observe carefully how the "self-debasing" and "self-regarding" impulses interact in ways that allow the Puritan to gain control over others while striking the pose of humility and sacrifice. The Puritan puts on the face of meekness merely to avoid arousing envy and resentment. But,

> having given his self-abasing impulse free rein, he is now in a position to exploit his self-regard. He has made himself right with the weak and slavish. He has fortified himself with their alliance. He now satisfies his self-regard by becoming proud of his humility and enjoining it on others. If it were self-control alone that made the puritan, he would not be as powerful as he is. Indeed he would be no more than the mild ascetic, who is all abnegation because his self-regarding mechanism is weak. But in the puritan, both impulses are strong. It is

control over others that yields him his satisfactions of power. He may stamp out his sex-desire, but his impulse to shatter ideas that he does not like will flourish wild and wanton. To the puritan the beauty of unselfishness lies in his being able to enforce it on others. He loves virtue not so much for its own sake as for its being an instrument of his terrorism.[38]

Mencken, Bourne, and other American critics of Puritanism were actually close to Weber's thesis that Puritanism at one time in history had a certain austere integrity of intellect before its principles succumbed to pleasure and its convictions gave way to compromise and the rewards of conformity. The idea that ethical idealism could evolve into capitalist materialism resonated metaphorically in Van Wyck Brooks's *The Wine of the Puritans* (1908), a book written in response to a symposium question, "What is America?" What indeed! "You put the old wine into new bottles," the narrator explains, "and when the explosion results, one may say the aroma passes into the air and the wine spills on the floor. The aroma, or ideal, turns into Transcendentalism, and the wine, the real, becomes Commercialism."[39]

A perfect Weberian formulation. Weber himself, as will be seen in the following chapter, had been influenced by America's Transcendentalist theologians; he would have had no difficulty recognizing that part of Calvinism retained its piety while the other half gravitated toward profits. And Weber would have agreed with Brooks that Emersonian Transcendentalism represented an "inverted Calvinism," the seeking of salvation by means other than formal religion.

Yet American thinkers assumed the Puritan heritage still weighed heavily on the nation's psyche, producing intolerance and bigotry, putting the creative and acquisitive impulses at war with one another, and allowing fundamentalist preachers to run amok. But Weber, like Tocqueville, believed that to understand America one must begin with its religious beginnings, and both discerned in Puritanism the vital passions of the heart beating against the threatening deadness of the world. The temptation in American intellectual history, however, is to regard the beginning as a curse rather than a blessing.

Was America misbegotten? Generation upon generation of American writers and intellectuals have assumed their country had been misconceived at birth. The theology of Calvinism, the religion brought to the New World by the Puritans of the Old World, sowed the seeds of capitalism and there followed America's fall from grace, a plunge into what the discontent like to call the alienated state of "pre-history": the rise of an exchange economy of trade and commerce, then industrialization and big business, and finally the massive structure of today's corporate society with its alleged "hegemonic" domination. Scholars often cite the work of Weber to demonstrate that New England Puritanism provided the "liberal rationalization of economic life."[40]

All this is in keeping with a persistent tendency in American historiography: tell me what you don't like about the present, and I'll show you how it came to be legitimated in the past. But such reasoning scarcely reflects the intent of Weber, who set out to understand the "heroic age of capitalism" as a moral proposition that depended on character and responsibility, an ethical "calling" to an inner-worldly asceticism. Spirited by "transcendental sanctions," the early capitalism that derived from Puritanism "enabled its adherent to create free institutions." Today much of what once gave us our freedoms has now become the enemy as early Protestantism and capitalism are blamed for producing "alienation," "schizophrenia," and "anal repression."[41]

Although no apologist for capitalism, Weber found in America's Puritan heritage a lost treasure, a concept of moral personality that he saw as disappearing from the world, a discovery all the more remarkable in that it was made by a sociologist. While many sociologists, in Europe and especially in America, were developing ideas of personality and the self based on theories of social interaction, Weber stood closer to his Transcendentalist and Calvinist predecessors in believing (as did Nietzsche) that one becomes who one really is by one's own efforts. Deriving from religious experience, genuine personality requires of the self "a systematization from within, and moving outward from a center, that the individual has himself achieved." Personality scarcely involves the development of the self by way of an outward "series of occurrences" but instead by having "an 'inner core,' an altogether regulated unity of life conduct, deriving from some central stance [*Stellungnahme*] of one's own." When Weber told Rickert that his work on the Protestant ethic aimed to find in Protestant asceticism a "modern *vocational* culture," he was seeking to recapture the older idea of the "calling" as a possible antidote to the corrosions of modernity. But how could duty and self-discipline come to be appreciated when modern sociology was expounding the notion that there is no inner self, no solitary "I" unaffected by social conditions, no transcendent mind to which conscience is accountable?[42]

In attempting to present to the modern world an older religious idea of ethical character, an idea based upon the premise that individuals choose the ultimate ideals to which they dedicate their lives, Weber can be described as "the last Puritan." In 1926, six years after Weber's death, George Santayana's *The Last Puritan* appeared, a commentary upon the American and German national characters with Calvinism serving as backdrop. The main character, Oliver Alden, embodies much of what Weber had in mind in resurrecting Puritan ethics. Instead of trying to experience everything, "he kept himself for what was best. That's why he was a true Puritan after all." Aware of the contingency of all things, Oliver will recognize circumstances as a prerequisite to changing them but he will not be a slave to the vagaries of social existence. Oliver, who voiced Santayana's desire for serene order and harmony, scarcely reflects Weber's vision of strife and conflict. But they both saw American Protestantism as an expression of romantic individualism, and, with respect to committing oneself to an ideal, Santayana's character represents precisely the quality of aristocratic liberalism that Weber articulated as a moralist if not a sociologist. "Either truth or nothing," declares Oliver at the story's end, a similar utterance to Weber's last whisper on his death bed. "I was born old," Oliver states, and

> I was born a moral aristocrat, able to obey only the voice of God, which means that of my own heart. My people went to America as exiles into a stark wilderness to lead a life apart, purer and soberer than the carnival life of Christendom. We were not content to be well-dressed animals, rough or cunning or lustfully prowling and acquisitive, and perhaps inventing a religion to encourage us in our animality. We will not now sacrifice to Baal because we seem to have failed. We will bide our time. . . . We will not accept anything cheaper or cruder than our own conscience. We have dedicated ourselves to truth, to living in the presence of the noblest things we can conceive. If we can't live so, we won't live at all.[43]

Of Anglo-American Puritanism it could be said that Weber represented both its wine and its aroma; the reality it became and the ideals that lingered on in the teachings of his own German household; that which had been effected by the passage of time and that which had been lost to modern thought and yet still made itself felt as an "agonized conscience." So burdened and so blessed, Weber faced the world prepared, like a true Puritan, to translate what he knew in his heart into what he formulated in his head.

THE SCHOLAR AS *LEIDENSCHAFTLICHER GENUßMENSCH*

Although few Americans came to know Max Weber on the basis of his trip to the United States in 1904, when he returned to Germany he enjoyed wide recognition. The talks that he and Marianne delivered at the "American Evening" sessions in Heidelberg took place among familiar faces. Some showed up to hear Weber talk for the first time after years of illness; others had heard of him and wanted to see for themselves.

Max Weber left a deep impression on anyone who encountered his riveting presence. Even before he spoke his physical features gave the effect of power concentrated and focused. An earlier photo of a young, beer-drinking carouser sporting dueling scars shows him thinner, his face free of the furrows so familiar to Weberian scholars. In a later and more telling photo he has the stern look of a Calvinist preacher. A thick beard covers the lower face and barely reveals softly curving lips; a pronounced, wide nose rests between frowning dark eyes that stare out with a scrutinizing severity; above them arches a brow wrinkled and weighted with worry.

His heavy, serious outward demeanor belies other hidden emotions that could be surprisingly tender. His letters to his wife reveal a sensitivity and affectionate caring that came from the heart rather than the head. One contemporary remembers his "golden sense of humor" and "deep sense of charity." The latter quality often had him stepping aside so that others could have access to academic appointments, even those who held different political positions. Curiously, Weber wrote about the springs of ambition that drove the Puritan to create, unintentionally, the roots of modern capitalism; yet Weber himself displayed little professional ambition in his academic career. Although many sociologists see the human desire for recognition and approbation as basic to social conduct, Weber scarcely seems to have felt it himself, even while acknowledging it in his work. He had no interest in writing best-selling books or in exploiting the lecture circuit. He seemed indifferent to reputation, status, and prestige. In a German academic culture full of pomp and ceremony, he never received an honorary degree and most likely never sought one.[44]

The historian Friedrich Meinecke remembers Weber as both a deeply serious scholar and a *Leidenschaftlicher Genußmensch,* a physical man of gusto with a lust for life. He could withdraw into the quiet of his study and emerge ready for conversation and a libation. He enjoyed the Alps as much as the archives. Whatever he did—whether research or recreation—he did with passionate intensity. The author of the "Protestant

Ethic" worked long and hard but seldom to the point of denying the pleasures of life. According to Meinecke, he had a "rousing social life" (*übermütiger Gesselkeit*), and after an all-nighter on the town he would "gladly" go for a swim in the Necker River.[45]

Self-driven, Weber's quarrel was as much with God as with society. Intellectually he was more a seeker than a scholar. "Weber had no philosophy," the philosopher Karl Jaspers wrote; "he was philosophy." Knowing truth had been lost to knowledge and its corrosive skepticisms, he dedicated himself all the more to knowing the unknowable. No subject was alien to his inquiring mind, a penetrating mind upon which nothing was lost.[46]

A complex personality, Weber had moods that swung between the sincere and the sardonic, and occasionally he had to fight off the "demons" that haunted his imagination as they had shadowed that of Goethe. He had, a contemporary observed, "a chivalrous ardour for doing the right thing that sometimes verged on the quixotic." A "political rowdy," Weber loved to combat the false and frivolous. Another figure, describing the World War I period when Weber was criticizing the German government, spoke of the "pugnacious character" of his daring use of words "which put his freedom and life in danger." Weber spoke so directly and passionately that even his opponents admired his frankness and intellectual honesty. "His words rang with force," recalls another, "a torrent flowing from all the pores of his being." But the strife and struggle behind his words was restrained, cool, a delicate balance between emotion and reason that seemed, to people listening to him, about to explode had it not been for his severe self-control. Sometimes his patience gave way to polemic and invective when he could no longer suffer fools smilingly. Philosophers who talked endlessly of a "higher synthesis," he quipped, should come down from the "clouds" and have their heads examined. When President Woodrow Wilson offered the formula "Peace Without Victory" to bring World War I to an end, Weber wryly remarked that every time the German army has a victory the world is further away from peace.[47]

Weber could hardly believe in a peaceful world without conflict. In some respects his outlook toward the world reflected his experience with his childhood and his family. In Weber's social and political reflections his philosophy often bespoke his biography and his struggles with life. Some clues to his life and mind may be found at the foot of the cradle.

TWO

"Man's Philosophy Is His Biography"

CHILDHOOD INSECURITIES AND CURIOSITIES

It was no easy birth. On April 21, 1864, Max Weber was born in Erfurt, a town close to Weimar. He was a firstborn child, often a portent of high achievement. Another possible sign was his head, too large for his frail body. His mother had contracted a fever and was unable to breastfeed him. She worried about his sickly condition in the following years, especially after he became dangerously ill with meningitis. During his illness, through bouts of cramps and congestions, "little Max's head grew conspicuously while his limbs remained girlishly small," wrote Marianne in her biography.

As a youth Weber had many "nervous peculiarities and anxieties" as a result of the disease. In adolescence he was tormented by the thought of dying or becoming an imbecile. Earlier, at the age of five, his mother would try to carry him into the ocean, thinking that the bracing salt water would strengthen him. But Max reacted to the roaring sea with screams of terror he would remember later as a grown man.[1]

Childhood insecurities subsided; his mother and grandmother were encouraged by young Max's resourcefulness and self-reliance. He would become absorbed in games and puzzles, and for hours he chattered to himself as he answered all challenges with a concentrated curiosity. From youth to adulthood Weber overcame his physical infirmities with cerebral intensity. Throughout his life he would frown upon weakness in anyone—man, woman, or child. Valuing autonomy and the strength to take independent stands, he subscribed fully to the adage "dependency begets servility." He would grow up to become the diagnostician of domination.

Yet Weber grew up carrying acute inner dualisms, such as the tension between freedom and power and emotion and reason, and these divided impulses in his mind and temperament reflected in part his parentage. His father came from a wealthy family of linen manufacturers in Bielefield. Max's grandfather, Karl August Weber, presided over a house with a proud kinship and conducted his commercial business in a relaxed, easy style. He showed up at the office just before noon. Weber's father, Max Sr., went into law and became active in politics as a member of the Prussian Landtag and the German Reichstag. The paternal side of Weber's ancestry lived for business and politics, the world of wealth and power and the contentments of material success.

Weber's maternal lineage had more to do with the interior sphere of affections and spiritual yearning. The grandmother, Emile Souchay, shy and frail, felt inadequate in the face of her more confident husband, a descendant of the French Huguenots who brought to Germany a Calvinist tradition. Emile drew upon her faith in God and the inner freedom of spiritual grace and communion. Weber's mother, Helene Fallenstein, had much the same character, a sweet soul of piety and patience, loved by others more than she could ever love herself. Through her sister, Ida, she met Max Sr. when she was sixteen and he twenty-four. They married soon after in the full bloom of romantic love. The wife and husband appeared happy. But Helene silently put up with her husband's overbearing ways as she produced seven other children after Max was born. Everyone was captivated by Helene's charm and natural goodness; few noticed the quiet doubts and crises of conscience. The sensitive Max Jr. felt the struggle within the household, as did his Aunt Ida.

Ida loaned Weber, when in his teens, the works of the American Transcendentalist William Ellery Channing. His mother had also been influenced by the Transcendentalist Theodore Parker. Both New England theologians believed that inner perfection was the prerequisite for any attempt at social reform. Although Weber's mother could never turn his mind toward religious matters, Weber became impressed with the "unassailable height of convictions" in Channing's religious philosophy, which looked to the "individual human soul" as the fount of value and energy that made up for the infirmity of the will. But Weber saw little use in Channing's antipolitical temperament and pacifism. The renunciation of violence, Weber wrote to his mother, may have been justified in the case of America's war with Mexico (1846–48), but in everyday life to listen to God more than to man is only a "formula for an older Christian martyrdom."[2]

Yet if Channing's pacifism offered no solution to the conflict between ethics and power, his philosophy did emphasize a vital connection between religion and the life of labor. As did Tocqueville, Weber would come to appreciate the voluntary character of Protestant institutions in America; in the pre–Civil War era labor was extolled as a Christian duty rather than stigmatized as mindless drudgery best left to servants, slaves, and field hands, as it was in the plantation South. To Channing the Christian imperative of self-denial was vital in a culture where "anxiety grows with possessions" to the point that the pursuit of riches unrestrained by spiritual grace could be the ruination of a country. Weber saw something special in American Protestantism, a "school of hardened asceticism," he would later call it, that was absent in German Protestantism. Weber had little patience with a Transcendentalism that looked upon reason as the faculty of moral perfection, but he could agree with Channing's dictum: "Nothing decides the character of a people more than the form and determination of labor." Channing praised America's middle-class republic, imbued with "habits of self-help" evolving from the "rough schools of labor." In mid-nineteenth century America virtue had more to do with work than wealth, with the demands of honest toil than with the drapery of social status.[3]

HEIDELBERG STUDENT DAYS

The idea that labor constituted the content of a nation's character would stay with Weber when he later investigated the condition of agricultural and industrial workers in Wilhelminian Germany. The principle of labor and productivity may also explain why young Weber remained more interested in modern America than in classical antiquity, where work and toil carried the stigma of slavery. At the age of fourteen, when many impressionable youths are looking for authority figures, he made it clear to his uncle, Fritz Baumgarten, that ancient Greek and Roman thinkers had little to teach modern society. Herodotus? Too sanctimonious to be a reliable historian. Cicero? Though a man of "extreme moral purity" (*überaus sittenreiner*) he gave speeches that lacked fierceness and determination, amounting to lamentations when what was needed were lessons. But the teenage youth at least paid the ancient authorities the respect of reading them in their original language.[4]

Weber enrolled at the University of Heidelberg shortly after turning eighteen. Thin and lanky, bookish and brilliant without being arrogant, he confessed what he thought were his limitations to his mother. "I don't flirt with girls. I don't write poems. What shall I do except read?" Like his father, he majored in jurisprudence with law and politics in mind. He also studied economics, history, and philosophy. Later, doing graduate work at the University of Berlin, Weber studied Roman law with the eminent historian Theodore Mommsen. At the defense of his Ph.D. thesis, "The History of Commercial Societies in the Middle Ages," Mommsen paid him the highest compliment. "When I come to die, there is no one better to whom I should like to say this: Son, the spear is too heavy for my hand, carry it on."[5]

Weber first worked as a barrister in Berlin courts and then as a *dozent* (lecturer without pay) at the university. In the period of the late 1880s Weber lived at his parents' house and was financially dependent upon a father he came more and more to dislike. In contrast to his uncle Baumgarten, who remained true to his political principles of 1848 and never reconciled himself to the Bismarck regime, the senior Weber seemed all compromise and no conviction, an amiable boor when not a petulant bully.

Max Weber could hardly model his life after that of his self-satisfied father, who lived for pleasure and looked upon politics as nothing more than wheeling and dealing. As a college student at Heidelberg, Weber rebelled against regulations and starched-collar respectability. With other fraternity youths, he spent freely, downed steins of beer, gambled at cards, while alone he searched for ideals that might elevate life above hedonism. He also indulged in dueling as evidence of manhood, looking upon sword cuts (*Schmisse*) as scars of honor. Once, upon returning from Heidelberg to his parents' house in Berlin, his mother opened the door and, barely recognizing the "scarred boozer," welcomed him with a slap across the face.[6]

Startled by the slap, Weber may have been pleasantly surprised as well. During his Heidelberg student days Weber had received from his mother letters regarding a certain "Frau X" who tended to cringe in the face of her husband's domineering presence. The son advised his mother that the wife's timidity and silence probably only increased the husband's mistrust in people for failing to deal honestly and openly with him. If she stood up to him he might become aware of how he has been suppressing her basic rights—"that of free thought and free speech; indeed the freedom of the person altogether." Although Weber admitted that no one can say for sure what might happen if the cowering wife suddenly challenges her husband, he remained convinced that the self-righteousness of those who wield power requires the shock of resistance on the part of those subject to it.[7]

In Weber the personal translates into the political. The submissive citizen was as repugnant to him as the withdrawing housewife. Germany's political culture had been shaped by Bismarck's *Staatskunst*. In Weber's estimate, Bismarck's rule rendered the bourgeoisie too content to make a bid for real political power as well as parliamentary representation. Bismarck had also intended to pacify workers through a smattering of welfare and social security provisions. Weber complained to his uncle Baumgarten that the German people had willingly acquiesced to both Bismarck's rule and the reign of the Kaisers as though the little liberty they enjoyed existed as a concession from authority. It is this "type of tactless servility," Weber exploded, that renders Germans so satisfied with Bismarckian material prosperity that they have become complacent when they should be defiant.[8]

The name of Max Weber is frequently associated with the idea of authority and its various theories. Yet what the authoritarian loves most Weber valued least—obedience. The young Weber grew up feeling a vague disgust toward conventional authority and those who go along with it in a state of mindless habit. In his first scholarly study, ostensibly so technical and statistical, he tried to awaken Germans to a passion for freedom by showing in what ways their own agrarian workers were unwilling to accept domination and servitude.

"WE MUST BEGIN TO LEARN ALL OVER AGAIN"

The 1880s were for Weber a time of considerable activity and divided attention on matters personal as well as professional. At the age of twenty-eight he was pondering his recent engagement to his fiancée Marianne, a step taken with some difficulty as he was still romantically attached to his adolescent sweetheart, Emmy Baumgarten, daughter of his uncle Fritz. Weber's first pangs of love erupted with Emmy, adding to the turbulence of his younger years. In the same decade he was holding down three jobs in Berlin—lecturing at the university, writing for and editing a journal, and representing an attorney at the Supreme Court (the Kammergericht). He worked daily from nine until seven in the evening. At the same time he yearned for a role in the governance of the nation. Yet none of the political positions existing in Germany seemed promising to Weber. The various theories of political economy struck him as little more than deductive delusions.

The socialists believed the stages of economic development would yield the truths and norms necessary to bring about freedom, harmony, and justice in modern society. Economists of the Manchester School relied upon self-regulating laws of the marketplace to fulfill the needs of the German people. Progressives assumed that the interests of workers and the power of capitalists could be supervised and regulated by a centralized state consisting of administrative officials who claimed expertise. To Weber political economy suffered from too much theory and not enough practical, empirical investigations. Weber had the opportunity to demonstrate the inadequacy of reigning theories when he took on the task of analyzing, interpreting, and evaluating a massive study on the conditions of agricultural workers in East Elbian Germany. The study had been commissioned by the Verein für Sozialpolitik, an organization founded in the 1870s to bring social science to bear on questions of public policy. The study derived from a wide-reaching survey of farmers, and was based on detailed questionnaires and special reports on field laborers in various rural districts. This resulted in three volumes of regional surveys supported by a staggering body of statistics. What did it all signify?

In his first effort at analyzing research data Weber not only showed how knowledge depends upon interpretive understanding; he also showed why the reign of Junker hegemony, the pride of the nation-state, will soon be replaced by the advent of commercial capitalism and why existing theories of political economy were no longer adequate in explaining the changes underway in Germany. After the publication of Weber's analysis, one member of the Verein admitted: "The predominant feeling aroused by the work is the sense that our knowledge is antiquated and that we must begin to learn all over again."[9]

Good research brought bad news. Addressing a Germany that had identified economic development with the progressive improvement of all classes, Weber reported that the transition to full capitalism (*Hochkapitalismus*) had not benefited the *Gutsherrschaften*, a form of manorial system under which peasants had labored for the lord in return for their own land. The arrival of agricultural machinery and the specialization of crops only disguised the damage economic changes had done to the rural system of labor among the *Instleute*, free contractual laborers who lived on large estates and who agreed to a one-year contract of work together with the "entire family of workers."

These laborers attracted Weber's curiosity as well as his sympathy. In conventional radical social theory workers were supposedly bound by a kind of class consciousness joining them together in sentiments of identity and solidarity. As Weber looked upon rural field laborers, they seemed almost incipient entrepreneurs, particularly when they hired the labor power of "corvee workers" or "day laborers" whom they themselves paid. Moreover, the *Instleute* spent a good deal of the year involved in sowing and reaping, and thus, in addition to a daily wage, they had as much interest in profits resulting from the annual harvest as did the estate owners. Were workers attempting to rise with their class or to break free from the class conditions that had been imposed upon them?

If Weber discerned individual aspiration at the bottom of society, he was not blind to class exploitation at the top. The agricultural laborers, even though they identified their future with the profit and prosperity accruing to the *Gutsherrschaften*, found themselves being displaced, as a consequence of the shift to a money economy, by cheaper wage workers coming from Poland and Russia. With the arrival of immigrant workers, class antagonisms between owners of the manor and older agricultural laborers broke out as rural life underwent its inevitable transformation. The implications of this situation went beyond economics and involved national security. With German peasant day-laborers migrating to the cities, rural Germany was further depopulated and the eastern countryside could potentially be opened to Slavic settlement, a development that endangered the "Germanness" of Germany and rendered the country vulnerable to foreign invasion.[10]

THE CRISIS OF POLITICAL LEADERSHIP

One can well understand why readers of Weber's report felt the need to learn all over again. The relationship of economics to politics had to be reconsidered since neither the hegemony of the Junkers nor their recent decline can be explained solely in economic terms. The estates constituted less a system of capital and labor than a relation of domination and subordination in which estate owners had all legal authority at their disposal. Historically the Junkers had won their ascendancy through Prussia's military victories and Bismarck's political achievements. As ruling elites they had little to do with the means of production. But if Weber's report caused socialists to rethink their premises, it also compelled capitalists to reconsider their promises.

Manchester theorists expected economic development to improve conditions for all classes. Weber demonstrated that economic change shattered the community of interest between worker and landowner; hence the transformation from a patriarchal organization to a capitalist system turned people against one another. "Between natural economic opponents there can only be struggle, and it is sheer madness to believe that a strengthening of the economic power of one party would benefit the *social* position of the other." Where many contemporary theorists of political economy saw progress arising from economic development, Weber saw tragic consequences for workers who were forced into becoming proletarians when they desired to be entrepreneurs. "His farm hands," Weber wrote of the Junker, "were by no means proletarians . . . they were, on a small scale, agriculturalists with a direct interest in their lord's husbandry. But they were expropriated by the rising valuation of the land; their lord withheld pasture and land, kept his grain, and paid them in wages instead. Thus, the old community of interest was dissolved, and farm hands became proletarians."[11]

Yet while it lasted the *Instleute* system allowed free contractual laborers to identify their interests with those of the estate. The laborer became a partner, a "small entrepreneur" in the master's world of producing and selling. "The strictly patriarchal leadership was tolerated because it corresponded to the economic foundations of the relationship." Clearly Weber sympathized with the aspiring field worker, the incipient capitalist who desired to escape his class situation only to fall victim to capitalism itself. Identifying with those determined to move upward, Weber's tragic sense protests against the restricting conditions of modern life that make class formations inevitable and the older feeling of personal responsibility impossible:

> Only a class can negotiate with a class; the relations of responsibility between the individual master and the individual worker disappear; the individual entrepreneur becomes, so to speak, capable of being substituted, he is merely a class type. The personal relation of responsibility disappears and something impersonal, which one used to call the domination of capital, takes its place.[12]

The older patriarchal hegemony at least rested on personal relations of domination; the new "impersonal class-domination" could only sever all human ties and bring about class hatred, itself a reflection of the irrational aura of money and the unconscious roots of economic desire that breed resentment. In his later years Weber would be accused of "fearing" the Left and the prospect of social revolution. The truth is he wanted to see human action become conscious; he wanted actors to know the motives for their actions. In the case of rural life he saw the disparity of wealth creating frustration on the part of those who, deprived of a decent level of existence and envious of the possessions of the privileged few, are tempted to destroy that which they desire. Although Weber had little patience with socialism, he scarcely subscribed to the opposite view: that the idea of liberty must stand and fall with capitalism. At least he could not subscribe to it until capitalism becomes conscious of the tragic consequences of its own actions.

In 1893 Weber delivered his report on agricultural workers to the general assembly of the Verein. The many layers of his rich analysis immediately earned him recognition as one of Germany's leading social scientists. The report brought to public attention how the rural economy was being penetrated by new rationalized entrepreneurial forces and how the dominant position of the Junkers was being assumed by a bustling new commercial class. This remarkable situation presented Germany with an unprecedented political crisis as the old order passed into history. Thus Weber's technical report also served as a text for the political education of a nation. With political authority at the top being subverted by new economic forces, Weber saw no capacity for leadership forthcoming, and he would soon address this vacuum as a class issue. The middle class was still in historical transition and the working class still waiting to form itself.

> The disturbing element in the situation which confronts us is that while the bourgeois classes as bearers of the power interests of the nation seem to be withering, there is no evidence to indicate that the working classes are in any sense qualified to replace them. . . . In our cradles we were visited with the most grievous curse that history can impose upon a generation: the cruel fate of being political epigoni.[13]

The fate that confronted Weber's generation was not only the alienation of workers from the fruits of their labor but the alienation of freedom from responsibility, an ironic result of the new economic liberty of the market breaking the older bonds of political authority. That the new entrepreneurial class would continue to import foreign workers indicated that it put its own interests above those of Germany. National loyalty and duty commanded little respect in a market economy. Weber searched for a way to accept economic modernity and at the same time cultivate necessary political beliefs. Specifically he recommended that the importation of Polish and Russian workers be halted and the large estates in the east be divided and supervised by the State. In seeking to link economic policies with political aims, Weber sought to enhance the power of the nation as the symbol of national ideals. While some scholars looked to laws of economics to deliver Germany from the weight of history, Weber looked to the human condition itself as it contends with particular historical situations. For such a challenge the moral education of a nation takes precedence over the claims of political economy. In his inaugural address, delivered at the University of Freiburg in 1895, Weber presented the first lessons of a nation's education and explained why it was important for Germany to reach for heights beyond itself.

THE FREIBURG INAUGURAL ADDRESS

The previous year Weber had accepted a chair at Freiburg in *Nationalökonomie* (political economy). Immediately students flocked to his seminar to learn his method of studying rural labor, and requests for Weber to lecture elsewhere in Germany arrived with the daily mail. When Weber gave his inaugural lecture the auditorium was packed with students, scholars, and journalists, some merely curious, others prepared to learn anew.

Weber began his address discussing in detail the results of various studies of agricultural labor. After describing the changing character of the nation's population as deadly serious, he took pains to point out that the political consequences of the problem were far more important than its economic causes. The assumption that the attainment of economic power qualifies a class to claim political leadership is a dangerous notion, "and in the long run incompatible with the interest of the nation when the economically declining class is politically dominant." The Junkers could no longer rule and Bismarck's reign failed to cultivate citizenship responsibilities among the German people. As a result, "the bourgeois classes, as repositories of the *power*-interests of the nation, seem to be withering, and there is still no sign that the workers have begun to mature so that they can take their place." Left without political guidance, Weber implied, his was a lost generation led astray by Junker obsolescence and a national habit of mass obedience.[14]

"I am a member of the bourgeois classes," Weber announced. "I feel myself to be a bourgeois, and I have been brought up to share their views and ideals. But it is the task of precisely our science to say what people do not like to hear—to those above us, to those below us, and also to our own class."

What was it Germany did not want to hear? In words that echo the political philosophy of Alexander Hamilton, Weber believed that the future belonged to an ascendant class and not to the Prussian Junkers (or, in the American context, the Southern planters). Weber also insisted, like Hamilton, that the social cohesion of the nation is the source of strength to which all other considerations must be subordinate: "A nation is favoured by destiny if the naive identification of the interests of one's own class with the general interest also corresponds to the interests of national power." But in periods of economic transition the political will atrophies and teachers of economic science cultivate a "feeble eudaemonism" in the guise of "socio-political" ideals. "And it is one of the delusions which arise from the modern over-estimation of the 'economic' in the usual sense of the word when people assert that their feelings of political community cannot maintain themselves in face of the full weight of divergent economic interests, indeed that very possibly these feelings are *merely* the reflection of the economic basis underlying those changing interests." Just as Hamilton believed that economic development should strive for unity rather than diversity, Weber insisted that Germany should avoid listening to economists who assume that different class interests can never be unified when each class gives priority to its own material pleasures. Economists offer a glib calculus of human happiness, Weber held, when what Germany needed was the challenge of greatness. Such a challenge cannot be found in a culture that puts the quantity of material goods ahead of the quality of moral life.

Weber informed the audience that divisive conditions prevail mainly during the social stresses of economic transformation. But in more immediate moments of great crisis, such as in war, it becomes clear that the nation-state rests upon "deep and elemental psychological foundations within economic dominant classes." Like Hamilton, Weber also believed that the elemental political instinct toward the public good "sinks below the level of consciousness of the masses" and, hence, must be articulated by a governing elite. Weber, too, was a conservative who refused to be guided by the past. "If our work is to retain any meaning it can only be formed by this: concern for the *future,* for *those who will come after us.*"

Weber is also closer to Hamilton, and further away from Jefferson, in rejecting the pursuit of happiness as one of life's aims and instead offering the strenuous ideals of duty and responsibility. Political economy deceives itself, he believed, with its "optimistic dreams of happiness." Remember, he enjoined, Dante's warning: "Abandon hope all ye who enter here: these words are inscribed above the portals of the unknown future history of mankind. So much for the dream of peace and happiness." From Dante Weber turns to Nietzsche. "The question which leads us beyond the grave of our own generation is not 'how will human beings *feel* in the future,' but 'how will they be.' In fact this question underlies all work in political economy. We do not want to train up feelings of well-being in people, but rather those characteristics we think constitute the greatness and nobility of our human nature." To this task the doctrines of political economy, with their concern for either the production of commodities or their distribution, scarcely touch the human condition. A true human science "investigates above all else the quality of the human beings who are brought up in the economic and social conditions of existence."

Reading the Freiburg address today, exactly a century later, one cannot help but feel the frustration that Weber conveyed about Germany's predicament. History's highest moments come only from leadership, yet leadership leaves people in a complacent torpor, and those later generations who come after, Weber observed, reiterating a sentiment voiced on previous occasions, feel that "history has bestowed on us as a historical baptismal gift the most burdensome curse which it could give to any people: the harsh fate of *following* the period of political greatness." After having turned to Bismarck to watch their country become unified, "the German bourgeoisie, intoxicated with success and thirsting for peace, was overcome by a peculiarly 'unhistorical' and unpolitical mood. German history seemed at an end." The "dominance of a great man is not always a means of political education," particularly when a nation is content to engage in the politics of power diplomacy and aspire to nothing more than playing international politics like a game of chess. While Germany dabbles in the "paltry manoeuvering of [its] epigone," the great challenge of world adventure, the romance of seeing the German flag following "overseas expansion," surpasses German's capacity for wonder. "The blazing sun which shone at Germany's zenith, and which caused the name of Germany to shine in the farthest corners of the earth—the sun was, so it almost seemed, too strong for us; it had burned away the bourgeoisie's slow growing capacity for political judgment. For what do we see?"

Weber continues with a close analysis of Germany's impasse. He chides the haut bourgeoisie for looking to a "new Caesar" to protect it from below against the rising masses and from above against the ruling elites. Meanwhile the petit bourgeoisie does not stir. It moves only out of petty economic concerns. And the workers? "*Economically*, the upper strata of the German working class are much more mature than the egoism of the property-owning classes might admit. Justifiably, therefore, they demand freedom, and even by means of organized and open struggle for economic power to defend their interests." Yet Weber, while defending workers, by no means sided with radical intellectuals who saw workers transforming themselves into a revolutionary proletariat prepared to carry out the "mission" of history Marx assigned to them:

> *Politically*, the working class is infinitely less mature than the clique of journalists who aspire to monopolise its leadership would have it believe. Much play is made with memories of a century ago in the circle of these *declassé* bourgeois: the result is that here and there the more timid souls see in them the spiritual descendants of the men of the Convention. However, they are infinitely more harmless than they appear to themselves: there is in them no glimmer of that Catilinarian energy of the act, nor certainly does there breathe in them any of that storm of *national* passion which blew through the halls of the Convention. They are pathetic experts in political triviality; they lack the deep instincts for *power* of a class that has been called to political leadership.

After Weber repeatedly describes labor as so immature as to be a "*politically* uneducated *philistine class*," and hence incapable of leading Germany into the twentieth century, he raises a troubling question. "Why is the proletariat of England and France to some extent differently constituted?" Weber answers his question with a characteristically ironic observation that went against the grain of his era. "The reason is to be found not only in a longer period of *economic* education, resulting from the organized struggle of the English working classes for its interests. It is rather a matter of the reverberations of world-power status, which constantly confronts the state with great problems of power-politics and which provides the individual with continuous political schooling."

Many radical thinkers of Weber's era regarded imperialism as capitalism pushed to its "highest stage"; Weber saw German workers remaining immature precisely because they had no will to imperial exploits, no interest in "German power-politics on a global scale." Ironically, where Marxists hoped that workers as a proletariat would rise in opposition to imperialism, Weber believed imperialism could hardly take place without workers marching with it.

"THE MAGIC OF FREEDOM"

The Freiburg address, with its many references to "world-power" and
"power-politics," has been interpreted by historians as a call for national
unity in which the might of the new industrial state would expand overseas and find its place in the sun of liberal imperialism. Some scholars find
Weber's "tub thumping" not a little arrogant and even "demagogic," an
ominous portent of the emotions on which the Third Reich battened on
its march to power.[15] The overtones are there, to be sure. But the Nazi
roots of the Third Reich lay in the post–World War I situation, which
had left Germany defeated and humiliated and, as will be discussed in the
last chapters, even with a sense of betrayal at the way President Woodrow
Wilson forced peace terms on Germany, only to allow France and England to violate them. Moreover, Weber opposed many of Germany's
annexationist war aims, and for much the same reason Lincoln had
opposed America's aims in its war with Mexico—he had no wish to see
other people dominated. In 1895, in contrast to 1919, Weber faced a different emotional situation: a country too satisfied with itself, "intoxicated
with success and thirsting for peace," as opposed to the later *Revanchismus*
which had Germany embittered with defeat and thirsting for vengeance.
Weber said nothing about resorting to war as a solution and even his reference to "overseas expansion" hardly indicates that he saw imperialism
as an expression of nationalism. From his earlier study of how the Junker
class welcomed foreign workers, to the disadvantage of Germany's own
workers, it would not be too difficult to conclude that economic elites
betray the interests of their own nation when they look abroad. Profitably
living by the laws of the market, the capitalist cannot afford to be a
patriot. Nor can the economic imperialism of the capitalist be so surely
seen as expressing the quality of political nationalism Weber had in mind.

Was Weber exhorting Machiavellian power politics so that Germany
could become a world power (*Weltmacht*) and dominate the world, or
was he advocating such "political schooling" in order that Germany not
be dominated by those nations determined to dominate? The first
interpretation characterizes Weber in ways that foreshadow Hitler and
the irrational lust for supreme power driven by supreme righteousness;
the second characterizes Weber in ways mindful of Hamilton and the
rational use of power with the limited purpose of promoting a nation's
interests and protecting its security. Sensing that freedom requires
power for its preservation as well as its realization, Weber would, years
later during the World War I era, ponder the dilemma of *Realpolitik* and
moral conviction. Such a dilemma would be only one of a number of

antinomies that haunted Weber. If power was his obsession, freedom was his passion.

The Freiburg address needs to be interpreted together with Weber's earlier report on agricultural labor. In both documents Weber emphasizes that Germany's enemies are not other countries but conditions in Germany itself, which had left the country in a smug state of arrested accomplishment. After the "youthful spree" of Bismarck's unification, now what? Can Germany ever again look forward to greatness?

Weber's refrain about the "quality" of human life had more to do with freedom than domination. By "quality" Weber meant an existence that is self-determining, active rather than passive, with the capacity of rising to consciousness and finding for oneself the meaning and significance of experience. Such a qualitative state derives from the individual's having felt socially worthy and having taken part in a *Sinnzusammenhang*, a nexus of meaningful connections and schemes of events that are purposeful by virtue of being freely willed. It is this quality that Weber perceived among the agricultural workers in east Prussia. Although Weber could have explained their migration into the city as a result of material deprivation—the decline of their diet and falling living standards—he chose to emphasize the moral impulse of liberation:

> Why do the German day-labourers move out? Not for material reasons: the movement of emigration does not draw its recruits from districts with low levels of pay or from categories of worker who are badly paid. Materially there is hardly a more secure situation than that of agricultural laborer on the East German estates. Nor is it the much-bruited longing for the diversions of the big city. This is a reason for the planless wandering off of the younger generation, but not for the emigration of long-serving families of day-labourers. Moreover, why would such a longing arise precisely among the people on the big estates? Why is it that the emigration of the day-labourers demonstrably falls off in proportion as the *peasant village* comes to dominate the physiognomy of the landscape? The reason is as follows: there are only masters and servants, and nothing else, on the estates of his homeland for the day-labourer, and the prospect for his family, down to the most distant of his progeny, is to slave away on someone else's land from one chime of the estate-bell to the next. In this deep, half-conscious impulse towards the distant horizon there lies hidden an element of primitive idealism. He who cannot decipher this does not know the magic of *freedom*. Indeed, the spirit of freedom seldom touches us today in the stillness of the study. The naive youthful ideals of freedom are faded, and some of us have grown prematurely old and all too wise, and believe that one of the most elemental impulses of the human breast has been borne to its

grave along with the slogans of a dying conception of politics and economic policy.

Weber had to deal with an awkward fact: While Germans fled their situation, Polish workers adapted to it. Did the Darwinian "process of selection" indicate anything about the two nationalities? Weber came close to
a racist slip when he explained why one nationality gives way to another.
"The German peasants and day-labourers of the East are not being
pushed off the land in an open conflict by politically superior opponents.
Instead they are getting the worst of it in the silent and dreary struggle
of everyday economic existence, they are abandoning their homeland to
a race which stands on a lower level, and moving toward a dark future in
which they will sink without a trace." But Weber has no desire to see any
part of the German population fade into oblivion, and thus the inaugural
lecture concludes with a peroration to accept the "sense of our responsibility *before history*." Our generation, Weber exclaimed to a riveted audience, must act without knowledge of how history will treat us. Will posterity recognize us as its predecessors?

> We shall not succeed in exorcising the curse that hangs over us: the pre-
> cursors of an even greater epoch. Will that be our place in history? I do
> not know, and all I will say is this: youth has the right to stand up for
> itself and for its ideals. And it is not years which make a man old. He is
> young as long as he is able to remain sensitive to the grand passions
> nature has placed within us. And so—you will allow me to conclude
> with this—a great nation does not age beneath the the burden of a
> thousand years of glorious history. It remains young if it has the capac-
> ity and the courage to keep faith with itself and with the grand instincts
> it has been given, and when its leading strata are able to raise themselves
> into the hard and clear atmosphere in which the sober activity of Ger-
> man politics flourishes, an atmosphere which is also pervaded by the
> solemn splendor of national sentiment.

The Freiburg address reveals some of Weber's most fundamental values.
His identification of freedom with migration and the desire of upward
mobility is less a paean to bourgeois ambition than a point of empathy
with farm laborers and their unwillingness to submit to the patriarchal
rule of the owning classes. Consider the contrasting sentiment uttered in
Frederick Jackson Turner's speech delivered two years before the
Freiburg address. Where the American theorist of the crisis of rural life
saw democracy as having sprung from the availability of free land, Weber
depicted the "magic of freedom" as expressed in the laborer's flight from

sod and soil. Here again Weber resembles the American Alexander Hamilton, who went so far in challenging the Jeffersonian myth of the independent agrarian yeoman as to show that rural life bred abject dependency, including slavery. Hamilton's vision of a developing state based upon rapid economic growth posed a threat to the Southern plantation aristocracy, just as Weber's descriptions of economic change taking place in Germany wrote the death sentence to a fading Junker aristocracy. Yet ultimately Weber's sense of freedom, which flouts authority's demands for acquiescence, had less to do with economics or politics than with resistance and defiance.

At times Weber comes close to returning to politics the one ingredient that many Enlightenment thinkers sought to purge from it—passion, not only as an irrational impulse but as the impelling desire to escape domination. That the answer to power is passion, and not necessarily institutions and theories of checks and balances, suggests that not only did Weber have no qualms in seeing the lawbreaker as a creator but he also valued innovation over tradition and saw the problem of history as the problem of continuity. For all Weber's sensitivity to historical conditions, what he saw as giving "quality" to our lives is not what conditions us but what we make of ourselves. More personally, Weber's equation of freedom with the right of young people to stand up for their own ideals bespoke an emotion he felt in the household of his own father. Weber's difficulties with authority are shadowed by a feeling of approaching tragedy.

BREAKDOWN: "DESCENT INTO HELL"

The aim of life, Weber believed in his bones, is to become the person that one is, and to do so requires will power. Such a Nietzschean dictum may help explain why he respected power more because he loved obedience less. When he later developed his three types of authority and their legitimations, only one commanded his respect, and significantly it had more to do with an emotion than an institution, with rebellion rather than submission. Weber was *sui generis*. A curious combination of anarchist impulses and conservative convictions, he would rebuke those who submitted consciously, or who simply went along with their subordinate status as though it were a habit, as if will had atrophied.

Weber became as preoccupied with authority as he was with power, and he moved from one concept to another in ways that made conventional distinctions between the two disappear. Knowing that authority had to be believed in order to command, he saw no essential difference between belief and legitimacy or between authority and power. Weber's uncanny ability to equate authority with power flew in the face of the more optimistic outlook of western political philosophy, which assumed that the Enlightenment's legacy had resolved the problem by defining all legitimate authority as deriving from voluntary consent. But the son who had no choice in selecting a father is apt to see patriarchal authority as tyrannical, as much so as the arbitrary power political philosophy promised to extirpate. In the bosom of the family a young boy has no inalienable right of consent.

"My father," Weber wrote to a close friend in 1887, "has always been sanguine, and his mood is often subject to abrupt changes, even if the outward occasion is a slight one." In recent years such shifts in temperament made "a really profound, painful impression upon my mother, one that she does not easily get over, even if the annoyance that occasioned it was only a fleeting one." Weber added that as a son of the house it would be out of the question for him to meddle directly in such family affairs.[16]

Weber stood by his mother Helene, realizing that her vulnerability to her husband's moods grew as she aged. Perhaps Weber sympathized with his mother, as well as with his sisters and his first love, Emmy Baumgarten, because he felt the same emotions that would come to charge women's consciousness: a desire for independence with respect to an abode and for fulfillment in respect to a meaningful occupation. When working as a lawyer and living in his father's house, Weber complained of not having a "roof" of his own and spoke of "earning his own bread" as the "foundation of happiness for a man."[17] In his early years it was uncertain that Weber would favor his mother's side in the domestic conflict. While at college he adopted some of his father's ways when he went in for drinking and dueling. Yet he came to reject his father's paternalist mannerisms and arrogance. He and his sisters resented the way the father let his wife wait on him while he held forth on the topics of the day as if he were an oracle. A good-natured bourgeois, Max Weber Sr. enjoyed life too much to be troubled by the problems of the world or the pains of others. He left the upbringing of the children completely to his wife, toward whom he behaved, on more than one occasion, less as a lover than a lout.

In 1896 Weber left Freiburg to accept a professorship at the University of Heidelberg, in the city that had been Helene's beloved home town. The following year Weber invited his mother and sisters to visit him and his wife. Helene did not have the strength to insist to Weber Sr. that she preferred to visit her son without him, as the invitation implied.

When she showed up with her husband, Weber could only conclude that once again his mother's freedom had been violated. In front of his mother and sisters Weber berated his father and demanded that in the future Helene be allowed to visit alone and be free of his father's controlling presence. Then Weber did the unthinkable: he ordered his father out of his house. Never again would Weber see his father, who died several weeks later of a gastric hemorrhage.

At first Weber showed no signs of self-reproach for his behavior. But a month after the funeral he became sick on a vacation in Spain. He recovered enough to resume teaching in the fall and immediately overloaded himself with work. Again he fell ill and spent the following summer in a sanitarium at Lake Constance. Once more he took on academic duties in the fall only to suffer another collapse, this time a complete breakdown, which was, his wife wrote, "only at the beginning of his descent into hell."

Weber's illness, which lasted for six and a half years (1897–1904), stymied medical specialists, who tried everything from hydrotherapy to metabolic treatment. He suffered from several neurotic symptoms: chronic back pains; insomnia, for which he would resort to morphine; weakness of limbs; inability to talk, concentrate, and read; and periodic visitations of "demons" that kept his mind in restless torment. At times he seemed broken, sitting for hours in *Stumpfanheit* (apathy), picking at his fingernails. Weber traveled to several locations to see if a change of scenery might help. In Lucerne, slouched on a sofa, semiconscious, he would stare out the window at the treetops filtering the glare of the lake. "What are you thinking about?" asked Marianne. "Preferably nothing, if I can manage it," he replied. Marianne felt it necessary to keep Max away from his similarly tormented cousin, Otto Baumgarten, who had an even more "lucid sense of helplessness" and would take his life a few years later. Did Weber himself contemplate suicide? "His soul," Weber wrote to his cousin's father, "was locked within the prison of his illness." He could do no other, Weber consoled his uncle. "He fulfilled what was demanded of him: a rich inner life, a spiritual refinement of his self, a strong-will endurance without complaint. Fate gave him no external assignments, and it deprived him of any opportunity to give some to himself."[18]

Weber's letter of condolence implied his own sense that he had survived by virtue of the "external assignments" that helped him overcome his personal torments. The idea that fate can deliver one from damnation to a redemptive occupation resembled the Puritan doctrine of the calling that Weber was working on at the time of his recovery. Thus his angst found an intellectual reference and historical significance, so much so that he could even regard early capitalism as a spiritual striving for salvation. Yet the exact nature of Weber's own breakdown remains a mystery.[19] Was his mental illness a precondition of his intellectual greatness? Whether or not Weber's genius had any connection with his neurosis, the circumstances of his breakdown had clear connections with the uniqueness of his social philosophy, his calling, which he was about to bring forth from a mind recovering from the tensions of neurotic conflict. This mind was peculiarly equipped to provide a tragic sense of society and its discontents. His antinomic mind was cursed with the blessing of Keats's "negative ability."

As a social scientist Weber perceived the world as constituted by fundamentally unresolvable conflicts. The tragic sense that life is a struggle between opposing principles also came to characterize the methodological writings he was working on while recovering from illness, writings in which contrary value systems are examined, each valid and good but incomplete in itself and fraught with irony. While most sociologists sought principles of integration and cohesion, Weber had an eye for the immiscible as tension (*Spannung*), which came to have a central place in his outlook. He took society apart and left it to others, moved by the mystique of organic metaphors, to put it back together again with explanations more soothing than the mechanisms of rationalization.

Weber was one of the first social scientists to remove the whole question of authority from patriarchy or from anything that suggested domestic relations. In the classical political philosophy of Aristotle, Hobbes, and Locke, the family constituted a "natural" social unit from which some rational principles of political order could be derived. If Weber remembered anything that had gone on between his pious mother and overbearing father, it was a memory of domination, power, and manipulation. Even more revealing, as a sociologist Weber gave less weight to society than did classical thinkers like Hobbes and Rousseau, who saw human beings driven by the desire to win approval from others. In Weber's analysis, familiar sociological principles like approbation, prestige, status, and class take second place to the needs of the soul, especially the "metaphysical need for a meaningful cosmos" that gave existence some purpose and significance.[20] Weber accorded value to those qualities that his father thwarted in his mother: spiritual piety and individual autonomy. Such qualities, of course, are also found in Germany's philosophical traditions. But while Weber shared Kant's commitment to autonomy as the precondition of responsibility, and while he could at least feel the pull of Hegel's sense of tragedy as the clash of dialectical opposites, he could hardly believe that reason would serve as the basis of motive or that the state was held together by a sense of nationality and society by the ties of community.

Nor could Weber believe in some of the ideas that were later attributed to him by American sociologists. Despite the distortions of his subsequent American disciples, Weber refused to identify social interaction as normative and to cast society itself as the foundation of authority. Rather than seeing consensus and solidarity in modern society, Weber saw conflict and coercion everywhere, the same forces that had conditioned his childhood household. "Every living thought represents a gesture toward the world," wrote the American philosopher John Dewey. His contemporary Walter Lippmann added a corollary: "We may add that the gesture can represent a compensation for a bitter reality, an aspiration unfulfilled, a habit sanctified. In this sense philosophies are truly revealing. They are the very soul of the philosopher projected, and to the discerning critic they tell more about him than he knows about himself. In this sense the man's philosophy is his biography; you may read in it the story of his conflict with life."[21]

Max Weber's social philosophy contains a rich array of living thoughts that represent both his conflict with life and life's own unresolved conflicts and contingencies. It could be said that Weber thought more as a philosopher or poet than as a social scientist. He concerned himself with individuals as seekers after meaning and with history as the drama of purposes and destinies seen through a glass darkly. He pondered the plight of organized institutions whose impermanence pointed up change and conflict, formation and disintegration, the past as the human spectacle of hopes and ruins. Weber's unique theory and methodology, long appreciated as a sociological analysis of familiar academic subjects, is also a meditation upon meaning. Weber's tragic mode, rather than offering a rational ordering of society, presents a dramatization of its antinomies as it confronts the many operations of power.

THREE

Authority and Its Discontents

"RESIST MUCH, OBEY LITTLE"

In April 1914, Max Weber, now fifty, writes a long letter to his
mother, now seventy, an old woman stooped from age and yet,
according to Marianne, with eyes still sparkling with kindness. Looking back, Weber writes of the difficulty growing sons have of opening up
to their mothers.

His own marriage to Marianne, Weber observes, has become "flour-
ishing" because he had come to understand "your life—hard on the outside, beautiful on the inside," the way it had to be at the time. During the
period of troubles with the father of the house, all who knew the situation could say of Helene: "She did what she could." As for Max Sr., he
did what he did as a member of a passing generation:

> Certainly all of us have a fair view of him today, and now that all the
> difficult tensions have been forgotten, we can rejoice at what he was in
> his surely uncommon, solid, bourgeois mentality. We know that the rifts

in his life were the tragedy of his entire generation, which never quite came into its own with its political and other ideals, never saw its own hopes fulfilled and carried on by the younger generation [of his era], which had lost its old faith in authority and yet still took an authoritarian view of matters where *we* could no longer take such a view. His life would have been a hard one without your love, which was ever aware despite all conflicts.[1]

Between the mother's love and the father's power, between selfless surrender and submission and arrogant assertion and domination, lies the problem of authority that would haunt Weber the rest of his life. He had also lost faith in authority but, unlike his father, he could no longer carry on as though the dull comforts of bourgeois existence would provide reasons for believing and obeying. Authority for Weber became an emotion as much as an institution. In seeking to give it a rational foundation in sociology, would Weber ever be able to respect authority?

The crisis of authority that Weber sensed reverberated throughout the intellectual world of his era. Combine liberalism with modernism and we are left with the overthrow of authority and the endless search for its substitute. Such was the dilemma formulated by the American political philosopher Walter Lippmann, who spent the first half of the twentieth century in a futile search for the foundations of legitimacy. During Weber's period of recovery, 1903–5, he had been involved in a similar search, but the institutions and ideas that once fulfilled the role of authority could no longer command credibility. Authority was once assumed to have an objective basis in God, nature, or reason. But Weber saw authoritative institutions as historical and contingent upon the conditions of their development. He asked readers to observe how authority gets itself accepted in modern society. "The reason for this fact lies in the generally observable need of any power, or even of any advantage of life, to justify itself."[2] Authority as power and domination relies upon reason not as critical reflection but as rationalization and conventional modes of legitimization. Forms of authority may institute themselves without reference to anything objectively true and authoritative.

While recovering Weber had been working on his now-famous thesis, "The Protestant Ethic and the Spirit of Capitalism." Its author described the modern market world of business transactions as evolving from an otherworldly theological angst long lost to history. The possibility that one could reverse the process and return from economics to religion as a source of authority was foreclosed in the essay: Weber saw this as impossible in the western world. In the past, Protestant religious convictions could inspire people to bring about a revolution in behalf of faith and to abide by church doctrines. Similarly, the authority of the State could be regarded as an "indispensable instrument . . . for the social control of reprehensible sins and as a general condition for all mundane existence pleasing to God."[3] With the coming of the Enlightenment, however, reason would soon replace God and science dismiss sin.

Weber had been working on methodological questions during his recovery, and it may have been his own illness that convinced him of the limits of reason, and that led him to think of the mind as more a dissolving acid than an integrating agency. Whether or not methodology would help Weber reestablish his identity, the self's freedom still depended upon reason as an analytical faculty. Reason was once regarded as the vessel that contained truth; in Weber's era it had become an empirical technique, a process of obtaining knowledge by eliminating error. Methodology itself could scarcely deliver the conclusive truths necessary to propping up authority. On the contrary, Weber's idea of inquiry aimed to interrogate what passed for truth in order to demonstrate that it had a functional status only, and that its existence depended upon it being believed without question. The capacity to criticize one's own beliefs, Weber wrote to the Dante scholar Karl Vossler, requires enduring criticisms that have no resolution. Later, in his essay "Science as a Vocation," Weber would explain how our beliefs are chosen rather than derived, and that their selection has no more basis than emotional preference. The realization that beliefs are purely subjective and personal is, he pointed out in another essay, the "fate of a cultural epoch that has eaten from the tree of knowledge."[4] The problem of authority is the problem of unbelief.

Nowhere in Weber's vast writings did he regard patriarchy or anything related to the family as the legitimate basis of authority. In Hegel's philosophy the reverent devotion (*pietät*) of husband and wife within the family extend outward into the community as the father carries the message of universal "Spirit." Closer to our age, scholars look to the family as the primary institution of socialization, where children received ethical education. In view of Weber's own moral education at the side of his mother as well as his aunt and uncle, it is revealing that he says nothing positive about maternal sensibility and piety. In later years, when he discusses, in manuscripts that would be posthumously published as *Economy and Society*, "The Household," the tone is coldly analytical and the subject treated as an aspect of organized economic life. Authority, to be sure, functions in the home and in religion as reverence for ancestors, but for the most part it is "the authority of men as against women and children;

of the able-bodied as against those of lesser ability; of the adult against the child; of the old as against the young."[5] Within the family authority imposes itself without resistance—lest one dare disobey and order the father from the house. Such manifestations of authority compel behavior but not belief.

To Weber the traditional German political state was as dubious a source of authority as the family. The autocratic rule of either Bismarck or the Kaiser left Weber as dejected as it left the German people passive, and he turned away from Hegel and the German organic vision of the nation-state as the highest expression of national life. Instead Weber adopted a vision of politics closer to Anglo-American traditions, in which the purposes of individuals take precedence over the universal claims of the state. "How can one possibly save *any remnants* of the 'individualist' freedom in any sense?" he would write in *Economy and Society*. "It is a gross self-deception to believe that without the achievements of the age of the Rights of Man any one of us, including the most conservative, can go on living his life."[6] Weber would have agreed with the poet who instructed Americans in four words how best to respect the authority of the political state: "Resist much, obey little" (Walt Whitman).

In 1905, a brave act of resistance came from a country that had never felt the full radiance of the Enlightenment and its legacy of liberalism and democracy. The Moscow uprising in December aroused the passions of many writers of the western world who identified with the Russian intelligentsia. To Weber in particular the struggle taking place in a backward country raised three crucial questions that many radical intellectuals dared not pose so starkly. Can freedom be born of revolution? Does authority disappear with the first blow of rebellion? Can the political state be anything more than organized force and power?

THE RUSSIAN REVOLUTION OF 1905: THE CONTINGENCY OF POLITICAL FREEDOM

In November 1905 the U.S. ambassador to St. Petersburg informed Washington that the turbulence in Russia—the general strikes, the Bloody Sunday massacre, the mutiny on the battleship *Potemkin* in Odessa—had reached desperate intensity. "The Russian nation appears to have gone temporarily insane; government practically helpless to restore order throughout the country." Earlier Weber had heard the news of Father Gapon leading a demonstration to the tsar's Winter Palace that ended in a bloodbath of workers and peasants. Saddened, Weber was hardly surprised. Unlike the American ambassador, Weber was struck less by the chaos that threatened to change Russia than by the force of inertia that would prevent change and postpone a country's confrontation with its tragic situation.[7]

As news of Russia reached Heidelberg, Weber put aside his scholarly work and followed the events, spellbound. He learned Russian in a matter of weeks, often studying in bed early in the morning. He had already known many of the Russian emigres in Heidelberg, who had formed an exile colony and built a Russian-language library. He admired the ideals of the Russian revolutionaries and even the few anarchists aroused his sympathy, no doubt because they all shared suspicion about any form of organized power. Although Weber sometimes referred to the supposedly alienated western intellectuals as "inkwell romantics," he respected the Russian intelligentsia and its consciousness of the tragic burden of Russia's history.

Russia occupied Weber's thoughts as Germany's neighbor and rival. Any possible revolutionary change that would bring down the tsar could alter European power relations, precariously balanced in Bismarck's system of countervailing alliances. But events in Russia also had implications for Weber's philosophy of history and theory of politics, which provided the framework for his two analytical articles, "Zur Lage der burgerlichen Demokratic in Russland" (The situation of bourgeois democracy in Russia) and "Russlands Ubergang zum Scheinkonstitutionalismus" (Russia's transformation to sham constitutionalism).[8]

Weber's judging Russia's proclaimed transformation from monarchy to democracy as more sham than substance suggests the richly unique way he perceived things. Democracy deceives itself if it expects a popular will to be generated through political activity aspiring to collective self-realization. Democracy aims to expand, absorb, include, encompass—and thereby it purports to represent all of society; power, in contrast, acts in the opposite direction. It gravitates into the hands of an elite and excludes others from its exercise. "The 'principle of the small number,' i.e., the superior political maneuverability of *small* leading groups, always dominates political activity. This 'Caesarian' stigma is inevitable" the larger the state.[9] If power follows its own logic and cannot be democratized, how could Russian transform itself simply by announcing it?

Some of the Russian intelligentsia hoped that even their own backward country could make the transition from despotism to democracy. Leon Trotsky, for example, tried to convince Marxists that the "law of combined development" enabled Russia to skip the liberal stage of history and leap from feudalism into freedom in a single sustained effort.

Weber saw power imposing its will regardless of historical stages. Democracy could scarcely serve as the initiating agency of social transformation, not only because of the ineradicable presence of power but also, even more, because of the inescapable presence of class. In Russia there existed no connection between a power elite and an ascendant economic class that could possibly represent the interest of the majority of the population while expressing its own political will. With no middle class there is no possibility the nobility can be challenged and the bond between crown and peasantry broken. When thinking about Russia Weber recalled some of the themes of his St. Louis address. In America middle-class values deriving from an earlier religious mentality pervaded society; in Russia a middle class had yet to be born and the orthodox Church had yet to live apart from the tsarist State.

The juxtaposition of Russia and America suggests that observation of developments taking place in two dissimilar countries was important to Weber. Skeptical about the prospects of genuine liberty in Germany and much of the rest of continental Europe, Weber saw liberty established in the United States and highly problematic in Russia in its efforts to forge a new civilization. Unlike some western economists, he did not see liberty and democracy emerging in Russia as a result of capitalist development. Yet the uprising in Russia opened up the possibility of a new starting point for a completely different evolution of human freedom, and Weber, in contrast to the German press, had great sympathy for the Russian liberals, the Constitutional Democrats (Kadets). As Weber saw it, Russia, backward, feudal, and despotic, had an inevitable rendezvous with modernization as the only way to catch up with and rejoin the political culture of the rest of Europe. "These are," Weber wrote in response to the events of 1905, "perhaps the 'last' opportunities for the building of a 'free' culture from the bottom up."[10]

In his analysis of the Russian situation Weber thought more like a Marxist than even Trotsky himself. The stages of historical development were the missing factor in Russia, observed Weber in offering a class analysis to demonstrate the absence of class formations. Without these stages Russia lacked a middle class that would assume the responsibility of political leadership. Without the social preconditions of liberal politics, authority would by definition become institutionalized in bureaucratic structures. Other factors, Weber noted, also hindered Russia in opening itself to the principles of western liberal democracy, particularly a divisive nationality question and a peasantry emotionally loyal to the tsar. But above all, history itself bypassed Russia, and history moves without plan or purpose, a chaos of causes and effects signifying nothing more than chance and contingency. To comprehend history, Weber held, is to grasp how conditioned and unfree humankind is. Only through struggle, Weber believed, could it realize freedom. Some people are blessed by circumstance, others cursed by being born of a nation in whose history reason and progress never awakened.

"Today," wrote Weber, "the chances for democracy and individualism would be very poor indeed, if we relied for their development upon the social laws of the effect of material interests." Nor should we listen to those "who live in continuous fear that in the future there could be too much democracy and individualism in the world and not enough authority, aristocracy, and office prestige." History shows that such institutions recreated themselves, and the movement of "interest constellations" suggests that the western world may be moving in "the direction of increasing lack of freedom." In 1905, a period of Progressive hope in America and Victorian optimism in England, Weber looked at Russia and shook his head:

> It is utterly ridiculous to attribute elective affinity with democracy or even freedom . . . to today's advanced capitalism—that inevitability of our economic development—as it is now imported into Russia and as it exists in the United States. Rather, the question can be phrased only in this way: How can democracy and freedom be maintained in the long run under the dominance of advanced capitalism? They can be maintained only if a nation is always determined not to be ruled like a herd of sheep. We individualists and partisans of democratic institutions are swimming against the stream of material constellations. Whoever desires to be a weathervane of a developmental tendency may abandon those old-fashioned ideals as quickly as possible. The rise of modern freedom presupposed unique constellations which will never repeat themselves.[11]

Among the constellations that converged to create the conditions of freedom were the episodes of overseas expansion whose "winds" blew through Cromwell's armies, the French Constituent Assembly, and Germany's own economic development. But continents were no longer available and populations were moving inward rather than outward. Other constellations included the social structure in place at the stage of early capitalist development, the rise of science, and "certain values that grew out of the concrete historical distinctiveness of a religious body of thought." Together with political circumstances and material preconditions, "these religious conceptions shaped the ethical quality and the 'higher culture' of modern man."

Weber's reflections may be read either as timely thoughts about the fate of Russia or as a theory of freedom and its possibilities. His writings also presupposed a philosophy of history that may be summarized as follows:

1. History as the story of western freedom is the product of a unique combination of conditions and unrepeatable circumstances that the birth and growth of democracy require.
2. Yet human will and resolution are essential for the sustaining of free society.
3. And this moral resource is all the more vital in view of the inevitable recurrence of aristocratic elites and authority systems.
4. How humankind acts and confronts historical conditions is more important than any theory of law supposedly governing history itself. Even those who, like the seventeenth-century Calvinists, saw their fate as predestined, chose resolution over resignation. History is what we make it.
5. We cannot forget that the North American continent had been formed by certain values, especially religious values, that shaped ethics and economics and later gave rise to democracy and science.
6. Ultimately character itself is a causal force in history (which makes Weber a moralist more than a materialist or, given his sensitivity to the enormous importance of structural conditions, an idealist contending with matter and the mechanical ordering of things).

Weber's theory of history seems almost paradoxical when considered solely in secular terms. The concurrence of conditions that brought freedom into existence cannot be repeated, yet humankind rises to dignity only by making history rather than succumbing to it. One is reminded of Reinhold Niebuhr's Calvinist dictum that fallen man is humanly condemned to sin yet spiritually challenged to overcome it. This Christian sense of paradox, which juxtaposed character to condition, freedom to determinism, choice to contingency, also contains implications for classical thought.

Of all the theories and tensions in Weber's commentary the most telling is the remark that one need not worry about any excess of individualism and democracy since aristocracy and authority will inevitably return in one form or another. This observation bears some similarity to classical political thought, where history was seen as cyclical, with tyranny returning to stalk republican liberty, with usurpation and despotism resulting in personal dictatorship. Weber's theory, incorporating a kind of cunning concerning the cycles of power, also posed a challenge to the more impersonal theory of Marxism, where history is seen as progressively evolving through class conflict into a higher synthesis. And Weber's observation departs from the political thought of some of the American Founders, where power was regarded as the antagonist of liberty and authority the antithesis of freedom. The "stream of material constellations" that Weber saw on the horizon would create new systems and structures operating independently of political consent and indeed of human consciousness itself. The question "Who governs whom?" can hardly be answered when the personal origins of authority have been obliterated by impersonal rules and regulations. After Weber's corrosive analysis, the idea of authority would never be the same.

TYPES OF AUTHORITY

Weber had good reason to describe political events in Russia as a "sham" or pseudo-constitutional democracy. Yet he took no delight in such an exposure. He had been upset listening to the contempt with which the German public greeted the struggle of the Russian constitutional movement. As Weber studied the new State constitution of April 1906, his curiosity turned to skepticism and his mood darkened from day to day. The tsar and Russia's ruling class, in an attempt to reestablish the country's credit status with Europe, allowed for a facade of constitutional reform, while at the same time clamping down on all independent political impulses in the country. Ostensibly the Duma was granted more power to legislate; the Church gained some independence from the State; language laws promised to deal with the nationality question; professors assumed they had won academic freedom; and unions and political parties similarly saw themselves as enjoying legitimacy and the right to participate in public life. Yet what took place in written documents would have little bearing on real life. Power, rather than following language, betrayed it.

All along the tsar had been waiting for a pretext to dissolve the Duma, and when he did Weber expressed no surprise. He discerned that, aside from the desperate deceptions of the tsar and his court sycophants, Russia lacked an essential consensus with which to reform itself. The Liberal Kadets, with their respect for private property, could scarcely speak for the great majority of peasants, with their land hunger and dream of agrarian communism. Unlike in America, the "tree of democratic individualism will not grow sky-high" in a country that seeks to modernize and adopt the fruits of advanced capitalism without having the necessary foundations in historical liberalism.

From an American perspective Weber's thoughts on Russia suggest two ironies. One is that the very limitations Weber saw in backward Russia Thorstein Veblen would see in Germany itself, particularly in a Prussian culture that borrowed its technology from England without adopting its liberal political institutions and habits of mind, leaving Germany potentially, even inevitably, a militaristic, dynastic state.[12] The second irony is that some American writers also sensed that their own history dealt them a case of historical deprivation. Specifically, what the novelist Henry James pointed to as the institutions that offered European intellectuals the rich materials of literature—court, church, aristocracy, hierarchy—were precisely those institutions that thwarted the possibilities for political freedom in Russia. Weber would, one speculates, be more sympathetic to Veblen than to James. While Weber sympathized implicitly with English political values, he had no sentimental attachment to aristocracy and scorned the Junkers as parasitical. With his tragic view of history, one in which the future must remain open to hope and the will to freedom and power, even if fated to defeat and frustration, Weber could only see in Russia an inevitable encounter with stagnation and domination. Yet Weber's vision was so prophetic that he saw the future being as problematic as the past, so darkened by the shadows of modernity that democracy itself may fall prey to the forces of institutionalized coercion. Where Veblen saw science emerging to challenge the power of the capitalist class, and where James assumed that an elite leisure class would preserve the values of the past, Weber had no such illusions. Instead of disarming power, science expands its sphere of domination; instead of preserving past customs, genuine ethics creates values in an act of choice.[13]

In Weber's thoughts the single force emerging in Russia that had gone unseen by other social philosophers, with the exception of the anarchists, was bureaucracy and its administrative apparatus. Weber wrote to a friend that "the 'definite' bureaucratization of the autocracy in the entire realm of domestic politics" would have profound consequences. The rise of bureaucratic officialdom will alienate the tsar from the peasantry and, in the long run, make the monarchial regime even more incoherent as power shifts from the crown to ministers and managers. By emphasizing bureaucracy Weber may have been getting back at the many Germans who, in their "self-satisfied arrogance and shallow realpolitik," remained indifferent to the "great human Russian fight for freedom."[14] Weber hardly hesitated to apply the term "sham constitutionalism" to the German state, where political parties competed for power as autocratic elites formed shifting alliances to ensure that parties would never wield it. Bureaucracy also preyed upon German society, where historically the growth of the power of central authority meant the expansion of executive authority and the reach of the state. But neither Germany nor any modern nation should assume itself immune from bureaucracy, a phenomenon that would stalk the future even more than it had stifled the past. Unless bureaucracy is to become the graveyard of democracy, freedom must learn the lessons of power as a normal tendency that moves through institutions in silent stealth. "Who would call it lust," wrote Nietzsche, "when what is high longs downward for power."[15]

"*Herrschaft*," observed Weber, "the prospect of finding obedience to a specific command, can rest upon a variety of different motives." Weber specified conditions of "interests" resulting in compliance, that is, "through purposeful and rational considerations of advantages and disadvantages on the part of the person obeying." Obedience also derives from the force of custom, a kind of "dull habituation," or it can be founded upon purely emotional inclinations of the dominated person. But a submission resting on such grounds would be relatively unstable. For the rulers and the rule relations of domination and subordination are cultivated much more through legal arguments, the grounds for "legitimacy," which gives rules and regulations the conviction of inward support. "The shaking of such legitimate beliefs can have far-reaching consequences."[16]

Weber's succinct description of *Herrschaft* was published posthumously in the *Preussische Jahrbücher* (Prussian yearbook) in 1922, and it became amplified in various sections of *Economy and Society*. When Weber's work was translated into different languages and scholars in the non-German-speaking world discovered him, they debated whether *Herrschaft* meant something so crushing as domination or possibly the more gentle idea of authority and adherence to rules. But authority in the Anglo-American sense—the right to rule based on consent—was not what Weber had in mind. Authority, as opposed to power, implies consent to being governed, whereas Weber suggested that compliance may be other than consent, and imply submission without resistance. Occasionally he referred to *Herrschaft Kraft Autorität* (domination by virtue of authority) to describe some acts of obedience deriving from a sense of duty. But Weber remained less concerned about the rightfulness of authority than the ways it had come to be legitimated in social action.

By the World War I years he would, as will be seen, go so far as to define the authority of the State as resting on little more than the monopoly of violence used to enforce its will. Other thinkers, such as the American historian Henry Adams, also saw that when authority loses its philosophical foundations it expresses itself as "police," and Randolph Bourne, the hero of the Greenwich Village Left, wrote a provocative (and unfinished) essay on "The State" during the war that is almost Weberian in illuminating the mechanisms of coercion.[17] But Weber would have agreed even more with Nietzsche's Emersonian dictum—One has only two choices: Obey oneself or be commanded. Like Nietzsche, and Emerson and Thoreau, Weber saw too much obedience and submission and wrote about authority to remind humankind what it was doing to itself. The concept of domination may be seen as Weber's liberal version of alienation: obedience breeds weakness and people settle for an amiable " 'adaptation' to the possible."[18] It may have been a Calvinist residue in Weber that led him to regard surrendering to society as alienating—a strange stance for a sociologist.

Weber was almost alone in his outlook in the early years of the twentieth century. Earlier Marx had promised his followers that the "furies of interests" would be extirpated with the elimination of private property, and the disciples of Adam Smith saw the activities of interests being "harmonized" in competitive market economics. While exponents of political economy saw little role for the intervening state, idealist philosophers like Hegel saw it as a mystical, unifying force, and the French sociologist Emile Durkheim looked to society itself as a healthy system of norms leading to moral integration. To Weber, interest, force, and coercion characterized all authority relations, and the idea that the state will "wither away" was as much a delusion of socialism as was the liberal assumption that power can be safely controlled once government becomes democratized.

In *Economics and Society* Weber developed a scheme for distinguishing three "types of legitimate domination." Weber emphasized that authority, to be credible, cannot rest on interest alone but must possess claims to legitimacy. To the frustration of later scholars, Weber made no distinction between obedience resulting from coercion and obedience that emanates from conviction, a distinction that would highlight the difference between brute domination and moral persuasion.[19] Motives for compliance, as Weber observed behavior, may be as varied as the character of the command that has its effect upon the ruled. But Weber felt no need to establish a criteria of "political correctness" in order to claim that certain expressions of compliance represent "false consciousness" or the seduction of "hegemony." He remained more interested in how types of domination had come to be accepted as legitimate. The three types he specified were the rational, the traditional, and the charismatic.

Rational domination signifies legal authority, in which obedience is owed to rules, statutes, contracts, court judgments, and other legally established proprieties that are impersonal and systematic in nature and are either imposed upon or agreed to by subjects. Traditional authority is sustained by long-accepted beliefs in the customary way of things and the legitimacy of whatever or whoever symbolizes immemorial conventions. Charismatic authority, in contrast, is established in neither law nor tradition but takes its significance from the manner in which it arises spontaneously to challenge conventions and win the allegiance of the people by virtue of the prophetic or heroic character of the leader.[20]

With modernity having stripped the western world of its illusions, Weber saw tradition fading and the struggle in the twentieth century taking place between the inexorable spread of rational-legal authority and its possible challenge by the appearance of a charismatic figure—whether a mystical savior or a revolutionary leader. Significantly, Weber worried most about rational authority because it alone had the potential for establishing and perpetuating a force of institutional domination. Such a force threatened the world with a permanent monocratic, one-dimensional life of deadly routine, an existence utterly dependent on papers and documents, peering out of the "iron cage" of bureaucracy.

BUREAUCRACY

In the classical political thought that influenced the American framers, passion, interest, ambition, and the desire for power and its corrupting effects posed the great threat to human liberty. The solution the framers devised in the Constitution was to reconceive government mechanistically, imposing a system of checks and balances that left America without a single source of sovereign authority. The Constitution came to be seen as a "machine that would go of itself," and Hamilton in particular looked to "energy in the administration" as the strength of the American government. Weber would have appreciated the framers' skepticism concerning democracy, not simply because of its alleged threat to property, which turned out to be more apparent than real, as Tocqueville would later make clear. More precisely, Weber's "principle of small numbers," the thesis that power gravitates from the many to the few because small groups are better organized and more maneuverable, was precisely what Madison invoked in warning the anti-Federalists:

> The people can never err more than in supposing that by multiplying their representatives beyond a certain limit they strengthen the barriers

against the government of a few. Experience will forever admonish them that, on the contrary, *after securing a sufficient number for the purposes of safety, of local information, and of diffusive sympathy with whole society*, they will counteract their own views by every addition to their representatives. The countenance of the government may become more democratic, but the soul that animates it will be more oligarchic. The machine will be enlarged, but the fewer, and often the more secret, will be the springs by which its motions are directed.[21]

Although the *Federalist* authors presaged Weber in seeing oligarchic tendencies growing out of democracy, Hamilton's own trust in "enlightened administrators" to lead democratic government may have been misplaced. From a Weberian point of view, the *Federalist* gave America a text that, in the name of preserving liberty, could as well beget bureaucracy, the new nemesis of political freedom.

Whence came this new nemesis?

In 1909, at a meeting of the Verein in Vienna, a speaker claimed that municipal transportation employees' pay compared favorably to that offered by private enterprise. Immediately Alfred Weber, Max's brother, a professor of political economy who believed in some measure of socialism, challenged the speaker and warned that the transfer of the means of transportation from private ownership to the state only increases the government's administrative apparatus. Max then rose to speak and those in the audience turned around in awe. "He was like an undammed stream of intellect that cannot stop flowing," recalled one member. "How good he looks!" remarked another, happy to see Weber recovered. "We take delight in his fire, but it is consuming him!" wrote another, of the audience's reaction, "but the young ones were enthusiastic."[22] Many of the older Verein members were socialists or Progressives who sought to staff government with the expertise of social science in order to influence government policy and bring private enterprise under some form of rational control. Weber exploded at the thought:

This passion for bureaucratization as we have heard it expressed here is enough to make a man despair! It is as though in politics a charwoman (*Scheuerteufel*), with whose mental horizon a German can get along best anyway, were permitted to run things all by herself, as if we intentionally were to become people who need order and nothing but order, who get nervous and cowardly when this order becomes shaky for a moment, who become helpless when they are torn out of their exclusive adjustment to this order.[23]

Weber went on to insist that he was opposing "only the uncritical glori-
fication of bureaucracy," that what really concerned him was Germany's
interventionist state and not necessarily the doctrinal disputes between
private enterprise and government involvement. Yet on other occasions
Weber cited the specter of bureaucracy in an effort to disabuse socialists
of their faith in a planned economy. "How will the life of the individual
be changed under Socialism?" Weber demanded to know, as he pro-
ceeded to answer his own question. To transfer ownership of the means
of production to a socialist state would allow politics to triumph over the
workers along with the entrepreneurs and would deny capitalism an
accounting of its own rationality. "The lot of the mine workers is not the
slightest bit different whether the mine is privately owned or publicly
owned."[24] Under socialism workers can still be dominated by union
councils and managerial agencies, as the centralization of authority aug-
ments the reach of bureaucracy. Technicians, executives, administrators,
and other new specimens of the age of science only enhance the dynamics of domination by means of organization and specialization.

In his writings on Russia Weber noted that Lenin offered the principle of "organization as a process" to replace faith in the spontaneous consciousness of the proletariat. Had he heard Lenin remark, after the bolsheviks seized power in 1917, "We must organize everything," Weber
would hardly have been surprised. "It is the sober fact of universal
bureaucratization," he wrote during the war years, "that is behind what
the literati euphemistically call the 'socialism of the future,' behind the
slogans of 'organized society,' 'cooperative economy,' and all similar contemporary phrases. Even if they aim at the opposite, they always promote
the rise of bureaucracy." The power residing in bureaucracies is relatively
autonomous and defies a Marxist class analysis based upon property relations. Even more telling, power issues forth from the very persons and
organizations that step forth upon the stage of history as enlightened
deliverers from premodern conditions:

> Wherever the modern specialized official comes to predominate, his
> power proves practically indestructible since the whole organization . . .
> has been tailored to his mode of operation. A progressive elimination
> of private capitalism is theoretically conceivable, although it is surely
> not so easy as imagined in the dreams of some literati who do not know
> what it is all about; its elimination will certainly not be a consequence
> of this war. But let us assume that some time in the future it will be
> done away with. What would be the practical result? The destruction
> of the steel frame of modern industrial work? No! The abolition of pri-

vate capitalism would simply mean that also the *top management* of the nationalized or socialized enterprises would become bureaucratic. Are the daily working conditions of the salaried employees and the workers in the state-owned Prussian mines and railroads really perceptibly different from those in big business enterprises? It is true that there is even less freedom, since every power struggle against state bureaucracy is hopeless and since there is no appeal to an agency which as a matter of principle would be interested in limiting the employer's power, such as there is in the case of a private enterprise. *That* would be the whole difference.[25]

A glance at Weber's six principles of bureaucracy should help indicate why he felt that the "whole difference" between capitalism and socialism may simply be a matter of accepting different conditions of oppression and domination. In *Economy and Society* he specified the following characteristics:[26]

1. The reign of rule and regulations through the jurisdiction of administrative office: actions originate in commands and orders are carried out in stable ways as official duties.
2. The principle of hierarchical office authority characterizes all bureaucratic structures, guaranteeing an ordered system of superiority and subordination in which higher desks supervise lower ones.
3. The modern office is managed by the flow of written documents, facilitated by a staff of subaltern officials and scribes and their bulging files.
4. Office management, especially modern specialized bureaus, presuppose comprehensive and expert training; executives, supervisors, directors, and other officials require occupational experience, degrees, credentials, the passing of special examinations, all of which assume that the bureaucrat's first loyalty is to the office.
5. Official business becomes the primary activity of the bureaucrat, who is not to exchange his services for profit or to extract rent or emoluments, as in the middle ages; instead the officeholder contributes faithful management and receives in return a secure existence.
6. The management of the office is a matter of knowledge; commands cannot be arbitrary fiats but instead must follow from general rules that can be learned, a code of operations that is abstract rather than personal, so abstract and separated from human consciousness that knowledge consists solely in accommodating itself to its instrumental role, accommodating itself to dominating or being dominated.

Weber cited ancient Egypt, China, the Roman Catholic Church, and the Diocletian monarchy as examples of the diverse forms of bureaucracy that could exist under absolutist regimes and premodern economic systems. But the bureaucratization of the modern world involved the full development of a money economy of world trade and transportation, as well as the advent of sophisticated technology and the growing size and complexity of corporations and governments and their administrative tasks. Although Weber saw bureaucracy as less characteristic of the United States, he regarded its development here as inevitable for three reasons.

Weber never subscribed to the idea of "American exceptionalism," and thus, unlike Tocqueville, he missed seeing that developments in the United States might take a different path than those in Europe. Instead Weber drew parallels between mass political parties in Germany and those in America, convinced that both were succumbing to increasingly closed bureaucratic organizations. So structurally determined would party politics be in the United States as well as Europe, Weber believed, that any hope for innovation and bold leadership would be defeated by faceless bureaucrats carrying out the chain of command to thwart change, to preserve the status quo. In four words Weber warned what bureaucracy would do: "this castration of charisma."[27] The tendencies of bureaucracy—specialization, careerism, hierarchy, nonownership of the means of administration—applied to business as well as politics, and hence Weber foresaw the convergence of similar bureaucratic structures in all advanced economic systems. In modern nation-states Weber expected the process of convergence to culminate in one form of administrative authority characterized by legality and procedural rationality. The outlook was grim, and in our times the term "Weberian" has come to mean power, submission, the tyranny of pettiness.

How prophetic was Weber's vision?

Around the time Weber was writing down his thoughts on bureaucracy in the massive manuscript that would become *Economy and Society*, the former American President Theodore Roosevelt bolted from the Republican convention of 1912, determined to form his own party, the "Bull Moose Party," and start his own presidential campaign on his own terms. Weber referred to this episode, as we have seen, and regarded Roosevelt as having escaped "castration" at the hands of party bosses. But the specter of bureaucracy continued to haunt him.

In view of the weakness of American political parties in recent years, one can look back with less fear of the staying power of organizations. Weber overemphasized the controlling presence of bureaucracy and rejected the possibility of political leaders breaking from party ranks and responding to the demands of the electorate. Similarly, in business some administrative skills turned out to be "firm specific," so that potential bureaucrats owed allegiance to the company rather than to the office.[28] As for government, similar rational bureaucratic structures could take different political forms as the state in various countries is subsumed by different societies and cultures. The rise of the welfare state in America had its bureaucratic features, but in the depression of the thirties it emerged as a response to citizens' demands that government do for them what economic conditions prevented them from doing by themselves.

Weber assumed that rational bureaucracies would prevail because they were technically superior to any other form of administration. But a bureaucratic party machine could hardly castrate the charisma of a Teddy Roosevelt, the two-fisted cowboy of American politics or, as H. L. Mencken described him, "a glorified longshoreman, engaged eternally in clearing out barrooms."[29] Toward the end of the war, as will be noted later, Weber began to look beyond the debilities of bureaucracy and democracy to focus on leadership, convinced that only dynamic charismatic figures can take the initiative in the service of a cause and at the same time be accountable for the consequences of their actions. T. R. could not have agreed more.

Although Weber's theory of bureaucracy cannot be regarded as accurately prophetic, it remains brilliantly perceptive when one considers the other two reasons why he saw bureaucratic rationalization as inevitable in America as well as Europe. The two reasons suggest some of the dilemmas of American society, in which capitalism and democracy, rather than being antagonists in the story of freedom, succumb to the same fate.

Bureaucracy emerges as an institutionalization of legal-rational authority, and as such it is entirely compatible with capitalism. Bureaucracy is not only more precise and efficient than older forms of authority, it also is more objective and equitable. Bureaucratic laws, as with the laws of the marketplace, have "no regard for persons" and, in theory, the principle of "neither fear nor favor" renders legal relations impersonal, calculable, systematic, responsive only to objective standards and indifferent to status and privilege. "Its distinctive characteristics," Weber wrote of bureaucratic authority, "which makes it so acceptable to capitalism, are developed all the more completely the more it 'dehumanizes' itself: that is to say, the more perfectly it succeeds in realizing the distinctive characteristics which is regarded as its chief virtue, the exclusion from the conduct of official business of all love, all hatred, all elements of purely personal sentiment— in general, everything which is irrational and resists calculation."[30]

Aside from accompanying the rise of both legal-rational authority and market economics, bureaucracy also sprouts from the political environment of mass democracy. The leveling of social differences, the demands for "equality before the law," the constitutional guarantee of procedural rights all result in more and more regulation, while popular demands made upon the state result in greater cash expenditure from the public treasury together with the proliferation of agencies to administer government programs and supervise budget allocations. Today we can see more clearly Weber's prophetic warnings. Democratization and bureaucratization go hand in hand as each professes the objective execution of authority, while the equalization of opportunity can only be met by the rise of professional administrators. Eventually, as noted in the Introduction, equitable administration becomes corrupted as the bureaucracy responds to specific interest groups demanding special programs and other advantages. As much as democracy and bureaucracy try to be fair and equitable, a rights-based political culture pressures government to serve particular constituencies. If "all politics is local," as the contemporary saying goes, can democracy be universal?

With Weber one senses no feeling for "negative liberty," the individual's desire to remain free of political authority and unmolested by government. Instead he saw democratic government as an extension of the party "boss system" and thus amenable to popular demands to provide services as well as protections. Weber would appreciate the irony that today greater democratization may bring about greater government control and surveillance. Of power, people clamor "to take it back" while at the same time requesting that government meet their needs with programs that require the bureaucratic expansion of power.[31]

Bureaucracy and legal-rational authority contain still a final irony: bureaucracy, the new nemesis of freedom, developed from precisely those procedures that were to protect freedom from older forms of tyranny and despotism. When the Enlightenment offered a government of laws to replace a government by men, it was assumed that the certitude of rules would serve liberty and protect property, thereby rendering life more free, sovereign, and autonomous. To be free meant to be immune to all arbitrary rule by man, not to be subjected to the will of others, to be safe from contingency and caprice. By Weber's description, bureaucracy left men and women secure and safe yet still unfree and alienated. Genuine authority, the will to authorize in order to be what one is, had yet to emanate from the people themselves. Could politics itself overcome the alienation of power from the will of its subjects?

DEMOCRACY AS TRAGEDY

"You blockheads!" On more than one occasion Weber wrote out the expression *Ihr Dummkopfe!* to convey his impatience with the Social Democrats and their illusions about political democracy as the means by which freedom is both realized and preserved. The Social Democrats refused to recognize that their party, indeed any modern party, cannot be other than a "machine in the American sense of the term," Weber wrote to Robert Michels in 1907. Michels, a scholar in Italy and a close friend of Weber, would later in his career formulate the infamous "iron law of oligarchy," which held that direct democracy was impossible since elites always rise to the top by virtue of strategic position, superior talent, or whatever it takes to bend an organization to the will of a closed minority. Weber saw power emerging from the technical imperatives inherent in the nature of modern organization. Thus whether parliamentary or syndicalist, Social Democracy cannot escape the bureaucratic fate that awaits all modern organizations. "The will of the people is a childhood illusion I gave up long ago," he advised. For Weber the term remained a "lingering fiction" one must abandon. Must democracy abandon its hopeful promises?[32]

At the time Weber was asking Michels to reconsider his perspective about democratic politics, American writers were coming to regard democracy as increasingly problematic because of the end of the frontier and free land and the rise of big business and its economic domination of government and society. Weber advanced an idea that Michels himself would soon endorse and even embellish: democracy is defeated not so much by conditions external to itself but by its own inner tendencies. The tragedy of democracy occurs when it cannot defeat the organizational forces that evolve, quietly and almost invisibly, to take possession of it. In the case of bureaucracy and political machines, the forces are less alien to the human subject than is its creation. "An inanimate machine is mind objectified," Weber declared.[33] The modern condition of power, rather than contradicting our essential nature, is its natural expression. Weber sees in politics the duality of democracy, the sense of struggle between the ideal born of spirit and the real produced by structures brought into existence by the rationalizing mind, the very conflict out of which tragedy generates its rebirth.

Weber's political views have been described by some recent scholars as partaking of an "elitism" that derived from his "fear" of the democratic masses.[34] Perhaps. But why would a thinker fear a "lingering fiction"? Although steeped in the subject of power, Weber himself had no instinct for domination and control, what he called the power drive (*Macht-pragma*). Yet he could hardly view democracy as a danger to oligarchies. "What is democracy today?" Weber would ask during World War I. "That no formal inequality clouds over the political rights of separate classes. But what consequential difference does that make?" Eliminating formal privileges and inequities to make the conditions of life relatively more fair and just requires the intervention of the administrative state and its hierarchy of offices and abstract legal provisions. In the name of expanding human equality democracy begets bureaucracy and "modern Social Democracy does not lead to anything else."[35]

Rather than fear Social Democracy, Weber tried his best to get social-ist scholars hired in the conservative German university system. He also remained more amused than alarmed by those who took socialism seri-ously, as though it represented a radical threat to normal political behav-ior. "I have not criticized Social Democracy but have only made fun of those who fear it," he wrote to Michels. Weber cited the example of the Socialist Party in Catania, Italy, to remind Michels that socialists behave as mercantilists and brokers once in office, and thus class politics "drives and must drive toward 'to-the-victor-the-spoils' politics." The party claims as a matter of right the fruits of success. Such behavior, Weber could only conclude, explains why democratic socialism, in its claim to be gradually transforming society by slowly penetrating it politically, will itself be transformed. That even a radical party claims the spoils of vic-tory only indicates that it had been conditioned to react to the behav-ior of its opponents, rather than creating a new politics of principled opposition.[36]

Weber's citing the "spoils system" of the Jacksonian era in American politics suggests further how much he drew upon American examples. Later, toward the end of the war, he would declare in his now-famous "Politics as a Vocation" (1918) that the professional politician is the "entrepreneur" of democracy, the boss a "capitalist" who buys and sells votes, and the party a vehicle for winning office and the spoils of patron-age. In the same address he emphasized how American political culture underwent change from the time of Washington, when the young repub-lic "was to be a commonwealth administered by gentlemen," to the time when John Calhoun and Daniel Webster retired from political life and Congress had lost almost all its authority and influence to party machines and their organizations and functionaries who live "off" politics rather than "for" politics.

Significantly, Weber was writing about the same era that produced Tocqueville's *Democracy in America*. Yet the Frenchman and the German seemed to be describing two different political cultures. Tocqueville saw American democracy as unstable, innovative, tumultuous, subject to the whim of the majority; Weber saw it as rigid, impermeable, timid, subject to the grip of party organization. Tocqueville, in addition, saw America as unique, an amorphous political culture with neither a feudal past nor a socialist future which rested on a broad liberal consensus; Weber saw the convergence of similar structural developments and thus wrote of the "Europeanization" of America and the "Americanization" of Europe as though people on both continents were cousins coping with the same conditions of life. In one respect the difference between Tocqueville and Weber was the difference between a hopeful liberal Catholic and a skeptical Calvinist modernist. The former told the French that democracy had a good chance in America because of the absence of aristocracy; the latter told Germans that America, despite its vaunted democracy, had its own version of an aristocratic elite—"a rough plutocracy of possessions."[37]

One could well compare Emerson's and Thoreau's essays on politics to Weber's thoughts to appreciate why the truth-seeking intellectual finds himself unable to identify with organized political parties. Weber could agree with the Transcendentalists that politics is all "cunning," the State a "trick," and democracy the "theatre" of the demagogue. He could also agree that modern life compartmentalizes the human subject into specialized parts to the point that consciousness risks being lost to external trivia. But Weber had his own reasons for looking askance at German political parties headed by his contemporaries.[38]

The National Liberal Party, the allegiance of Weber's father who looked up to Bismarck, seemed sensible to Weber in accepting the indispensibility of capitalism; yet it lacked a social conscience, and Bismarck's iron rule stunted the citizenship capacities of the German people and left them disposed to Kaiser Wilhelm II, "the crowned dilettante."[39] Weber sympathized with Gustav Schmoller and the support academic socialists gave to social welfare programs; but he had no patience with their premise that capitalism was destined to disappear from history. He shared the democratic ideals of left-wing liberals like Theodore Mommsen, only to find them too indifferent to nationalism and patriotism. More attractive, at least for a time, were the Christian Socialists associated with his friend Friedrich Naumann. When teaching at Heidelberg Weber came to know several theologians and he began to see a role for the spiritual consciousness of Protestantism in modern politics. Yet as Weber watched Naumann attempting to turn the Evangelisch-Soziale Verein into a formal political party, he sensed a lack of political instinct and a surfeit of

Christian benevolence that appealed to his mother and aunt, who financially supported Naumann's efforts to win a seat in the Reichstag. The son believed politics had more to do with duty than with mercy. Weber esteemed Naumann, the "poor people's pastor," but he reminded his political followers that "modern workingmen want more than forbearance, compassionate understanding, and charity; they demand the recognition of their right to reflect about the same thing, and in the same way as the so-called educated people."[40] Addressing the Fifth Evangelical-Social Congress in 1894, Weber took issue with Naumann's previous speech. "We are not engaging in social politics in order to create human happiness," he lectured an audience of devout Christians. Then, waxing Nietzschean, he explained what he sought from politics: "We want to cultivate and support what appears to us *valuable* in man: his personal responsibility, his basic drive toward higher things, toward the intellectual and moral values of mankind, even where their drive confronts us in the most primitive form." Weber saw Christian Social Democracy as a contradiction in terms. To act charitably on behalf of workers stunts their own potential autonomy while sustaining the pretentious moral superiority of the upper class. What the working class needed, thought Weber, is what Germany itself needed: self-respect earned by effort and struggle, the capacity to take action on behalf of one's own causes, to be able to say with Nietzsche: "I have willed it thus."[41]

Weber failed to see exemplary behavior not only in the working class but in the broad German middle class, which had acquiesced to Bismarck and the Kaiser, and even in the Junkers who, in his estimate, had betrayed the nation's interests by hiring Polish workers. "They might be all right in a card game or a hunting party," Weber remarked of the Junkers, "but otherwise they don't amount to anything."[42] Where, then, did Weber stand on democracy? Given his imagination for the noble, Weber sensed that to know the positive value of democracy was also to know the negative forces that would frustrate its promises. To Weber politics itself dramatized the conflict between the desirable and the possible.

Many of Weber's thoughts on politics and democracy were conveyed in correspondence with Michels, Naumann, and others in the first decade of the century. Just before the outbreak of World War I he began developing a sociology of parties, but it was not until the later years of the war that his political views found a public audience. By that time, as the last chapter will indicate, Weber placed his hopes in leadership, convinced that only a single individual could undertake great deeds in acting boldly yet responsibly. But Weber's theory of politics involved more than a simple faith in the *Führernatur*.

"Your work is moving entirely in a direction which appears to me to be as fruitful as it is hitherto unexplored," Weber wrote to Michels in 1906.[43] Michels had started out as a syndicalist who believed that the means of production should be transferred not to the state but to workers' unions. Michels was troubled by the disappearance of the ranks of the middle class from the workers' movement. By the time he wrote *Political Parties* in 1911, he had come around to Weber's view that the realization of democracy would be thwarted by tendencies inherent in growth and expansion; Michels formulated one of these tendencies as the "iron law of oligarchy." Although Weber remained skeptical of fixed, teleological laws, he became Michels' mentor in more ways than he was aware.

When Weber advised Michels how to go about studying the German Social Democratic Party, no mention was made of socialism itself or of anything ideological in the nature of platform shibboleths. Instead Weber recommended investigating what "relevant interests" created the party's formal basis, how the effects of the distribution of power relate to constituent demands, the ways ideas get represented and influence is exercised, and other aspects of interdependency that illuminate "the reciprocal weight of the structural components of the party" and the chain of command "from 'fellow travelers' to the 'party faithful' all the way up to the officers in Berlin." Application of "cui bono" interrogation to the "anatomy" of parties had been lacking up to now, Weber observed, noting that the only pioneering work in the sociology of party life had been James Bryce's *The American Commonwealth*.[44]

In the period 1906–10, when Weber was corresponding with Michels and others on the question of social democracy, he saw politics as neither the socialist striving for justice and solidarity nor the classical commitment to virtue and civic duty. Classical republicanism rested on the ancient premise that politics would prevail over economics and curb the excesses of commerce and luxury. Weber no longer could see a distinction between politics and economics, the public and the private, when he described politics itself as a form of *Betrieb*, a business operation sustained by its own managerial momentum and aiming at successful transactions. As to socialism, Weber ridiculed the slogan "the end is nothing, the movement everything" as less a guiding principle than an incitement to confrontation. The syndicalist is so caught up in the mystique of the strike itself that he only manages "to squint at the outcome." All talk that socialism will end "the domination of man by man" through the "farce" of revolution is "utopian." Even through parliamentary means it remains doubtful that socialism will create a new man willing to renounce bourgeois pleasures. Once anyone wants to live as a "modern individual" and demands the comforts of his "daily newspapers, railways, and electrical appliances," he indeed has renounced all revolutionary ends and ideals and lives only for the movement and its momentary satisfactions.[45]

While Weber dismissed socialism as the wish of the misguided intellectual, he took democracy more seriously as both a political proposition and as an intellectual condition. To Weber party politics must be seen as appropriation, the struggle of interests to gain strategic position, the maneuvering of coalitions to gain power and its rewards. Did the view of human existence as power relations (*Herreshaftsbeziehungen*) mean that the forces of domination left no role for democracy? Can there be a theory of politics if democracy is little more than a succession of forces each trying to be the strongest? Curiously, one role Weber assigns to democracy is that of a tribuneship: the means by which people protect themselves from actions of their representatives and leaders. Democracy cannot lead but it can judge; it cannot produce effects but it can evaluate them.

Invoking the fiction of the "will of the people," Weber instructed Michels, is exactly as "if one wanted to speak of the will of the boot consumer who sets the standards for the way in which the shoemaker devises his techniques. The consumer does indeed know where the shoe pinches but never how it should be made better."[46] Far from turning citizens into consumers, Weber endows them with the authority of being the best judge of their own interests. Although there exists no unified rational will in the expression "the people," and therefore democracy cannot be considered directly self-governing in the sense that people collectively issue orders they are to obey, the people are still capable of evaluating which decisions harm or benefit them. Here Weber is close to the *Federalist* authors in insisting that the will of the people may be a fiction yet people are still sovereign to the extent that government rests on the consent of the governed and its elected leaders are accountable for their performance in office. Although skeptical of democracy as an institution, Weber was far from an elitist who wanted to see people ruled. Marianne records a scene that took place between Weber and the German leader Erich von Ludendorff:

LUDENDORFF: There you have your rightly praised democracy! You and the *Frankfurter Zeitung* are to blame for it. *What* has improved now?

WEBER: Do you think that I regard the *Schweinerei* (unholy mess) that we now have as democracy?

LUDENDORFF: If you talk that way, maybe we can have a meeting of the minds.

WEBER: But the *Schweinerei* that preceded it was not a monarchy either.

LUDENDORFF: What is your idea of a democracy, then?

WEBER: In a democracy the people choose a leader they trust. Then the chosen man says, "Now shut up your mouths and obey me. The people and the parties are no longer free to interfere in the leader's business."

LUDENDORFF: I could like such a "democracy"!

WEBER: Later the people can sit in judgment. If the leader has made mistakes—to the gallows with him![47]

Like other aristocratic liberals (Tocqueville, Henry Adams, John Stuart Mill), Weber recognized that democracy must be accepted as an inevitable aspect of modernity. During the war years he defended universal suffrage as necessary to the equality of status that German citizens had been gaining. He would also come to value a strong parliamentary democracy as a training ground for the selection of politicians with leadership talent. In addition, democracy could give people some means of controlling an otherwise autonomous administrative *apparat*.[48] Ultimately Weber, for all his brooding preoccupation with power and domination, could hardly deny democracy without denying citizens the freedom they needed in order to be responsible for the future of Germany.

What democracy needed was an aristocratic sense of duty which would induce individuals to accept the burdens of history. But democracy itself was, like monarchy, oligarchy, and other past systems of rule, a form of domination, and no amount of popular participation could rid it of its ironies. Politics, even democratic politics, would be tragic in that its very activities to promote liberty would result in institutions that pose a threat to it. This "tragedy of culture," as Georg Simmel called it, became even more pronounced in religion than in politics. It is in the spiritual realm that humankind had its ultimate "fall." Capitalism had its "ideal foundation in ascetic religion, specifically in the repudiation of all idolatry of the flesh."[49] Capitalism, too, would undergo an inversion of human purpose.

FOUR

Calvinism and Capitalism: The Irony of Unintended Consequences

THE RISE OF CAPITALISM AND THE DEATH OF GOD

In the period 1902–3, five years after Weber's breakdown, he had not yet recovered, although he could now sleep without taking pills. He and Marianne traveled to Switzerland and Italy in search of solitude and repose, but occasionally he would relapse into restlessness and depression. On his thirty-eighth birthday he returned home, "an eagle with broken wings," Marianne sighed. Back in Heidelberg, he asked to be dismissed from his full professorship and reclassified as an *Honorarprofessor* (adjunct professor). But the faculty and administration so esteemed Weber that they extended his old status with department membership and voting privileges.

Weber's unstable mental condition continued to haunt him, and he occasionally became annoyed with those who crossed his path. He tried traveling alone. In 1903 he took six trips, looking always to stay in towns free of the rattling noise of the new automobiles. He liked to observe people he scarcely encountered on campus: workers, artisans, merchants, the doers and makers of the world. Italian towns could be noisy with the people's chatter and bustle. But in Scherenigen, a beach resort outside the Hague, he wrote Marianne of the quietness and cleanliness of the Dutch. "Today they are scrubbing the outside of the houses, as high as they can reach; all this has a very soothing effect."[1]

Watching others dutifully at work could be soothing to one who had yet to regain his own capacity for strenuous activity. Whether or not Weber still felt any guilt over expelling his father from his house, his prolonged inability to engage in sustained research and writing made him feel useless. During this period Weber's estimation of himself sunk, now that he was drawing a salary from the university even though he had been released from teaching duties and department responsibilities. What "torments him most," Marianne observed citing his own expressions, was "the unworthy situation" in which he had to endure idleness. In a letter to a friend Weber wondered: "Shall I ever be able to work?"[2]

Unworthiness and idleness! Seventeenth-century Calvinism was about to captivate a twentieth-century agnostic.

In 1903 Weber's younger colleague Edgar Jaffe had just acquired the scholarly journal *Archiv für Sozialwissenschaft und Sozialpolitik* (Archives for Social Science and Social Policy), and he asked Weber to serve as a co-editor, together with himself and Werner Sombart. At first Weber had reservations. "It is really quite doubtful whether I can participate; it is repugnant to me to let the others work and parade my name without holding out the prospect of a certain quantity of work." But Weber signed on and reestablished contact with the scholarly world. The prefatory editorial to the first number, drafted by Weber, announced that the scope of the journal would expand beyond questions of legislative policy; it would take "the historical and theoretical recognition of the general cultural significance of capitalistic development as the problem to which it will devote itself." In the first issues Weber published articles on methodology and welfare policy in regard to agricultural workers. At the same time he was absorbed in the preparation of a larger study, "Die Protestant Ethik und der Geist des Kapitalismus," which appeared in the summer of 1904, just before his trip to the United States. Part two appeared the following year upon his return.[3]

The Protestant Ethic and the Spirit of Capitalism, which was not published in book form in English until 1930, has become a controversial text in the literature of social science. It emerged out of a historical context that was itself controversial. Toward the end of the nineteenth century capitalism arrived in Germany with an intense and unsettling suddenness. Whence did it come, and what did it signify?

Werner Sombardt's two-volume *Modern Capitalism* (1902) offered a historical analysis to suggest that the forces of secularization that undermined religion made possible the worship of money and the accumulation of capital. The search for gold in the age of exploration reflected this new attitude toward wealth, and in the modern age profit making seized shopkeepers and retailers, especially Jewish merchants—a thesis Sombardt later developed in his anti-Semitic *Juden und das Wirtschaftsleben* (Jews and the Economic Life) (1911).

It was not only Sombardt's thesis that Weber had in mind when he set out on his own research and reflection. Throughout centuries of western civilization the pursuit of wealth as an end in itself was regarded with suspicion. Classical republican traditions looked on commercial activity as incompatible with the *res publica*; hence the tension between "interest" and "virtue." Christianity condemned the seeking of riches as the sin of avarice, a sure sign of the fallen state of the soul. When Adam Smith wrote *The Wealth of Nations* in 1776, he and other Scottish philosophers rejected classical thought for failing to see that commerce constituted a creative activity that expressed humankind's social nature and contributed to a county's material well-being. During Weber's era, in both America and Europe, the debate over political economy dealt mainly with the role of the state in controlling the economy or in allowing the "invisible hand" of laissez faire to regulate commerce according to laws of supply and demand. But with Weber the problem of capitalism would have less to do with political authority than with religious morality.

Weber's relating of religion to economics in order to treat capitalism as a cultural phenomenon enabled him to study the values that motivate action and illuminate meaning. Perhaps his personal experience led him to believe that religious emotions—guilt, shame, fear, and awe among them—needed to be taken seriously. To many of the leading intellectuals of the day such emotions were epiphenomena, symptoms of behavior rather than its cause. Many thinkers believed that they could be relegated to the museum of ancient superstitions. Marx and Freud, each for different purposes, saw religion as an illusion, while Durkheim saw it as a function to be explained sociologically and Nietzsche viewed religion as a crutch for the morally crippled. How did Weber approach religion?

According to some Weberian scholars, Weber's bringing religion to bear upon economics derived from his mother Helene and his aunt Ida, both devout women who had been influenced by the American Transcendentalist theologians William Channing and Theodore Parker. Early in his career Weber did value religion in the spirit of his family. In a letter to his brother Alfred, written on the occasion of his confirmation in 1885, Weber praised Christianity as a religion of duty and responsibility, "a social bond of world-encompassing brotherhood."[4] This early note of advice expresses the Transcendentalist idea of religion as moral development, mutual obligation, and self-determination. Yet the Transcendentalists rejected the doctrines of their philosophical ancestors, the Calvinists, along with the idea of original sin and predestination. In turning toward Channing and Parker, Helene and Ida sought a religion of hope and inspiration; in discovering Calvin, Weber, whether for personal or intellectual reasons, found himself drawn to a theology of fear and intimidation.

Why this was so has yet to be explained. Moving away from Channing's trust in God's benevolence and humankind's excellence, Weber traces the origins of capitalism to emotions that have to do with the omniscience of an angry God and the anguish of a helpless, fallen human nature. This turn to Calvinism can hardly be attributed to the more gentle spiritual atmosphere of the female side of Weber's household. Nor does it signify an evolution in his own thinking. His earlier studies of economic history—on ancient Roman agriculture, craft workers of the middle ages, and the modern stock market—place little emphasis on religion.[5]

The pivot on which the Protestant ethic essay revolves is the Calvinist doctrine of predestination. In this gloomy doctrine the majesty of God thunders down as threat and terror. Human creatures are, to use the imagery of Jonathan Edwards, "Sinners in the Hands of an Angry God" whom He dangles over the fiery pits of hell. All human beings are predestined even before birth to either heaven or, most likely for the majority, hell. The torment over the fate of one's soul created in the Puritan what Weber described as "a feeling of unprecedented inner loneliness," since the individual was alone, without the mediation of church, priesthood, sacraments, or rituals of magic.[6] Again and again ministers told the Puritans that God was everything and humankind nothing, and that pain and suffering, even that of the innocent, is good and righteous altogether.

Why was Weber so receptive to such a gloomy, outmoded, prescientific way of looking at the world? Actually, Calvinism, which continually reminds its followers that the mind can know nothing of ultimate value and the will cannot will what it most wants, anticipates much of the modern sensibility of Weber's intellectual circle in Heidelberg. His contemporary Paul Honigsheim, aware that Weber had believed deeply in individual autonomy and self-determination, precisely what Calvinism had denied as the sin of pride, wrote that it was "unavoidable that Max Weber would be preoccupied with Dostoyevski."[7] Like the author of *The Brothers Karamazov*, Weber became absorbed in the paradoxes of Christianity and the riddles of theodicy that tried to explain the ways of God to suffering humanity. Nietzsche, another name invoked in Weber's circle, was perhaps more a Calvinist than he was aware when he observed that nothing can be known about God's will except that it is irrevocable. Capitalism, according to Weber, grew out of that torturing thought.

Weber once remarked to Marianne that he was "tone deaf" to religious doctrinal issues. The truth is, as Marianne herself noted, that the Protestant ethic text had more to do with theology than with economics. It is religion that illuminates what sort of creature the human being has turned out to be, and like Dostoyevski and Nietzsche, Weber would interrogate religions to see if they made people weak or strong. In his study of world religions he would explain how a specific belief system served to justify either good fortune or inevitable suffering. Capitalism had something to do with fear of God's judgment, and hence Weber remained curious. "Why," he asked the Dante scholar Karl Vossler, does God actually allow "the damned to look into the future?"[8]

CAPITALISM AS THE CREATION OF SIN

The two essays on the Protestant ethic, later expanded to book length, illuminate the workings of Weber's mind and temper. From the seeming chaos of historical data Weber sought to establish historical connections, the task of any scholarship that aspires to the status of theory. Beginning with a few rather ordinary observations, Weber is moved by extraordinary curiosity, and ranges broadly over the complexities of social phenomena until he brings patterns of history into bold relief. Yet the argument remains incomplete, a fragment awaiting further analysis and more corroborating evidence. Not only the Protestant ethic thesis but all of Weber's major writings ended up as fertile fragments, as though he were less interested in convincing others that he had the right answer than in convincing himself that he had posed the right questions.

One would never guess from the opening of the first essay what the thesis is about. A glance at the occupational statistics of any multireligious country, observes Weber, brings to light that business leaders and owners of capital are predominantly Protestant. Among Catholic populations there is relatively less upward mobility in various occupations, although reverence for religion subsides among both Catholics and Protestants in their respective higher class strata. Within Protestantism itself Lutherans appear less immersed in business enterprise than are Calvinists and such early American sects as the New England Puritans, Quakers, Baptists, and Mennonites. Weber has yet to reveal the question that is behind his inquiry: Why did capitalism belong to the west?

In order to establish what he means by the "spirit" of capitalism, Weber quotes a number of maxims regarding time as money and credit as credibility of character:

> The most trifling actions that affect a man's credit are to be regarded. The sound of your hammer at five in the morning, or eight at night, heard by a creditor, makes him easy six months longer; but if he sees you at a billiard table, or hears your voice at a tavern, when you should be at work, he sends for his money the next day, demands it, before he can receive it, in a lump.

Weber then informs German readers he is quoting from Ben Franklin, whose attitude toward wealth is contrasted to that of Jacob Fugger, a merchant lacking in civic conscience and interested simply in making money. In late medieval and Renaissance Europe, the Fuggers were to Germany what the Medicis had been to Italy, great merchant bankers whose influence seemed at times to surpass that of church and state. Compared to these giants of world finance, Franklin seems a humble man of virtue. Weber is aware that Franklin's reasoning is utilitarian. True, he advises youths to appear honest and industrious as expedient to success. But Germans are wrong to dismiss such opportunism as "pure hypocrisy." The equating of utility to virtue is something of a "divine revelation which was intended to lead him in the path of divine righteousness," and it shows that "something more than mere garnishing for purely egocentric purposes is involved."

> In face, the *summum bonnum* of this ethic, the earning of more and more money, combined with strict avoidance of all spontaneous enjoyment of life, is above all completely devoid of any eudaemonistic, not to say hedonistic, admixture. It is thought of so purely as an end in itself, that from the point of view of the happiness, or utility to, the single individual, it appears entirely transcendental and absolutely irrational. Man is dominated by the making of money, by acquisition as the ultimate

purpose of his life. Economic acquisition is no longer subordinated to
man as a means for the satisfaction of his material needs. This reversal
of what we should call the natural relationship, so irrational from a
naive point of view, is as definitely a leading principle of capitalism as it
is foreign to all peoples not under capitalist influence.

Why does the capitalist drive himself so hard? Weber cites Franklin
referring to the Bible of his youth. "Seest thou a man diligent in his business? He shall stand before kings." The earning of money is evidence of
moral character and industry, "and this virtue and proficiency are . . . the
real Alpha and Omega of Franklin's ethic, as expressed in the passages we
have quoted, as well as in all his works without exception."[9]
Weber may have taken Franklin's writings more seriously than
Franklin himself, whose own epicurean style of living could hardly be
regarded as "irrational" or pleasureless.[10] But Weber had his own reason
for insisting that "it will suffice for our purpose to call attention to the
fact that without doubt, in the country of Benjamin Franklin's birth
(Massachusetts), the spirit of capitalism (in the sense we have attached to
it) was present before the capitalist order." By turning to Franklin's origins in Puritan New England, Weber could begin to concentrate on
Calvinism, and as he does the text moves from enigma to paradox, culminating in capitalism being born without having been conceived.
Weber made it clear that greed, avarice, aggression, and the acquisitive
impulse had existed since the human species came down from the trees.
He was also aware that in the middle ages Catholic Italy and Spain knew
the passion for pecuniary gain, and even with the Protestant Reformation some of the older strictures against profit and usury remained. But
with Luther a new attitude developed, focusing less on wealth than on
work, especially on the idea of *Beruf*, a calling or vocation that expressed
the inner worldly fulfillment of duty through an occupation, in contrast
to the otherworldly monastic ideals of medieval Catholicism. But the
"calling" itself, although it gave ethical dignity to mundane activity, could
hardly have created the intensity, indeed the "anxiety," behind the "spirit"
of capitalism, the irrational drive that compels man to try to do what is
rationally impossible. The key is the doctrine of predestination, God's
foreordaining everyone's fate, which remains unresponsive to all human
effort, coldly indifferent to prayers, sacraments, and good works. Ironically, the Calvinist, with no recourse to church or community, sees the
self standing alone, desperately hoping to be God's instrument who has
been ordered to reshape the world ascetically and rationally without
enjoying it sensually or socially. No longer able to distinguish between

laboring upon the materials of existence and seeking the salvation of the soul, Calvinists assume they are carrying out God's will through a life of discipline and systematic self-control, by an "inner-worldly asceticism."

How could such methodical asceticism usher in capitalism, which equates wealth with material happiness, the very pursuit condemned by the Puritans? According to Weber, wealth came to be seen as a sign not of enjoyment but of abstinence, the result of hard work, frugality, and self-denial, precisely what was necesssary for capital accumulation. Weber quoted the English Puritan Richard Baxter: "You may labor to be rich for God, though not for the flesh and sin."[11]

With the restraint against profit removed by the Calvinist spirit of capitalism, the rising bourgeoisie saw their striving as virtuous, and later Franklin, having left religion behind in Massachusetts, sees his exemplary life in Pennsylvania as prudent and moral. Eventually the moral sensibility disappears entirely from capitalism and wealth becomes less an indication of character and virtue and more a measure of consumption and vice. In discussing the phenomenon of rationalization at the end of the chapter, we shall return to the tragic fate of the capitalist "spirit" in modern times. But first let us discuss the criticisms of Weber's Protestant ethic thesis.

A number of early critics took Weber to task for several reasons: his misunderstanding of various aspects of Protestantism (the Pietists and Luther and the doctrine of the calling), his refusal to recognize that Catholic Europe fostered the growth of capitalism as much as did Calvinism, or his exclusion of Jewish merchants as producing wealth without the wages of sin. More recently it has been pointed out that Calvinism had an Arminianism offshoot that rejected predestination in favor of free will and that Calvinism was not only anti-Mammon but its doctrine of grace precluded the possibility that one could earn salvation through work. It has also been pointed out that Weber focused on America and avoided studying Germany, where the presence of monarchial authority prevented Protestant religions from adopting a methodical way of life and where capitalism emerged independently of Calvinism. The case of Scotland also complicates Weber's thesis. There the structural changes allowing for a market to emerge were present, as was a Calvinist ethos; yet capitalism arrived largely as an English import.[12]

Of all the criticisms two in particular frustrated Weber the most: that he had failed to prove a causal relation between Calvinism and capitalism, and that he had sought to disprove Marx by implying that capitalism had its origins in religious ideals rather than in historical materialism. According to Marianne, Weber "expressed great admiration for Karl

Marx's brilliant constructions," and he believed that neither the materialist nor the idealist approach to history are of much value in getting to the bottom of things.[13] As to causal linkage, Weber announced in the Protestant ethic manuscript itself: "We have no intention whatever of maintaining such a foolish and doctrinaire thesis as that the spirit of capitalism . . . could have arisen as a result of the Reformation, or even that capitalism as an economic system is a creation of the Reformation."[14]

Many recent scholars critical of Weber seem to be tempted by what might be called the fallacy of dissimilarity: the assumption that because two discrete phenomena have no resemblance to each other they cannot possibly have any historical relation. Thus it has been argued that Weber tried to connect two incompatible temperaments: the "repressed" and suspicious Calvinist and the "liberated" trusting capitalist. With such an assimilation, Weber then translated spiritual angst into worldly striving solely in the economic realm, when in reality Calvinism resulted not in capitalism but in the political "Revolution of the Saints" under Cromwell.[15] Such reasoning presupposes that in history two phenomena must have similar characteristics in order to have a necessary causal relation. Hence a recent scholar has insisted that "the frequent failure of capitalism to create or even coexist with Calvinism proves that Calvinism cannot be the creator of capitalism."[16]

This manner of reasoning has been applied specifically to colonial America as a case study. The Great Awakening, writes one historian, "dissolved the affinity between Calvinism and capitalism postulated by the Weber thesis." That historian cites another: " 'Where capitalism flourished,' among the merchants of the American seaports and in European cities . . . 'Calvinism declined.' And, where Calvinism flourished, in the New Light Congregationalist, Presbyterian, and Baptist congregations in the rural hamlets of New England and Virginia, capitalism was viewed with suspicion, if not distaste."[17]

The above quotes may indicate why Weber and his critics could never resolve the issues dividing them concerning the Protestant ethic. Given Weber's sensitivity to the irony of unintended consequences, one can interpret capitalism as the unsought outcome of Calvinism, even though devout Calvinists remained suspicious of capitalism and the capitalist personality could not flourish until freed of such suspicion and guilt. Weber indicated that anxiety over salvation led to actions that had Calvinism as their indispensable condition, actions that in the long run brought about results that had no bearing on or similarity to the mentality from which they had distantly sprung.

Historically one thing can lead to another without these things existing in simultaneous compatibility, and the birth of a new mentality is not necessarily explained by the conditions that gave rise to it, especially if those conditions stood in the way of its birth. Weber's idea of "elective affinity" proved misleading to the extent that the expression was taken to mean something like a mutual attraction (whereas Weber often had in mind the phenomena of different beliefs having similar consequences), and it is hard to see how capitalism evolved from Calvinism since there was little affinity to begin with and less election and choice. But "elective affinity" (*Wahlverwandtschaft*) signifies rather institutions that are historically independent of one another, such as a religion on the one hand and an economic system on the other; it signifies that they are related in that one proceeds from the other but not necessarily by design or intent and thus a theological belief can produce a contradictory vocational ethic. In history causes do not always resemble their effects and human motives and purposes do not always impose their character and design on things, particularly when motives produce ironic consequences and developments occur only once in history and thus there is no way to establish whether unique events have an invariable sequence. Weber asked us to consider Puritans as agents of their own thoughts and actions, but his sense of irony and contingency precluded him from establishing causal relations in the form of laws that explain the emergence of capitalism as a necessary occurrence.

Weber may have been aware, as he seemed to be when he later turns to studying nonwestern religions, that the social scientist has no way of holding structural conditions constant while testing to see if the religious variable of Calvinism issued in capitalism. But whatever "caused" capitalism, Weber's thesis is consistent with the notions of a Calvinist, who rejected the idea of justification by works and, hence, would scarcely be surprised to see capitalism as the effect of sinful humanity trying to do what God wants while forgetting there is no way of knowing what God wills. To use the language of religion rather than that of social science, one might say that the transformation of Calvinism into capitalism had more to do with actualization than causation; it was a process of emanation that, proceeding from the spiritual to the material, turned the Puritan into a Yankee. Thus a New England colony whose leaders detested private wealth seeking as threatening to the community still expounded a life of hard work that set in motion forces that would undo the community. Eventually ambition and mobility came to be valued and the older covenant community gave way to individualism and the cult of success.

How accurate was Weber's characterization of American Puritanism?

His use of the terms *ascetic* and *inner worldly asceticism* may have been too austere a description of the Puritan way of life in at least two respects: marriage and sexual activity, education and the life of the mind.

The use of the term *ascetic* to signify "the destruction of spontaneous, impulsive enjoyment" scarcely described the Puritan man and wife. Puritan preachers affirmed the pleasure of marriage as more than procreation and filial duty. Although husband and wife were not to lose self-control, erotic attachments were regarded as natural. While Richard Baxter, the Puritan Weber cited and analyzed, stands out as a prude, other preachers openly acknowledge the carnality of conjugal life.[18]

Asceticism is also misleading in regards to the Puritan life of the mind, which did more to delight in the world than to reject it. Although the Puritan status of the will may have been predetermined and hence could not be regarded as self-determining, the intellect was determined by what it knows, the mind's objects, and Puritan intellectuals, who founded some of America's greatest universities, studied everything that nature had to offer. The Middle Ages condemned curiosity as a vice, the sin of pride, but some of the Puritans were passionately curious about all things and, instead of simply accepting the doctrines they had inherited, they deliberately challenged those who were content to, as Perry Miller put it, "let sleeping dogmas lie." The theologian Jonathan Edwards, a contemporary of Franklin, emphasized the affections of the heart that "ravish" the mind. "Without exaggeration," Miller wrote of one of Edwards's essays that was read widely in England as well as America, "one may say of the *Narrative* that it did for bewildered English Nonconformists in 1736 what Goethe's *Werther* did for young German romantics: it perfected a formula for escape from an intellectual dilemma by opening an avenue into emotion and sensibility."[19] New England Puritanism produced capitalism and, as well, a possible "escape" from its resulting rationalizing mechanisms.

It may be unfair to criticize Weber for paying insufficient attention to American intellectual history, particularly to political ideas as well as religious doctrines. But the Protestant ethic thesis, whatever its validity in respect to comparative case studies, resonates in an early American political culture pervaded, as it was, by Lockean moral precepts. As with Calvinism, John Locke's God also commands us to labor upon the materials of earth and to make industry our duty and "calling." Locke, like the New England Puritans, saw political society as voluntary so that individuals are free to reject or accept the values of the community, even to the point of remaining in the sinful state of nature. Puritanism in America, to be sure, started out with the intent to be communal and spiritual, but as Perry Miller noted, the Lockean contract, like the Puritan covenant, implied voluntary consent, and thus what had once been regarded as pre-destined could hardly thwart initiative and enterprise. Between the Calvinist and the Yankee, it may have been Locke who served as the true midwife of capitalism.[20]

Was it faith or fish that brought the Puritan to America? The modern temper, noted Miller, would prefer to quote from *Magnalia*, published in the Massachusetts village port of Marblehead, as evidence that America's earliest settlers were on the make as diligent fishermen. But the omnipresence of the New England *Jeremiad* suggests, Miller observed, that Puritans shouldered guilt and anxiety as they pushed ahead driven by their own ambition. "The jeremiahs came from something deeper than pious fraud, more profound than cant; they were the voice of a com-munity bespeaking apprehensions about itself." Hence the Puritans could barely make up their minds whether change meant progress or perver-sion, whether success was a sign of salvation or damnation. "Why did they fill their diaries with self-condemnation?" asked Miller of the pillars of the Puritan community. "Why did a John Hull or a Samuel Sewall accuse himself, even while hastening along the road to wealth? Why, when they assembled together, did they hunger and thirst after a method-ical analysis of their imperfection?"[21]

THE RELIGIONS OF THE WORLD

"An educated Chinese would simply refuse to be continually burdened with 'sin,'" wrote Weber in *The Religion of China: Confucianism and Tao-ism*. "The concept of 'sin' is usually felt as shocking and lacking in dig-nity by genteel intellectuals everywhere. Usually it is replaced by con-ventional, or feudal, or aesthetically formulated variants such as 'indecent' or 'not in good taste.'"[22] Insofar as Weber had set out to show that capi-talism never took root in a historic China that knew nothing of sin, guilt, and the hunger for salvation, a question poses itself that perhaps only God can answer: Is capitalism born in sin?

Weber's investigations of world religions, which began just before World War I and were published to little attention in the *Archiv* while the war was going on, were in part responses to criticisms of the Protestant ethic thesis. If western Puritanism provided the basis for the possibility of a rationally organized economic system in the west, did it not follow that religious beliefs in other parts of the world might have impeded the emergence of capitalism? In a series of studies later published in English as *The Sociology of Religion* and then as several books on specific topics, Weber explored Hinduism, Buddhism, Islam, and ancient Judaism, along with Confucianism and Taoism.

Yet the word "sociology" in the title is a little misleading. The sociologist is more concerned with structures and systems than with origins and causes, the domain of the historian. To discern causes is to turn theory into knowledge in order to grasp how transformations take place. In this enterprise Weber was, curiously, both a postmodernist and a premodernist. In the first instance, he depicted the Puritans as spiritually driven creatures who knew what they were doing even while having no awareness of the world they were making. The capacity of human action to remain obscure as to its meaning fascinated Weber long before the postmodernist philosophers and literary critics of our time. Yet even though the Protestant ethic thesis falls short of clear causal analysis for its verification, Weber himself remained committed to searching for causes and human motives as a means of finding out how people experience their social world through religious emotions. Aware of the limits of reason and that there can be no science of the particular, Weber nevertheless remained a premodernist rationalist who sought to understand historical phenomena by establishing the specific conditions for their development.

Weber had been thinking about religion during the war years, during which his brother Karl lost his life at the front along with other relatives and a number of friends and former students. At Christmastime in the first year of the war Weber stood before a tall Christmas tree in his Heidelberg house and looked into the eyes of soldiers on leave as he spoke of fate and mortality. Weber reminded the young warriors that in everyday life death has no rational meaning but death on the battlefield is graced with dignity and glory. While Weber was not so insensitive as to declare that man's noblest vocation is to suffer, he did understand that a sense of tragedy springs from sympathy. The soldiers' eyes, Marianne recalled, were moist with emotion.[23]

During the war years, when Weber worked as a hospital administrator, he put aside an hour a day for his studies on religion. He had more time after he resigned from his job in 1916, and to research Hinduism and Buddhism he went to the university library in Berlin to obtain English census reports and missionary literature on Asian countries. After digging through documents in English, French, and German, Weber still felt he had only begun to scratch the surface. He thus began his writing with a characteristic apology: "Only a small portion of the documentary sources and inscriptions have been translated and that is a great handicap for the non-Sinologist. Unfortunately, I did not have an expert Sinologist to cooperate in the text or check it. For that reason the volumes are published with misgivings and with the greatest reservations."[24]

Although Weber is often cited for his "grand" theories and typologies, his own scholarship is dense with minute data, as though he believed that truth lies embedded in the ordinary details of everyday life. The study on China starts out with a discussion of coins and minting, proceeds to comment upon monastaries, cities, and feudal dynasties and their hereditary characteristics, and moves on, after an examination of subjects ranging from the literati to the static bureaucracy, to concentrate on the peculiar mentality that grew out of the Confucian worldview. Confucianism meant an "adjustment *to*" the world in contrast to Protestantism which meant "mastery *over*" the world. The ethic of the literati, again in contrast to the angst-ridden Calvinist, aimed to achieve an inner harmony that left the social order as it was. The Confucian outlook, although partaking of an "inner-worldly mysticism" as opposed to the Puritan's hard-driven asceticism, could be practical and rational. Chinese life was characterized by filial piety and patriarchal authority, with a merchant class as methodical as its western counterpart. But Confucianism itself lacked a concept of sin and hence an emotion of guilt. The literati also differed from western intellectuals in being concerned neither about the plight of the masses nor about their own salvation as they quietly cultivated the art of self-perfection. Where the western mind found itself alienated from God, in the east there is no dualism of flesh and spirit. "Completely absent in the Confucian ethic was any tension between nature and deity, between ethical demand and human shortcoming, consciousness of sin and need for salvation, conduct on earth and compensation beyond, religious duty and socio-political reality."[25]

Buddhism, propagated by "strictly contemplative mendicant monks," obliterated the tension of dualism even further by surrendering the will to the cycle of permanent rebirth. While Buddhism became absorbed in mystical contemplation, Taoism practiced rites of magic and Hinduism established a Brahmin class that cultivated an indifference to the world and to the misery of the masses. As to the mideast, Islam created a "warrior" religion and its leaders remained more interested in immediate booty and conquest as symbols of status than in products of economic development as a sign of salvation, a process that would require a formal legal system along western lines. The religion of the Jews, Weber pointed out in *Ancient Judaism*, was more western in retaining the dualism between God and humanity, in accepting a covenant of social obligations, and in eliminating magic from its cosmogony. Yet Judaism never became an important religion in the development of capitalism since its people remained marginal, a "pariah" minority that could wander over the European continent but never dominate it.[26]

Weber's investigations of religions by no means implied that he was subscribing to an idealist as opposed to a materialist intepretation of history. The believer, whatever the belief, could hardly be interpreted as renouncing interest for some transcendent goal beyond self-preservation. Even the eastern idea of reincarnation is more consoling than the western existential idea of annihilation. Religion promised to ward off evil forces and to provide a supernatural afterlife free of worldly woes. To reach such a state required various assumptions of magic, whether the Indian doctrine of kharma, the Protestant idea of the calling, or the Catholic service of sacraments. Magic may be rational. Clearly it purports to fulfill worldly desires that are comprehensible, but the means to realize such ends as happiness are irrational in that there is no scientific basis of producing what is promised through prayer and ritual. Protestant religion, in contrast, is rational in respect to the means of labor and work, but such activities have no relationship to spiritual salvation, an irrational end that defies human reason and effort. Nevertheless, the priest as well as the magician has a role to play: to provide a systematic procedure of sanctification in order to accommodate the needs of believers with a meaningful worldview.

But only in religions where animism and magic have been curbed does one find the first development of capitalism and the furthest development of rationalization. In modern rationalized society human life submits to systematic control and aspires toward rational ends no longer distinguishable from the instrumental means to reach them. Work, once regarded as a means to salvation, has become an alienated way of life, a dreary economic necessity in a consumer society. Work loses all memory of the "calling," once a moral compulsion based upon a religious conviction. In driving out magic, science and modernity have also driven out religion. The life of labor ceases to be divine.

FROM RELIGION TO RATIONALIZATION

Weber's comprehension of how religion came to be defeated by the forces of rationalization is far from fully developed in the early versions of the work on the Protestant ethic. But it would soon enter his thoughts in almost any subject he wrote about. It is fitting that Weber returned to earlier centuries to read Calvinist sermons. What better way to learn how humanity condemns itself by its own actions?

Weber's understanding of the fate of the Protestant ethic, his conviction that what he had discovered in the seventeenth century was now lost to modernity, had impressed itself upon him during his visit to the United States:

"Couldn't the old man be satisfied with his $75,000 a year and rest? No! The frontage of the store must be widened to 400 feet. Why? That beats everything, he says. In the evening when his wife and daughter read together, he wants to go to bed. Sunday he looks at the clock every five minutes to see when the day will be over—What a futile life!" In those terms the son-in-law (who had emigrated from Germany) of the leading dry-goods man of an Ohio city expressed his judgment which would undoubtedly have seemed simply incomprehensible to the old man. A symptom of German lack of energy.[27]

The old man, in contrast to the young son-in-law, still retained a remnant of the Protestant ethic and hence could not relax. Why does Weber seem to prefer the older generation and its addiction to unrelenting labor? Some writers Weber admired (Goethe, Tolstoy, Channing) regarded work as either a simple biological function or as an ethical activity that sees fulfillment not in the present but in the future. Weber exhorted the soldiers at Christmastime: "Those who do not come back will be the seed corn of the future. A hero's death for the freedom and honor of the people is a supreme achievement that will affect our children and children's children."[28] Calvinist workers, like contemporary soldiers, also face life heroically and see fulfillment in what they were forced to do as they struggle to achieve a holy purpose. A sacred activity dedicated to the future lifts life's deadening monotony. But in today's world labor has no spiritual relish. Thus in the final section of *The Protestant Ethic and the Spirit of Capitalism,* Weber abruptly turns from analyzing the past to a jeremiad about the present human condition: "The Puritan wanted to work in a calling; we are forced to do so. For when asceticism was carried out of monastic cells into everyday life, and began to dominate worldly morality, it did its part in building the tremendous cosmos of the modern economic order." What began in willed moral discipline ended in a world of industry and technology and human lives are now determined by mechanisms rather than by meaning. The transformation of work from a calling into a compulsion was inevitable in that the productive deeds by which the early Puritan tries to win his salvation produce the worldly goods that absorb his heirs. Weber quotes an English Calvinist: "In Baxter's view the care for external goods should only lie on the shoulders of the 'saint like a light cloak which can be thrown aside at any moment.' But fate decreed that the cloak should become an iron cage."

In its rise early capitalism at least had a tragic dignity as the Puritan defied the doctrine of grace and turned to the futility of good works in a desperate effort to escape the curse of predestination. Born in violation of God's commandments, capitalism as an economic proposition still embodied a spirit endowed with tension and moral aspiration. But today all trace of asceticism is gone from economics and religion has lost its intrinsic shaping power and work its meaning:

> Today the spirit of religious asceticism—whether finally, who knows?— has escaped the cage. But victorious capitalism, since it rests on mechanical foundations, needs its support no longer. The rosy blush of its laughing heir, the Enlightenment, seems also to be irretrievably fading, and the idea of duty in one's calling prowls about in our lives like the ghost of dead religious beliefs. Where the fulfillment of the calling cannot directly be related to the highest spiritual and cultural values, or when, on the other hand, it need not be felt simply as economic compulsion, the individual generally abandons the attempt to justify it at all. In the field of its highest development, in the United States, the pursuit of wealth, stripped of its religious and ethical meaning tends to become associated with purely mundane passions, which often give it the character of sport.

In these and other often-quoted passages from the end of the *Protestant Ethic*, some of which were added when Weber revised the manuscript shortly before his death, the author appears almost as "The Last Puritan" warning of the self-defeat of human pride. Woe unto "this nullity," these "hedonists without heart" and "specialists without spirit," who cannot see "victorious capitalism" for what it is.[29]

Modern society would not be surprised to be told that religion was a thing of the past. But Weber sought to make us conscious of the loss of reason as well. If religion once promised to save the world, reason promised to liberate it. But reason, the Enlightenment's "laughing heir" that once mocked religion, suffers a similar fate in its rendezvous with rationalization.

In the Enlightenment knowledge promised to deliver humankind from domination since knowledge, in order to be validated as true, had to be scrutinized under conditions free of all coercion. But Weber sees knowledge as more responsive than reflective, always actualizing the mind's tendency to react to the natural chaos of the world by organizing its energies, always analyzing, measuring, and calculating external events for purposes of control. Weber saw some forms of rationality as necessary for relating means to ends and living by standards and rules. But rationalization itself leads to the idolatry of the real, and science seemed to prove that the real had no reality beyond itself. Thus rationalization, born of the proud promise of reason, ushered in *die Entzauberung de Welt* (the demystification or disenchantment of the world), stripping life of all transcendent purpose and supernatural significance, rendering the universe a chilling, metallic "causal mechanism," turning the capitalist into a creature as much controlled as controlling in a wanton world of "sport."[30]

That humankind is the free agent of its own confinement to the routines of institutionalized existence is a Weberian insight with Emersonian overtones. From Puritanism to capitalism there occurs a "fall" into the processes of rationalization, which in turn result from the will to mastery and control, not of the self but of the world. Paraphrasing Goethe, whom Emerson admired, Weber depicted Protestant asceticism as the drive "which ever seeks the good but ever creates evil."[31] The indeterminate mysteries of religion give way to purposive-rational action directed toward ends, and the conscious striving to master reality involves the organizing imperatives of modernity; of forming, structuring, enframing; in short, of constructing the conditions of our own internment. Weber's worry about the "instrumentalization" (*instrumentierung*) of life had also worried Emerson. Knowing about the "Fall of Man," Emerson warned, "ever afterwards we suspect our instruments."[32]

Weber's most famous book, *The Protestant Ethic*, has perhaps as much to do with the human condition as with the origins of capitalism.[33] That he added the notion of the "disenchantment of the world" to the text suggests the extent to which religion, in allowing itself to take on the calculating instruments of reason, allowed capitalism to desacrilize life perhaps even beyond redemption. Thus for Weber society would be little more than the forces that take possession of its institutions. But Weber was no fatalist; he did see three tendencies that could upset the spectacle of complete rationalization: the breakthrough of charismatic authority, the passionate devotion to a "calling," and the eruption of ecstasy and even erotic life. "Nothing has any value for man as a man which he cannot do with passion," instructed Weber, who recognized, with Nietzsche, that value is created rather than found, an act of will and self-reliance.[34] The spirit of freedom and value must be asserted against the forces of fate, which at every turn threaten to appropriate history and its subjects. The theorist of domination would himself not be dominated.

FIVE

Human Action and Its Meanings

THE HEIDELBERG CIRCLE

They came from all over Europe—from Italy, France, Switzerland, Poland, Hungary, Russia. The intellectual pilgrimage to Heidelberg had much to do with the city's distinguished university, the most liberal and cosmopolitan institution in Germany in the years before World War I. The "Heidelberg Circle" would frequent the Cafe Haberlein and also Weber's home, a white brick dwelling overlooking the River Neckar. Every Sunday afternoon philosophers and social scientists gathered at the Webers to take tea and cake before plunging into some esoteric discussion. Sometimes, weather permitting, guests would spread out in the shade of the old, tree-lined garden. The Weber salon attracted men and women of diverse political persuasions, ranging from feminists to chauvinists, from anarchist activists to elitist poets. It was a "*salon des refusés*," Weber once quipped to suggest how his open-minded gatherings differed from Germany's aristocratic conventions.[1]

Although Weber hardly saw himself in the role of guru or even as an intellectual guide, students and scholars flocked to his house in the hope that they might catch a word of wisdom from Heidelberg's leading intellect, a legendary figure who no longer, after his breakdown, taught at the university or gave public lectures. Members of the Heidelberg Circle spoke of Weber's "golden humor" and his intensely vital and passionate temper and joy of life. Joseph Schumpeter remembered Weber as "one of the most powerful personalities" ever to enter academic life. "The profound influence of his leadership," Schumpeter added, was due to a "chivalrous" character ready to fight for the good cause. Weber's physical presence exuded the strength of his convictions. When he felt things strongly his voice, recalled Karl Jaspers, thundered "like a lion's roar."[2]

A list of members of the Heidelberg Circle reads like a "Who's Who" of German academic life. In addition to Georg Jellinek, Weber's close friend and pioneering analyst of international relations, there was Ernst Troeltsch, author of the seminal *Social Teachings of the Christian Churches;* Friedrich Naumann, the theologian and Protestant social reformer; Gustav Schmoller, economist and planner of Germany's early social welfare state; Werner Sombardt, fellow editor of the *Archiv* and theorist of modern capitalism; Robert Michels, the anatomist of social democracy and its theoretical problems; Ernst Toller, the anarchist-pacifist playwright; and some followers of Stefan George, the poet who had his own competing circle of writers.[3]

Marianne Weber remembers the salons of the Heidelberg Circle as convivial and pleasant. People chatted with one another "lightheartedly and freely without any sense of being held to what they said." In certain discussions, however, Weber himself held other thinkers to the positions they articulated, and this was particularly true of conversations with *Kathedersozialisten,* academic socialists who believed Germany's social problems could be overcome by means of economic planning and state regulation of industry. Weber would also take seriously the chatter of two other figures who turned up at his home at 17 Ziegelhauser Landstraße in stately Heidelberg—Ernest Bloch and Georg Lukács.[4]

Weber at first tolerated Bloch and Lukács as voices prophesying new intellectual movements emerging over the horizon; he was always ready to listen to any ideological proposition that promised to be fresh and exciting in its extreme departures from the familiar. Bloch the Jewish theologian and Lukács the secular Marxist both hungered for a transforming apocalypse that would answer the metaphysical need for meaning. Both were impatient with Weber's skepticism concerning all chiliastic visions, and their presence could often imbue the Heidelberg Circle with an atmosphere more eschatological than convivial. One contemporary joked of their portentous posturing: "Who are the four Evangelists? Matthew, Mark, Lukács and Bloch."[5]

Weber may have been deeply interested in religion, but Bloch's evangelical anti-intellectualism he disliked. At one Sunday occasion at the Webers, Bloch interrogated Friedrich Naumann, a close family friend, with questions that only a fellow apocalyptic could follow, and everyone present squirmed in discomfort. The genteel atmosphere of the Sunday gatherings was being jeopardized by Bloch's outrageous behavior. Weber had no "ear" for Bloch's prophetic rantings about God and religion that demanded unconditional acceptance. "Very well," Weber remarked to a friend who was trying to put in a good word for Bloch, "but the man who wants to be called a philosopher is obliged, if you please, to construct an epistemology as a basis for his assertions; then we shall see if he is a philosopher or not." When Bloch would make pronouncements on eschatology at the Sunday gatherings, Weber would frown and pull at his beard. But Bloch's boorish behavior, even more than his outlandish speculations, disturbed several people at the salons to the point that they stopped coming. Frustrated, Weber told one of his students: "I would like to send a porter to his house to pack his trunks and take them to the railroad station, so that Bloch would go away."[6]

Bloch, who had his differences with Weber over interpreting music as well as religion, soon found out that Weber had come between himself and his friend Lukács. "How can a man like him," Bloch asked Lukács of Weber, "who has so little idea of my abilities, of my whole *Spezificum* . . . how can this man be so intellectually close to you?" How indeed![7]

The Webers had befriended the young Georg Lukács, who had come to Heidelberg in 1912 intending to pursue postdoctoral studies in philosophy. At that time Weber was one of the only nonreactionary professors in Germany, if not the only one, and Weber considered it a moral imperative to help talented youth "with something to say" who had been subjected to political, religious, or ethnic discrimination. Weber attempted to advance Lukács's academic career, and at first they shared a common philosophical outlook and saw values existing apart from empirical reality. But with the outbreak of war in 1914, the Webers were shocked to discover that Lukács had denounced the war as barbaric and the beginning of the "age of complete sinfulness." Before long Weber and Lukács found themselves completely estranged from one another and intellectual as well as political differences began to emerge. Lukács's disposition toward collectivist experiments made him ripe for Marxism, turning him into a supporter of the bolsheviks in 1917 and later a member of the Soviet government in Hungary after the breakup of the Austro-Hungarian empire. "Most

esteemed friend," Weber wrote to Lukács in 1920, "of course we are separated by our political views! (I am absolutely convinced that these experiments can only have and will have the consequence of discrediting socialism for the coming 100 years.)"[8]

Such warnings scarcely troubled Lukács, who would go on to write
books indicating that, no matter how much he still respected Weber, he
learned almost nothing from him. Where Weber described workers
becoming more integrated into their respective nation-states, Lukács
would claim that Lenin's party dictatorship embodied the genuine spirit
of class consciousness; where Weber saw reason as succumbing to the
forces of rationalization, Lukács saw reason objectifying itself in history
and hence posing a solution to alienation and reification; where Weber
turned to religion for a "theodicy of misfortune" to explain the psychic
stresses that planted the seeds of capitalism, Lukács saw tragedy as inherent in the nature of existence and capitalism as "pre-history's" last stage.
But these later differences eschew the intellectual problems that Weber
and Lukács shared in the years before the great war. A few of these problems are recorded in Lukács's once-lost *Notizhefte* (Notebooks).[9]

In 1911, before Lukács turned to a Hegelian-Marxism that dialectically
dissolves all philosophical antagonism into "higher" syntheses, he apparently shared Weber's dualistic sensibility. He had no objection to Weber's
contention that each individual must choose values and that no one can
teach others what they "should" do but only what they can do and might
want to do. He also agreed that all knowledge of cultural reality has
already been conditioned by a specific historical point of view held by
authors. As a result the values and interpretive perspectives that authors
bring to a subject constitute a hindrance. In six words Lukács wrote out
Weber's dictum: "Where values begin, science leaves off." Later Lukács
would dismiss such dualisms as the "antinomies"of the bourgeois class.[10]

"HIATUS IRRATIONALIS"

At the Sunday salons two words could often be heard over the buzz of
polite conversation: *Naturwissenschaften* and *Geisteswissenschaften*. Often
the words would be pronounced with such exclamatory force that it
almost seemed a philosophical issue was being resolved by simply nam-
ing it. But the repetition of these heavy terms indicated that Heidelberg
had been infected by a disease of the intellect. "Something like a methodological pestilence prevails over our discipline," wrote Weber of social
science.[11]

Ever since the Enlightenment it was assumed that true knowledge lies in the capacity of science to experiment with data and observe the outcome. Facts are to be ascertained and classified and the behavior of the physical world explained through generalizations, perhaps even law-bound deterministic properties that the factual data exhibit. Can a discipline whose methods illuminate the physical and biological world be applied to the sphere of human action? The question preoccupied, indeed almost obsessed, a German intellectual life steeped in the philosophy of Immanuel Kant. Weber's neo-Kantian contemporaries, reacting to a lofty Hegelian metaphysics that made no effort to assimilate natural science, sought to find ways to use philosophy in order to have access to truths about history, society, and culture. Such discussions could occasionally turn the relaxed atmosphere of the Sunday gatherings at the Webers into a *Methodenstreit*, a "battle of the methods" to be applied in the study of human phenomena. This "battle" reflected an intense Germanic will to know and a deep desire to understand what it is one understands when something is said to be understood.

In the Weber circle the name Wilhelm Dilthey often came up whenever a discussion turned on the relation of inner experience to external reality. Son of a Protestant minister, Dilthey had been nurtured on music and romantic theology as well as history and philosophy; he once described German intellectuals in words that could have applied to Weber specifically—"all these thinkers hid poetic souls behind their furrowed faces." Like Weber, Dilthey felt acutely the gap between the world of nature and the world of human action. He based his philosophy on the radical difference between the ways of knowing proper to *Naturwissenschaft* and those proper to *Geisteswissenschaft*. While the first category referred to the external world of nature, the latter had no direct equivalent in English, and hence it has been interpreted as the science of spirit, as the field of human studies, or as culture itself. Dilthey's aim was to defend the autonomy of cultural sciences against the encroachments of the more exact physical and biological sciences by reminding us that history itself is "spiritual" in that it partook of human thoughts, purposes, and actions. Rejecting older religious orthodoxies and newer scientific methodologies, Dilthey insisted that the world can only be truly comprehended historically once we see how humankind manifests itself in various ways and in different contexts and how a specific social phenomenon can be understood by knowing the conditions of its growth and development. That human mental life appears to be infinitely diverse ruled out the possibility that *Geisteswissenschaft* conforms to any generalizations or hypotheses found in *Naturwissenschaft*, where behavior is physical and takes place in a continuum that can be explained by establishing causal connections. Thus Dilthey drew a distinction between two realms: "We explain nature, but we understand [*verstehen*] mental life."[12]

What do we understand when we claim to have understood history and society? In nature deterministic, predictable behavior can be explained by observing patterns and sequences; but human activity is motivated by free agents whose thoughts must be inferred. The meaning they give to their experiences must somehow be known. Can we understand without explaining? Such questions Weber would have to grapple with in his own theory of understanding as interpretive comprehension.

In this heated *Methodenstreit* over the epistemological foundations of new disciplines like sociology, two other contemporaries of Weber sought to overcome the crisis of knowledge by redefining the terms of discourse. Wilhelm Windelband went beyond Dilthey's explanation/understanding dichotomy and insisted that the difference between the natural and human worlds had more to do with method than object. Nature constitutes a "nomothetic" science that aims to establish lawful uniformities and predictable patterns. Human society, by contrast, is "ideographic" in that inquiry into its nature deals with elements that are particular and individual, so specifically diverse as to deny universal explanations. Dilthey believed Windelband's distinction between the two realms would deprive history of significance since human behavior becomes meaningless if it cannot be understood as exhibiting regular recurrences or at least some sense of rational sequence. If there can be no science of the particular, how can a general truth be derived from a specific fact?

In his methodological writings Weber often drew on Heinrich Rickert, a former student who became close to Marianne. Rickert's and Weber's parents had worked together in the National Liberal Party. The sons had known each other since their youth and Marianne came to admire Rickert's wife Sophie, a graceful sculptor, "a new type of woman with an artist's soul, a woman who expended the same emotional strength on her artistic creation that she did on being a wife and mother." Marianne also attended Rickert's seminar, became a devoted student, and kept her husband informed about what she had been learning—"the object of knowledge" as the "meaning of life and the world." Weber himself had facilitated Rickert's appointment to the University of Freiburg in 1896, and a half-dozen years later he found himself steeped in Rickert in preparation for his own forays into methodology. "I just finished Rickert," he wrote to Marianne from Florence; "he is *very good*."[13]

Rickert could scarcely bring himself to return the compliment. Karl Jaspers recalled a conversation he had with Rickert in Heidelberg shortly after Weber's funeral. Rickert deprecated the value of Weber's work and scoffed at the idea that he deserved to be called a "philosopher." Jaspers, still distraught over Weber's death, angrily replied: "If you think that you and your philosophy will be known at all in the future, you may perhaps be right, but only because your name is mentioned in a footnote in one of Max Weber's works as the man to whom Max Weber expresses gratitude for certain logical insights."[14]

The insight that Weber shared with Rickert would come to be called, a century later in Anglo-American philosophy, "anti-foundationalism." Reality, supposedly the ground upon which we stand, has no ontological status, no knowable existence independent of the act of knowing it. Rickert had studied with Windelband and the two, along with several others, became associated with the Baden or Southwest German School of Neo-Kantianism. Following Kant, Rickert maintained that the object of knowledge depends upon the mind's operations to such an extent that reality is not "given" bare to the mind but instead is constituted by it. Thus the distinction between nature and culture turns on how each is perceived. "Reality becomes nature if we consider it in regards to what is general; it becomes history if we consider it in regards to the particular or individual."[15] How phenomena are considered is a matter of the concepts that are brought to bear on the object under investigation.

In *Die Grenzen der naturwissenschaftlichen Begriffsschildung* (1902), Rickert addressed the title of his book: "The Limits of Concept Formation in the Natural Sciences." Rickert went beyond Windelband's position that history involves the particular and contingent and thus that it cannot be explained by general laws. Individual behavior, Rickert observed, can be illuminated by general concepts (class, culture, religion, politics, and so on) which are formed to represent them. Particular aspects of human action become objects of knowledge when brought under a concept. Knowing an object is made possible by the ability to form a concept of that object. An event in history becomes a genuine object of knowledge when it is brought under a concept or when concepts are formed to represent the event. Such concepts are constructions and hence have no basis in reality, the foundation on which truth was traditionally believed to rest. But there can be no correspondence between knowledge and its object once we become aware that reality eludes our grasp, "an inexhaustible manifold," a void that seems to become greater and greater the more deeply we delve into it, and thus cannot be known as it really is. Without mediating interpretive concepts—what Weber would call "ideal types"—reality remains as inscrutable as Melville's white whale. The real, the goal philosophy once aimed to arrive at, is beyond reason itself. Between the thinker and the object he or she is trying to get at there exists a *hiatus irrationalis,* an unbridgeable gap between thought and thing, idea and reality.

Rickert attempted to resolve this hiatus by insisting that the chasm between reality and concept be regarded as a challenge to our cognitive limitations rather than as an ultimate impasse. While natural science may yield predictable truths, human culture is richer in that a nonrecurring individuality alone is endowed with value since free human agents cause change rather than existing as insignificant incidents to whom things happen. Unlike natural phenomena, particularly the realm of physical sciences where bodies are moved by forces beyond themselves, human culture moves by purpose and creative choice. Values not only inhere in the objects of cultural studies, they influence the scholar's point of view. Values have no basis in reality any more than the concepts employed to explain it. But values are attributed to entities and activities, and in this sense scholarly inquiry is value-related in that personal, subjective values provide the scholar with principles of selection when faced with the amorphous, indeterminable heterogeneity of reality.

Value-relatedness need not jeopardize the scholar's objectivity, which would be threatened when crude value judgments are made about this and that. All cultures have their own value schemes and need not be evaluated by standards external to them, and even significant values within a culture are incommensurable. The value of values lies neither in their validity nor their veracity. Their existence is to be recognized as a methodological necessity in the process of forming concepts about an essentially unknowable reality. Thus what seemed a hiatus to other thinkers—the disconcerting thought that reality eludes conceptual representation—presented a healthy challenge to Rickert, a cognitive burden that may turn out to be a moral blessing by returning value to conscious choice and creativity, not the "is" of physical reality but the "ought" of human possibility.[16]

The work of Dilthey, Windelband, and Rickert provided the methodological ideas that were discussed in Heidelberg at the turn of the century. Using them as a point of departure, Weber attempted to resolve theoretical issues that today still perplex the social scientist. If value-relatedness need not entail evaluation, if one may study value-driven behavior without judging it, can objectivity be maintained and relativism avoided? Can values themselves be made intelligible so that modern culture might rest on a rational consensus?

ACTION AND MEANING

While Rickert remained convinced that such theoretical questions could be answered affirmatively by postulating the existence of transcendent values, Weber doubted that anything but a specific culture's own values existed. By his view, then, modern society found itself with no possibility of evaluating experience from a superhistorical position. Instead of aiming at judgment, inquiry should recognize only the value-related principle that governs how facts are selected and described, the subjective and ephemeral values and interests that are behind an investigator's own concerns and curiosities. Weber's conviction that the decision what to research and make worthy of knowing is personal and practical has some resemblance to American pragmatism. "The value of a work," Weber wrote to Karl Vossler, "which presupposes a polyhistorical range of knowledge, is in the end conclusively determined by the value of the problems posed, by the degree to which questions are correctly and therefore originally asked. A 'shoemaker' or 'dilettante' will often come up with the correct answer, as well as, or even better than, a thinker."[17] But while Weber saw inquiry as an exercise in practical problem-solving, he did not share the pragmatist view that knowledge rested on experience, or, to be more accurate, that one looks to experience to verify ideas about truth and reality.

In this respect Weber had to go beyond *verstehen*, Dilthey's notion of understanding the purposeful actions of particular individuals through an exercise in emphatic reexperiencing. The processes of *Einfühlen* (empathy) and *Nacherleben* (reliving) may help objectify knowledge, Weber noted, but to know what has been experienced "can be answered only by a *theory of interpretation*." Experience without concepts can lead to an "inchoate stupor" until theoretical reflection intervenes. But conceptual understanding need not be confined to culture. The study of human action also has an empirical content in that it too can be explained in terms of causality. Weber conceded the *hiatus irrationalis* insofar as reality refused to yield its secrets to the human concepts that aspire to know it. But Weber turned Galileo's telescope around, so to speak, and advised his contemporaries to look through the opposite end at the observer and his motives and purposes. What the social scientist aspires to is not to know the ultimate nature of reality but the "subjectively intended meaning" imposed on reality by humanity in its attempt to orient its behavior, in order to realize its aims and purposes. Conduct becomes meaningful when the means of human action are considered together with the ends to be realized. To Weber understanding becomes possible through the discovery of causal relationships that relate concrete results to intentions. "The question of the appropriation of the means for achieving a given end is understandably accessible to scientific analysis."[18] One need neither accept nor reject a particular value at the basis of a specific behavior to apprehend a person's purposes in order to explain what causes him or her to act. The ultimate springs of action may be irrational but ends may be rationally pursued. The Puritans sought salvation and got Mammon!

Are reasons causes? Georg Simmel, another Weber contemporary, believed in what came to be called the reference theory of knowledge—a person's reasons only have meaning to the extent they refer to something beyond language, and hence have an objective meaning; this is in contrast to the understanding of the motives that lead persons to speak and act in a certain way, the subjective meaning. Weber had reservations about extending the concept of meaning to the objective criteria of science. He believed that understanding by means of motivational explanation need not set sociology apart from science as long as causal analysis was involved. Weber remained convinced he could explain behavior by ascertaining the agent's conception of what he or she is doing, as opposed to explaining it by reference to some objective criterion of understanding. The meaning of an action depends upon an analysis and interpretation that people themselves give of their own actions or of those of others. Science may explain causes and connections but social investigation would find behavior meaningless if action could not be related to an intended purpose. Thus a social scientist who discovers rules and regulations operating in a community cannot assume that such rules "cause" behavior without knowing why its members are willing to abide by such rules:

> Let us suppose that two men who otherwise engage in no "social relation"—for example, two uncivilized men of different races, or a European who encounters a native in darkest Africa—meet and "exchange" two objects. We are inclined to think that a mere description of what can be observed during this exchange—muscular movements and, if some words were "spoken," the sounds which, so to say, constitute the "matter" or "material" of the behavior—would in no sense comprehend the "essence" of what happens. This is quite correct. The "essence" of what happens is constituted by the "meaning" which the two parties ascribe to their observable behavior, a "meaning" which "regulates" the course of their future conduct. Without this "meaning," we are inclined to say, an "exchange" is neither empirically possible nor conceptually imaginable.[19]

To his more empirically oriented critics Weber denied that a concern for causal investigation should remain only within the domain of natural science. Weber insisted that behavior itself is caused, and to interpret the behavior is to interpret the meaning of overt action by getting at the motives behind it. Against his more romantic contemporaries, like the historian Heinrich von Treitschke, who saw freedom expressing itself in the mystery of personality; or the economists Wilhelm Roscher and Karl Knies, who saw behavior as free precisely because it is unpredictable, Weber devoted all his energies to proving that behavior is capable of rational interpretation to the extent that motives, and even what appears to be irrational motives, lend themselves to explanation and comprehension. And recognizing that meaning is intended only by people themselves, Weber takes us into the consciousness of his subjects. At the turn of the century Weber had great faith that knowledge of human action turned on establishing the conscious intention of the actor. Like a criminal investigator, he would interpret the meaning of an act by coming up with the motive.

PRINCIPLE OF ACTION

In the many *Methodenstreit* discussions that went on in Heidelberg Marx and the Marxist philosophy of history could often be heard voiced to counter Weber's position. A Marxist, or at least one who still retained a Hegelian sensibility, saw history as moving in ironic ways and even independently of human consciousness in accordance with certain laws of development. Weber remained convinced that a causal analysis of the interrelationship of means and purposes could be based not on laws and concepts, but on regularities observed in social behavior and historical experience. He aimed to explain historical change not by going beyond society but by reference to what people do and why they do it. Although ultimate metaphysical reality remains unknowable, human beings become real and knowable by virtue of their actions: *Hinter der Handlung steht der Mensch* ("Behind the action stands the human being"). And actions can be analyzed on the basis of the reasons human beings impute to the meanings of their actions. And if people have no reasons?

Weber's focus on motives and purposes may have derived from his Kantian commitment to personal autonomy and moral responsibility. But to some writers the shocks of World War I undermined belief in rational explanations for behavior:

What an odd thing—to be in the Italian army.
It's not really the army. It's only the ambulance.
It's very odd though. Why did you do it?
I don't know. There isn't always an explanation for everything.
Oh, isn't there? I was brought up to think there was.

Ernest Hemingway, A Farewell to Arms

The "Great War" led many intellectuals in the western world to hold a new view of history as irrational, absurdly random, with the relation of cause and effect obliterated by the "guns of August" and human reason left dumb to explain human action. The shocks of war led the novelist James Joyce to write that "history is the nightmare from which I am trying to awake." But for Weber, as well as for Joyce, the irrationality of events could heighten rather than blunt conscious awareness, and the irony of intention and consequences may limit the scope of rational control without paralyzing the intellect's drive to comprehend the apparently incomprehensible. Ultimately Weber could never believe that life lacked "qualitative existence," the inner meaning and significance people give to their experience. It was up to the social scientist to penetrate this *Sinnzusammenhang*, the sense of connections and the structure of meaning in the scheme of things that make life worth studying as well as living.

Weber accepted the challenge, and quietly in his unpublished manuscript fragments he worked out a four-part scheme to enable scholars to comprehend conduct according to the following principles of action:

1. *Zweckrationalität.* Instrumental action taken in respect to a goal ("purposeful rationality") in which the actor calculates the conditions or means to attain a desired end and the consequences of succeeding or failing.
2. *Wertrationalität.* Value rationality in which action is taken for the sake of some overriding ethical, aesthetic, or religious principle, regardless of its chances of success.
3. Affectual. Behavior springing from sheer emotion.
4. Traditional. Behavior following from "ingrained habituation."[20]

In contrast to natural science, the challenge of social science is the challenge of *verstehen*, of understanding meaning, and Weber formulated such categories to rise to that challenge. Social behavior can be made comprehensible in light of its meaning as experienced by the subjects who act from intentions and purposes. Understanding requires interpreting what people are doing, what their actions mean and signify. Weber's categories are provocative but it would have helped matters if he had supplied concrete examples. How would he have answered Freud's question: "What does woman want?" Do we observe what women do or listen to what they say? Furthermore, must the interpretation of the sociologist be acceptable to the subject he or she is studying? During World War I, as we shall see, Weber believed he could interpret the unwise basis for Woodrow Wilson's diplomatic actions and for V. I. Lenin's revolutionary aspirations. Could he?

Years after the posthumous publication of *Economy and Society*, some scholars found Weber's four classifications lacking in explanatory depth and predictive power. Admittedly it is difficult to distinguish between a goal and a value and an emotion and a tradition. As an institution marriage is an "ingrained habituation," but the decision to take the step (or "leap" or "plunge") may involve rational premeditation and planning while the head weighs the consequences of the goal and at the same time the impulses of the heart rush to fulfill its own longing regardless of the prospects of failure. Had Weber himself gone through divorce he might have agreed with Oscar Wilde that you can't reason someone out of what they had not reasoned into. Yet Weber would have been the first to point out that his categories are neither rigidly systematic nor mutually exclusive. "The individual can participate in a variety of types of social action in one and the same act," he observed:

> An act of exchange, which someone completes with X who is the representative of Y, which is perhaps the "organ" of society, contains (1) a language; (2) a written association; (3) an exchange association with X personally; (4) similarly one with Y personally; (5) similarly one with the social activities of the members of the society; (6) as an act of exchange is oriented to the expectations of potential action on the part of others aware of the exchange (competitors of both sides) as conditions of the act and to the corresponding assumptions of legality.[21]

By emphasizing the simultaneity of action rather than its sequence, Weber illuminates the multiple meanings of action in all their complexity. Thus the New England Calvinist acts in response to his conscience, which in turn feels the presence of God, while his activities are oriented toward the expectations of society and its members. Skeptical of reductionism, Weber refused to regard any specific reality as the only reality. Capitalism was more than economics—at least in the beginning.

Far from being descriptive categories, Weber's principles of action offered constructions of possibility to assist in the forming of hypotheses.

Such constructions could be "ideal types," heuristic categories that serve the purpose of posing questions and clarifying concepts. Ideal types are meant to be exaggerated simplifications of the complexity of historical data so that behavior may be analyzed in view of its approximations or deviations from the model or "ideal," that is, its complete attributes. Thus value-rational action entailed undertaking some goal on the basis of conviction in which the fulfillments of conscience are more important than the calculation of consequences. During World War I Weber drew on this particular categorical imperative to analyze critically both the pacifists who renounced power and the liberals who would pursue peace through it.

In theory Weber's categories were to be used for purposes of analysis alone, without any imposition of moral judgment. But a controversy began to emerge in his time that is still debated today regarding Weber's idea of *Wertfreiheit*, freedom from value judgment. Closer to our time the conservative philosopher Leo Strauss would criticize Weber for denying the possibility of objective norms and separating fact from value. But the "value-judgment dispute" first broke out at a conference in Vienna in 1909. Some of the members of Heidelberg's Weber Circle were attending the meeting when representatives of the "Austrian School" of economics presented a treatise on "productivity" as though it were strictly a scientific concept. When Weber insisted the concept was value-ridden, a heated debate broke out and another *Methodenstreit* was under way.

Weber had little support from fellow social scientists in developing his essay on "The Meaning of 'Ethical Neutrality' in Sociology and Economics." When the essay later appeared in 1917, it had some resonance in the midst of World War I, when the need for objectivity was greater than ever. But earlier the notion of excluding ethics seemed puzzling. Had not Weber himself taken a moral stand in his inaugural address at Freiburg in 1895, when he called upon Germans to make uppermost the interest of the nation-state? Although Weber had shown the importance of religion in history, his methodological theory of inquiry seemed to eliminate religious values from the historian's work as a scientific investigator, a stance his admirer Friedrich Meinecke was unwilling to take.[22]

But Weber was a dualist who believed factual analysis alone could never yield ethical standards. No hierarchy of values can be derived from empirical research, nor can reason resolve conflicts between different ultimate values, which Weber often referred to as a "war of the gods." The ideas with which we form concepts in order to understand reality may have a rational capacity to organize data, but the ideas themselves are subjective in that they spring from our desire to know this rather than that, a selection based upon a value decision:

> The *objective* validity of all empirical knowledge rests exclusively upon the ordering of the given reality according to categories which are *subjective* in a specific sense, namely, in that they present the *presuppositions* of our knowledge and are based on the presupposition of the *value* of those *truths* which empirical knowledge alone is able to give us.... But these data can never become the foundation for the empirically impossible proof of the validity of the evaluative ideas. The belief which we all have in some form or other, in the metaphysical validity of ultimate and final values, in which the meaning of our existence is rooted, is not incompatible with the incessant changefulness of the concrete viewpoints, from which empirical reality gets its significance. Both these views are, on the contrary, in harmony with each other. Life with its irrationality and its store of possible meanings is inexhaustible.[23]

Weber's controversial stance on ethical neutrality suggests how a political position is sustained by a philosophical conviction. In the 1890s Weber took public stands against socialists who sought to nationalize the economy and liberals who desired to increase the concentration of power in the State. Weber worried that a state-controlled economy would simply increase the power of civil servants. Such demands, he noted, had been made in his own organization, the Verein für Sozialpolitik, and the "predilection for bureaucracy which exists among us in varying degrees, is a purely moral sentiment: namely, the belief in the unshakability of the undoubtedly high moral standards of Germans." Weber delighted in depicting the scientific pretenses of bureaucrats, but since the Verein had been established to engage in empirical research upon which normative policy decisions could be made, it was a little inconsistent for him to insist that scientific methodology must be free from value judgment. Nonetheless, Weber had good reason for later amplifying the meaning of ethical neutrality, particularly during World War I when, as we shall see in subsequent chapters, German professors would legitimate their political stance by invoking the "objective" state of their academic discipline.

Years earlier, in 1904, Weber wrote " 'Objectivity' in Social Science and Social Policy," an effort to show why the scholar should think twice before passing judgments of a political nature. Those who do engage in such judgments assume they are objective out of a deep presupposition that the naturally right is synonymous with the immutably existent, as in positivism, or with the inevitably emergent, as in Marxism and Hegelianism, where social ideals are seen as progressing toward rational ideals as part of history's philosophical mission. Weber had a Nietzschean suspicion for thinkers who profess to discover the truth of things in their research when in reality they are imposing their own opinions and norms. The dilemma is that knowledge makes us aware that ethical values cannot be derived simply because they are politically or normatively desirable:

> It is the fate of our cultural epoch which has eaten of the tree of knowledge to be aware that however completely we may investigate history we can not read its real meaning, and that we must be content therefore to create our own sense of history; that our *Weltanschauung* can never be the product of the progressive knowledge of experience, and that thus the highest ideals and those which move us most deeply, work themselves out permanently only through conflict with rival ideals which are quite as sacred to other individuals as ours are to us.[24]

Weber became convinced that knowledge never could or should claim to ground itself in authority, that all ideals rival one another, that all action is potentially tragic ridden in that it involves choice of one thing to the exclusion of the other, and that if the social scientist maintains his neutrality by standing in the middle he loses his responsibility for refusing to take sides. "Irony is the pathos of the middle," observed Thomas Mann. Neutrality scarcely meant indifference or inaction to Weber. Actually his ethical stance stood him between two thinkers who themselves straddled the conscience of the modern mind.

BETWEEN GRACE AND GREATNESS: TOLSTOY AND NIETZSCHE

Seldom did a Sunday gathering at the Webers go by without the name of Dostoyevski coming up, recalled Paul Honigsheim. "But perhaps even more pressing," he added, "even inflaming, was the necessity of coming to grips with Tolstoy."[25] A third figure with whom Weber would have to come to grips was Friedrich Nietzsche, the German philosopher who has become associated with nihilism yet a thinker so sensitive to human weakness that he sought to rescue genuine morality from mendacity and mediocrity and locate it in the sovereign individual. Tolstoy, Weber, and Nietzsche all viewed history as essentially meaningless, an absurd succession of forces and effects that would remain without significance until the thinker strove to make sense of events. The different ways Tolstoy and

Nietzsche interpreted history dramatized the conflicts between ethics and power at the heart of Weber's tragic vision of politics.

Weber began his explorations into methodological issues in the latter stages of his sick period, 1902–3; the following year, when he had recovered enough to make the trip to the United States, the first section of his Protestant ethic thesis appeared, indicating that he was steeped in religiosity as well as methodology. Tolstoy's writings had been translated into German beginning in 1885; in Heidelberg in the first years of the next century Weber had discussions with Russian and Russophile intellectuals that became more intense with the Russian Revolution of 1905. During the period 1912–17, the Hungarian philosopher Lukács would show up at the Sunday salons and inform the Weber circle that Dostoyevski and Tolstoy offered an alternative to western culture with its Kantian ethic of duty and individual responsibility. Weber recognized that Tolstoy indeed had an alternative vision to offer the world, and the Russian thinker resonated in his thoughts for personal as well as political reasons. "Life with you," he wrote to Marianne from Florence in 1908, "is like the soft light and warmth of the spring sun which—as Tolstoy only all too optimistically hopes—will spring from the power of human love."[26]

With the revolution of 1905, Weber keenly followed the daily events in Slavic emigre publications, having learned Russian in a matter of months. He identified with the aspirations of the Russian people and displayed unusual sympathy for the anarchists, possibly because they distrusted all systems of organized authority. Concerning the Marxists, however, Weber could only wonder why their ideals had any chance of gaining ascendancy in a backward country that lacked the conditions to make the transition to socialism. Marxists were hungering for action and success, "the thirst for the deed," in the face of a philosophy that called for patience, practicing a "pragmatic rationalism" that could be flexible and adjust means to achieve ends. The concern for action and pragmatic consequences contrasted with Tolstoy's stance, which regarded means as sacred regardless of the outcome of a course of action. Marxists, in contrast, were willing to adopt almost any means, assuming they could transform Russian society and move it in a progressive direction. Weber described the tsarist state as a bureaucratic machine of the "terrible objective meaninglessness" of a system that knows no goal beyond that of self-preservation. Reading Tolstoy's novel *Resurrection*, Weber could only wonder about the fate of Russia. With the conscience of conviction dead, with reverence for power replacing reverence for God and nature, would the despotism of the tsarist state give way to the tyranny of the revolutionaries? Reformers themselves presume to be correcting evil without being aware that it lies within themselves. What is to be done?[27]

The cataclysmic politics of the moment, Weber prophesized, cannot hold back the logic of bureaucratization and the fate of modernity. The conditions for freedom may have bypassed Russia. An idea or movement makes its appearance once in a set of circumstances and cannot be repeated in a different context. As noted earlier, Weber believed that the historical origins of modern freedom entailed a "certain conjunction of unique and unrepeatable conditions," and such conditions as the expansion of overseas commerce and the rise of parliamentary government never made their appearance in Russia, with the result that western liberalism scarcely penetrated her political culture. Above all, the conscience of Calvinism has been bypassed in Russia and thus economic development under Marxism can only be a material achievement without a moral foundation:

> Among the masses, the "respectable" Social Democrats drill the spiritual parade, and instead of directing their thoughts to an otherwise worldly paradise (which according to Puritanism should also inspire respectable achievements in the service of this-worldly "freedom"), they turn their minds to a paradise in this world, and thereby make of it a kind of vaccination for the vested interests of the existing order. They accustom their pupils to a submissive attitude toward dogmas and party authorities, or to indulge in the fruitless play-acting of mass strikes or the idle enjoyment of the enervating howls of their hired journalists, which are as harmless as they are, in the end, laughable in the eyes of their enemies. In short, they accustom them to an "hysterical wallowing in emotion," which replaces and inhibits economic and political thought and action. The only plant which can grow on this infertile soil, once the "eschatological" age of the movement has passed and generation after generation has vainly clenched its fists in its pockets or bared its teeth towards heaven, is that of spiritual apathy.[28]

Weber could hardly accuse Tolstoy of spiritual apathy. Tolstoy represented the opposite extreme to the pragmatic Marxists who would use any means to realize an end that is itself unrealizable, even evolutionary, piecemeal reforms that leave workers wallowing in emotion and the ruling classes untouched. The question of realizing ends scarcely troubled Tolstoy, whose goals were not of this world. Tolstoy preached an inflexible adherence to a single methodical means regardless of the consequences. Did Russia need Tolstoy more than Trotsky?

Tolstoy began to occupy Weber's *Zwischenbetrachtung*, a running commentary recorded in his manuscripts of the World War I years. With the issue of value freedom uppermost in his thoughts, Weber became interested in Tolstoy's writings, which seemed to hold out the possibility that there could be an ethical stance that rejects all cultural values yet is itself free of corruptions and contradictions. Weber once told Marianne that he felt inner mystical promptings, and thus Tolstoy's concept of the Kingdom of God lying within oneself he could feel all the more. Particularly intriguing was Tolstoy's aesthetics of salvation, especially his renunciation of possessive individualism (*individueller Besitz*), the moral nourishment of work, and the radical limitation of needs. It almost seemed that Tolstoy represented the original spirit of capitalism; that he was a moralist who could work on matter without being corrupted by materialism. Weber noted the manner in which sections of the socialist movement had championed Christian as well as secular opposition to militarism and violence. Thus with the outbreak of World War I, Weber observed that the pacifists had failed to abide by what he called "The Tolstoy Consistency" as they voted for national defense measures in their respective countries or allowed violence-prone anarchists to be included in proposed international courts of arbitration.

Toward the end of the war, in 1918 when he gave his now-famous address "Politics as a Vocation," Weber would explain why such a consistency constitutes an impossible proposition. But it hardly took the war to illustrate the inadequacies of Tolstoy's pacifism. Earlier Weber had been intrigued by Tolstoy's sense of Christian brotherhood and the imperative of powerlessness because, among other reasons, Tolstoy's notion of religion represented the opposite of Calvinism. In contrast to the angst-driven Puritan, the contemplative mystic as the vessel (*Gufäß*) of spirit need not attempt to prove himself in this world. Weber shared Tolstoy's existential view that a life undergoing endless adaptations has no ends, and thus can only be wearily endured but never fulfilled. Yet Weber saw Tolstoy's pure inner-worldly perfection as equally meaningless. Tolstoy's evocation of the "Sermon of the Mount," the injunction to "resist not evil" in order to refrain from opposing power with power, seemed to Weber to lead to a "radically anti-political saintly mysticism." Tolstoy's ethic had no relevance to contemporary politics, and the more he struggled to bring it to bear on the human world, the more he succumbed to, in Edith Hanke's words, "more introversion, quietism, and finally to flight from this world—the last consistency."[29]

Tolstoy represented one category in Weber's four principles of action: the *Wertrational*, or behavior motivated by an intense consistency of moral intention irrespective of success, the intrinsic value from which action supposedly originates. Consciousness informed by conscience is the politics of conviction. Or is it a conceit parading as a principle?

"That the value of an act should depend upon what preceded it in *consciousness*—how false that is! And yet morality has been measured that way, even criminality." Measuring the value of an act "by its origins implies an impossibility, namely *knowing* the origin." Thus spake Friedrich Nietzsche.[30]

Nietzsche approximated Weber's favorite principle of action, *Zweckrationalität*, instrumental action undertaken with expectations of probable behavior of objects and other human beings so that purposes and outcomes can be rationally pursued. But even Nietzsche may not have been so certain that results can be known prior to acting. Utilitarians tell us, he warned, that since we cannot know the origins of an act we must measure its value by its consequences:

> But does one know the consequences? Perhaps as far as five steps. Who could say what an act stimulates, excites, provokes against itself? As a stimulus? Perhaps as the ignition spark for an explosive? The utilitarians are naive. And in the end we would first have to know what *is* useful; here too their vision extends for only five steps. They have no conception of any great economy which does not know how to dispense with evil.[31]

Utilitarians, positivists, and pragmatists all assume that the useful and practical can be known as a matter of methodological steps. Weber shared Nietzsche's conviction that nothing could be known factually but only interpreted from varying perspectives. In Nietzsche he also found an answer to Kant's ethical imperative that sanctioned only actions that originated in conscience and reached out to humanity as a whole. While Tolstoy sought to internalize moral behavior, Kant sought to universalize it; yet neither showed how acting on the basis of ethical duty can produce desired results. As did Nietzsche, Weber became convinced that a true morality must be able to anticipate consequences so that the actor is responsible for what he or she has wrought. Only instrumental action sufficiently assesses means in relation to ends in order to understand the antecedents and consequences of an action. Morality involves events as much as emotions.

Weber would go beyond Nietzsche by looking to science in order to think in causal sequences so that future outcomes might be calculated. But Nietzsche's meditations had planted themselves too firmly in Weber's imagination to be extirpated as unscientific. Ironically, Weber saw in

Nietzsche some of the values he had appreciated in historical Calvinism: a heightened sense of responsibility to which the kingdom of life would rise. As Nietzsche indicated in the example of ancient Greece, Weber also spoke of "guilt" as a source of strength that comes from accepting the burden of responsibility. Weber also agreed with Nietzsche that modern life has become flat, dull, and monotonous, and hence in need of heroes and great personalities. But Weber refused to subscribe to Nietzsche's disdain for democracy and aristocratic contempt of the masses. On the subject of religion the two German thinkers part company even further. Weber agreed with Simmel's judgment that Nietzsche "completely misinterprets Christianity."[32]

As though quarreling with Calvinism, Nietzsche restored to the human condition knowledge and will power and courage and strength, thereby replacing Christian humility with aristocratic nobility. Nietzsche also restored the most dubious sin of all—pride. Weber could hardly interpret Christian charity as the altruism of submission, nor could he dismiss Christian ideals of social justice as reflecting the "resentment" of the lower classes. What Weber identified with in Calvinism was its spiritual alienation that provided the psychological grounds of yearning for salvation. Weber stood closer to Tolstoy in sensing Christianity as a theology of strife rather than of submission.

The differences between Weber and Nietzsche involved politics as well as religion. In Weber's concept of *Augenmaß*, the notion of visual, detached judgment, lies the concept of distance: "distance to things and to men" and for all cases "distance in opposition to one's self." Nietzsche referred to the "pathos of distance" as a sensibility that grows in aristocratic society, setting people of rank apart from one another on the basis of differences and making possible "that other more mysterious pathos, that longing for ever greater distance within the soul itself, the evolving of ever higher, rarer, more spacious, more widely arched, more comprehensive states—in short: the heightening of the type 'man,' the continued 'self-mastery of man' to take a moral foundation in a supramoral sense."[33] To Weber the pathos of distance required in politics subduing normal human emotions like prejudice and vanity. The challenge was to fuse passion with proportion as the first requirement of objectivity. Such an effort would require an almost superhuman capacity for devotion without distortion, a politics of passion at the pitch of perception, a self aware of itself in all its conceits and deceptions.

Between Nietzsche's aristocratic pride and Tolstoy's Christian humility lies Weber's tragic vision of politics. In Nietzsche human nobility lies in its strength for self-mastery and individual accountability. In Tolstoy, human salvation lies in mystical self-surrender and adherence to inner convictions. Would choosing conviction to the neglect of consequences necessarily mean that righteousness would prevail over responsibility? Tolstoy's ethic called for scrutinizing one's motives with little regard for their effects in worldly experience. Nietzsche denied that one can know the "origins" of acts yet he assumed that all motives and their effects are power-driven. One thinker sought to renounce power, the other to recognize it in all its ferocity; one aspired to grace, the other to greatness. Weber could not help being drawn toward Nietzsche's aristocratic sensibility, which saw man's noble vocation as suffering, but he also realized that from the "flame of pure intention" sprang spiritual ideals. Christianity arrived on earth to bring peace among men; but politics can realize its ends only through violence, a thought that scarcely troubled Nietzsche while it drove Tolstoy to despair. In 1918, as World War I came to its gory conclusion, Weber could only wonder whether religion and politics, both historically having set out to convert the world, are not only mutually incompatible but each inadequate to its respective mission.

Tolstoy would abolish all the conditions of modern culture in order to save humanity from itself; Weber believed that the only way to deal with the world in its own terms was to give up hope of salvation. Yet politics could still be the "imitation of noble actions" since it would remain a state of unending conflict. Moved in different ways by both Nietzsche and Tolstoy, Weber offered politics as a tragic calling, the drama of fate and freedom, proportion and passion, the dynamic of the real in the name of the ideal, an act of the moral imagination with which we can appreciate that "man would not have obtained the possible unless time and again he had reach out for the impossible."[34]

Weber's Christian piety, and his romantic attachment to aristocratic ideals like chivalry and duty, suggests how far removed he remained from modern democratic politics and its "art" of compromise. Like Nietzsche, Weber loathed pragmatic adaptability, adjustment, and accommodation; like Tolstoy and the old Calvinists, he dismissed politics as the "pursuit of happiness" as a "flabby eudaemonism." Nor should politics aim solely at establishing institutional structures, whether to balance power or to benefit the general welfare. Politics has more to do with cultivating the quality of character than with responding expediently to circumstances. Politics is the "pathos of distance," the will to stand alone, the strength to withstand the pressures of the moment, to live for conviction without shirking the demands of action. Politics, like tragedy, must have a hero.

SIX

The Dignity of the Academic Calling

THE GERMAN PROFESSOR

S o must teaching have its heroes. In some ways the "calling" of the profession of teaching requires more ideals than does politics. Weber once remarked that although the politician "must make compromises, the scholar must not cover them up."[1] The philosopher Karl Jaspers esteemed Weber as a philosopher who, rejecting absolutism on one side and nihilism on the other, believed that teaching and scholarship involved an incessant struggle to try to know what may be unknowable. Weber portrayed the scholar as driven by curiosity, as a seeker.

Although sociologists have claimed Weber as one of their own, and he occasionally referred to himself as a sociologist, his primary interests were religion, politics, and economics and their respective histories in various cultural environments. He went from an early interest in the study of law to a later meditation on the end of philosophical reason and its transformation into a practical instrument. He also devoted himself to theoriz-

132

ing about teaching, a profession he entered reluctantly in the 1890s, withdrew from a decade later due to illness, and returned to only in 1918, two years before his death. To Weber teaching as a vocation represented a challenge to the character and integrity of the professor, the one agent in society responsible for training the minds of the future. Weber took teaching as seriously as he did his research. Instead of seeing the modern intellect has having been rendered obsolete by the rationalization of modern society, Weber saw that figure as more relevant than ever. It could be said that Weber hoped the academic would fulfill the role that Tocqueville saw lawyers fulfilling in a democratic America without an aristocracy: the role of the thinker committed to objectivity, free inquiry, and love of truth.

Weber's joining the responsibilities of teaching to the human desire for learning had much in common with the older Protestantism that established education in colonial America. "College lecturing is a duty—not to be pleasant, not in the least," he wrote to Mina Tobler in 1920. But whether lecturing was a matter of writing or speaking, the "wicked young" students "should indeed take notes, and I know how good that is."[2] Neither Weber nor the New England Calvinists believed that education must identify with the inevitable rise of democracy. Education would have less to do with the "pursuit of happiness" than with cultivation of mind, exercise of will, demands of veracity, and readiness to accept discipline and assume the responsibilities of leadership. The Enlightenment dictum that the truth shall make us free had little place in Weber's philosophy of education. Nevertheless, realizing that knowledge could demonstrate at best that the foundations of freedom are fortuitous, Weber devoted his life to the quest for truth.

Weber overworked himself in his academic involvements. In his first position at the University of Berlin, he taught nineteen hours of lectures and seminars weekly (today's average in American and German universities is about five hours). Until the end of World War I, he commanded the admiration of students who heard him lecture or gathered at his Sunday salon in Heidelberg. "The young attached themselves to Max Weber, drawn to his personality and intellectual honesty," wrote Ernst Toller.[3] The arduous teaching assignments apparently took little toll on his lectures, which impressed students with their lively intensity and vigorous body-language:

> Max Weber lectured with great emphasis, his hands accompanying the swing and rhythm of his address like a conductor, a hand noticeably delicate for so strong a man. I heard the great lectures, on "Social and Eco-

nomic History," presented by him, and took part in his seminars. I know the ideas developed in Weber's book, *Wirtschaft und Gesellschaft*, give students such difficulty today that they are scarcely able to penetrate through the abstract formulations. But at that time we followed with suspense, indeed with exciting expectation, the short sentences, which offered definitions, abstract interpretations, and concrete examples, as though whipping into shape a relentless logic, rendering meaningful each idea and relating it to the latest findings. I have never observed a lecturer so conscientious in the transmission of knowledge, and neither before nor after [have I been] so deeply conscious of having learned.

Another student remembers Weber, who hated to see professors "prophetizing from the lectern," beginning his presentation by looking out over the jammed audience and, citing Stefan Georg, declaring "Your numbers are already a crime." He paid little attention to oratorical abilities but his categories had the lucidity of precision. "As far as I remember the lectures gave the picture of inner-worldly asceticism, pure definitions and explanations: like dry wine, quality proof, drawn from the cellar."[4]

The *élan vital* that Weber brought to German academic life impressed itself on many of those who witnessed it as a rarity in a regime of uniformity. In the late nineteenth century the German university remained a timid, authoritarian institution whose purpose was to serve the needs of the state. The American historian Henry Adams, who went to Berlin with the eager expectation of studying civil law, found the university atmosphere torpid with the passivity of rote learning based on the antiquated lecture system. "The professor mumbled his comments; the students made, or seemed to make, notes; they could learn from books and discussion in a day more than they could learn from him in a month, but they must pay his fees, follow his course, and be his scholars, if they wanted a degree." The students barely seemed to mind and went through the motions of being educated while rarely taking the professor seriously. That the students were more interested in poetry, beer, and girls delighted Adams. But as for education, "To an American the result was worthless."[5]

Weber would hardly have allowed himself to reach such a conclusion about university education in Germany, but he, too, resented its bureaucratic structures and dreary imposition of authority. In the 1880s, when Weber was an undergraduate, the German university, despite Adams's disappointments, continued to be the mecca of the academic world and scholars from all over flocked to it to study research methods and *Wissenschaft*, pure theoretical learning as opposed to technical training and the application of political policies. But when Weber himself became an academic he remained distressed by the thought that professors, in with-drawing into the world of scholarship, had become servants of the state and were hence dependent upon politics for research funds and even pro-motions. Such problems made more relevant the situation of American universities, and Weber, recalling his trip to the United States in 1904, would remind his colleagues that many eminent American colleges owed their existence to religious sects. In 1911, at the Conference of German University Teachers meeting in Dresden, one of the themes was the orga-nization of North American universities and the features that distin-guished them from their German counterparts. A Columbia University professor had sent ahead a list of questions thought to be pertinent to German academics, questions involving such matters as the division of labor between teaching and research and the fact that American univer-sities were not primarily concerned with the education of future public officials. Weber submitted his own list of questions:

1. Since the president seems to serve as rector, trustee, and cultural minister, what does the president actually do?
2. What are the consequences of the apparent democratization of the faculty?
3. What leverage does the full professor have in respect to his assistants?
4. Under such circumstances, how was the formal freedom to teach in the manner one wished worked out?
5. What were the prospects, here or there, for the broad stratum of teachers, and the outlook for the most competent?[6]

During the course of the conference Weber articulated some of the differences between German and American universities. German frater-nities, "increasingly insurance institutions for connections and advance-ment," may have something in common with those of America. But the emergence of business colleges in Germany may be more deleterious than in America where students are not so stuck on tradition. "The impetus behind these colleges is the circumstance that their interns are primarily concerned with gaining social status and its trappings—a few dueling scars, a bit of student life, a break with the habit of work—all things of which I must ask myself: Are they really going to assist our younger generation of businessmen in competition with the great com-petitive peoples of the world, especially the American?"[7]

American education, founded upon Protestant religions, would remain more individualistic and less reliant on the state. In Germany the univer-sity teacher, who had to work as a *privatdozent* without pay in his early years, would rise in the ranks only to become equivalent to a government official. Less and less will intellectual interests attach to science and scholarship. Will the seat of learning go so far as to subordinate itself to the state? By 1914, the German professoriat had come to serve, as one of its members quipped, as the Hohenzollern dynasty's "intellectual bodyguard."[8]

ANTI-SEMITISM

In Munich in 1917, standing before an audience of students, journalists, and public officials, Weber lectured on both the challenges of being a professor and the dispiriting dilemmas of going about it morally. Should a professor encourage a young instructor to undertake the "Habilitation"? This procedure involved the submitting of a research document indicating work done after receiving the doctorate and the presentation of a series of lectures in which the aspiring academic is questioned. Should research have priority over teaching?

> According to German tradition, the universities shall do justice to the demands both of research and of instruction. Whether the abilities of both are found together in a man is a matter of absolute chance. Hence academic life is a mad hazard. If the young scholar asks for my advice with regard to habilitation, the responsibility of encouraging him can hardly be borne. If he is a Jew, of course one says *lasciate ogni speranza*. But one must ask every other man: Do you in all conscience believe that you can stand seeing mediocrity after mediocrity, year after year, climb beyond you, without becoming embittered and without coming to grief?[9]

Weber's abrupt remark about the grim prospects of Jews in the university, with reference to Dante's advice about entering Purgatory, "Abandon all hope," followed quickly by mention of the depressing spectacle of mediocrity, may have been a coincidence. But the juxtaposition is richly ironic. Some of the wisest and worthiest minds in German society were being denied entry into the academy, and as a result students in the audience must deal with mediocrity when what they really need is meritocracy.

The presence of anti-Semitism restricted Jews from entering the profession of university teaching, and they were also excluded from the ranks of the bureaucracy and military. In Wilhelminian Germany anti-Semitism was perhaps no more virulent than in other parts of Europe. But in Germany it not only partook of a typical fear of foreigners; it also had a disturbing historical legacy and intellectual legitimacy through Martin Luther's attack on Jewish synagogues, Heinrich von Treitschke's defense of Germany as an Aryan nation, and Richard Wagner's diatribes against the "wandering Jew," which Nietzsche suspected harbored as much admiration and envy as resentment. Like Nietzsche, Weber could scarcely deny Wagner's musical genius but he found distasteful *Parsifal's* cheap mixture of sensuality and spirituality as a means of exploiting Christianity for theatrical effect.[10] Weber's own family background was free of anti-Semitism, and his mentor, the eminent historian Theodore Mommsen, opposed the bigotry of Treitschke and other anti-Semites.

In 1905, when Heidelberg was alive with east European refugees as a result of the unsuccessful Russian Revolution, Weber came to know many Jewish students of diverse nationalities. In their circle Weber was overheard remarking: "When I am again healthy, I will only allow Russians, Poles, and Jews in my seminar, no Germans." The Jews present replied: "That's our Max."[11] Although the comment may have been half in jest, Weber retained an abiding interest in Jewish affairs. He was somewhat ambivalent about Zionism. He felt that the colonizing of Palestine economically did not necessarily guarantee the dignity and power of the Jewish nation, particularly when it lacked a unified symbol of authority, such as the Pope.[12]

Weber wrote a study, published as a series of articles in the *Archiv* during the war years, of the Talmud, the Book of Solomon, and other pre-Israelite and Israelite sources, which would be published posthumously as *Ancient Judaism*. Perhaps because of such explorations, which made him appreciate the staying power of a people without a territory, Weber became particularly sensitive to the issue of the Diaspora. But in the study Weber skirted around the possible relationship of Jewish faith to capitalist economics—the thesis of his contemporary Werner Sombardt in his anti-Semitic tract, *The Jews and Economic Life* (1911). In Weber's estimate Jews, unlike Protestants, never confused religion with economics; they were content to make money and spend it, not to spiritualize it by saving and accumulating it. Rather than torturing themselves with the problem of evil and the paradoxes of an imperfect world and a perfect God, Jews accepted the world and avoided all irrational quests for salvation.

At the same time Weber was writing on this subject, the American Thorstein Veblen was writing on the "intellectual preeminence" of Jews in European history. Veblen believed it was the Jewish thinkers' isolation from conventional cultures that made them skeptical of existing orthodoxies and placed them in "the vanguard of inquiry."[13] Weber saw Jews in the same situation but drew no cultural or intellectual conclusions. He perceived Jews as a "pariah people," inhabitants always separated, subject almost to a "guest status" in the land in which they found themselves. Weber used such terms sympathetically to invoke what later came to be termed in sociology "marginality," the condition of those who remain outside the consensus of mainstream culture while cultivating their own ethnic pride and status. In *Ancient Judaism*, a text unfinished at the time of his death, Weber rendered a comment on the cause of anti-Semitism. Little was said about the alleged nomadic restlessness of European Jewry—an interpretation prevalent after the Nazi era due in large part to the writings of Hannah Arendt. Weber specified the Jews' social isolation, which generated suspicion among the gentiles, and their penetration into the economic world of trade and finance, which generated competitive hostility.[14]

The frequent exclusion of Jewish scholars from German academic life distressed Weber. He never forgave Dilthey, Rickert, and Windelband for blocking the appointment of Georg Simmel. He also tried to help Georg Lukács and Ernst Bloch find positions. Although Weber was only tenuously connected to the university, being mostly a kind of adjunct professor on leave because of ill health, he was often consulted on appointments. To one officer of a search committee he wrote out some recommendations, and of the possible refusal of one professor he stated: "I would very much regret it especially if his descent stood in the way."[15]

Although Weber's frustrations in helping Jewish scholars left him disappointed, he managed to keep his sense of humor. "I value standing somewhat outside the university system," he told Paul Honigsheim, "because I become an expert at the service of the Chancellor. Then I happen to have two lists and occasionally I describe them. The first list contains only the names of two Israelis, the second lists only two non-Semites. The person who is marked second in the Jewish list still stands above the other who is first on the non-Jewish list. Nevertheless, I know exactly that the choice would be made from the non-Jewish list."[16]

The situation of the Jews on the German campus was no laughing matter at the end of World War I. After 1918 anti-Semitism grew vicious in an atmosphere of military defeat, national humiliation, and economic dislocation. With the forthcoming peace treaty terms, right-wing parties spread the stab-in-the-back legend and Jews were blamed both for the loss of the war and the danger of bolshevism. Weber's political positions at this critical moment in Germany's history (the subject of the last chapters) offended many students and even fellow professors, caught up in the rising opposition to Allied demands and convinced that pro-western liberals had betrayed Germany.

Weber was not alone in protesting the spread of reactionary hatreds. In January 1919, more than three hundred professors signed a *"Erklärung!"* (declaration) in the *Heidelberger Zeitung* against the "malicious rage" directed toward "our Jewish citizens." It stated that all military, political, and economic misfortunes that had come down on "our fatherland" are being attributed to them, and that the racial outbursts were doing great harm to both domestic freedoms and Germany's reputation abroad. "We shall combat every injustice, wherever we find it," it concluded.[17]

Although Weber tended to use ethnic categories in his research investigations—and occasionally pejoratively, as in his study of Polish migration to east Prussia and later when mention is made of the "Slavic menace" arising from bolshevism—he had little patience with the concept of race as a relation of superior to inferior. Although a nationalist, Weber eschewed chauvinism and refrained from identifying the German state with the dominant position of a unified, coherent people based upon a common nationality. Rather than view biology as destiny, Weber saw the contingency of ancestry. He once defined race as "hereditary types bred of communities of reproduction," only to add, "I feel at a point of intersection of more and more races as of yet special ethnic national characters: I am part French [his mother was of Huguenot descent], part German, and as French certainly somewhat infected with the Celtic. Which of these races blossomed in me?"[18]

With his hybrid ancestry and rich cosmopolitan curiosities, Weber befriended many Jews and sought out such black leaders as Booker T. Washington and W. E. B. Du Bois. In some of his last thoughts, when he was writing on the sociology of religion in 1919–20, Weber concluded that thinking of hereditary attributes in discriminatory terms would prevent science from ever being a moral institution.

The political atmosphere in which Weber jotted down what would be his last thoughts was growing tense, ugly, threatening. On the evening of January 21, 1920, Weber was to give a lecture at the University of Munich's "Maximum Hall." A witness, then a student, recalled the scene a half-century later:

> Scarcely had Max Weber entered the lecture hall than he was greeted with a chorus of whistles and cat-calls, which made it completely impossible for him to be heard. He crossed his arms and stared down at the raging mass, his face smiling mockingly. Without acknowledging it to us, this upholding a laughing mask for almost a hour in this completely unavoidable grotesque situation gave a light touch to the tension in the air. In view of the well-organized character of the disrup-

tion, it was completely impossible to make contact with Weber, who, surrounded by some demonstrators sitting on stage scaffolding, remained oblivious to the situation, unaware that not everyone was seated in solidarity. Yet there was no simple way to resist the sit-in. It would remain that way until anger calmed down and the general confusion subsided. That had little chance of succeeding by calling in the Rector, who, in any case, could not be heard. I still remember to this day, how his mouth opened only to close again. . . . Then the Rector wrote on the blackboard that if silence is not possible he will switch off the lights. There followed a shout from someone in my immediate vicinity: "So much the better, then we can beat up the Jews in darkness." The lights went off, the hall cleared out. The organized terror of Hatreds had won.[19]

ACADEMIC FREEDOM

Weber heard nothing of the remark about beating up Jews. He left the auditorium together with the departing demonstrators and went on to a social gathering where he was seen enjoying himself. Then he returned to his apartment and, in the words of Marianne, "slept splendidly."[20]

In the German university Weber was in some ways less troubled by the behavior of riotous students than by that of compliant professors. Rather than functioning as an autonomous institution sustained by the spirit of critical inquiry and governed by its own professional ethics, the university, often with the willing submission of the faculty, came close to being an appendage of the state. Weber was too much a German to make a rigorous distinction between society and government; he would have found a little silly Tom Paine's differentiation between a society that answers to our "wants" and a government to our "wickedness." With Hegel Weber saw that state and civil society existed in varying reciprocal relationships and that authority emanated from government, either as a body of institutions and laws or as the force of personal leadership. But education was the one area of life most vulnerable to manipulation from without. Within the university itself committees may operate professionally in keeping with the "bureaucratic ideal of transmitting specialized knowledge." But we need to be aware, Weber wrote, that "that area which everywhere provides the most important opening for the impact of domination upon culture [is] the field of education."[21]

In 1918 a lengthy, unsigned article appeared in the *Frankfurter Zeitung*, "Der Fall Bernhard" (The Bernhard Affair). The anonymous Weber described the "scandal" that had just come to the attention of the academic community. The thirty-three-year-old Ludwig Bernhard was appointed, with a promotion from his previous positions at several provincial campuses, to a full professorship of economics at the University of Berlin, Germany's largest academic institution. The appointment bypassed faculty procedures which had been designed to conduct a search and forward recommendations to the administration. Although Weber praised Bernhard's scholarship, he implied a certain insensitivity on the part of an academic who was willing to be appointed in such an unprofessional way. In my time, Weber explained, referring to his years as a beginning professor, "one of the most elementary requirements of academic decency was that anyone who was invited by a ministry to take up a professorship made certain, above all else, and before he decided, that he enjoyed the intellectual confidence of the faculty—or at least of the most outstanding colleagues in his field, whose cooperation he would need."[22] The Bernhard affair represented an attitude becoming more and more common: the breeding, in the ranks of academics as well as administration, of the "operator" who plays by the unspoken rules of patronage and cronyism in order to climb the greasy pole of promotion.

When Weber himself was starting out as a young academic he ran up against Friedrich Althoff, the rapporteur for academic personnel in the Prussian Ministry of Education. Althoff thought highly of Weber and planned to arrange his appointment to Freiburg as a springboard to a major position at Berlin—an unusual route as Weber had yet to establish a reputation in scholarship. But Weber made it clear that he would never allow himself to be imposed upon a faculty. Thereafter he became convinced that Althoff's autocratic legacy (he died in 1908) did damage to the university system, a conviction confirmed by the behavior of Bernhard, who had been one of the minister's proteges.

Weber stuck like a thorn in the side of academic complacency in matters of principle as well as standards. At conferences on academic freedom he would remind colleagues of the socialist as well as Jewish scholars who had been shut out of the university. He challenged the manner in which Gustav von Schmoller controlled all important appointments in economics. He tried to obtain chairs for Simmel and Sombardt. He especially singled out Robert Michels, who had been told that there was no chance he could proceed toward the habilitation since he was a member of the Social Democratic Party. But Michels was able to do so, Weber reported sarcastically, at the University of Turin, where Italy's standards are strictly scholarly in contrast to those of Germany, where they are not only political but religious. Another reason for his disqual-

ification, Michels was told, involved his refusal to allow his children to
be baptised.[23]

Max Weber, the social scientist who saw power and domination everywhere, would not allow it to prevail in institutions dedicated to knowledge and culture. What was at stake was the contamination of one calling by another, the vocation of learning by the profession of politics, the
integrity of knowledge by the molestations of power. To use a graceless
sociological term, what Weber feared was the delegitimization of higher
learning. He complained of education falling into the "custody of personally friendly but frightfully inferior and petty 'operators.' " Such rule
by bland functionaries will only "create a favorable 'market' for the ascent
of [the] compliant academic in accordance with the law by which, as
experience shows, one mediocrity in a faculty brings others in its train."
Once this trend takes hold faculty members "will be incapable of offering any resistance to public opinion or to the government because of the
weakening of their moral authority."[24] Where Tocqueville feared that
mass democracy would be the grounds on which the "tyranny" of public opinion grew, Weber saw the same threat to freedom coming not from
outside the campus but from within its own institutions, run by the
spineless leading the complacent.

In the German academic milieu Max Weber was a rarity. Where most
professors fell into categories established according to disciplines and
taught from a familiar political point of view, Weber defied definition—
an awesome scholar who pleased almost no one and confounded almost
everyone. He refused to affirm both the adequacy of Germany's political
institutions, thereby perplexing the Right within the university, and the
creative strength of the proletariat, thereby perturbing the Left outside
the university. The philosopher Karl Jaspers has insisted that Weber was
not a philosopher, because he felt no need to find the absolute, nor a historian, because he would not seek the whole of human existence. Instead
Weber represented a kind of rich "floundering" of fragmented perspectives, which made him more a scientist, for whom truth is tentative, revis-
able, and incomplete.[25] But Weber was also a dualist, one who sees the
world divided into radically incompatible spheres that cannot be reconciled. It has been said of modern thinkers that they try to reconstruct in
their hearts what they have overthrown in their heads. In January 1919,
Weber wrote to Else Jaffé about a forthcoming lecture he would deliver
but was having trouble writing. He remarked, referring to what would
be "Science as a Vocation," "It will go badly. It clings to me as different as
the calling of the head and the heart."[26]

Again one sees in Weber's mind and thought a penchant for immiscibility, a sense of antinomy, contradiction, incompatibility as a state of disassociation (*Unvereinbarkeit*). Some scholars believe that Weber's critique of the university reflected a quarrel with authority that had roots in his youth and his uneasy relationship to his father. Perhaps. But what made authority illegitimate for Weber was the confusion of realms as one expression of authority assumed to speak as a sovereign, irresistible voice and claimed to represent the totality of things. It was Weber's dualistic sensibility that enabled him to discern disharmony and conflict and to resist the tendency, so marked in the German tradition that produced Hegel and Marx, to see history as overcoming tensions and antagonisms and moving toward newer and ever higher syntheses. The same sensibility motivated his academic struggles against the encroachments of bureaucracy and the state. Weber's defense of academic freedom had as much to do with epistemological uncertainty as political liberty. Rather than unifying our outlook toward the world, knowledge fragments it as the nature of its object calls forth different concerns and perspectives. Weber saw different institutions harboring different spheres of value; thus the university and the state made different demands upon the individual. Even within education itself Weber saw divisions and dichotomies; he would question the tradition of *Bildung* that assumed that general education and cultural development went hand in hand with specialized training.

Yet because ideas and institutions may mutually exclude each other's presuppositions does little to invalidate their respective contributions to knowledge. Hence Weber could appreciate the teachings of thinkers who were incompatible since for him provocation is as essential to education as resistance is to power. "The honesty of a contemporary scholar, and above all, a contemporary philosopher, can readily be ascertained by his stance toward Nietzsche and Marx," Weber told some students on his way home one evening in Munich in 1920, a few months before his death. "Those who do not admit that they would be unable to undertake major parts of their own work without the contributions made by these two men, deceive themselves as well as others. The world in which we intellectually exist has been shaped in far-reaching ways by Marx and Nietzsche."[27] Although neither a Marxist nor a Nietzschean, Weber could appreciate both thinkers for offering no illusions about the pretenses of philosophical reason in a world of conflict, whether the conflict be a democratic struggle between labor and capital or an aristocratic struggle between a Dionysian impulse to freedom and an Apollonian impulse to order.

In 1918, Weber accepted a position at the University of Munich, the first chair he had held in almost twenty years. With Marianne active in the Women's Federation and about to be elected to represent Baden-Baden in the new postwar government, Weber's location in Munich enabled him to be close once again to Else Jaffé, with whom, as will be indicated in the following chapter, he had a romantic involvement. Weber's lectures were packed and students flocked to his office hours for advice. Weber was rejuvenated, delighted at occupying the famous chair held recently by the eminent scholar Lujo Brentano, pleased by the presence of admiring young scholars who looked to him for leadership in Germany's time of crisis. But once again Weber worked himself into exhaustion preparing lectures, revising the Protestant ethic manuscript, researching world religions, giving talks on the peace settlement, and writing for the *Frankfurter Zeitung*. Small wonder he felt acutely the immiscibility of differing occupations. Shortly before delivering his lecture on "Politics as a Vocation," Weber wrote to Else of his divided, enervated condition. It became clear to him "that I must naturally pay all of the responsibility of my teaching position out of my 'political' healthiness, because I cannot achieve both."[28]

"WHAT SHALL WE DO AND HOW SHALL WE LIVE?"

Weber's earlier, companion lecture, "Science as a Vocation" (November 8, 1917), brought to fruition ideas about education that had been fermenting in his mind for a quarter century. The subject became more acute during World War I, which raised ethical as well as educational questions, and Weber addressed them in such papers as "Zwischen zwei Gesetzen" (Between two laws) and "Der Sinn der 'Wertfreiheit' der sociologischen und ökonomischen Wissenschaften" (The meaning of value-freedom [or freedom from moral judgment and personal evaluation] in the sociological and economic sciences). The period 1915 to 1920 was an epochal, tumultuous time in Germany's history, a period of war, military defeat, and political upheaval. It was a time rife with worries about postwar reconstruction; apprehension about bolshevism, dramatized by the Spartakus uprising in Munich; and fear of the rise of right-wing nationalism and anti-Semitism.

Weber's public lecture "Science as a Vocation" was addressed primarily to students who had organized a series of talks on choosing a vocation in what appeared to be a new world facing an uncertain social and political order. Other lectures would involve politics, education, art, and religion.

Weber's lecture was as much about education as science, particularly the choice of a teaching career; by the end it turns into a philosophical discourse on the twilight of reason and the older truths that no longer hold true. As a kind of sermon, it also warns students to practice value neutrality in order not to judge that which they may have yet to understand, and, at the same time, to hold themselves to the highest standards of intellectual integrity. The Christian maxim warns not to judge lest you be judged; Weber warns not to judge lest you not judge yourself. Only with critical self-judgment does one become aware that value judgments are a matter of will rather than knowledge. By a curious irony, Christianity's relegating judgment to God and Weber's excluding it from science presents a situation in which ancient truths and modern doubts come together to deny the right to judge.

The address—which has come to be appreciated as one of the great documents of twentieth-century modernity, a meditation on the fate of Occidental rationalism[29]—opens with some prosaic remarks. Weber explains to students in the packed audience the differences between the German *privatdozent*, who has job security but no easy expectation of advancement, and the American assistant professor, who has no security until he obtains a tenured position by demonstrating achievement in research. In Germany, therefore, young instructors must rely upon independent means and be able to cope with the hazards of occupation. Whether one should advocate habilitation for every *privatdozent*, and whether teaching should be given valuation equal to research, Weber hesitated to say. But he did state that he favored the principle that any graduate student who took his degree with him should demonstrate his worth elsewhere and habilitate at another university. "But," he wryly added, "as a result, one of my best students was rejected at another place because no one believed that this was the reason for his attempt to habilitate there."[30]

After describing work conditions, Weber turns to a subject of more pressing concern—the tendency of German academic life to become more and more "Americanized." Such developments meant that research would become a "state capitalist" enterprise in order to pay for the necessary equipment and other resources. The technical advantages of modern education will not only mean more bureaucracy and mediocrity due to the "law of cooperation" in faculty and administrative bodies; it also means more democracy and its accompanying standards of popularity, which produces the opposite tendency, "the most ludicrous sort of competition," as faculties and universities themselves vie for student enrollments. Lecture fees, Weber complained, are already being affected by a course's "drawing power." The question of whether a professor is a good teacher is determined by attendance, the numbers of which may reflect idiosyncracies on the part of the lecturer, his temperament, tone of voice, and other qualities that may have more to do with performance than pedagogy. "After quite extensive experience and sober considerations, I am very suspicious of large audiences, however unavoidable they may be. Democracy should be practiced where it is appropriate. Scientific training, however, if we are to carry it on in accord with the tradition of German universities, implies the existence of a certain type of aristocracy." Warming to his subject, Weber then stated that it was time to shift from the external conditions of the academic's vocation to something deeper, "namely, the *inward* calling for science." Are you, Weber asked the audience, capable of rising to its demands?

One requirement is the ability to live in full knowledge that the pursuit of knowledge fails to fulfill one's deepest needs. Only the narrow specialist ever attains a sense of achievement in carrying out the details of an investigation. The interdisciplinary, speculative theorist, such as the sociologist, must proceed by hunches and conjectures that have no immediate means of verification. "Whoever lacks the ability to put blinders on himself, so to speak, and to convince himself that the fate of his soul depends on whether his particular interpretation of a certain passage in a manuscript is correct, will always be alien to science and scholarship. He will never be able to 'experience' a sense of what is involved in scientific work. Without that rare intoxication, ridiculed by those on the outside, without this passion, this feeling that 'thousands of years must pass before you enter into life and thousands more wait in silence'—depending on whether your interpretation is correct, science is not your vocation and you should do something else. For nothing is worthwhile for a human being as a human being which he cannot do with passionate devotion."

To what end all this fervent dedication? Here Weber suggests some irrational paradoxes existing in science as he earlier had seen in Calvinist religion. Students are wrong to think science is only a matter of technique and calculation. Instead it involves "inspiration" and "imaginative insight." Diligent effort may possibly lead to a breakthrough but most likely an original idea comes as it pleases and is a matter of "chance." By describing science as contingent, Weber separated it from the classical idea of virtue as residing in a combination of knowledge, will, and perseverance, and made the vocation as irrational as other human endeavors. Like art and poetry, science may require invention and even the faculty of divination; but a work of art stands for itself and is not meant to be superseded. Every scientific achievement, however, "raises new questions and *asks* to be surpassed and outdated." The scientific intellect, so proudly born of the rebellious spirit of Prometheus, must contemplate its own obsolescence.

Earlier Weber had demonstrated, to his own satisfaction, that the Puritan work ethic had brought about a consequence opposite to what had been intended, as the New Englander transformed himself from a Calvinist in search of heavenly salvation into a Yankee content with worldly satisfaction. Ironically, science has a similar paradoxical outcome. Ask a scientist what he does and he will probably reply that he improves the conditions of life by making it more efficient and rational. But does "intellectualist rationalization" make life more comprehensible in the process of making it more comfortable and calculable? Like a good Calvinist, Weber warns students that progress humbles pride when we ask whether scientific work is important in the sense that it is "worth being known":

> Does it mean that we, today, for instance, everyone sitting in this hall, have a greater knowledge of the conditions of life under which we exist than has an American Indian or a Hottentot? Hardly. Unless he is a physicist, one who rides on the streetcar has no idea how the car happened to get into motion. And he does not need to know. He is satisfied that he may "count" on the behavior of the streetcar, and he orients his conduct according to this expectation; but he knows nothing about what it takes to produce such a car so that it can move. The savage knows incomparably more about his tools. When we spend money today I bet that even if there are colleagues of political economy here in the hall, almost every one of them will hold a different answer in readiness to the question: How does it happen that one can buy something for money—sometimes more and sometimes less? The savage knows what he does in order to get his daily food and which institutions serve him in this pursuit. The increasing intellectualization and rationalization do *not*, therefore, indicate an increased and general knowledge of the conditions under which one lives.

As if students in the audience were not disturbed enough at being told that the advancement of scientific knowledge alienates the mind from the conditions of life, Weber went on to introduce an even more disturbing thesis. In nineteenth-century romantic thought, in the writings of Lessing and Herder in Germany and Burke and Wordsworth in England, it was assumed that society and the nation were so organically rooted that the interference of the analytic intellect posed no threat to culture and its ongoing continuity. But Weber introduced a thought that had been implicit all along in some of his writings and now found poignant expression: the "disenchantment of the world" brought about by scientific analysis of its forces and mechanisms, the demystification of everything spiritual and sacred, the triumph of mastery at the expense of mystery. In dealing with the technical world of matter and motion and energy and power, science cannot answer ultimate questions of meaning, and Weber turns to Leo Tolstoy to drive home the point that science is silent in the face of God, the riddles of the soul, the hunger for immortality, and the purpose of life itself. "Science," Weber quotes Tolstoy, "is meaningless because it gives no answer to our question, the only question important for us: 'What shall we do and how shall we live?' "

Weber had been haunted by Tolstoy years earlier when he was exploring the implications of scientific methodology for the human sciences. The quote from Tolstoy could not have been more apt; in nine words it went to the heart of the heartless matter. The quote makes it clear that the question "what" shall we do with our lives precedes the easier question of "how" to go about living well. The thrust of science, however, is to reverse the formulation or perhaps to split it in half: consider the "how," the means and methods of dealing with the forces of nature, and regard humankind as inseparably born from that same nature, and the "what," the meaning and significance of it all, will take care of itself. Without meaning, without human finality and purpose, will science save the universe from nothingness? Can education have a moral end?

Another figure haunted "Science as a Vocation"—Friedrich Nietzsche:

> After Nietzsche's devastating criticism of those "last men" who "invented happiness," I may leave aside altogether the naive optimism in which science—that is, the technique of mastering life which rests upon science—has been celebrated as the way to happiness. Who believes in this?—aside from a few big children in university chairs or editorial offices.

"Big children in university chairs"? One can only wonder how that scathing remark was received. Nietzsche's "last man" is he who craves physical security rather than intellectual integrity, he who, instead of enduring loneliness and gazing steadily into the void of unanswerable metaphysical questions, "blinks," steps back, and retreats to join the rest of humankind as happy animals who rub up against one another to feel they belong, preferring coziness to curiosity, warmth to wisdom.

Weber asks students to heed the wisdom of Tolstoy and Nietzsche, the moralist and the nihilist, and refrain from demanding that teachers serve as authorities and answer questions about meaning, purpose, and value. Science can clarify issues and establish the facts upon which decisions may be made without judging which ought to be made. Other thinkers like Georg Lukács, Weber noted, have turned to aesthetics to see if the problem of truth and meaning has a resolution; but art also can do little in guiding us toward ethical choices. German students make the mistake of craving a leader instead of a teacher, a sage who will propound conclusive truths instead of an inquirer who will critically analyze them. American students have no such craving:

> The American boy learns unspeakably less than the German boy. In spite of an incredible number of examinations, his school life has not had the significance of turning him into an absolute creature of examinations, such as the German. For in America, bureaucracy, which presupposes the examination diploma as a ticket of admission to the realm of office prebends, is only in its beginnings. The young American has no respect for anything or anybody, for tradition or for public office— unless it is for the personal achievement of individual men. This is what the American calls "democracy." This is the meaning of democracy, however distorted its intent may in reality be, and this intent is what matters here. The American's conception of the teacher who faces him is: he sells me his knowledge and his methods for my father's money, just as the greengrocer sells my mother cabbage. And that is all. To be sure, if the teacher happens to be a football coach, then, in this field, he is a leader. But if he is not this (or something similar in a different field of sports), he is simply a teacher and nothing more. And no young American would think of having the teacher sell him a *Weltanschauung* or a code of conduct. Now, when formulated in this manner, we should reject this. But the question is whether there is not a grain of salt contained in this feeling, which I have deliberately stated in extreme with some exaggeration.

Weber by no means advises German students to emulate American students and the mundane American view of education as a relaxed exchange of tuition for instruction. Ultimately the questions for which students seek answers are questions of meaning and value that only religion could once address before modernity dispelled God from the universe. Earlier thinkers foresaw the dilemma; hence Augustine's dictum that one believes not what can be demonstrated as true but that which is accepted as "absurd." Faith is acceptance, even submission, a surrender requiring nothing less than "intellectual sacrifice." At this point Weber expresses some respect for the mystics who are willing to sacrifice the demands of the mind to arrive at a higher spiritual level. But he wonders whether the "dignity of purely human and communal relations" will be enhanced by the illusions of transcendence or whether such illusions are merely an escape. In the modern age the attempt to create new religions through artistic endeavor or academic prophecy may create, instead of a genuine community, "miserable monstrosities" and "fanatical sects."

Characteristically, Weber concludes on a note of ambivalence, recognizing that while modernity compels us to deny all preexistent beliefs, humanity compels us to appreciate the need to believe and the desire to transcend the modern condition. The only sin is the pride of the academic who, instead of meeting the "demands of the day" without illusions, sees himself as a prophet out to save the world without recognizing that such existential yearning has always been a timeless description of the human condition rather than a solution to it. And to those who give in and heed their needs rather than their values, Weber is forgiving, preferring, it would seem, the quiet consolations of religion to the ideological conceits of politics, where the weakness of relativism is no better than the weariness of resignation:

> To the person who cannot bear the fate of the times like a man, one must say: may he rather return silently, without the usual publicity build-up of renegades, but simply and plainly. The arms of the old churches are opened widely and compassionately for him. After all, they do not make it hard for him. One way or another he has to bring his "intellectual sacrifice"—that is inevitable. If he can really do it, we shall not rebuke him. For such an intellectual sacrifice in favor of an unconditional religious devotion is ethically quite a different matter than the evasion of the plain duty of intellectual integrity, which sets in if one lacks the courage to clarify one's own ultimate standpoint and rather facilitates this duty by feeble relative judgments.

A Munich evening newspaper described the lecture as "from beginning to end extraordinarily lively, brilliant, absorbing in its personal insights; a shame if anyone had been truant from it." The news reporter ended with the observation that science has no answer to the question: "What shall we do?" But Karl Löwith praised the address as the consummation of a life of learning, with the words themselves striking him as a "deliverance."[31]

PURITANISM WITHOUT PRAGMATISM

Weber's "Science as a Vocation," so stunningly disturbing, has been generally viewed by recent scholars as a discourse on modernity and the "disenchantment of the world," an expression of the estranged human condition that comes directly from the mind of darkness that belongs peculiarly to European intellectual history. True enough. But the address may be more telling when one considers it in light of developments in American intellectual history.

Years earlier, when Weber was writing on the Russian Revolution of 1905, the origins of capitalism, and Protestant sects in North America, he made many favorable references to America and its democratic traditions that derived from Puritanism. By 1917, however, Weber no longer looked to America for guidance or inspiration, at least not when he is discussing issues in intellectual history. The war being fought between Germany and the United States may only partly explain this reorientation. In "Science as a Vocation" Weber satirizes American education for regarding college as little more than a commercial transaction and for confusing technique with knowledge, mistaking specialization for cultivation, methodological procedure for moral development.

It is worth recalling that many American philosophers of pragmatism, especially John Dewey, placed great hope in education as well as in science. But in "Science as a Vocation" Weber sees the limitations of both endeavors. Here one confronts a hitherto unraised question. Why would Weber have such admiration for the seventeenth-century America of Puritanism and remain aloof from the modern American culture of pragmatism? To try to answer this may help us determine whether Weber became what American social scientists would later make him out to be—a sociologist of systems and structures, or what came to be called a "structural functionalist." Was Weber happy simply to describe how things functioned and how people adapted to their social roles and how society itself slouches toward equilibrium? To the extent that Weber saw the mind as replete with antinomies, and modern sociology influenced by Dewey sees it as an organism of adjustment and adaptation, a question poses itself: If Weber admired Puritanism, why could he not also admire pragmatism?

The most striking thing about "Science as a Vocation" is what goes unsaid. Weber, the leading sociologist of the twentieth century, refused to advocate "the sociological turn" in modern thought. In much of western culture many thinkers, faced with the "end" of philosophy as epistemology and metaphysics, advocated moving on toward the study of language

("the linguistic turn") or the study of science or social relations or whatever discipline that required no philosophical foundations. Several American pragmatists were happy to see philosophy give up its claims to truth
and step aside in order to make room for science and sociology. None felt
the loss of religion as painfully as Weber did. Perhaps that explains why
other intellectuals had less difficulty in turning to surrogates. John Dewey
in particular assumed that belief in religion could be sustained without
committing what Weber called "intellectual sacrifice." In *A Common
Faith* Dewey contended that religion should no longer be identified with
anything supernatural and transcendent that would return the curse of
dualism. The aim of philosophy, even scientific philosophy, is as meaningful and as valuable as that of religion: to help humankind regain its
"unified wholeness." Referring to William James's psychology of religion, Dewey wrote: "It is pertinent to note that the unification of the self
throughout the ceaseless flux of what it does, suffers, and achieves, cannot be attained in terms of itself. The self is always directed toward something beyond itself and so its own unification depends upon the idea of
the integration of the shifting scenes of the world into that imaginative
totality we call the Universe."[32] By conceiving humankind as an instrument of adaptation and integration, Dewey convinced himself that science and sociology would succeed where philosophy and religion had
failed.

Weber could no more follow this American turn of thought than he
could cling to German philosophy and its conceits of academic prophecy
in ignorance of its own inadequacy. "Science as a Vocation" reads less as
a call to the professor of sociology than as a philosophical lyric to remem-
brance of lost truths and vanished values that could no longer be sustained. For it was German philosophy, especially the Hegelian sense of
unity and totality found in Dewey, that steered American thought away
from the abyss of modernity, while Weber, following Nietzsche, wanted
the modern mind to stare into the abyss without blinking. Weber left
open the door of the old church for contemporary social philosophers
who could not bear the burden of doubt and despair. But Weber discerned the end of reason as a philosophical concept along with the death
of God. Hegel incorporated "Reason" into the movement of history, not
only to make the real rational and the rational real, but, more important,
to assure himself of the continued presence of God. Weber asks us to feel
the absence.

Weber's "Science as a Vocation" carried a message that had considerable meaning for America, especially for American intellectuals who had
rallied to support of America's entry into the war against Germany in

1917. When Weber observed that a true scientific vocation must adhere to aristocratic values, he was perceiving a problem that American progressive thinkers would scarcely allow themselves to face: that science, democracy, and politics are separate realms and cannot be forged together in the name of progress. The authority of science corresponds to its distance from politics, especially democratic politics, which is more a popularity contest than a truth test—is even "a ludicrous form of competition." Dewey and many of the pragmatists assumed the opposite, convinced that science could join politics now that experimental intelligence had replaced philosophical reason. So armed, America would make the world safe for modernity as well as democracy, an exercise in militant diplomacy that a Calvinist could only regard as a dangerously un-Puritan mission. Weber warned of the "naive optimism" of those who believed in the "technique of mastering life which rests upon science." The Puritan knew that any hope for salvation rested elsewhere.

SEVEN

"A Joyous Triumph over Rationality": Women, the Erotic, and the Power of Status Politics

Marriage is a long conversation. When marrying, one should ask oneself this question: Do you believe that you will be able to converse well with this woman into your old age? Everything else in marriage is transitory, but the most time during the association belongs to conversation.

Friedrich Nietzsche

KNOWING WOMEN

"He who knows women only through man," observed Henry Adams, "knows them wrong."[1] Max Weber knew women through a series of relationships with them, experiences that began in the family to which he was born, continued into his married life, and, in two instances, extended beyond marriage in affairs that suggest something about the volatile spirit that lay beneath his scholarly demeanor.

Helene Weber, Max's mother, was the first woman to have an effect upon him that stuck to his memory. Although Helene devoted her adult life to her children, Max found it difficult to return the maternal love. He would not allow himself to be coddled by her intense moralism and coverted to what at times seemed her pietistic resignation. The presence of Weber's more critical and independent Aunt Ida indicated that women need not submit to patriarchal domination. What Weber saw as suffering in his mother's life was the sacrifice of unborn principles, a spectacle that his wife Marianne would later record in a feminist text.[2]

A sensitive feminist such as Marianne saw the household as a struggle between man's need for authority and woman's need for autonomy. Helene's submission to Weber Sr. troubled Max as much as it did Marianne. Did the sad spectacle have a lasting effect on Weber's attitudes toward women in general?

Although Max, together with his brothers and sisters, made every effort to escape Helene's desire to impose her own inhibitions on their lives, the oldest son did acquire a distaste for sensuality that endured, despite his rebellious, hedonistic years as a college student. His first love, for his cousin Emmy Baumgarten, appears to have been Platonic even though the engagement lasted six years. Weber was twenty-three and she eighteen. Emmy's mother, Aunt Ida, adored Max but worried that he might prove too forceful for Emmy's tender, fragile nature: "Would he not crush her spirit?" Marianne recalled fretting about the same emotions that troubled Ida.[3]

Yet Max's letters to Emmy brought out his soft side instead of his tumultuous passions. With a Rilkean sensitivity, Weber explained to her the harmony of the good and the beautiful as the imagination awakens to the emotions of the heart. He also could be lighthearted. Once he suggestged to her that philosophy has the "feminine shape" of both an "Amazonian logic" and an "air balloon"—fierce argument and lofty flight.[4] Weber was taken by Emmy's beauty, but her Madonna-like tenderness signaled a frailty that often gave way to melancholic depression. Emmy began to distance herself from Max, fearful that her medical condition would become a burden to him. Years later, when Emmy heard of his engagement to Marianne, she wrote a brief, cordial note of congratulations, and Max replied with a soul-stirring letter. "As you know, I have always measured the women and the girls who have crossed my path against your personality, and for my roughhewn nature it was a blessing that I felt inwardly constrained to view the opposite sex through your eyes."[5]

Marianne Schnitger, a distant relative—granddaughter of Weber Sr.'s elder brother—arrived as a guest in the Webers' house in 1892. The family had no inkling that she fell in love with Weber while he was still making occasional visits to Emmy in a sanitarium and while, at the same time, a friend of Weber's courted her, with the encouragement of his mother Helene. This period, which lasted almost a year, Marianne would later describe as an "abyss." When they married the following year, Max was twenty-nine and Marianne twenty-three. Some members of the Weber family welcomed the marriage, relieved that the relationship with the mentally unstable Emmy could now be forgotten as a youthful fling. But Weber's letter proposing marriage to his new fiancée reveals a mind wracked with doubt and guilt. "Read this letter, Marianne, when you are calm and composed, for I have things to tell you that you may not be prepared to hear."[6]

It is not true, Weber begins assuring her, that "we are through with each other and that I shall banish you to the still, cool harbor of resignation in which I myself have lain at anchor for years." After an oblique reference to his own years of impotence in a house ruled by his father, Weber declares he cannot ask of her that which he wonders whether he can ask of himself—"the divine compulsion of complete unconditional devotion." Weber then confesses that he has trouble taming the "elemental passions nature has endowed in me," which had made him a "problem child" to his mother, and hence "I knew well that her love for me—which forced me to silence because I cannot repay it"—derived from his inability to live up to her moral expectations. "For years the idea that the rich heart of a girl could come close to my sober nature never occurred to me. This is why I was blind and certain of my opinion even in your case," he admits to Marianne, as though he had had trouble distinguishing one woman from another.

What occurs in the next paragraphs is a confession that he not only failed to respond to his mother's love due to his "sober nature" but that possibly he has no capacity for love at all. After mentioning that he probably hurt his friend, Marianne's suitor, by now coming between them, he turns to the delicate subject of Emmy. Having thought the relationship over, doctors recently informed him that her illness may be due to her "still" being secretly in love. Weber is now in agony over the thought that her recent recovery possibly resulted from his having aroused false hopes by visiting her. But is it "hope or renunciation" that is strengthening her? "Whatever the reason, I could not accept cool renunciation or resignation from her either. I cannot be dead for her if I am to live for another, and that is why I must look into her eyes and see whether her heart beats sympathetically when I receive from another girl the happiness that she would have given me if prejudices, my outward hopelessness . . . and also my weaknesses had not intervened."

But Weber has no intention of returning to Emmy to look into her eyes to see what it is he wants to see and perhaps does not want to see. Instead, in the concluding paragraphs, Weber proposes marriage in a passage that could have been written by a tense logician rather than a tender lover:

> And now I ask you: have you inwardly renounced me in recent days? Or resolved to do so? Or are you doing it *now? If not, then it will be too late*, we shall then be bound to each other, and I shall be hard toward you and not spare you. I say to you: I shall take the course that I must and which you now know. And you will take it with me. Where it will lead, how far it is, whether it will lead us together on this earth, I do not know. And even though I now know how great and strong you are, you proud girl, you may still succumb, for if you go with me, you will not only bear your burden but mine as well, and you are not used to taking such paths. Therefore, test both of us.
>
> But I believe I know how you will decide. The tidal wave of passion runs high, and it is dark around us—come with me, my high-minded comrade, out of the quiet harbor of resignation, out onto the high seas, where men grow in the struggle of souls and the transitory is sloughed off. But *bear in mind:* in the head and heart of the mariner there must be clarity when all is surging underneath him. We must not tolerate any fanciful surrender to unclear and mystical moods in our souls. For when feeling rises high, you must control it to be able to steer yourself with sobriety.
>
> If you will go with me, then do *not* answer me. In that case I shall quietly press your hand when I see you again and not cast down my eyes before you, something that you should not do either.
>
> Farewell; life is coming down hard on you, you misunderstood child. This is all I shall say to you now: I thank you for the wealth you have brought into my life, and my thoughts are with you. And now once more: Come with me, I know that you will come.

A marriage proposal, like most love letters, usually ends with a burst of affection; Weber's concludes in an arid contract. The word "love" is mentioned only twice; once when he admits he cannot "repay" it to his mother and again when it is speculated that Emmy may still be in love with him. Love goes unmentioned in respect to the receiver of the letter, as does any thought about happiness and the pleasures of the body, or any "surrender" to whatever may threaten control and the sobriety of duty. Weber's metaphor of marriage as a voyage into the high seas of treacherous emotion suggests no place for the exquisite confusions of romantic love or the delectable swoons of erotic sex. Would marriage, too, be an iron cage?

It may be going too far to claim that he who fears love fears life. But clearly for Weber the bonds of wedlock would be tied by something other than eros. In view of his dual temperament, the struggle of the "elemental passions" against the need for prudent sobriety, his decision to marry Marianne represents the prevalence of the rational over the romantic in a marriage that led obviously neither to children nor apparently to sexual consummation.

Yet Weber's relationship to Marianne was, as one infers from the voluminous correspondence, sensitive, affectionate, endearing, and deeply caring—sentiments that remained marvelously steady and did not wither away as year after year of marriage turned the rare into the familiar. In the period 1906–8, Weber often wrote to her, "*Meine Liebstes Schnauzel*" (my dearest puppy), of springtime in Italy, of trying his luck at the casinos of Monte Carlo, of searching for hotels away from the dust and noise of traffic, all the while reminding her not to overtax herself with work and writing. In his letters he could mention the "L" word missing from his marriage proposal. On his birthday, April 18, 1908, Marianne had sent him a greeting, describing her husband as the most wonderful human being she ever encountered, and saying that she "loved him as one loves a work of art or of nature." Bashfully referring to her description as a "Tower of Babel," Weber exclaimed "how great your love is" and then gushed forth lyrically: "Life with you is like the soft light and warmth of the spring sun which—as Tolstoy only all too optimistically hopes will flow from the power of the [abstract] love of man—quiet and certain, dissolves all the icebergs of life and melts away all the snow coverings, while the wild storm of my ardour is only able to shake the flakes and the pinecones."[7]

"Marriage—a problem. This too has become a problem, as everything else has, with time." Thus spake Thomas Mann, who in the earlier twenties remembered that of all the marriages he had seen, ninety percent of them were "unhappy."[8] That of Max and Marianne, one might assume in a kind of Cupid's wager, belonged to the happy ten percent.

FREUDIANISM

Happy, but incomplete—at least for Max. As for Marianne, she felt that her happiness in the marriage would depend upon developing a sphere of "independent intellectual existence" as she absorbed herself in her own academic studies and in women's causes. The Webers had what she took pride in as a *Musterehe*, a marriage of moral example.[9] Perhaps, as Marianne implied, the sensuous possibilities of marriage remained circumscribed by the rigorous moralism of Helene, Max's mother, who came close to equating bodily pleasure with sin and whose repressive child-rearing, which upheld the good and the pure, continued to inhibit her son even as an adult. Significantly, Max's own sensuality seem to have expressed itself only when he gathered with men in *Bierhausen* or other refuges from respectability.

Although a forceful personality, Weber could become awkward and uncomfortable in the presence of women. "I can rarely communicate my feelings to others and have to force myself to do it," he wrote to Fritz Baumgarten a few years after his marriage.[10] He struggled to overcome shyness in the company of women, and flirting became more of a heavy ordeal than an easy dalliance. Was Weber incapable of intimacy? Did the world of women remain for him what one recent scholar has called a "magical garden," all the more enchanting because he dared not enter into it?[11]

Marianne suspected otherwise. Years after Weber's death she asked the philosopher Karl Jaspers, an admirer of Weber who had known him as a student, whether her husband had had a love affair. Jaspers first dismissed the possibility, confidently assuring her, "Max Weber was the truth itself." Yet curiosity compelled Jaspers to write to Else Jaffé in 1967; thereupon he was made aware of Weber's infidelity. Jaspers was shattered at the thought that a man so apparently virtuous could have led, however momentarily, a life of duplicity. "What happens with a man to whom truth is above everything else?" Going over once again Weber's vast writings, Jaspers now saw "a titanic trouble in emptiness."[12]

Jaspers's distress in discovering that Weber had failed to live up to the heroic portrait that many of his contemporaries saw could perhaps provoke Nietzsche's phrase, "human, all too human," reminding us that the homage we pay to genius may be little more than projected consolation for our own insignificance. With the belated discovery of Weber's moral imperfections he becomes more humanly complete.[13]

Weber met Else Jaffé when she became his student. At the time she still bore her maiden name. She was the daughter of Baron von

Richthofen, a Prussian officer who fought in Bismarck's army in a war that created the German empire. Her sister was Frieda von Richthofen, a legendary figure, a passionate champion of sexual freedom who ran away from her husband and children to marry D. H. Lawrence. Else's temperament was decidedly different from that of her sister and in some respects closer to Weber's. She shared, at least at first, the conviction that social responsibility often required self-denial.

Else was Weber's first female student at the University of Heidelberg. Marianne also attended Max's lectures and became Else's close companion; Marianne and Else remained lifelong friends, well after Weber's death. In her student years Else looked up to Marianne as a model who never for a moment believed that marriage excluded women from the men's world of work and politics. As did many women activists of the era, Else sought employment as a factory inspector and became acquainted with other reformers such as Friedrich Naumann. But to the disappointment of many of her friends, she gave up her career around the turn of the century and withdrew from a life of activism. In 1901 she was briefly engaged to Alfred Weber, Max's brother, who had long been in love with her. But the following year, without explaining her change of mind, if not of heart, she married Edgar Jaffé, a political economist and fellow editor with Weber of the *Archiv für Sozialwissenschaft und Sozialpolitik*.

Five years after her marriage to Jaffé, Else had an affair with Otto Gross, whom she had met through her sister Frieda, who had also been carrying on sexually with him. A sybarite posing as a sage, Gross was the leading exponent of the theory of eroticism as an idea whose time had come. Gross had grown up in a household dominated by an insensitive father, and had an ultrasensitive mother who submitted to her husband, a childhood environment that had some similarity to Weber's. But Gross drew on anarchist ideas and psychoanalytic theory to argue that the true individual, as an antagonist to the state, could be completely free through sexual liberation and orgiastic openness. Gross's championing of "The Erotic Movement" drew considerable attention in the pre–World War I years, attracting Americans like Mabel Dodge and Isadora Duncan.

In 1907 Else sent Weber an article by Gross to be considered for publication in the *Archiv*. The topic could not have been more timely: a critique of Freud's theories of the necessity of repression, inhibition, and sublimation. Weber returned it directly to Else, reporting that he could hardly bring himself to recommend it to the editorial board. Was Weber being discreet in not passing on to editor Jaffé a submission by an author who was having an affair with his wife? Was Marianne being discreet when, years later, she edited the letter and eliminated all mention of Gross, referring instead to "Dr. X"? Whatever the case, Weber informed Else that while all social philosophers "are in our theories ethical monsters," Gross is especially one of the "counsellors of confusions" in going beyond his specialty and imposing a "worldview" as he becomes a "moralist" instead of a "scientific investigator." Judging Gross an intellectual "Pharisee" for his censorious disdain for ordinary society, Weber then used the letter to open his thoughts to Freudianism and to Freud himself.[14]

Weber granted that Freud's thought had the potential for becoming an important source in the study of cultural history, particularly with the possibility of an "exact casuistry" to deal with issues of conscience, which in his day, he emphasized, did not yet exist. But Weber objected to the assumption that a new discovery in a field, in this instance psychoanalysis, necessarily leads to a new worldview and a new system of morals. Every theoretical discoverer may see himself as a "missionary" ready to reform existing culture. But "Freud's adherents" like Dr. X (actually Gross was an apostate) turn to "metaphysical speculations" that end up reducing themselves to practical "childish questions" such as "will this taste good?"

Why wash the "diapers" of this infant science in our *Archiv*? queried Weber: they may serve as dainty tidbits for the reform of sexual ethics, but baby diapers they remain. What else, he asked, are we to call an ethics which, in Dr. X's terminology, is too "cowardly" to admit that it seeks to promote a banal "nervy show-off" (*Nervenprotz*) who will discredit any kind of norms whose observance threatens those precious nerves? Like a modern-day Calvinist, Weber then shows why courage lies in controlling fear and cowardice in its expression.

> If every "suppression" of emotion-laden wishes and impulses leads to "displacement" and "repression," . . . and if repression is as such, ostensibly because it signified the inner untruthfulness of "error and cowardice," in reality because from the viewpoint of the nerve hygiene expert it raises the danger of hysteria, compulsive neurosis, phobia . . . if such repression is the greatest evil—then this nerve-struck ethic must exhort, for example, the freedom-fighting Boer to forsake the cause of freedom and take to [his] heels, otherwise [he] will repress [his] anxious emotions [and react to war even more irrationally and pathologically].

Weber did not explain to Else the details of the Boer War in South Africa, where the British used scorched-earth tactics to drive the Dutch settlers into a position where they had to stand and make a fight or flee and surrender. But in a footnote he does patiently explain to her that Gross's theory would make one a coward in the conventional sense of succumbing to fear so that one would not become a coward in the modern neuro-medical sense of repressing an anxious emotion and rendering it unconscious. Weber came close to out-Freudianizing the Freudians by suggesting that it was not repression that creates anxiety but the prior presence of anxiety that generates the inhibiting mechanisms of repression. What was modern man anxious about?

> To the husband or lover or respectively the wife or mistress who, by sudden changes of perception, is overtaken by attacks of jealousy [the new ethic] must shout "Let them out," à la Othello, or through a duel or any form you prefer—it is better to be "mean" (from the point of view of new sexual ethics) than that you resist [repressed emotions] and risk the formation of a mad delusion. [The ethic] must in every situation be courageous enough to recommend to me that I yield to every animalistic, vulgar impulse of my appetites or of my sexual life, and that means to allow this stirring of desire any adequate form of satisfaction, for otherwise my precious nerves could harmed. This is the typical and all too familiar attitude of the medical philistine.

Did Else catch the sarcasm? Weber's disdain for an "ethic" that recommends as an act of courage the insouciant yielding to every temptation suggests the mind of a moralist. But for how long would Weber himself be able to resist the stirrings of desire? Why did he go to such lengths to refute the theories of a psychoanalyst who taught Else and other women the delights of an erotic deliverance from guilt?

Weber's letter to Else continues with a lengthy discussion of ethics and its dilemmas. Weber denied that psychiatrists can serve as authorities on matters of ethical choice. He distinguished two ethics: the "heroic," involving an endless striving after and approximation of moral principles; and the "average," which entailed only the routines of everyday life, an ethic that makes no demands. Only the former can be called idealism in the Christian and Kantian sense. The "psychiatric ethic," says Weber, is merely confessional: "Admit to yourself what you are like and what you desire." Freud's revelations from the unconsciousness can shed no light on ethical choice; it cannot distinguish value from fact, the normative from the descriptive. How does one know that his or her physical desires are morally desirable? Weber then elaborates reasons why he can only conclude that Dr. X's version of Freudianism is less a science than a sermon and must be rejected as an article. But before concluding that psychoanalysis only gives legitimating force to our wishes, Weber evaluates Freud in ways that tell us a good deal about himself:

> Whoever deceives himself about himself (and wants to be deceived), and has forgotten how to remember the things in his life he had been ashamed of, and which he can remember to the extent he wants to, he will not be helped ethically by spending six months (a minimum tour of duty with Freud) lying on Freud's couch and recalling to consciousness the "infantile" and other experiences of a shameful variety that have been repressed (Note well! always under the vow of confidentiality of the doctor.) Freud's cures may appear to have hygienic value for him, but what, for instance, am I supposed to gain ethically if I were to be recleansed of some kind of sexual mischief, which, say, a servant girl had enjoyed with me (Freudian examples!), or of a lurid impulse which I had repressed and forgotten and [which was] now to be revived? I don't know. Leaving aside the hygienic angle of the issue, I confess in toto, without the feeling that there is something "terrible" about the confession, that nothing human is alien to me, and thus in principle I am surely learning nothing new.

Weber's extensive letter to Else rejecting Dr. X's article has been viewed by scholars as either an attempt to protect the von Richthofen sisters from Otto Gross by exposing his pansexual theories as pseudoscience, or as a concealed competitive rivalry on the part of Weber, who was about to fall in love with Else. More telling may be Weber's own "confession" that he would feel neither guilt nor shame if his childhood sexual encounters were brought to consciousness; a testimony somewhat at odds with the self-analysis he had written out at the time of his breakdown, when he admitted that his insomnia—which would continue as an intermittent sleeplessness until his death—derived partly from fear of uncontrolled nocturnal ejaculations.[15] But the letter to Else reveals more than it conceals. While he chastises Gross's ethics of sensual pleasure, he can reassure Else that anything emanating from his own sexual impulse would not be alien to him.

ASCONA: "A TERRIBLY EMOTIONALLY WEARING POLYGAMY"

The year following Weber's letter to Else on Dr. X and Freudianism, Max and Marianne corresponded over the delicate subject of the von Richthofen sisters' affairs with Gross. Weber agreed with his wife that such behavior was "deeply immoral" and that Gross's intention to seek treatment for his cocaine addiction was all the more reason the relationships should end. Frieda's marriage to Ernest Weekly, and Else's to Edgar Jaffé, signified a new era when women could claim the right to affairs. But Else now found herself in a "terribly painful" situation, Marianne informed Max. She can hardly say that her affair is acceptable because Edgar agreed to it and at the same time admonish her sister: "You may not deceive your husband!" Gross had told Else, Marianne wrote, that eroticism is necessary in order to work out tensions in friendships. Marianne wanted Max to intervene since he had already formed a sufficient impression of Else to discern whether her relation to Gross had now become completely asexual and unerotic, as she had been led to believe. But Weber had little patience with erotic emancipators who sought to liberate society from hypocrisy only to continue among themselves a life of duplicity. He also doubted it was proper to meddle in the private affairs of others and to make ethical pronouncements; he did not want the Webers to serve as a "Greek chorus."[16]

Weber's own attraction to Else had been building for years, although he behaved properly while she was his student. Then in 1910, two years after Max and Marianne had exchanged letters about the affairs of the von Richthofen sisters, Max conveyed his deepest feelings to Else while on a trip to Vienna. Perhaps because of loyalty to Marianne, Else turned aside his amorous declarations, and the following year she took up again with Alfred Weber, Max's brother who had earlier pursued her and could continue to do so openly since he had no wife. The Webers would occasionally travel with Alfred and Else as a foursome, but the tensions became too great and after a quarrel, Max and Else remained apart until 1917, whereupon they resumed their friendship, this time to the point of physical intimacy.

Despite the initial rebuff, Weber's opening up to Else in 1910 marked something of a turning point. He would now become less censorious and more tolerant of carnal pleasure, less highminded about moral duty and more intrigued about human possibility. The following year he began a relationship, soon to be erotic, with Mina Tobler, a Swiss pianist who had been prominent in the Heidelberg circle of intellectuals. During World War I Weber wrote to Else and Mina of his difficulties reconciling conflicting demands, not only personal but also political and professional.[17] As Weber approached his last years at the end of the war, he was almost as much in the company of Else and Mina as of Marianne. At his deathbed Else and Marianne hovered outside the door, waiting to see whom he would call for in his delirious state.

Years earlier, when the scandals of the von Richthofen sisters had reached Heidelberg, Weber asked Marianne to send him some writings of Oscar Wilde.[18] Perhaps even more than D. H. Lawrence, Wilde had represented a true challenge to conventional Victorian gender relationships. Questioning the double standard that separated male from female, Wilde wrote plays in which women are businesslike, politically astute, and sexually adventuresome, and men sentimental, impractical, and sexually diffident. Something like this "art of inversion" animated the atmosphere of Ascona, a Swiss-Italian town on the eastern shore of Lake Maggiore that became the site of anarchist and free-love communes in the years before World War I. Ascona had been visited by the Russian anarchist Peter Kropotkin and by followers of Max Stirner, the mid-nineteenth-century philosopher who had cast the individual ego as the single absolute beyond all good and evil. But even as a disreputable site of bohemianism and uninhibited eroticism, Ascona could attract the respectable and curious Webers.

Marianne records that she and her husband could scarcely condemn Ascona out of hand. Max in particular became much interested in the effects of amoral eroticism upon the total personality. The Webers recognized the harmful effects Gross was having on his female conquests. "Even though all this seemed like a delusion to the Webers," writes Marianne, "they could not turn away in indignation since they felt deep concern for the noble and lovable human beings involved. . . . They wanted to learn to understand this strange, unbourgeois world of adventurism and to carry on an intellectual dialogue with it." The tolerance on Weber's part derived from his admiration of those who live by and for convictions, though he never lost sight of responsibility as well, and thus always looked to the consequences of behavior together with intent. Ultimately the Webers arrived at the following judgment: "The ethical ideal of monogamy as it ought to be, as the highest form of erotic community remained. But it cannot be forced upon all types of human beings and their lives. And no principles can be formulated for the ethical handling of the manifold concrete situations into which human beings stumble outside and in addition to marriage."[19]

Marianne's account is in large part correct, for Weber would judge the behavior of Ascona's libertarians rather severely; he was especially harsh when considering the consequences for their children, left without intact families. But Weber was a romantic as much as a scientist, a thinker interested not only in the prosaic data of the world but perhaps even more in his own emotions. As a rationalist Weber retained his objective standards when looking upon the new underworld of the forbidden; as a romantic he could hardly deny that his capacity for wonder had been fired by passion, and he would soon be pondering the meaning of the erotic, the one experience that cannot be routinized without losing its mystical ecstasy.

Weber's thoughts on sexuality were heightened by two visits he made to Ascona in the spring of 1913 and 1914.[20] Weber traveled there at the request of Else's sister Frieda, who had married Otto Gross and had accompanied her husband to Ascona in 1910 to establish a free college on Monte Verita. Ascona had been inhabited by nudists, healers, nature lovers, and writers and artists. The arrival of Otto Gross had an unsettling effect. Some residents remained skeptical of his call for "sexual revolution"; others participated in open sex that for a few led to breakdowns and, in the case of one of Gross's own lovers, suicide. In intellectual circles rumors quickly spread of the bohemian bedlam at Ascona led by the drug-addicted and mentally ill Otto Gross.

In 1913, Professor Hans Gross ordered the police to arrest his son Otto as a menacing psychopath (C. G. Jung signed a certificate to that effect) and had him taken to Austria to be committed to an insane asylum. The father had also petitioned Swiss authorities to be made legal guardian to Otto's son. The arrest of Otto became a cause célèbre among some bohemians who viewed him as a martyr, as they did Frieda, who, threatened with deprivation of her maternal and marital rights, continued to champion psychosexual freedom and even invited the anarchist Ernst Frick to live with her.

Max Weber brought to Ascona character references written by himself, Marianne, and others to support Frieda's case for custody. Writing to Marianne in Heidelberg, Weber describes finding Frieda Gross "very affectionate" and "basically in good humor" though her "flimsy scarf [was] peppered with cigarette burns."Yet he could not get through to her. "I sit on the garden bench at the roadside looking over the lake. She talks to one about God and the world, also about X. I answer: I am morally quite prepared to strike X dead, that's not morally reprehensible but only the decent thing. Unfortunately, our crazy laws forbid it and I could not do something other for love of E."

Curiously, Weber could tell his wife that he would like to smack Gross if it were not for love of Else, without having to say whether his motive was jealousy or retribution. But Weber recorded the effects of the extramarital adventure: "Her life is wrecked. How so can be quickly told. Dementia praecox was already diagnosed before her marriage to Otto Gross, the parents had to conceal this from her. Then it went . . . she became totally obsessed, completely and wretchedly eaten up, and on top of this—which she confesses—a terribly emotionally wearing polygamy.

Once you start this it cannot stop. She simply cannot meet the demands of her husband, she has become a complete nervous wreck, and *must* have the other."[21]

Whether or not a "wearing polygamy" has no limits in that sexuality, unlike love, tends always to vary its object, would Frick ("the other") be any better choice? A disciple of Gross, Frick had served ten years in prison for setting off a bomb in Zurich as a political protest. "And the case of Frick?" Weber wrote to Marianne. "He also has a 'religious belief' in a future society free of jealousy, of really 'free' love, that is free within. She also theorizes about this, but when I say (1) that noble action in respect to jealousy is a beautiful thing but how could one find it chivalrous to give everything to a man whom one has come to blame for so much? (2) Whether this cry for love will not lead to a crazy waste of psychic strength—this brings the response: *Yes*, it is terrible and completely hopeless and her strength is gone." Weber then tells Marianne that the boy has come to hate both his father and his mother's lover. As for Frieda Gross, "it is lamentable to see this faded yet still delicate being in a coquettish and recklessly disordered realm."[22]

On Weber's second visit Frick had been released from jail and was living with Frieda. The situation threatened Frieda's custody, and Weber reminded her of how legal authorities might look askance at overt promiscuity. Weber also had a conversation with Frick, whom he found less disposed to sexual ecstasy than to political eschatology. "He waits for the moment of great inner illumination when he will do the whole Great Prophet thing. The poor fellow, everything turns on him . . . he is convinced of the absolute wickedness of the basis of society; Frieda cannot explain why he overvalues these ideas so. He wants goodness and brotherly love to be brought to perfection through the acosmos of the erotic. I've already told Frieda why it won't work, and she admits the specific consequence is a Tolstoyan asceticism, to which he is further inclined."[23]

Whether or not Asconian libertines could be capable of taking up "Tolstoyan asceticism," Weber himself often had recourse to the Russian novelist for a philosophy of life that would offer an escape from sexual as well as political conflict. In his interjected observations in his manuscript (*Zwischenbetrachtung*), Weber noted that Tolstoy had described sensual love as the "worst form of passion." Tolstoy ridiculed the notion that one could redeem the soul through the pleasures of the body. The spheres of the erotic remained alien to spiritual brotherliness because they were spasmodic and ethically unrestrainable. Weber wondered whether "pure passionateness" (*rein Leidenschaftlichkeit*) might be as characteristic of religion as of sex.[24]

EROTICISM

In 1915, a year after he had returned from Ascona, Weber opened up his massive, untitled manuscript, turned to the section on religion and ethics, and added a new discourse on sexuality and the erotic. In the conversations he had with Gross's followers at Monte Verita, he scorned any chance of success in their aim, as he put it to Marianne, to practice "perfect kindness of brotherly love by taking an acosmistic view of eroticism." In his present thoughts on religion he noted that an "acosmistic ethic" of any kind represents a flight from the real world of power into the realm of mysticism. Such "apolitical emotionalism" characterizes all forms of eroticism. "Indeed, the power of the sphere of eroticism enters into particular tensions with religions of salvation. This is particularly true of the most powerful components of eroticism, namely sexual love. For sexual love, along with the 'true' or economic interest, and the social drives toward power and prestige, is among the most fundamental and universal component of the actual course of interpersonal behavior."[25]

In modern times sex and religion appear to be opposing drives answering to differing needs; earlier in history they were closely related. In discussing, however briefly, the history of eroticism, Weber undertook the role of genealogist in showing us how cultural attitudes, seen in their own time as fixed, divinely ordained relationships of authority, are actually contingent upon the historical circumstances that produce them. But ultimately Weber is struck, as always, by the presence of power, even within an experience as pleasurable as sex.

Sexual intoxication, Weber begins, has functioned in many systematic religions to control reproduction, just as ancient phallic worship and temple prostitution are found among orgiastic cults that enjoyed ritual dances to achieve a state of ecstasy. Only with the appearance of the chastity of priests do certain types of tension between sex and religion emerge. Sexual abstinence is seen in some religions as essential to contemplative withdrawal from the world, and the Catholic church needed to demand celibacy of the clergy to preclude the inheritance of benefices by possible heirs of the priests. The Confucian ethic downplayed sex as disturbing to the mind's inner equilibrium; Mosaic and Hindu laws condemned adultery. The major world religions have looked to some form of marriage as a means of regulating free sexual experience, which would otherwise mean the loss of self-control. But such inhibitions, on the part of institutions as well as that caused by human development beyond the natural and organic basis of sexuality characteristic of peasant societies, only refines and sublimates eroticism all the more. The "total being of man" has become alienated from the organic cycle of peasant life and in modern times eroticism is raised into the "sublime sphere" of "conscious enjoyment," and because of this "elevation," it "appeared to be like a gate into the most irrational and thereby real kernel of life as compared to the mechanisms of rationalization."[26]

The degree and manner in which eroticism came to be valued has varied enormously throughout history. Weber, with his characteristic wide-ranging curiosity, takes his investigations everywhere, from Hellenic society to the middle ages, from the Renaissance to the salon cultures of the French Enlightenment. The latest accentuation of the erotic occurred with the rise of modern intellectualist culture of professionalization and specialization. An overrationalized life drove out religiosity, leaving modern man in search of secular sources of salvation. Eroticism now signifies a "joyous triumph over rationality," and with the new ethic "the triumph of spirit over body should find its climax precisely here."[27] Erotic love differs from religious salvation, which is devoted to a supra-mundane God, renunciation of the body, and the practice of brotherhood and neighborly love. The sexual ethic of eroticism thus competes with religion in a struggle to claim the body.

Under such conditions, Weber continues, "the erotic relation seems to offer the unsurpassable peak of the fulfillment of the request for love in the direct fusion of the souls one to the other. The boundless giving of oneself is as radical as possible in its opposition to all functionality, rationality, and generality." Far more radical than capitalism, which is about accumulating, or science, which is about calculating, or religion, which is about worrying, erotic love as "boundless giving" rests upon the possibility of "communion which is felt as a complete unification, as a fading of the 'thou.'" This experience, Weber notes, may be ineffable and close to mysticism. He then suggests an element of desperation. "As the knowing love of mature man stands to the passionate enthusiasm of the youth, so stands the deadly earnestness of this eroticism of intellectualism to chivalrous love." An eroticism that knows itself is no longer innocent about romantic love. But the lover knows himself to be in a sphere inaccessible to any rational endeavor, his body and emotions delivered from the mundane and the monotonous. "He knows himself to be freed from the cold skeleton hands of rational orders, just as completely from the banality of everyday routine."[28]

Having described what appears to be the supreme heights of erotic love, Weber proceeds to show its limitations and illusions. Attaching itself, as it must, to another person, erotic love has no room for genuine love of others and instead smiles upon the world from the pose of its own bliss. "The euphoria of the happy lover is felt to be 'goodness'; it has a friendly urge to poeticize all the world" in its own state of bewitchment. But the genuinely religious, Weber notes, citing Tolstoy, meet such romantic nonsense with "cool mockery," seeing it as subjective, indulgent, exclusive, incommunicable, and unreliable. Erotic love and religious brotherly love inhabit two different worlds.[29]

The great danger of erotic love—wrote Weber to himself, as though he has been recently through it and barely escaped without succumbing—is the illusion of fate and the resulting loss of will, both of which conceal from the partners the presence of power.

> From the point of view of any religious ethic of brotherhood, the erotic relation must remain attached, in a certain sophisticated measure, to brutality. The more sublimated it is, the more brutal. Unavoidably, it is considered to be a relation of conflict. This conflict is not only, or even predominantly, jealousy and the will to possession, excluding third ones. It is far more the most intimate coercion of the soul of the less brutal partner. This coercion exists because it is never noticed by the partners themselves. Pretending to be the most humane devotion, it is a sophisticated enjoyment of oneself in the other. No consummated erotic communion will know itself to be founded in any way other than through a mysterious *destination* for one another: *fate,* in this highest sense of the word. Thereby, it will know itself to be "legitimized" (in an entirely amoral sense).[30]

Within the most emotional bonds of intimacy Weber sees not romantic fulfillment but human manipulation and exploitation. This arresting observation raises a question: By whom? Feminist scholars assume Weber had in mind primarily men, who play upon the woman's desire to please not herself, but always and everywhere "the other."[31] Perhaps so, but whether Weber was speaking from personal experience or social observation he had no intention of legitimizing brutal gender coercion that allegedly follows sexual arousal. Significantly, the final passages on the section on eroticism conclude by defending marriage.

As an established institution marriage answers to the uncontrolled frenzy of erotic love. A "rationally regulated marriage" is accepted as "one of the divine ordinations given to man as a creature who is hopelessly wretched by virtue of his 'concupiscence.'" After the Fall, Weber continues, we are all creatures of sin and passion. "According to Luther, God, in order to prevent worse, peeks at and is lenient with these elements of passion." What's a man to do?

From a purely inner-worldly point of view, only the linkage of marriage with the thought of ethical responsibility for one another—hence a category heterogeneous to the purely erotic sphere—can carry the sentiment that something unique and supreme might be embodied in marriage; that it might be the transformation of the feeling of a love which is conscious of responsibility throughout all the nuances of the organic life process, "up to the pianissimo of old age," and a mutual granting of oneself to another and the becoming indebted to each other (in Goethe's sense). Rarely does life grant such value in pure form. He to whom it is given may speak of fate's fortune and grace—not of his own "merit."[32]

One may interpret Weber's meditations on carnal knowledge as strictly scholarship, part of his thoughts about the mystical dimensions of religious experience, with the aim of showing that eroticism cannot be translated into an ethical proposition and that therefore it has, contrary to what the Asconian libertines claimed, no political significance. Or his meditations may be more personal, an attempt to explain to himself the volcanic temptations of love affairs and the deeper value of his own marriage. Did Weber believe, along with some other agnostics, that we must feel the sting of sin in order to grow? As Georges Bataille has observed, consciousness of the self requires transgression. "If we observe the taboo," Bataille writes of prohibitions against erotic pleasure,

> if we submit to it, we are no longer conscious of it. But in the act of violating it we feel the anguish of mind without which the taboo could not exist: that is the experience of sin. That experience leads to the completed transgression, which . . . in maintaining the prohibition, maintains it in order to benefit by it. The inner experience of eroticism demands from a subject a sensitiveness to the anguish of the heart of the taboo no less great than the desire which leads him to infringe it. This is religious sensibility, and it always links desire closely with terror, intense pleasure and anguish.[33]

With Weber we are in the presence of a religious sensibility, an anguished conscience that could never take itself beyond good and evil. If marriage requires sacrificing erotic fulfillment, romantic affairs result in the brutality of power and manipulation. What, then, to do if only the erotic can free the self from the "cold skeleton hands of rational order"? Can there be sex without guilt? "The topographical position of the erotic must be determined," Weber instructed Georg Lukács, who, after his mistress had committed suicide, was experimenting with the proper place of eros in literary form, "and I am anxious to see where it is going to be in your work."[34]

THE WOMEN'S MOVEMENT IN GERMANY

Get some well-deserved rest, Weber advised Marianne in 1908, when she was recovering from an illness in a hospital. "Two hours reading is already somewhat much. You should simply vegetate. And for God's sake, keep your paws off the woman question and the ### moral laws! The general's daughters," he continued, referring to two patients Marianne was conversing with, "would be much more impressed if you acted as if you knew nothing at all about women problems, and it would be much better for you, since discussions at this stage [of illness] are very harmful and so unproductive. So please don't do it."[35]

Marianne could no more keep her hands off the woman question than her husband could keep his mind off it. In addition to joining his wife as a political reformer of women's rights, Weber also remained an inquirer intrigued by differences and diversity. His writings on sexuality suggest a mind perplexed by what passes for normal gender relations. In a fragment dealing with the "Treatment of the Problem of Sexuality," written around 1912, Weber saw unresolved contradictions in the institution of marriage to the extent it had anything to do with romance and the passions of the heart. Love, the belief in eternal value and the "attending paradox of everlasting happiness," submits itself in marriage to a contractual promise of duration, so that the responsibility of love and loving for the soul of another becomes a sort of "legalistic deficiency" on the worth of it all. "There can scarcely be a more devastating critique of ethical formalism than such an unavoidable banality."[36] A legal marriage vow, unlike a personal covenant, represents not the ultimate consummation of love but its likely waning.

Skeptical of socialism and its claims of a future egalitarian society, doubtful that democracy can fulfill its promise to represent the will of the people, Weber became an ardent champion of the women's movement as one cause he could support. As a young professor in Germany's conservative academic world, he was almost alone in advocating the admission of female students. He also protested to the *Frankfurter Zeitung* when certain officials, afflicted with a case of male chauvinism (*männlicher Geschlechtseitelkeit*) refused to hire female factory inspectors.[37] Perhaps more revealing, he defended women's need to venture beyond society's confining conventions. In 1908, Weber exchanged ideas about women's sexual freedom with Heinrich Rickert, the neo-Kantian philosopher whose seminars Marianne had attended. As mentioned earlier, Marianne became close to Rickert's wife Sophie, seeing her as "a new type of woman" with the soul of an artist and the sensibility of a responsible wife and mother.[38] But Sophie's husband Heinrich disapproved of woman challenging the double standard that allows men to be promiscuous and requires women to be virtuous. "You sought to demonstrate," Weber wrote Rickert in reference to a conversation he had had with Marianne,

> the different relevance of sexual freedom to the genders, using as experience the respective statements of friends. My experience has been the exact opposite. I have known women who took *precisely* that position on these things, that you found so abnormal in Frieda Gr[oss]; however, not merely in theory at the suggestion of the man; instead in practice as a deep personal conviction by women who lived and wanted to live according to it. I assure you, were I able to introduce you to these people, you could, upon getting to know them better, see differences between them but find their personalities and "femininity" just as little affected as that of those men who, as you described them to my wife, regard the sex act (with the whore) as "merely a one-time irrelevant release."

Such liberated women, Weber continued to advise Rickert, tower over our male acquaintances, for they live according to a principled conviction, be it ever so abstruse. Eliminate the child-bearing fate of women and is there any difference in moral disposition between the sexes? "Indeed, while men speak of the 'irrelevance' or ethical 'indifference' of their own conduct, such modern women I know," standing above the conventional virtue of "proper" women, "have more of a sensitivity to difference," an understanding that different means of evaluation are necessary to push their limits outward beyond existing society. Identity is predicated upon difference.[39]

Around the turn of the century feminist politics in the western world looked to the Left for the little support it enjoyed. Socialists saw women's oppression deriving from capitalism and its supposedly historically doomed institutions of private property, while some liberals regarded feminism as the deferred commitment of political democracy, to be fulfilled with parliamentary representation and the right to vote. Weber's involvement with women's causes was more aristocratic, a matter of seeing the female species as capable of achieving values that may approximate the height of human qualities; independent women with an inner sense of freedom; active rather than passive agents who look upon sexuality as a source of strength and identity rather than shame and weakness. "Max Weber took part most warmly in his share of the work of the women's movement," Marianne wrote in her own memoirs. "He helped me when there were always difficulties; chivalrously supportive. Indeed, recognition of the woman as determined by a fully worthy intellectual nature became a close and urgent matter to him."[40]

Discussions of the women's movement animated the intellectual hothouse of Heidelberg's "Weber Circle." Marianne herself became one of the leading feminists in Germany and came to know such American activists as Jane Addams and Florence Kelley. At a time when women were excluded from teaching in the German university, Marianne won the status of a scholar with the publication of articles and books on subjects ranging from Marxism, marriage, the patriarchal basis of German law, women and education, and the problems peculiar to working-class women. Marianne took issue with Charlotte Perkins Gilman's *Women and Economics* (1898), which had been translated in German as *Mann und Frau*. The American reformer believed modern technology made possible the liberation of the wife from the household; Marianne insisted the goal of the women's movement cannot simply be the replacement of the mother at home by the working wife, whose low wages could barely meet the needs of family and children. Instead of looking only to the economic emancipation of women, Marianne advocated reform of marriage laws to insure legal and economic equity against the husband's power.[41]

Max Weber gave full support to Marianne's writings and activities on behalf of the women's movement. Both husband and wife were leaders in Der Bund für Mutterschutz (The League for the Protection of Mothers), which advocated assistance to unwed mothers, establishment of hostels, child care, access to contraceptives. At the end of World War I Marianne would be elected to political office and made president of Der Bund Deutsche Frauenvereine (The German Women's Federation). All along the women's movement had its detractors in Germany as well as elsewhere. *Übermäßig!*—Outrageous! That love could be moral without marriage, and marriage immoral without love; that women are either mothers or whores, happy and fulfilled or hysterical and frustrated—such claims charged the atmosphere of those parts of German society where feminism was debated as a matter of morality and personal identity.

Many women with illegitimate children were also cultural rebels who championed sexual freedom as well as women's rights. These revolutionary demands for a new life-style free from traditional conjugal constraints posed a challenge to the Webers' definition of marriage and family. It was as though a new permissive ethic arose to replace the older Protestant ethic. The Webers often drew upon each other's language to describe the ideals of marriage partners for whom sexual fidelity is nothing less than an ascetic principle, the original "beautiful moment" that binds husband and wife "up to the pianissimo of old age." But Weber himself was as curious about eros as he was concerned about ethics, and in the quiet of his study he wrote down thoughts in which he anticipates the advent of the "postmodernism" of our times, seeing modern capitalist society spawning mutants of irrational pleasure in opposition to the mechanisms of rationalization. With the economy requiring disciplined production, and society, assaulted by advertising, demanding hedonistic consumption, Weber sensed the coming of what would be called, a half-century later, the "cultural contradictions of capitalism."[42]

In 1910, at a celebratory conference of the German Women's Federation at Heidelberg that attracted much attention, many men felt threatened by this challenge to their patriarchal ways. A young lecturer at the university published a defamatory article on the convention to the approval of the majority of Heidelberg's male population. The author charged that the feminist movement consisted only of women without husbands, Jews, frigid females, and those who had no intention of accepting the duties of motherhood. Since Marianne was childless and responsible for organizing the convention, she seemed to be the target of the attack. Max was furious, and Marianne demanded a retraction in the press. When the author refused, she issued a public chastisement under her name, but the citizens of Heidelberg recognized Max as the unnamed co-composer. The author of the attack now complained that Weber was hiding behind his wife in order to avoid being challenged to a duel. Weber immediately lashed back, stating that he stood behind everything his wife had written and accepted the prospect of a duel. The author backed down, and there followed a protracted lawsuit involving issues of slander that became the talk of Germany.[43]

Weber's writings on sex and eroticism and his sympathy toward feminist causes reflected his intellectual concern about the much-discussed position of women in modern society. Rival circles in Heidelberg, especially that of the poet Stefan Georg, were hostile to the women's movement and its emancipatory notions that seemed to threaten the marriage bond. Weber could support the movement even as a conservative. In his estimate, what was essential to understanding women's situation was the notion of status, a sociological concept that went beyond the socialist emphasis on class and the liberal emphasis on rights.

THE THEORY OF STATUS AND STATUS POLITICS

The subject of women concerned a number of Weber's contemporaries, especially such sociologists as Emile Durkheim, Ferdinand Tonnies, and Georg Simmel. Many social scientists, accepting conventional bourgeois attitudes toward gender inequality, assumed that conjugal institutions were necessary for society's organic solidarity. Other scholars saw communal forms of gemeinschaft rendering the household women's proper sphere; still others believed the idea of a genuine female culture would be unimaginable in a reified world created by the alienating work of the predominantly male working force.[44] While in some respects Weber was no less conservative than other sociologists, especially earlier in his life when he agreed with Marianne that marriage was a moral responsibility and sex an ethical act, he would depart from familiar sociological categories when thinking about women. The prevalent idea of class, so fundamental to a Marxist analysis, could only with difficulty be applied to the condition of women, whose situation may not be determined by either the ownership of the means of production or by a proletarian need to sell their labor power. Similarly, a liberal analysis based on the promise of political rights may be incomplete, particularly when women's rights and privileges were greater in the hereditary kingdoms of Hellenistic Greece than in democratic Athens, an era that witnessed the complete subjugation of women.

When Weber discussed women, he usually used the term "status," instead of "class" and all the implications the latter term had historically, especially in the struggle between merchants and workers over the price of labor. The term "status" derived from the Latin root *stare*, to stand, which literally designated an individual's or a group's standing in the eyes of others. Status was a matter of perception, and its changing, contingent features suggested why Weber remained skeptical of any social science that presupposed the natural order of things.

Thus the differing positions of women throughout history did not turn exclusively on either their relation to markets or their participation in politics. Much of it had to do with marriage customs, the institution of the family, and the quality of life accorded wives and daughters, which in turn often expressed deep-rooted religious convictions. In past historical eras specific religions, eastern and western, shaped attitudes toward woman and her place in a given community. Functioning within religious customs were economics, property relations, and military conditions, in which women are obtained through exchange or purchase, excluded from inheritance, or captured in warfare. Weber recognized that matriarchy and matrilineal rule of succession occasionally occurred. But woman's position improves to the extent she becomes identified with a household and the mother takes primary interest in her own "legitimate" children. "As status aspirations and the corresponding cost of living rise the woman, who is regarded as a luxury possession, receives a dowry; at the same time this represents the compensation for her share in the household—a purpose clearly stipulated in ancient Oriental and Hellenic law—and provides her with the material means of destroying the husband's unlimited discretion, since he must return the dowry if he divorces her. In time, this purpose was achieved, in different degrees and not always through formal law, but often so successfully that only an endowed marriage was considered a marriage proper."[45]

That the dowry rendered women desirable indicated that status cannot be separated from economics and the distribution of power. Although Weber saw status distinctions to be less pronounced in America, he would have agreed with the American Thorstein Veblen that the wealth of the leisure class, in which wives remained idle status symbols of affordable consumption, enjoyed social prestige because of that class's conspicuous display of luxury and waste. In America, Weber observed, "submission to fashion" is stronger in an egalitarian setting as one "puts forward a claim to qualify as a 'gentleman.' "[46]

Some status groups remained closed, as in the Indian caste system, in which hereditary membership is most important and fraternization is banned. Capitalist cultures, in contrast, "know nothing of honor" as the market and its unpredictable rewards upsets established orders of stratification. Nor does the allocation of status necessarily follow the distribution of wealth, as witnessed by the low regard in which the nouveau riche is held compared to an impoverished aristocracy.

Reduced to essentials, Weber's new definitions left class behind with economics while relating status to the more problematic vagaries of culture and social esteem. Classes may be stratified economically by their relation to the production and acquisition of goods; status groups take their positions as spenders and consumers exhibiting special styles of life.

Status, honor, prestige, social deference, the stratification of esteem—such categories had more relevance than class in explaining ethnicity, racism, gender differences, and intense nationalistic sentiments, all of which separate people and frustrate the formation of class solidarity. Certain people who cultivate belief in their own ethnic community, Weber observed, jealously preserve not only a sense of their own worth but even a superiority toward other groups. The Marxist view that further pauperization will polarize people along class lines failed to consider that workers more often found their identity in ethnic, racial, and regional loyalties. Perhaps they even chose not to regard themselves as proletarian workers condemned to an endless life of labor. "Quite generally, among privileged status groups there is a status disqualification that operates against the performance of common physical labor. This qualification is now 'setting in' in America against the old tradition of esteem for labor."[47] As a potential status-seeker, the worker desires to emulate the life-style of classes immediately above. If class consciousness was supposed to arise as history moves from the bottom up, status consciousness moves from the top down in a society that honors the conspicuous waste of wealth rather than its honest production.

Although he predicted neither, Weber's concept of status enables us to understand both the decline of the labor movement as a result of the exhaustion of class politics, and the more recent rise and relative success of the women's movement as a result of status politics. But the latter development contains a rich irony, particularly when modern feminists must use conservative means to reach radical ends.

Although Weber hardly saw status politics as genteel, in contrast to the ferocity of class struggle, he did tend to view it as defensive rather than aggressive. Status groups seek to mobilize power by using their privileged position in ways that continue to increase opportunities for themselves while restricting access to others. This strategy of exclusion traditionally employed criteria of descent and lineage.[48] Today, however, in the women's movement gender criteria are used to open up opportunities for one sex even if it means the exclusion of the other. The new status politics, whether that of gender or ethnicity, requires criteria of eligibility that depend more upon biology than ability and more upon ancestry than achievement. Weber did not fully anticipate the ways in which the state and its laws could be bent to the political purposes of groups engaging in what today is called "identity politics." But to the extent that status groups appear to be more effective in mobilizing their members than do economic classes, and to the extent that such groups use the resources of government, we are witnessing today status-bloc politics determined by administrators, court orders, and other agencies that Weber foresaw as the coming dictatorship of "officialdom."[49]

How would Weber view the gender-bloc politics of women today? Ironically, the feminists of Weber's era saw themselves primarily as pacifists who advocated benevolent cooperative communities dedicated to caring, loving relationships—which he tended to dismiss as utopian. At that time the suffrage movement, in America as well as in Germany, rested on the claim that access to the voting place and the professions would enhance women's unique capacity for nurturing and moral sentiment. Once women entered the world of men, the world itself will become less harshly competitive and more humanly compassionate. History, it seems, has switched its tracks once more, to use Weber's metaphor. Again things have turned out differently. Just as the "calling" turned the historic Puritan into his opposite, the recent feminist cause has turned the modern woman into her historic opposite. With ambition replacing submission, the present scheme of human employment leaves no room for moral sentiment.

Contemporary feminists in America are more Weberian in analysis, if not conviction; they are less utopian and more realistic about tactics. All sentiments about older ideals of pacifism, socialism, and even democracy are no longer as important as an identity politics that is gender-specific and status claims that rest on definition and self-description. Under whatever banner they march, modern women are ready to use bureaucracy and administrative fiat to advance their own causes; whatever the rhetoric of their "discourse," they are more than willing to look upon politics as struggle, power as the monopoly of force and its enforcement, success as limiting the adverse actions of others, and freedom as striving toward values of independence and autonomy. In their achievements feminists have succeeded by working through and with the institutions of power and authority, the Weberian realities of the modern world.

But the women's "revolution" of our times is one of the strangest revolutions in history. Women activists used the rules and regulations of the bureaucratic state to win their right to be inside the "iron cage." Yet the scenario is perfectly Weberian. Like the seventeenth-century Puritans who felt foreordained to a fate they refused to accept, the modern women, too, altered the "world-image" that had once determined their lives and, out of a need for power and self-determination, renounced one part of an existing self to realize a yet unborn self. Thus the story of American history continues, with modern women winning the war against biological determinism just as our ancestors won their war against theological determinism. Calvinism is a success story in more ways than one.

EIGHT

Subjectivity in Morals, Willfulness in Politics: Germany, America, and World War I

THE GORE OF AUGUST 1914
___

It was June 1914, a time of tranquillity when it seemed as though news of the world could be dismissed as a nuisance. In that month Walter Lippmann, the American political philosopher and journalist who would be one of the architects of American policy toward Germany, had sailed for England a few days after the Austrian Archduke Ferdinand had been assassinated at Sarajevo. A few weeks later Lippmann went to Brussels and bought a ticket to journey through Germany and Switzerland, planning to spend the rest of the summer hiking the splendid Alpine mountain passes. "I remember being astonished and rather annoyed when I went to the railroad station and found that the German border was closed because Belgium had had an ultimatum." The shock of the war led Lippmann to put aside his preoccupation with domestic reform and to now turn to foreign affairs. "So I know at least one young man who was not mentally prepared for the age he was destined to live in."[1]

Marianne Weber describes the same serene setting in Heidelberg in summer 1914: the Shakespeare comedy festivals in the warm evenings, the picnics in the castle park at Schwetzangen with a Greek temple as background, the "radiant young" enjoying the midsummer gaiety, lolling on the "sylvan soil" in the opening bloom of life. "Delighting in the artistic spirit of their class, people moved easily and freely in the summery blue; the earth was fair."[2]

When news of the assassination reached Heidelberg, people, old and young, gathered in the Webers' parlor, most of them hovering around Weber himself. He had, as a child of six in the very same room at the same time of year, experienced the outbreak of the Franco-Prussian War of 1870. In the earlier war the die had been cast in the youth's memory; in the present situation it still seemed possible to "play with fate." But when the moment of truth came everyone knew what their duty was. Without anyone voicing it, a sense of brotherhood and community spread among the people. Marianne describes returning with Max from a meeting in the center of the city where people gathered to receive the news that Germany was at war:

> On their way home the Webers paused at the upper end of the old bridge for a moment; a radiant summer evening lent perfection to everything around them. The setting sun glowed like a firebrand on the windows of the houses on the mountain slope, and the soaring sky imparted its delicate blue to the river. The earth rested blissfully in its beauty. Soon it would drink in the blood of thousands. It was going to shroud in darkness the eyes of the young people who delighted in it, still ignorant of its full wealth, and dim the summery splendor of mature manhood. With a shudder, human beings now stood on the edge of reality. And even more touching than the fate of the youth was the fate of the men who now moved knowingly and soberly from the height of life into the darkness.[3]

Unlike the American Lippmann, Weber was hardly unprepared for the world of darkness that descended over Europe with the guns of August. Seeing a world of power and conflict, Weber felt he was seeing history becoming conscious of itself. Nor would he make a distinction between domestic politics and foreign affairs; he would have had no trouble accepting Carl von Clausewitz's dictum that war is politics by other means. Although Weber remained convinced that capitalism emerged from Puritanism, it was not the creation of wealth that interested him but instead the more problematic spectacle of power. Like Alexander Hamilton, Weber believed that national power was more important than society's economic wellbeing, security more vital than opulence; thus military objectives should extend political purposes. But as Lippmann well knew, American political culture had been shaped not by Hamiltonian realism but by a Jeffersonian aversion to the reality of power and to the necessary presence of the nation-state. It was the ideals of Jefferson that Wilson would bring to Europe to end World War I. The stage of diplomacy was set for tragedy.

World War I illuminated the relation of forces in international politics, and German statesmanship seemed to have lost touch with reality. The German government, Weber complained, allowed itself to be surrounded by hostile powers and strategically outnumbered. As a theorist of *Realpolitik* who believed that conflicts are usually settled by resorting to force, Weber was hardly in a position to claim that war could have been avoided by more intelligent negotiation. But the war brought to the surface the weakness of the Bismarckian legacy, which Weber had all along criticized for rendering the German people passive and Parliament supine. The diplomatic implications were just as troubling. As a strategy of international statecraft, the nineteenth-century Bismarckian system, which assumed that Germany could be strong as long as she remained one of three world powers, could only balance power in a world without bipolarity, precisely the configuration that the country began to face in the twentieth century. Along with Germany Weber faced a new, uncertain world.

In the early months of the war, however, Weber was caught up in the patriotic spirit and martial élan. The sudden confrontation with the Allied powers gave to the German people a sense of unity and spirit of sacrifice that made the war appear to Weber what John Adams had seen in the American Revolution and Lincoln in the Civil War: a "proving ground" that would put a country's national character to the ultimate test. "Whatever the outcome, the war is great and wonderful," he wrote to a friend. Despite all its ugliness, the war "is worth experiencing. It would be even more worthwhile to participate in it, but unfortunately they cannot use me in the field as they would have used me if it had been waged in time, twenty-five years ago."[4]

DUTIES AND DEATHS

Weber was fifty at the war's outbreak. Having unsuccessfully volunteered for military duty, Weber accepted a commission as captain to take charge of the Reserve Military Hospital Commission in Heidelberg. Weber plunged into work and managed the economy and the rules and regulations of nine different hospitals. For the most part he worked seven days a week for twelve hours a day. So upset was Weber at being judged unfit for military duty that he joked to Edgar Jaffé that all his labor was meant to "prove to myself that I am not good for any work." But Marianne knew better and regarded his strenuous daily work schedule as a "miracle," and final evidence that he had recovered from mental debility and no longer worried about deadlines, self-doubts, and noctural "demons."[5]

But the work could be monotonous, and he had no patience with bureaucratic routines that stood in the way of efficiency. A request for a itemized list for hundreds of items needed for a hospital led Weber to reply with a tedious, almost four-foot long telegram. When a commissar asked why a telephone had been installed, Weber exploded that any "normal" person knows for what purpose a phone is used. Weber approved of a visit to the central hospital by "Her Royal Highness and Grand Duchess," but he let it be known that he would not waste his time escorting her.

Weber served in numerous capacities. He had to overlook budgets and deal with doctors, nurses, Red Cross officials, orderlies, custodians, and cooks, while finding some time in the evening to offer adult education classes. He served as arbiter and judge, issuing reports on discipline under the changing conditions of war. The scholar who would later be recognized as a master of "grand theory" knew a few things about the grubby details of daily life. He had to intervene in endless squabbles: an inspector mistreating nurses, the theft of food and wine, the mistress of a senior surgeon committing an impropriety, a batty cook found washing her hair in a stewpot. But Weber's analytical powers and organizational skills remained intact: he wrote a report on the reasons for increased alcohol consumption in times of war and supervised the distribution of gifts and donations brought to patients by townspeople.[6]

In early 1915 Weber asked to be discharged from the hospital service, realizing that a reorganization of staff by the military left his position ill-defined. When he departed doctors and staff members presented him with a souvenir album of photos of all who had worked under him. During his half-year at the hospital Weber had witnessed the soldiers returning from the front with mangled limbs and bandaged heads. Arranging space for the wounded, organizing care for invalids, Weber also instructed his German staff and their patients to treat lame enemy soldiers, particularly the French, with respect. Despite the disgruntled complaints and personal bickering, Weber believed the war was bringing out the best in the German people; it could also bring out the worst in Weber, as when he refers to Africans whom the French recruited from their colonies to fight in the war: "We have demonstrated that we are a great civilized nation," he wrote his mother. "People who live in a highly refined civilization and then nevertheless are equal to the horrors of the war out there (which is no achievement for the Senegalese!) who despite this come back like that, as thoroughly decent as the great majority of our people—such people are genuine human beings, and this must *certainly* not be overlooked amidst all the obtrusive activities of a disagreeable kind. This experience will definitely last, no matter what the outcome may be."[7]

The news of the deaths of friends and relatives deeply stirred Weber. No doubt he grieved upon hearing the horrible messages. But the letters of sympathy he wrote suggest that one who found existence existentially meaningless could almost look upon death as giving life purpose and significance.

The death of his brother-in-law, struck down in a battle near Tannenberg, led Weber to meditate on the life this man, Herman Schafer, who, having struggled to live in the shadow of his brilliant father, a famous architect, welcomed the coming of the war and enthusiastically joined up as an officer. Weber writes to his youngest sister, Lili, reassuring her that her husband's eagerness to serve his country indicates that "death in the war is not something he would have wanted to evade." The "spirit of the soldiers" he had seen at the hospital makes Herman part of a noble legacy. He told Lili that she and her children should remember: "To have fallen in these battlefields is worth even a beautiful and rich life."[8]

The loss of a philosopher and fellow-professor led Weber to further reflection. Emil Lask was a Jewish scholar who believed in universal truths while having a reverence for the infinite varieties of life. "When he was gripped by the magic of love for living beauty," wrote Marianne, "his entire being glowed and his surrender turned into self-effacement." Although friendship and loyalty could inspire sacrifice in him, he was hard on himself, often struck by the impermanence of all things and caught up in melancholy hesitation when confronted with a decision. Yet with the outbreak of the war Lask did not opt for a professor's deferment or claim the disability of poor eyesight; he went directly to the front as a noncommissioned officer and took a fatal bullet. When Weber wrote to

Lask's family, he first expressed some bitterness at the senseless sacrifice. But one thing was certain. "It is not entirely senseless if a man validates what he has taught his students by the manner of his death." Without illusions, he accepted the burden of duty, living up to the ideals he taught without prating of them. In the young Lask Weber saw the convergence of character, fate, and destiny. "Though he would have liked to go on living—this we know—he would be equally in tune with himself if he were able to look back on his end." He could have rationalized and convinced himself that it was "more appropriate for a man who was so courageous by nature but simply was unwarlike to devote himself to his profession." Yet he could never face himself knowing others took the more manly course. "In his profound honesty with himself he knew this quite well, and that is why, after a brief period of hesitation, he went."[9]

Weber's moving letters of condolence reveal the human values he most esteemed. Not often does a social scientist know what conscience is. For Weber it was far from a socialized faculty of adjustment and adaptation, and it had no Shakespearean connotation of the doubt and hesitation that makes "cowards of us all." For Weber it was more Germanic and romantic, closer to Schiller's dictum that a brave man would risk his life to save his conscience. To act on principle (*Gesinnungsethik*) had always been uppermost to Weber and, indeed, had earlier drawn him to the ethical world of the Puritans and their healthy "agonized conscience" (Santayana).

The loss of Karl Weber, Max's young brother, was wrenching in ways that had as much to do with life as with death. Max and Karl had been estranged from each other as youths. Karl had no interest in school and seemed a problem child. But of all the Weber children he loved their mother Helene most dearly and eventually her gentle influence took hold. He became disciplined and dedicated, studying architecture under the famous Karl Schafer. By the time the war broke out, Max had recognized his qualities and, upon his death, wrote to his mother of them: "The refined inner objectivity, the ability to deal with things in silence, the relinquishment of 'recognition.'" His coming into his true moral self, Weber wrote in praise of his mother, resulted from his "having completely understood and grasped you. And finally, he had a beautiful death in the only place where it is worthy of a human being to be at the moment."

To wrest beauty from death! Such associations bespeak Weber's hope that the greatness of the human spirit will survive the calamities of history and that tragedy must have a hero in order to accept, rather than merely renounce, the world in which it occurs. But was Weber sentimentalizing military glory? Or was he, like Lincoln, using a tragic war as the occasion for meditation? A letter Weber later wrote to Karl's fiancée illuminates not only his outlook on life but his deepest feelings about the "bonds of understanding" that draw people toward one another and toward themselves.

Weber tells the fiancée that he has been rereading Karl's letters and, sensing the "great genuineness and depth" and "delicacy of feeling" in his brother's emotions, he regrets more than ever the misunderstandings of their youth. The "injustice" that Weber did Karl, he laments, was his failure to realize that Karl's behavior was not simply the theatrics of an adolescent but the coming into being of a genuine artist. But Karl's "ardent love for you" had brought forth an "enchanting second bloom as the fulfillment of a life that was longingly reaching for the highest things." Karl could then face his weaknesses and strengths and even have an "honest avowal of his religious attitude, an attitude that is keeping with the fate of our time. This," Weber emphasizes,

> is particularly valuable to me, because it shows me that there too he did not delude himself, which is what so many people are doing today, particularly artists, weak souls who cannot bear the face of today's life. That he was strong enough not to do this and did not lose himself in the harshness of his fate and all his harsh self-criticism is evidence of such great inner strength that one has to love him for this alone.
>
> And that is why we thank . . . you for this wonderful flowering which you gave to the man who was already marked for death in such beauty, something that is expressed in every line of these touchingly beautiful last letters. *If you remain open to the splendor of this life, which was great despite everything, you will live a life that will be most nearly in his spirit.*[10]

That Weber could write so sensitive and poetical a letter in time of war, and even approaching defeat, illuminates the character of one who has too often been associated with the heartless world of power and domination and the petty trivialities of bureaucracy. His letters almost seem to answer Nietzsche's challenge to provide the meaning of human suffering. In a time of strife and chaos, his thoughts remained consistent and continuous. Just as he tried to give death a redeeming personal dignity in World War I, Weber continued to try to give politics a moral foundation.

WAR AIMS, THE U-BOAT, "BETWEEN TWO LAWS," AND THE CLAIMS OF AMERICAN DEMOCRACY

Is there a disparity between Weber's long-developed social theory and his political positions during World War I, between his theorizing about the inexorability of power and then advocating a policy of prudent restraint? Given his definition of political action as the claim to the right to dominate a territory, and of power as the possibility of resorting to the use of force against the will of an adversary, one might think that Weber would have seen the war as the opportunity for Germany's imperial expansion. In the years before the war he favored expansion into parts of the non-western world; he also encouraged military development and specifically the naval buildup. Perhaps due to his conviction that Germany would always face a threat from the east, he was insufficiently sensitive to the reaction to Germany's maritime *Weltpolitik* by England, the country he admired most, next to America. But when the war occurred Weber stood apart from the jingoists who gathered at the Imperial Palace in Berlin, and as the war continued he would fulminate at Kaiser Wilhelm II, describing him as "like an emperor whose scepter has been stolen." So critical did Weber become toward the Kaiser and the patriotic bombast of the era that he was often labeled a "defeatist" (*Flaumacher*).[11]

But he was less a defeatist than a pessimist. From the beginning of the war Weber had doubts about its outcome and conceived it as defensive only, an effort to protect German interests through diplomacy. He expected no German triumphal entry into the leading ranks of world power, and hence all the bloodshed seemed—even though he might endow death with dignity in his personal letters—a horrible waste and the result of a German foreign policy based more on arrogance than prudent analysis. Thus instead of extolling power politics, Weber became critical of German leaders and institutions for their ineptitude and for refusing to see that an eager resort to military force may be a sign of political weakness. The exposed weakness of Germany's political institutions would be, as indicated in the next chapter, the basis for Weber's advocating a restructuring of the whole system of government for the new Weimar Republic.

Weber's view of the war as limited and defensive could be sustained in the first few months of combat. No important western thinker, including Weber, had seen the enormous significance the war would have for world history. Not until it stalemated in the bloody trenches did the war begin to seem more than an interlude and take on a tragic meaning, a painful awakening that convinced many writers what Weber had known for some time: that history may not be governed by human reason.

But Weber was no fatalist, and toward the end of 1915 he began writing out his thoughts on Germany's "war aims" in an essay intended for the *Frankfurter Zeitung*, though they ended up in his desk drawer probably because of censorship. Earlier he had opposed the annexation of Belgium and regretted the "preventive march through Belgium, which was painful for every German in spite of its compelling necessity" as a preemptive tactic to establish defensive positions.[12] But the old Pan-German League was now fanning nationalist emotions and advocating limitless war aims for Germany, including absorption of Poland and Russian border regions, resettlement of non-German populations, and postwar reparations. Edgar Jaffé, attempting to check the annexationist fervor, invited Weber to Brussels, where he had been officially observing the German occupation. At first Weber declined, for he was still at his hospital post in Heidelberg and, perhaps more important, he had no wish to create the impression that war provided the opportunity for him to leap into politics. But in August 1915 Weber arrived in Brussels, and, once aware that his vision of Germany's political relations with her neighbors were nowhere to be heard, he openly took part in the war aims debate.

The passionate demands of right-wing parties for unlimited annexation Weber regarded as nothing less than catastrophic. Not only were such demands unrealistic but they stood indifferent to consequences that could only result in lingering hostility. Weber suspected that the annexationist clamor, which only served to keep countries at war with one another, had as much to do with self-interest as with nationalism. The Right, he observed, feared that the economic effects of the war's ending would force political democratization of Germany's class-weighted suffrage system. Drawing upon Bismarck, Weber called for Germany to pursue a policy during the war that looked foward to the stability of future alliances afterwards, a policy altogether impossible with a peace "whose main result was that Germany's boot stood on everyone's toes in Europe."[13]

Weber's policy of reconciliation in Belgium and the west derived from his conviction that no lasting threat would come from France and England. With Russia on the eastern front the question of national security had to be considered, and there was no turning back Bismarck's effort to develop an alliance with Russia at the cost of suppressing the Poles. Thus Weber called for Polish and Baltic "autonomous" states in the east with Germany having the right to build "garrison fortresses," develop strategic railways, and establish custom unions. Weber envisaged a network of small nation-states in the east that could be "played off" (Mommsen's expression) against a Russia that would remain expansionist as long as the tsarist state refused to concede drastic reforms. Later, when the Brest-Litovsk peace treaty with Russia was announced in 1918, Weber had reservations about Germany's dictated, unyielding terms, which violated nationality principles in the east and reinforced the image of Germany's drive toward world power.[14]

Nowhere was Weber's sense of the tragic dimensions of politics more evident than during World War I. Once again his philosophy resembled that of Abraham Lincoln, who told Americans during the Civil War that the ghastly campaigns had to be fought so that the Union could be saved. Weber also believed that those who recoil from power and resort to violence fail to see that the life of a nation cannot allow itself to perish by a scrupulous loyalty to principle at any cost. That the logic of power is in conflict with the laws of morality, Weber believed, is a tragic truth that must be faced. Weber faced it in an open letter to the magazine *Die Frau* in February 1916. "*Zwischen zwei Gesetzen*" (Between Two Laws) was written as an answer to an article by a Swiss Christian pacifist who had challenged Weber's friend, Gertrud Baumer, a leader of the feminist movement in Germany, about the inevitability of conflicting duties in wartime.

Only people living in small countries, Weber wrote, specifying Switzerland, Denmark, Holland, and Norway, can easily renounce the use of power without suffering its effects, since such countries lacked effective power to begin with. Such small countries provide the soil on which the bourgeois virtues of citizenship and artistic achievement are valued rather than military prowess. But Germany's situation is different. "Because we are a *Machtstaat* (power state) and can therefore, in contrast to those 'small' nations, throw our weight into the balance of this historical issue, is why we, and not they, have the accursed duty and obligation to history, which means posterity, to resist the inundation of the entire world by these powers [Russia, France, and England]. If we refuse this duty, the German Reich would be a frivolous luxury, inimical to culture, an indulgence which we should not have supported and should dispense with as soon as possible by the '*Verschweizerung*' (Swissification) of our statehood, dissolving into little, impotent cantons, perhaps with provincial courts supportive of the arts, all the while waiting to see just how long our neighbors would allow us to continue this contemplative cultivation of the cultural values of a small nation, which would be the meaning and purpose of our existence forevermore."[15]

While Weber insists that there is no escape from the reality of power, he is far from advocating the triumph of power as an end in itself. Thus

he reminds readers of Jacob Burkhardt's dictum that power is "diabolical" to whoever wields it; and he expresses admiration for Tolstoy for his
consistency, not only his renouncing power but his forsaking living off
the exploited labor of others. The Gospels are also "absolutely unambiguous" about renouncing the laws of the comfortable world of the
flesh. Thus Weber had scorn for those who claim the ideals of the spiritual world and live by the conventions of the mundane world. "The
pacifism of American 'ladies' (of both sexes) is truly the worst cant ever
to have been proclaimed—quite naively—from any teatable, combined
as it is with the pharisaical attitude of the parasite who is making good
profits from supplying war materials towards the barbarians in the
trenches."

Patronizing, perhaps, particularly as it appeared in a women's magazine.
Weber probably had in mind American feminine pacifists whose husbands worked on Wall Street. Whether the impression had any basis in
fact, his larger point is that the United States, like Switzerland, has been
so geographically situated that the American people lack an understanding of "the law of 'power pragma' that governs all political history." So too
is a sense of tragedy lacking. "In the anti-militaristic 'neutrality' of the
Swiss and their rejection of the power state there also lies occasionally a
good bit of really pharisaical lack of understanding of the tragedy of the
historical obligations of a people that is now organized as a power state."
The historical obligation is to live between two laws, those of spiritual
conscience and those of worldly reality. Weber characterizes this as a
Christian burden that Germany accepts:

> The old sober empiricist, John Stuart Mill, once said that, simply on the
> basis of experience, no one would ever arrive at the existence of one
> god, and it seems to me, certainly not a god of goodness—but at poly-
> theism. Indeed anyone living in the "world" (in the Christian sense of
> the word) can only feel himself subject to the struggle between multi-
> ple sets of values, each of which, viewed separately, seems to impose an
> obligation on him. He has to choose which of these gods he will and
> should serve, or when he should serve the one god and when the other.
> But at all times he will find himself engaged in a fight against one or
> other of the gods of this world, and above all he will always find that he
> is far from the God of Christianity—at least from the God proclaimed
> in the Sermon on the Mount.[16]

Weber's tragic vision of politics scarcely implied that he resigned himself
to the inevitable. One possibility that he did his utmost to avoid was
America's entry into the war. The thought appalled him not only because

it would assure Germany's defeat but also because it would complicate whatever plans Germany might have for securing stability in the eastern front on a realistic basis. In February 1917, he wrote to Karl Löwenstein that pacifist sentiment in America was strong and there was little enthusiasm for going to war. Weber angrily opposed Admiral Alfred von Tirpitz and his demagogic call to resume the U-boat campaign. He dubbed one military advisor an "ass" for miscalculating the likelihood of America's entry. "The danger of war with America is at a high point," he wrote in March 1916. "It seemed to me as if we are ruled by an insane horde." Those who once said, "Ah! the Americans will never strike," will soon say, "Ah! the Americans wanted to be in the war in any case, as completely as did the Italians."[17]

With World War I America once again loomed significantly in Weber's thoughts about politics and history. In April 1916, Weber prepared an address with the Tocquevillian title, "Democracy in American Life." Two years later, in March 1918, he wrote an address with a title more Weberian, "Democracy and Aristocracy in American Life." Tocqueville doubted that an aristocracy would emerge in America because there existed no feudal remnants that clung to an ancien régime. But Weber, now that the United States and Germany were at war with one another, had good reason to dig deeper to find evidence that America was not all that democratic, particularly the America of Woodrow Wilson, the president who two months earlier than Weber's address had offered the 14 Points as the "moral climax" that would settle "this final war for human liberty." Weber delivered his address before a Heidelberg group called "The People's Association for Freedom of the Fatherland," an organization that sought to make the peace terms representative of the interests of all Germans and to renounce the government's excessive war aims. The text of Weber's address is missing but the substance of his comments received full coverage in three Heidelberg newspapers.

After recalling his trip to the United States in 1904, Weber spoke of some of the unsavory aspects of American life. First, he said, was the breach (*Bruchstelle*) made in the American democratic character by the treatment of the Negroes, who are segregated into separate train compartments and waiting stations as well as sections of city parks, denied the right to vote, and forbidden to marry whites. The South in particular, he noted, operates on a double standard (*zweifache Wertung*) for human beings based on the old feudal scorn for labor. Landed estates still carry influence, and as society secularizes the old status of the church has been replaced by a whole slew of exclusive clubs. Democracy is without respect for anything except personal achievement; the conditioning already begins in school classes, where children are inculcated to the point of valuing only money standards. Yet social mobility is more difficult than ever, and for this reason Americans have boundless respect for the "self-made man." Decades ago America was a "paradise" for workers; today, with the end of free land, the formation of trusts, and the waves of immigrants, conditions have so deteriorated, said Weber, that he would warn German workers against going there.

Out of this peculiar democracy, Weber continued, now grows gradually an aristocracy, a society where one belongs to various strata of subordination, where rules of fashion determine the dress in the street, where claims to ancestry, whether the Pilgrim or the Indian, confer status, and where student life in the universities begins and ends with sports. "The war will Europeanize America further," Weber explained, as recounted by a reporter from the *Heidelberger Neuesten Nachrichten*:

> And it is a fact that we have learned nothing of older democratic America. Over there the romance of numbers [*Romantik der Quantität*] rules the soul, and a strong hope in the future lives in every American. What the aim of that hope is no one knows. What this land lacks is historical destiny. America's existence is in no side threatened, and the American cannot put himself in our situation; he does not see our adverse geographical position with restless neighbors on our boundaries. The American who is now fighting in the West knows actually nothing wherefore he dies. But *our* soldiers *know it*, and that is the majestic thing, that the German war has this emotion, to fight and bleed for the native country and the security of the land. That will be our duty, to arrange the homeland, as the soldiers hope to find it when they return from war. We want the democratization of the franchise and to strengthen the right of parliamentary representation.[18]

The accuracy of Weber's description of America is less telling than the irony. Both Weber and President Wilson wanted to see Germany democratized; but Wilson was a Southerner indifferent to those "aristocratic" features of American life that conditioned race relations, and like his fellow Virginia ancestor Thomas Jefferson, he was more dedicated to bringing democracy to white Europeans than to black Americans. More telling is Weber's observation that the German soldier knows why he is fighting but the American soldier does not know why he may die, because he knows nothing about his hopeful aims for the future in a land that lacks a historical sense of destiny. But how could Weber be so sure that Americans lacked consciousness of what they were doing in the trenches?

Significantly, three leading American thinkers wrote books at the outbreak of the war to argue just the opposite in the case of Germany; to insist, that is, that Germany's very philosophy of history imbues the nation with a mentality that renders it unaware of the character and meaning of its own actions. Thorstein Veblen, George Santayana, and John Dewey all sniffed something rotten in Germany. The three authors would suggest to American soldiers that they are fighting two enemies: German monarchy and German philosophy. The speculative reflections of these American authors arose in response to the cannons of 1914, just as a century earlier Hegel was moved to meditation after observing Napoleon in the battle of Jena. If Hegel had seen "an Idea on horseback," Santayana saw "philosophical idealism" culminating in "big battalions."

AMERICAN PHILOSOPHERS AND THE MIND OF GERMANY

Americans read about the plight of Belgium during the German occupation with anger and tears. The outbreak of World War I, after it turned into carnage, provided a kind of delayed shock in America, particularly among American intellectuals who had looked forward to the twentieth century as a cultural renaissance. "Regeneration seemed to be everywhere at hand," wrote the Greenwich Village literary radical Randolph Bourne. "The pessimism and restlessness of the *Weltschmerz* (world affliction) seemed to have given place everywhere to an outburst of élan." Then came the horror of August 1914, and Bourne confesses that his generation "had not really believed that there existed in the world an initiative capable of willing the World War, and we had to learn not only that there was such a power, but also the persistent ruthlessness of its initiative." Wherein lies "such a power"? Bourne and his generation focused on the one symbol that seemed the antithesis of everything democratic:

> In the first shock of disillusionment, when the world seemed to turn black and sick around us, all this civilization that we had been so hopefully watching, turned a ghastly mockery in the presence of this grim superhuman power, so eternal, so indomitable. Once more we had to learn that it had conquered. We had to taste all the bitterness of the truth that this incredible, which everybody feared and nobody expected, had happened. The precise combination of all the evil coincidences had occurred, and in the presence of the opportunity, this militarism, which for forty years had been playing with the fate of nations

was to be like adamant against all those human and rational considerations that our hopes and good wills had been creating below it. One
had only to hear the Kaiser speak to "his people" on that historic day
in Berlin, and see that sinister, helmeted figure, the very personification
of nonhuman, irrational force, to realize how little weight all those
notions of personal, social, or even national welfare would have against
the grandiose ideals of prestige, aggrandizement, and imperialism incar-
nated in him.[19]

How exactly did the "precise combination of all the evil coincidences"
culminate in German history and result in a war whose coming no one
dared contemplate? At this juncture in American history most writers
had little doubt Germany was responsible for the war—in contrast to the
post-Versailles era when, feeling guilty about America's entry into the
war and the alleged betrayal of the 14 Points, the contrite in America
deemed Germany an innocent victim and England the aggressor whose
propaganda manipulated America to join the Allied powers. Yet the three
American intellectuals who came forward with books implied that Germany and America faced one another on the battlefield because each
country inhabited entirely different philosophical universes: Thorstein
Veblen, *Imperial Germany and the Industrial Revolution* (1915); John Dewey,
German Philosophy and Politics (1915); George Santayana, *Egotism in German Philosophy* (1915).

Veblen's critique of Germany was not that far removed from Weber's
own critique, but with an ironic twist. During the war years, when
Weber was advocating that Germany reform its parliamentary institutions
by looking to England as a model, Veblen was arguing that Germany
would emerge as a dangerous world power precisely because its Prussian
traditions bypassed western liberalism and identified economic development with the authority of the state. England was suffering "the penalty
of taking the lead," Veblen prophesied, as Germany borrows her technology and moves ahead unimpeded by England's political habits and
institutions. Weber would agree that Germany posed the paradox of having a retarded political culture and an advanced technological mentality,
along with a highly bureaucratized state and educational system. But
while Weber sought to overcome the deficiency by having Germany
turn to political liberalism, Veblen saw science and technology as the salvation of modern industrial society.[20]

John Dewey was less interested in Germany's peculiar stage of historical development than in her "philosophical absolutism" that deifies the
State. Kant's "Gospel of duty" instructs people to do their duty and obey

without specifying what their duties are. As a consequence and, as Dewey acknowledges, a distortion of Kant, people have nowhere to turn to obey and carry out their obligations other than to the seat of political authority. While Kant rested ethics upon moral intent and seemed almost indifferent to practical consequences, Fichte and Hegel denied Kant's separation of the two worlds (the unknowable noumena and the observable phenomenal) and instead united the two in order to identify "Absolute Spirit" with the State. The result of this synthesis has been, Dewey noted in descriptions similar to those of Veblen, a "combination of self-conscious idealism with unsurpassed technical efficiency and organization in the varied fields of action," a combination that blurred the distinction between ends and means and endowed Germany with a dangerous sense of historical destiny.[21]

George Santayana addressed an issue that would later, after the Nazi era, become a deadly riddle: How can Germany enjoy the "highest *Kultur*" and be possessed by the lowest instincts? In *Egotism in German Philosophy* Santayana describes the German mind as exalting emotion above reason and regarding egotism—"subjectivity in thought and willfulness in morals"—as something to be glorified rather than disciplined. German philosophy suffers from superhuman ambition in which the mind mistakes itself for the cosmos and the German people are easily led by philosophy to see in military means the expression of idealistic ends. "In this philosophy imagination that is sustained is called knowledge, illusion that is coherent is called truth, and will that is systematic is called virtue." Santayana named names. Fichte's theory of race, which depicted the German people leading the rest of the world out of the past and into the future; and Hegel's theory of history, which went so far as to read egotism into the dialectic so that "everything involves its opposite" and things are made to conform to words—all such pretentions sustained the conviction that Providence and Prussia were one and the same and that history has "its beginning in Eden and its end in Berlin."[22]

What Santayana scarcely considered in his book is that the egotism he attributed to the German mind could as easily have been found in the American—in, for example, Emerson's doctrine of the "Oversoul" and Whitman's "cosmic consciousness." It may even be seen when Woodrow Wilson's utter, absolute trust in democracy becomes "subjectivity" in politics and "willfulness" in diplomacy (the subject of the next chapter).

But the larger issue is that the three American thinkers had no knowledge whatsoever of Weber's writings—Veblen and a few others knew the Protestant ethic thesis, but none were familiar with Weber's vast treatises on world religions and his essays on philosophy and methodology. When

Santayana's book was published in France the translator wryly placed on the title page: "*Je Suis, donc tu n'est pas.*" Weber could not have agreed more about such epistemological egotism; it is not difficult imagining him saying to contemporary Hegelian philosophers: what begins in spirit ends in solipsism. How accurate then was the American assumption that the war somehow sprang from Germany's philosophical arrogance?

At the very time these American books came out in something like a philosophical assault upon Germany, Weber was quietly writing essays and revising his thoughts on subjects that suggested the limits of knowledge, the diversity of cultures, and the incommensurability of all values. Sensitive to the "crisis of historicism," Weber refused to conceive of history as a meaningful continuum that carried a uniform set of evaluative criteria as well as an unfolding telos. Rather than seeing history beginning in Eden and culminating in Berlin, Weber allowed his curiosities to take him to the four corners of the earth.

During the war years, Weber expanded his study of Protestantism and began to investigate various world religions. Where the Hegelian looks for unity and totality, Weber saw diversity and variety, as though truth lies not only in the details but in the distinctions that could be discerned in different beliefs, churches, sects, charismatic manifestions, and mentalities of asceticism and mysticism. His differential analysis of Judaism, Confucianism, Buddhism, Islam, and other religions aimed to explain, in light of the claims of universal history, the uniqueness of phenomena and the varied pace of change and development. If Weber implied that western development represented the highest form of civilization, he had no commitment to the view that the western pattern was special and irreversible. His vision of modern rationalization, the reduction of all life into institutionalized systems and structures, played havoc with Hegel's idea of "Reason" and "Spirit" coming to consciousness in the course of history.

American philosophers contributed to the impression that the German mind suffered from the hubris of certainty as it identified its own subjective will with the objective course of events. Another impression also emerged, particularly soon after the war in such books as *All Quiet on the Western Front*, that the academic calling in Germany had succumbed to nationalistic fervor as professors prostituted themselves to the grandiose promises of patriotism. Although Weber felt deeply the stirrings of patriotism, and hardly discouraged students from going off to fight for their country, during the war he never lost his cool prudence about politics and the life of the mind.

An example of Weber's capacity for sobriety amid the heady passions of the war years may be seen in an essay he revised sometime around

1916, "The Meaning of 'Ethical Neutrality' in Sociology and Economics." The essay was directed in part at Gustav von Schmoller and other
academic socialists (*Kathedersozialisten*) who had been teaching the
virtues of the "expansive state" as part of the "socialism of the future."
Such teachings, Weber charged, simply read into history the emotions
and prejudices of the teachers themselves, who ignored any objective
appraisal of such developments in view of the realities of bureaucracy, and
thus allowed themselves to be led into "abjuring not only the consecra-
tion of German philosophy, but also of religion . . . that is nothing but a
disgraceful lapse of taste on the part of self-important literati."[23]

Weber's advocacy of "ethical neutrality" was articulated at the same
time President Wilson advocated diplomatic neutrality as the best way of
keeping the United States from going to war. But for Weber neutrality
did not signify a refusal to take sides or even a disinterested reluctance to
become involved in the issues of the day. What neutrality signified was
the imperative of resisting the temptation to impose personal values in
the guise of scientific data, the duty to recognize that moral judgments
belong to one sphere of human activity and logically deduced and
empirically observed facts to another. Yet students and fellow professors,
Weber noted, have been insisting that passion and the promptings of conscience are essential to any knowledge endeavor that allows the complete
person to express his whole being. How can one be neutral and at the
same time be human? Does not objectivity rule out personal commitment? Did not Hegel teach us that the object and the subject are one in
the same?

Weber made it clear that passion and commitment were important, but
that they were to be directed to the requirements of the task and the
demands of the object one is studying. Authentic learning, he believed, is
less a matter of personal satisfaction than professional devotion, a matter of
allowing our beliefs to be influenced by something beyond ourselves, what
is without rather than what is within. Thus Weber sustains the separation
of spheres that American philosophers saw German philosophy as having
collapsed into a dangerous illusion. Objectivity (*Sachlichkeit*) he saw as
demanding commitment to the object (*Sache*), for genuine knowledge is
compelled by its object. The practical import of all this is that professors
should leave their predilections behind as they enter the classroom and students should cease confusing "being a personality" with being a scholar
dedicated to a discipline:

Like everyone else, the professor has other opportunities for the prop-
agation of his ideals. When these opportunities are lacking, he can eas-

ily create them in an appropriate form, as experience has shown in the case of every honourable attempt. But the professor should not demand the right as a professor to carry the marshal's baton of the statesman or the cultural reformer in his knapsack. This, however, is just what he does when he uses the unassailability of the academic lecture platform for the expression of political—or cultural-political—sentiments. In the press, in public meetings, in associations, in essays, in every avenue which is open to every other citizen, he can and should do what his God or daemon demands. The student should obtain, from his teacher in the lecture hall, the capacity to content himself with the sober execution of a given task; to recognise facts, even those which may be personally uncomfortable, and to distinguish them from his own evaluations. He should also learn to subordinate himself to his task and to repress the impulse to exhibit his personal sensations or other emotional states unnecessarily. This is vastly more important today than it was 40 years ago when the problem did not even exist in its present form. It is not true—as many have insisted—that the "personality" is and should be a "whole", in the sense that it is distorted when it is not exhibited on every possible occasion.[24]

A timely message, published in *Logos* in spring 1917—about the same time President Woodrow Wilson, a former university professor, went before the U.S. Congress to declare war on Germany.

NINE

"Peace Without Victory" and "Gambling on Gratitude": Woodrow Wilson and Max Weber

"DISMAL DAYS OF DISGRACE"
—

In fall 1916 Max and Marianne took a brief vacation at Lake Constance, a few days of escape from the stresses of supervising a hospital for almost a half year without respite. A little earlier Ernst Troeltsch had found Weber on edge with his colleagues and attributed the tension to his working twelve to thirteen hours a day. On one occasion Weber became "so irritable that our relations suffered a severe blow," wrote Troeltsch to his publisher as he described the temporary parting of ways. At first Lake Constance had a soothing effect. The soft blue color of the water and the autumn fragrance of the woods offered a few, rare moments of relief from the real world. "But," noted Marianne, "dark memories obtruded themselves upon the harmonious images. It was on the lake that Weber had vainly sought recovery eighteen years before and had had a premonition of his long suffering."[1]

In the war years the unaddressed problems of German history caught up with Germany. Weber grew impatient with the failure of political leadership in Theobold von Bethmann-Hollweg, the Chancellor who bungled peace negotiations with Russia. The military situation was also beginning to look grim. On the eastern front the German army withstood the numerically superior Russian forces; but on the southern front the Italian army held its own on Austrian territory; and in the west the war of attrition had no end in sight and no guarantee that the German lines would not crack. Such a stalemate angered Weber all the more as he felt his own potential contribution to the war effort had been rejected by mediocre government officials. "Does one have to be an ass or a careerist to be accepted by the authorities?"[2]

The issue on which Weber's advice had been disastrously rejected involved the decision to resume U-boat warfare. In spring 1916 Germany faced a dilemma: the military had advised the government that isolation of England would be impossible without the massive employment of submarines. Yet that policy certainly meant American intervention. Perhaps if carried out suddenly, the strategic surrounding of the British Isles by subs would be effective before America could mobilize an all-out war effort. Weber, together with a Viennese scholar, composed a declaration against intensified U-boat employment that he sent to high public officials. Weber held that Germany's enemies would be better persuaded to consider a cease-fire if Germany publicly renounced its annexationist war aims. In April, when the French passenger ship *Sussex* was torpedoed, and the United States demanded an end to such attacks without warning, Weber became incensed, describing the sinking as "an unparalleled dirty trick (*Schwenerei*), the most stupid thing that could have been done," as he noted that men, women, and children of several nationalities were on board. "If things go on like this—I hope not!—we are certain to be at war with the whole world."[3]

Germany did concede to American demands, but the concession depended on America asking England to grant "freedom of the seas," which meant lifting the blockade on the Continent. Weber saw the futility of asking a neutral to intercede against an adversary. Besides, why should the safety of American lives on the high seas, wondered Weber, be dependent on the uncertain relations of two belligerents? Germany found herself in a pattern of aggressive acts and contrite confessions, only to be followed by a proviso that such attacks may occur again if need be. All this, Weber complained, "gives Wilson a chance to say, 'I'm doing *nothing*, but I shall wait and see whether you behave well, and then, we shall see.' And then the *Sussex* affair; these stupid denials and the subsequent obligation to confess are extremely unfortunate." What Germans cannot comprehend, Weber warned, is that they are dealing with an American political leader who refused to compromise principle regarding freedom of the seas and the rights of neutrals. If Germany does not wish war with America, its leaders should cease gambling on the assumption that other political cultures behave in the same ways. "In his pedantry, which is so unfortunate for us, Wilson has remained absolutely true to himself. That is just what people here do not understand, that someone should carry on a *purely* formalistic policy, like a jurist in a lecture course or a doctoral examination, and conclude even his note with a sentence that surely came out of his notebook on responsibility in international law. We, on the other hand, are so proud of our *Realpolitik*, which we have turned into a theory. The President pursues policies like a juristic discussion in a scholarly dispute."[4]

Weber would have to cope with Wilson again and again as the war drew to a close. The first thoughts between the two scholarly thinkers, one an absolutist and purist, the other a dualist and skeptic, gave a prophetic hint of things to come. For when Wilson went before the U.S. Congress to declare America's entry into the war in April 1917, Weber recognized that the balance of military forces had shifted decidedly in favor of the Allies. As Weber gave up making pronouncements on foreign policy and implicitly began to contemplate Germany's defeat, he expected the United States to emerge as a world power. Herein an ironic confrontation was in the making. With the prospect of surrender, Germany would have to relinquish its traditional *Realpolitik*; with the prospect of victory, America would assume, for the first time in history, a role of world leadership without a traditional *Realpolitik*. What tradition, then, could once-formerly isolated America draw upon to implement its peace terms?

For Wilson the tradition would be the principle of national self-determination, a legacy deriving from America's Jeffersonian states-rights tradition, which had deep roots in Wilson's own Virginia background. That tradition had once identified with racist sentiment and state sovereignty as the last means of resisting the authority of the national government. No doubt Wilson viewed the principle of national self-determination as progressive and liberating. But the doctrine of states-rights, the substratum behind the principle, rather than establishing the basis for peace, led to the Civil War.

In late fall 1917 Weber traveled to Vienna on personal business. Immediately he was approached about taking a teaching position. Earlier, colleagues at Munich also had offered him a lectureship. Weber strongly rejected it, telling Marianne, who had encouraged him to return to teaching: "Terrible that you should still entertain the notion that I could get on a lecture platform!"[5] But as a change Vienna was more attractive, and in 1918 Weber agreed on a trial basis to take a chair in political economy at the university.

In the midst of World War I Weber had already returned to some of the studies he had earlier explored, taking from his files old manuscripts abandoned at the war's outbreak. Once again he entered into questions of social organization and power, comparative studies of business ethics and world religions, and ancient Judaism, which led him to reflect upon the historical role of the prophet.

Weber was struck at discovering that the old Hebrew prophets made no claim to omniscience, or to knowledge of the supernatural, or to a "metaphysical gnosis and interpretation of the world." Israelite prophecy confined itself to this world. German statesmanship should be familiar with this subordination of soaring transcendence to practical technique. "For Bismarck the exclusion of all metaphysical rumination and in its stead the psalter on his night table was one of the preconditions for conduct unbroken by philosophy. Likewise the Jews and the religious communities influenced by them were affected by this barricade against pondering the meaning of the cosmos."[6]

Indifferent to philosophical issues, prophets are invariably caught up in politics, Weber noted, for they appear when a homeland is threatened by a foreign power. Yet unlike the Christian prophet, the Jewish one is a solitary figure who need not depend upon a spiritual following. The prophet of doom is feared, and even if events prove him right, he can never feel triumphant after the disasters he predicted come to pass. The lonely prophet, observed Weber, no doubt with thoughts of his own predicament in mind, implores God to release him from prophesying misfortune that can only have been willed by a Supreme Being who refuses to explain the why of the world. In a chapter titled "Warfare and War Prophecy," Weber notes that the utopian, pacifistic fantasies of a prophet undergo a change of image among intellectuals in time of martial conflict; they take on a bloody connotation created by those who need not face the battlefield: "Just as today, in all countries, we find the highest measure of war thirst among those strata of literati who are farthest from the trenches and by nature least military."[7]

Least military, perhaps, but no less militant. In his addresses on education and science, Weber condemned professors who took on the role of prophet and claimed the "gift of grace" as seers and sages who knew the meaning of the universe and the direction of history. In the World War I years the "literati" voiced the various -isms with a vengeance, as though history was vindicating ideology. Socialism as the promise of international brotherhood proved to be an illusion when socialist parties in various countries voted to support war preparedness in their respective parliaments. But the world might still be redeemed by pacifism, anarchism, syndicalism, and, after October 1917, bolshevism. Two months after the October Revolution in Russia, Weber wrote to a friend that the present generation would lay claim to the resurrection of Germany in which he had once believed. He himself still hoped for "a third youth" (Treitschke's phrase) of the German nation, which again might arise and be admitted to a leadership role. "Never has it been so deeply regarded as a gift of fate to be a German as in these dismal days of disgrace."[8] But while Weber was attempting to salvage dignity from the disgrace of impending defeat, he believed all the more that politics required cool prudence rather than ideological headiness.

Before Weber took the chair at the University of Vienna, he spent the previous summer and fall at Lauenstein Castle in the Franconia forest in central Germany. The towering medieval castle had been refurbished and made into a cultural center for artists and writers and a think tank for academics. It was a strange setting. Some of the most modern thinkers in German intellectual life walked the hallways amid "dim tapestried chambers where ancient worm-eaten furniture loomed ghostly in the dark . . . feeling like medieval knights, missionaries of the Holy Ghost."[9] Residents occupied rooms looking out on dramatic wooded mountain slopes and met for discussion in the castle yard or the *Rittersaal*, the hall of knights. Well-known scholars and cultural figures argued whether Germany could find its salvation in art, religion, or politics. The older men had been shaken by the catastrophe of war, the younger were impatient with soul-searching and hungering for a new vision of the future. While sympathizing with the youths' idealism, Weber scorned the therapy of open communal confession and their demand for immediate answers to ultimate questions, which only "give rise to gabbing talk and sensationalism and nothing more." Confessions belong in the intimacy of a small circle of people, not the public courtyard. "Only a prophet or a saint and (in his language) an artist acts differently and is allowed to act differently."[10] According to Marianne, the students at Lauenstein Castle pleaded with Weber to become their leader and show the way to Germany's salvation. But Weber reminded them he was a scholar, not a prophet, and it was their fate to live in a godless time, to endure, not prevail.

One student who argued with Weber as much as he admired him was Ernst Toller, the pacifist poet whose verse radiated the primal goodness and solidarity of the human race. Toller was also an anarchist, one who affirms the future and looks forward to total statelessness, in which all structures of authority (fated, according to Weber, to always be somewhere) disappear into nowhere. Weber realized that anarchists had no future in a world where all politics is resolved by power in some form, where even persuasion and manipulation amount to coercion of the mind. Although Toller and other anarchists had their heads in the clouds, Weber admired them because of their uncompromising spirit and willingness to live for principles rather than whoring after power. Toller especially lived up to Weber's ideals, even to Weber's surprise.

A courageous, legendary figure, Toller was always running afoul of the law. Weber intervened twice to secure his release from jail. The first time Toller had been arrested for agitating for a general strike against the war. The second arrest, far more serious, resulted from Toller's role in fomenting the uprising in Munich in November 1918, when the Bavarian state had been called a "Soviet Republic," or what some of its creators called *ein Kaffeehausraterepublik*, a coffeehouse city hall republic led by the literati. When Toller was incarcerated in a military prison, written statements in his defense testifying to the ethical slant of his writings came in from eminent German intellectuals, including Thomas Mann. Weber, trained in law, appeared in court to give testimony. Weber's defense was on the basis of, in today's American legal terms, "diminished capacity" on the part of one who cannot think things through to the end.

In his testimony Weber expressed "deep sympathy for the defendant," a man of principle and "of entirely upright character." But Toller acted out of "an ethic of ultimate ends" without considering the consequences of his actions. A talented poet, Toller was unstable and, in the name of helping humankind, allowed his emotions to be carried away to the point of losing all sight of original intentions. Weber told the court he had earlier counseled Toller to distance himself from the mass politics of the street. With a wry, Calvinist irony, Weber then added, "God in His wrath chose Toller to be a politician."[11]

To the surprise of Weber and the court, Toller and his counsel rejected Weber's reasoning and characterization. Not only did Toller claim to know the realities of the political world, he rejected Weber's distinction between an "ethic of ultimate ends" and an "ethic of responsibility" (which, as will be discussed, became central to Weber's seminal essay "Politics as a Vocation") by denying that there were any mitigating circumstances and declaring that he was prepared to take full responsibility and be accountable for his ideals, even at the risk of receiving a death sentence.

Weber could not help but admire Toller as a person of pure conviction and unswerving responsibility. Toller was sentenced to five years' imprisonment. "I had committed high treason, but with honorable intent," he wrote in his memoirs. But Weber left Toller pondering the riddle of means and ends. "Was Max Weber right in saying that if we do not wish to resist evil by force, we must live like St. Francis, that for the absolute demand there is only one way, the way of the Saint?"[12]

THE PEN AND THE SWORD

In winter 1917, six months after the United States had entered the war and Weber started to sense Germany's defeat, a saying could be occasionally heard in private meetings and public assemblies: "The pen restores what the sword has ruined." The epigram abbreviated a similar one heard after the defeat of Napoleon and the Congress of Vienna in 1815, to the effect that diplomats must not be allowed to restore what common soldiers had valiantly brought to an end on the field of battle. When the saying was attributed to Weber, he wrote an angry letter to the *Heidelberger Tageblatt,* making explicit what he did say: that the German military must by all means not allow itself to become politicized "lest someday you have allowed that which you have achieved with the sword to be ruined by letting yourself be dropped into the bustle and onto the thin ice of domestic party struggles."[13]

Already the suspicion was growing that Germany's surrender would be neither easily understood nor readily accepted, even if conditionally negotiated in good faith.

Although an ardent nationalist, Weber was far from an arrogant chauvinist. Karl Jaspers described Weber as the "last national German," a thinker whose idea of the nation had little room for a fanatical worship of the supremacy of the state. The idea of the nation was more an "inner feeling" than an external entity. "Of course," Jaspers conceded, nation and state, the "internal and external are relative to one another." Still, for Weber one represented the "spirit," the other the "form."[14]

Jaspers was trying to dissociate Weber's nationalism from the brutal excesses of the Third Reich's Fatherland cult. But the distinction between spirit and form could hardly be maintained as Weber turned his attention to the future reconstitution of Germany. With the end of the war in sight in 1918, Weber became involved in two struggles that would

shape the course of history. The first task was to redefine the nature of
Germany's political institutions so as to influence the drafting of the new
constitution; the second was to have some voice in accepting the conditions of surrender so as to leave Germany secure rather than vulnerable
and, in addition, to challenge accusations of Germany's war guilt. The
second issue, to be taken up in the next section, had Weber confronting
Woodrow Wilson and American liberalism; the first, discussed below, had
him confronting the ghost of Bismarck and German conservatism.

Weber had to face a daunting challenge in his writings on Germany's
future: How to reassure the German people that their political culture is
worthy and unique but not so exceptional or superior that it could
remain viable without adopting foreign ideas? Ever since his Freiburg
inaugural address in 1895, Weber thought of Germany's "responsibility to
history," and that obligation made him impatient with pacifists who
would renounce all power, without which such responsibility could
never be faced. At the same time it was the pacifists who were cosmopolitan and universalist in their loyalties. Thus Weber's challenge was
to strike a balance between nationalism and cosmopolitanism. "The Germans should peacefully and without reservations," he wrote in 1915,
"cultivate their unique qualities in the context of the *Volkerband*." And
yet he argued against those who contrasted the German spirit—"as
unique, self-sufficient, and higher"—against the democratic individualism of western Europe and America.[15] In advising Germany to look
abroad for some measure of political guidance, and to reexamine its own
political system in the light of day, Weber was also going against Germany's Hegelian tradition, which insisted that "it is absolutely essential
that the constitution should not be regarded as something made, even
though it has come into being."[16] Once again Weber was behaving differently and not engaging in the dangerous metapolitics that American
philosophers saw as the curse of the German mind. In writing about
Germany's political reconstruction, Weber never suggested that the origins of a nation's political authority must remain veiled in secrecy until
the progressive movememt of history allows thought to become conscious of itself; nor did he believe that the war was about the evils of Germany's monarchy as well as its philosophy:

> People *abroad* imagine "autocracy" is to blame. At *home* the childish
> speculations of our litterateurs have led many to the opposite view,
> namely, that a conspiracy of international "democracy" against Ger-
> many has supposedly brought about the unnatural coalition of the
> world against us. Abroad they use the hypocritical slogan, "Free the

Germans from autocracy!" At home those with vested interests in the status quo—we shall get to know them better—speak with equal hypocrisy of the need to preserve the "German spirit" from the stain of "democracy," or they look for other scapegoats.[17]

Weber faced the task of explaining to his country why the time had come to accept parliamentarization and democratization at a time when Germany was fighting parliamentary democracy. He undertook the task in five articles in the *Frankfurter Zeitung* that later appeared as a pamphlet, *Parlament und Regierung im Neugeordneten Deutschland* (Parliament and government in a newly constituted Germany). These articles, bringing to light the faults and defects of a government in time of war, rendered Weber dangerously close to other "*Vaterlandlöse Gesellen*" as he too appeared to be in the company of literati without a homeland who allegedly had no loyalty to their government. But Weber was trying to save Germany not only from its enemies but from itself.

That Germany allowed itself to be surrounded by rival powers Weber attributed to the nation's lack of political education and to the "politics of national vanity" on the part of its leaders. Under Bismarck's rule Germans lost all opportunity to develop a sense of participatory citizenship in an electorate that might have cooperated in making decisions affecting its own political destiny. Intolerant of conflict and disagreement, Bismarck reduced Parliament to self-abnegation and the masses to complacent passivity. Weber even suggested that Bismarck's use of American patterns of patronage, the granting of pensions on the assumption that gratitude (*Dankbarkeit*) would enhance pro-state sentiment (*Staatsgesinnung*), had no success since politics has more to do with struggle and might than sentiment and memory. Whatever Hegel was supposed to have done to unify the actuating force of things in Germany, according to American philosophers, Bismarck, according to Weber, did the opposite and left Germany fragmented and without the two qualities necessary for a politics of dignity—intellect and will.[18]

Weber's analysis of parliament and government in Germany has some resemblance to the earlier critiques of American democracy leveled by Tocqueville and James Fenimore Cooper. Weber too complained that politics thrives on opinion and manipulated impression when it should express truth, character, and integrity. Politics has no place for born leaders, the wisest and the worthiest, statesmen who live for convictions rather than settle for convenience and compliance. But whereas Tocqueville and Cooper attributed the "courtier spirit" to the pressures of mass democracy that result in social conformity and political demagoguery, Weber saw the problem of mendacity and mediocrity as less democratic than bureaucratic, less the responsibility of the masses than the debilitating positions held by professional politicians, salaried party officials, advocates, and other "satraps" who would never think of sacrificing their office to their convictions. Weber worried less about democracy than about modernity. The "active democratization of the masses" may lead to a distasteful politics of aspersion and demagoguery, but this is a result of politics being institutionally restricted to the "rule of conservative officialdom."[19] It is bureaucracy that impersonalizes politics and deprives it of its potential values of dignity and responsibility. Political activity suffocates under hierarchical arrangements of offices, which conceal the personality of the agent behind a plethora of rules and regulations. Politics as an activity of freedom and accountability is incompatible with bureaucracy as a system of subordination and rationalization. And it was the bureaucratic structure of the German government that made it impossible for parliament to restrain the vanities of the Kaiser and his military advisors and their disastrous foreign policy.

In calling for a thoroughgoing reform of parliament, Weber did not hesitate to charge the Prussian conservatives with seeking to pass legislation during wartime to secure their land holdings to the disadvantage of farmers and the interest of the nation. To oppose their power Weber advocated the end to the three-tier suffrage system which, by allowing the richest taxpayers to elect the same number of representatives as the other two classes, had enabled the East Elbian landed aristocracy and big industrialists to predominate in Prussian politics. Weber had all along advocated extending the suffrage to German workers in Prussia, realizing that the materialist needs of the socialist laborer, despite the radical rhetoric of the Socialist Party, were conservative and satisfiable short of revolution. The war provided the opportunity to insist that soldiers at the front, indeed anyone qualified to wear a uniform, deserves the ballot. Weber saw democratization not only as a means of wresting power from the Junkers but also as a way of preempting the temptation of war-weary Germans to make social revolution, a possibility that could not be ignored after 1917, when Germany suffered catastrophic food shortages and some striking workers could look to revolutionary Russia as a beacon.

Weber stood against proportional representation, pluralism, "particularism," and any arrangement that would privilege a specific occupation, ethnic group, class, or intellect (literacy tests). Such preferences could scarcely reflect the ever-changing nature of the electorate while at the same time placing power in the hands of economic interest groups and accelerating the process of bureaucratization. Any arrangement that constrains political activity by misleading people into assuming that they are adequately represented by political professionals and desk-bound officials was anathema to Weber. His ideal of politics sprang from the spirit of volunteerism, which in turn derived from American sources.[20]

Weber's investigations of religion in America, especially the essay he wrote after the study of Protestantism and capitalism, the article "Churches and Sects in North America," became an important aspect of his subsequent thoughts on politics and society. Weber distinguished a church, which is corporate and authoritarian and functions like an "endowed foundation" with membership obligatory, from a sect, which is a voluntary association with membership a "religious probation" on the part of those morally qualified. In advising Germans to look to older Puritan ideas, even to "the American 'club' and associations of every kind based on selective choices of members," Weber hoped to see politics as voluntary and spontaneous, arising from character and will and serving ultimate values.[21] An American perspective could well describe the emphasis on liberal individualism as the Jeffersonian side of Weber. But as noted earlier, in the Introduction, there is also a Hamiltonian dimension in Weber that emphasizes the need for strong government and dynamic leadership and a citizenry less interested in the will to freedom than in the imperatives of duty and responsibility. In light of these contradictory tendencies in western liberalism, which contains both a politics of realization and a politics of subordination, was Weber influenced by America in his rethinking the nature of Germany's government?

Weber had serious doubts about the American party system. Thriving on patronage and the spoils system, party politics made, Weber noted with perhaps a little exaggeration, "the interests of more than a hundred thousand office seekers ride with the result of each election." Germany has "*Weltanschauung* parties," themselves just as opportunistic in shifting platforms to satisfy constituencies. Representation in America is also "inimitable" for Germany, since the Senate has the same number of votes for each state regardless of size; Delaware, Weber exclaimed to German readers, was "barely one-thirtieth the size of New York"—not exactly, but Weber saw clearly how geography trumped demography, giving rural America more power than its numbers warranted. In America popular elections reduce the citizen to an occasional voter, increase the power of party bosses and political corruption, and cater to the emotion of the mass, which "thinks," Weber observed, quoting an unnamed source, "only as far as the day after tomorrow."[22]

England's "venerable parliamentary system" impressed Weber more than America's popular democratic government. Parliamentary democracy produced better leaders who were more independent of both the electorate and, at times, the party, and its older gentry tradition of recruitment, though perhaps now fading, preserved England from the bureaucratization of government that befell other countries. In his wartime writings on parliament and government Weber had in mind the British system as the best means of protecting individual liberties and promoting political responsibility among the people's chosen leaders.[23]

Toward the end of the war, however, Weber became emphatic about a subject only hinted at in his earlier writings—the superiority of plebiscitary democracy to parliamentary democracy. Although he had earlier believed that parliaments could constitute a check on the ambitions of a "Caesarist leader who enjoyed the confidence of the masses," he now advocated, in his article "*Der Reichspräsident*" and elsewhere, precisely what he had once warned against—a popularly elected president who leads by gaining the trust of the people and who is thereby free to carry out his own convictions, as opposed to an elected official who must act according to the latest whim of the electorate. What accounts for Weber's change of mind?[24]

The closer Weber moved away from theory to face reality and the more he served as an advisor to the committee on Germany's new constitution, the more he believed that parliament would be beholden to sectional interests and party divisiveness. Somehow Weber believed that politics could emanate from spontaneous volunteerism and lead to unity, purpose, and direction. Yet like the *Federalist* authors, especially Hamilton, Weber doubted that representative government could rise above the centrifugal forces of economics. Parliament would continue to be dominated by wheeling and dealing, the "horse-trading" of favors and contracts, what in contemporary America is called "pork barrel" politics. Germany had only two choices, Weber insisted: a plebiscitary president, hopefully with some "inner charismatic qualities which made him a leader" capable of commanding the support of the people, or the competition of "party malcontents" who settle for the "rule of cliques."[25] One makes freedom a measure of conviction, the other leaves it to chance.

Ironically, Weber's advocacy of plebiscitary democracy led him, as Mommsen has noted, to embrace what he had earlier condemned in Bismarck: the "personal rule" of a dominant figure who leads the nation at the expense of leaving the electorate submissive and passive.[26] What Weber came to value in leadership was independence, freedom from restraint so that the policies of the nation-state could be determined by ideals higher than the pluralistic grub politics of electoral satisfaction, whose only purpose is to reassure one's reelection. Weber's idea of the

Reichspräsident reigning above parliament would later create the impression that he was responsible for article 48 of the constitution of the new German government of the Weimar Republic, which allowed in 1930–33 President Paul von Hindenberg's authoritarian rule and supposedly made possible the "führer principle" and the charismatic dictatorship of Hitler. (This controversial subject will come up in the Epilogue.) More immediately, it should be noted here that Weber's notion of a plebiscitary leader who would speak over the heads of parliament and government to reach directly the people themselves, and a leader convinced of the righteousness of his own aims and principles, would characterize none other than the American president Woodrow Wilson when he went to Europe to redeem Europe of its own sins.

WILSONIANISM VERSUS WEBERIANISM

To such a task we can dedicate our lives and our fortunes,
everything that we have, with the pride of those who know that
the day has come when America is privileged to spend her
blood and her might for the principles that gave her birth and
happiness and the peace which she had treasured. God helping
her, she can do no other.

Woodrow Wilson, April 2, 1917

It is immensely moving when a *mature* man—no matter whether
old or young in years—is aware of a responsibility for the
consequences of his conduct and really feels such responsibility
with heart and soul. He then acts by following an ethic of
responsibility and somewhere he reaches a point where he says:
"Here I stand; I can do no other." That is something genuinely
human and moving.

Max Weber, January 28, 1919

Weber is not referring to Wilson, and the American leader, a potential mediator who would ultimately let Germany down, knew nothing of Europe's most learned social scientist. Yet both Wilson and Weber cite Martin Luther's declaration to the Diet of Worms, "God helping me, I can do no other," to dramatize the taking of an ultimate, irrevocable stance. Wilson's words were spoken in his momentous speech to the U.S. Congress seeking approval of a declaration of war upon Germany and the Axis powers; Weber's words were uttered in his now-famous address "Politics as a Vocation." Ironically, Weber held that only one who was willing to follow Luther's injunction and engage a sinful world of power can fight evil on its own terms. "Insofar as this is true, an ethic of ultimate ends and an ethic of responsibility are not absolute contrasts but rather supplements, which only in unison constitute a genuine man—a man who *can* have a 'calling for politics.'"[27] Weber saw evil as an inescapable component of history and power politics, a vision that endowed his thoughts with a sense of tragedy to the extent that evil cannot be eliminated by the innocent claims of goodness and virtue. But Wilson went to war to fight power with piety. Did he have a "calling for politics"?

The backgrounds of Wilson and Weber are similar in several respects. Both were born and died within a few years of one another (Wilson, 1856–1924; Weber, 1864–1920) and thus lived to witness the emergence of modern industrial society. They were also reared in devout Protestant households and studied law before entering the academic profession, where they similarly engaged in issues of curriculum and administrative reform. Each admired the English system of government and became passionately devoted to the moral reformation of their own respective governments. The German and the American also assumed that such a reformation depended upon the discipline of social science and that freedom had no future without an understanding of history, even if the past has no necessary bearing upon the present. Finally, both believed that good government should speak to its people in the name of knowledge and reason rather than interest and power. But it is here, on the question of the nature of representative government, where Wilson seems more Weberian and Weber more Wilsonian.

In his articles on parliament and government, written prior to his advocating plebiscitary democracy, Weber saw in representative government a beneficial "division of labor," for the exercise of power by officials engaged in the techniques of administration "rests on *knowledge*." Weber justified parliamentary committees as educational in that their members needed to possess "technical *specialist knowledge*" acquired from fact-finding investigations and cross-examining witnesses and from having possession of concrete facts by means of access to files and other resources of the official apparatus. Thus he believed it essential that parliament had the "right of inquiry" (*Enqueterecht*). Armed with such knowledge, members of parliament can scrutinize administrative ruling and render government accountable.[28]

Weber had all along, as noted earlier, defended parliamentary government as a training ground for future political leaders. But here a quandary arises. How can qualities of leadership emerge from the mundane day-to-day operations of parliament by officials whose work is investigative and procedural rather than combative and political? The parliamentary official, Weber insisted, takes pride in subduing his own predispositions in order to be objective and to execute conscientiously the tasks assigned to him by the definition of his committee duties. A politician, in contrast, leads by allocating assignments, clarifying issues, and speaking and acting out of conviction. "It would be quite astonishing if abilities which are inwardly so disparate were to coincide within one and the same political formation. As we have said, *it is not the task of an official* to join in political conflict on the basis of his own conviction, and thus, in the sense of the word 'engage in politics,' which always means fighting."[29]

Although it is unclear how an official functionary who has no calling for ideological warfare can emerge from the dreariness of parliamentary duties to become a political leader, Weber defended committees as beneficial to a nation's political culture. Political maturity arises only when a nation is well-informed about how its elected representatives conduct their affairs. "The committees of a powerful parliament are the only possible places from which that educative influence can be extended." Lacking such well-trained committees, parliaments would be mere "talking shops" with their members delivering "set-piece speeches" advocating this or denouncing that, and politics would be little more than the babble of language uninformed by knowledge and intellect.[30]

In his writings on the virtues of parliamentary committees, Weber's instinct at ferreting out the grasping paws of power and the organizational tendencies of inertia seemed to have failed him. When one glances at Wilson's *Congressional Government* (1885), one may see some of the realities in the structural arrangements of representative political institutions that Weber missed taking into account. Wilson demonstrated that in a government with a plethora of standing committees leadership is lost to the labyrinth of office upon office and as a result no politician can speak for the nation as a whole. Where Weber saw no realm of political combat or struggle taking place among office-loyal committee members, Wilson observed that "chairman fights against chairman" for the public rostrum and for claims on government resources on the part of "selfish warring elements." Wilson's perception is almost Weberian in seeing that as different assignments are given to different committees, authority becomes so dissipated in the process of being delegated that all trace of responsibility disappears. The qualities that Weber valued in a politician—independence, integrity, conviction—Wilson saw suffocating under the "disintegrate ministry" of committee government where strategy of position conceals weakness of character. His disgust at congressional government without presidential leadership even had a Weberian ring. "Eight words contain the sum of the present degradation of our political parties," Wilson wrote; "no leaders, no principles; no principles, no parties."[31]

That formulation Max Weber could readily accept. But when Wilson leaves behind his somber wisdom about the limits of congressional government in the United States and takes America into the war, he also leaves behind his critical scholarly mind and becomes more rhetorical than analytical. Where Weber attempted to develop a theory of politics through a rigorous conceptualization of its impediments and compromises, Wilson sought to bring democracy to Europe by reiterating its ideals, as though cherished principles could rely upon political language alone, as though power could be made to yield to persuasion.

How did freedom come into existence historically? On this question Weber and Wilson held different perspectives. Weber believed that the historic liberty that evolved into modern democracy arose out of past circumstances so contingent they may be unrepeatable. When he earlier observed of the Russian Revolution of 1905 that this event may offer the last chance of liberty being born "from the bottom up," he was recognizing that more frequently in history the story of liberty is the story not of its evolution but its devolution. The first struggle of liberty takes place at the top, so to speak, with ruling elites vying with one another as power moves downward to an ascendant bourgeoisie and outward from controlling elements at the center. Freedom moves with power and has its origins in the ability to resist the exercise of domination against one's will. The scenario of freedom involves struggle, resistance, the overcoming of power by virtue of gaining access to countervailing power. So close was the relationship of power to freedom that Weber often saw revolution itself as an act of usurpation that cloaks itself in legitimacy.

The Wilsonian perspective lacks Weber's imagination of the omnipresence of power and its tendency to expand by excluding its rivals, a tendency so treacherous that the only difference between power and freedom may be who wins and who loses, who ends up commanding and who submitting. It may have been due to America's having skipped the feudal stage of history that American liberalism regards democracy as "born free" (Tocqueville's expression) without having had to undergo the class struggles of the old world. It almost seemed that Wilson saw freedom being born in the processes of nature rather than in the struggles of history, as though it arose organically with the forces of life bursting forth from nature's womb. How shall people find the true meaning of freedom?

Wilson answered his own question with the rhetoric of renewal and resurrection. "A people shall be saved," Wilson exclaimed, "by the power that sleeps in its own bosom . . . shall be renewed in hope, in conscience, in strength, by waters welling up from its own sweet, perennial springs. Not from above; not by patronage of its aristocrats." Wilson's populist rhetoric asked Americans to let a thousand flowers bloom. "I tell you, the so-called radicalism of our times is simply the effort of nature to release the generous energies of our people. This great American people is at bottom just, virtuous, and hopeful; the roots of its being are in the soil of what is lovely, pure, and of good report, and the need of the hour is just that radicalism that will clear a way for the realization of the aspirations of a sturdy race."[32]

After such innocence, what could Germany expect from America? Indeed Weber anticipated exactly the predicament in which Wilson would put both Germany and the United States when he went along with the Entente's conditions on ending the war. Wilson's 14 Points for a just peace settlement were articulated in January 1918; before accepting them Germany embarked upon a major offensive, and when that failed in April, Germany offered an armistice. Weber then observed the Entente responding by insisting upon Germany's complete disarmament as a prerequisite for an armistice. Although Weber's observations went unheeded, and he played no significant role in the peace settlement, his perceptions proved prophetic:

> There is no doubt among the informed people in Germany about President Wilson's sincerity. It seems, however, that he does not take enough notice of the following: if his wish that the German government is to accept armistice conditions that make further military resistance impossible is fulfilled, then not only perhaps Germany, but also, on a larger scale, he himself would be eliminated from the series of factors decisive for the conditions of peace. His own position as an arbiter of the world rested on and rests on and only on the fact that German military might is at least significant enough that it in no way can be forced into submission without the assistance of American troops. If this were otherwise, undoubtedly the absolutely intransigent elements in the remaining enemy states would gain the upper hand and would be in a position to push the president smoothly aside with a polite thanks for his previous help. *His role would be played out,* unless he resolves himself to war against his present allies.[33]

Weber would have liked to have seen Wilson play poker power politics against the Allies, with Germany kept as the ace in the hole. England and

France alone cannot defeat Germany's military might, and thus Wilson could use the presence of American troops, and even the possibility of negotiating a separate peace with Germany, to compel the Allies into being more flexible and less intransigent with the terms of peace. For with Russia's leaving the war, Germany's defeat no longer looked so impending. Thus Allied leaders knew their situation was hopeless unless American troops arrived en masse, particularly after the Brest-Litovsk Treaty (March 1918), which had the potential to enable Germany to shift many divisions to the western front. "There can be little doubt," Lloyd George wrote to Wilson in April, "that victory or defeat for the Allies depends upon the arrival of the American infantry."[34] As Weber rightly summed up the situation, if Germany lays down its arms, Wilson's hand is lost.

The worlds of Woodrow Wilson and Max Weber could not have been more different. Since each represents two distinct versions of liberalism—indeed, since Wilson stood in Weber's mind as pure sincerity alone, while Weber himself believed that the man who had a genuine "calling" for politics must fuse an ethics of intent with a calculation of consequences—it may be worthwhile to highlight the contrasts.

Wilson told the world that America would strive for "a peace without victory"; Weber observed of Germany's military situation that "every victory brings us further away from peace."[35] Wilson believed peace and the cessation of hostility would lead to international harmony; Weber had earlier observed (in his Freiburg inaugural) that "economic struggle between the nationalities follows its course even under the semblance of peace."[36] Wilson assumed that capitalism required a laissez faire government; Weber believed it perfectly possible for industrial capitalism to secure its goals within an authoritarian system. Wilson declared "we are at the beginning of an age in which the same standards of conduct and responsibility for wrong shall be observed"; Weber observed that "to look down from the pinnacle of thought to the flux of events" is to see no single standard but instead an implacable struggle between the "gods" and the demonic forces of conflicting cultures.[37] Wilson believed that America could command respect by virtue of its democratic ideals; Weber held that a state can neither be defined nor win respect with reference to its ends but only by its means.[38] Similarly, Wilson assumed that the people of Europe would be grateful for America's contribution to a "war to end all wars"; Weber observed: "Whenever a policy has been undertaken as a gamble on gratitude, it was from the start condemned to failure."[39]

To reduce these many differences to the practical proposals regarding ending the war, one could put it this way: Wilson wanted peace and democracy, assuming all remaining conflicts could be later worked out in a spirit of cooperation rather than combat; Weber wanted justice and security, assuming nothing would be forthcoming without playing the card of power.

Weber never regarded America or Wilson as Germany's enemy, and he continued to remind his countrymen that "our undoing was submarine warfare." Germany guaranteed to cease the sinkings as soon as the peace conference, based on Wilson's proposals, convened, Weber wrote at the end of 1918. But the Entente deliberately delayed, realizing that time would be on their side once American divisions arrived. The war had weakened England, Weber noted, but he saw no advantage to Germany in America's now emerging as the leading Anglo-Saxon nation. Everything turned on Wilson, and Weber could not help but wonder whether the president's sincerity would turn out to be a virtue or a fatality.[40]

As the war followed its tragic course, Weber became more impatient with Wilson, who, instead of using the deployment of American troops to win concessions, went along with the Entente's position that peace negotiations could not take place without a cease-fire. As much as the silencing of weapons is desirable to end the "useless bloodshed," the armistice need not be pushed to the foreground on such terms, Weber reflected. In any event, discussion must continue even if the Entente insists upon the "continuation of the slaughter."[41]

"Can anyone believe," Weber implored, "that peace comes through procession [*Umzuge*]?" It seemed that Wilson had in mind a course of proceedings such as takes place in the civility of a courtroom. "Perhaps peace yet lies in the hand of an international law professor," Weber sarcastically wrote of Wilson, formerly of Princeton. "That is the characteristic destiny of the world, that the first actual world ruler is a professor. How much a professor he is one sees in the blunders he's made. . . . If he forces it through that Germany arrives at the peace negotiations entirely weaponless, it will signify that his own dominating influence has ended. French generals will simply say: we are very grateful; now we are ready to deal with the Germans without you."[42]

In October 1918, the German government agreed to an armistice with Wilson, accepting his 14 Points as a basis of peace. Germany as well as the Entente had been prompted in part by fear of bolshevism, which, spreading from Russia and exploiting devastation and despair, had more to gain if the war continued. When the armistice was announced the following month, workers' uprisings in Munich, Berlin, and elsewhere ignited the sparks of a tense revolutionary situation that continued throughout the following spring as peace talks were taking place in Paris. Weber believed that the revolution had made Germany even more defenseless than the peace, and had rendered the country open to its enemies. He disdained the heady proposals of the revolutionaries as economically insane. For an immature proletariat to usher in on its own universal socialization is "imbecilic" (*Blödsinn*). Germany's economic life could not be restored without the business class and without the American credits the country sorely needed for postwar reconstruction. Yet Germany's precarious position made it impossible to carry out Wilson's peace proposals, for to do so France would presume that Germany has yielded to its conquerer and is no more dependent on America's assistance, and thus could be dealt with more harshly than the proposals intended. The crux is that Germany surrendered conditionally to America without having lost the war to England and France, countries in no condition to be anything but unconditional.[43]

THE 14 POINTS AND WAR GUILT

To emphasize only the contrasts between Wilson and Weber is misleading. Actually Weber harbored certain political ideals that put him closer to Wilson than to other European statesmen. The Entente leaders—England's Lloyd George, France's Georges Clemenceau, Italy's Vittorio Orlando—behaved like spineless cynics. After Germany acceded to Wilson's demand to guarantee the maintenance of the Allies' military superiority as a requisite for the armistice, making Germany completely powerless and turning Weber into what Machiavelli would have called "a prophet unarmed," the Allies repaid Wilson by scoffing at his peace proposals. Although discussed in the press, Wilson's 14 Points arrived in Europe only to be met with feigned surprise by Allied leaders who refused to even acknowledge their existence. As Machiavelli might have predicted, a neutral, in intervening to settle a war, falls prey to the victor.

While Weber was frustrated with Wilson, particularly for refusing to see that he could hardly be an arbiter between the great powers without maintaining Germany's armed forces as a bargaining chip, he became furious with the French. Writing in 1919, Weber recalled to his readers that when war broke out five years earlier German and French neighbors went off to war giving each other a farewell handshake and saying, "See you later on the field of honor." Today, Weber lamented, all discussion between the two countries is as hopeless as it is mindless.[44]

Weber accepted the spirit of the 14 Points. The principle of national self-determination comported with his own belief in autonomy. He recognized that under the League of Nations Danzig and German Bohemia would have to be given up and Alsace-Lorraine made into an independent state. "But I hope that Wilson's vision will shield our fate," he exclaimed, insisting that no one should place a barrier to the unification of all German people under the German flag and that "haggling" (*erschachern*) over border issues will betray the dignity of future world peace. He enthusiastically endorsed a democratic republic with systematic referendums to keep both parliament and the president in touch with the people. He also advocated paying off Germany's war debts through property taxes and through a new economic order directed toward the interest of the nation and rid of old feudal and dynastic elements.[45]

Thus the 14 Points, one of which demanded Germany's transformation from a monarchy to a republic, reinforced the constitutional reforms of Weber, who had already called for the Kaiser's abdication and for democratization and parliamentarization. But the timing was disastrous insofar as the coming of democracy would be associated with defeat. "In the future," Weber predicted even before the war had ended, "they will say at home that 'the outside world forced democracy upon us.' That is a miserable heritage." Thus what was regarded in Wilsonian terms as the rise of freedom could readily be seen in Germany as surrendering to the powers that be (*Obrigkeitsstaat*).[46]

Ultimately it was the points that came after the 14 Points and indeed violated them that aroused Weber's greatest concern. Germany had agreed to the armistice on the basis of "no punitive indemnities" and with an understanding that Germany bore no unique responsibility for the outbreak of the war, as Wilson himself had earlier emphasized. At the Paris Peace Conference, however, England and France saddled Germany with heavy reparation payments, the total amount of which was so incredibly high and so disputed it was left to future Allied commissions to determine. The reparations were imposed over the objections of Wilson and his advisors, who desired to see a prosperous Germany reintegrated into liberal-capitalist western Europe. A "war guilt" clause was also forced upon Germany, blaming her for aggression and for all the damage and loss of lives. As did Germany, Weber saw the clause as the ultimate insult, a "dictated peace" (*Diktatfrieden*) requiring his country to admit under duress that Germans who had died in the war had perished for an unjust cause.

This compounding of defeat with injury and insult Weber addressed directly in "Zum Thema der 'Kriegsschuld'" (On the subject of war guilt) in the *Frankfurter Zeitung*. The way in which he answers the accusation indicates the brilliance of his theoretical thinking working on the practical problems of the day.

As to Germany's invasion of neutral Belgium, Weber reminded readers that the plan had been made public as early as 1912 in the event of war as a defensive maneuver to cover Germany's flank. The anger of the Belgian people is understandable, Weber acknowledged, while reminding them that at the outbreak of the war the Chancellor admitted it was an "unjust" act and Germany promised to make amends once her military goals had been reached. In regards to U-boat sinkings, Weber pointed to international rules of war governing the conduct of neutrals. Was America behaving neutrally in shipping munitions to England, whose blockade around Germany, confined as it was to the Baltic Sea, also made the blockade selective rather than uniformly applied? Germany took responsibility for using U-boats on its understanding of the proper legal interpretation of the issue, while President Wilson insisted that responsibility cannot be linked to a policy but is separate and specific to each incident. As a consequence of Germany's defeat, Wilson's interpretation of the rights of neutrals will prevail, Weber admitted. But it is wrong to say that the Germans risked going into war for purely arbitrary and willful reasons. On the contrary, Germany had a firm belief in a certain legal interpretation, even if that interpretation had "intractable consequences" (*nicht durchführbare Konsequenzen*) in that it could not be carried out without producing unruly results. Thus the German interpretation may be seen as "objectively false" but it is still neither dishonest nor deceptive.[47]

Weber is willing to acknowledge mistakes on the part of Germany's diplomacy, particularly the Zimmerman letter (in which the Foreign Office secretly tried to enlist Mexico to join the Axis with the promise of winning back land lost to the United States), but the decision to go to war cannot be attributed to Germany alone. Weber cited precipitating events in the east, particularly Austria's ultimatum to Serbia and Russia's mobilization. But what is more telling is Weber's distinction between the objectively false and the subjectively true, a point that recalls his distinction between the two ethics that inhere in his theory of human action. The Allies contended that Germany consciously plotted war; Weber replies that Germany's intentions were moral and legal and her early military actions as much defensive as offensive, although the intentions and actions produced unintended consequences. Weber knew that an actor could be held responsible for outcomes he did not intentionally cause, which made him all the more determined to insist that Germany had behaved for reasons that cannot be judged as immoral and in clear violation of international law. Although it was buried in his argument, Weber asked fellow Calvinist Woodrow Wilson to consider the goodness of the rational will and judge not the ironies of history and its irrational ways.

Responsibility, yes; guilt, no! Those four words might sum up Weber's position on this bitter issue. When a pacifict professor demanded, as a precondition for moral regeneration, that each German individual, and especially the intellectuals, acknowledge guilt for the war, Weber replied:

> I have kept silent about the "guilt" of *others* in wartime, and I have not participated in the disgusting moralizing, which is equally loathsome on both sides. This gives me the right to say now that this wallowing in guilt feelings which I encounter in a number of places is a *sickness*—just as flagellation is one in the religious area and masochism in the sexual sphere. The policy of the past two years was an outrage—not because it was a war policy, but because it was *frivolous* and *mendacious*. Our policy before the war was *stupid*, not morally reprehensible—it certainly cannot be called that. This is my judgment.[48]

The war brought out, perhaps even more than his scholarship, Weber's keen capacity for perception, a talent for allowing his emotions to be congruent with the state of affairs being addressed and even sharing the feelings of others, including one's recent enemies. Thus when explaining events from the point of view of America, Weber told his readers that the "war ideology" in the United States had little to do with "the dollar." Weber cited Veblen's *The Theory of Business Enterprise* (1904), a good, characteristic book for "young America." Veblen had foreseen that the time was coming when it would be a "sound business view" for nations to take world trade from one another by war, only to discover that war itself, as Veblen knew, arouses a spirit of dignity more honorable than dreary money-grubbing.[49] Weber then mentions certain symptons of "aristocratization" in America, such as dueling swords he saw on college campuses when in the United States, that may explain its fighting temper. But Weber concludes by suggesting that Germany is perhaps more blameworthy since the United States was reacting to her actions. "With the masses" of Americans, Weber writes in an effort to describe what Americans experienced in response to events, "what created the mood for war was finally, above all else, the subjective but completely sincere belief in the absolute depravity of the German case (Belgium!), of the devious obduracy of German diplomacy, and of the inconsiderateness of German war methods."[50]

But Germany, rather than instigating the war, should be seen as responding to the dangerous movement of armies in the east, particularly to Russia, with its ruling classes and tsarist system, both antiquated systems of domination. Yet Weber was less interested in pinpointing blame than in freeing Germany from accepting "a peace of shame" so that democratic liberalism would not bear the stigma of defeat.

In February 1919, a group met at Weber's house in Munich and organized a "Heidelberger Vereinigung für eine Politik des Rechts" (Heidelberg Association for a Policy of Justice), in an effort to draw upon well-known figures who could command respect for earlier opposing annexationist policies and who could thus help present the case for Germany to the world. Weber sought to establish a commission to investigate the actions of leading figures in German government at the time of the outbreak of the war. His efforts were opposed, but he was asked to participate in the Committee for the Peace Negotiations, a commission of experts who were about to formulate Germany's detailed reply to the Allied charge of war guilt. Weber joined hesitantly, first believing that the guilt issue could never be rationally resolved and then discovering that German officials planned to repudiate all responsibility for the war. For months Weber wavered between recommending that the peace treaty be rejected, which could mean foreign occupation and the resulting "awakening" of Germany's "inner resistance," and recognizing the consequences of such an action, which could lead to further acrimony and radicalization throughout the country. Finally accepting the treaty as inevitable, Weber lamented that "misery had only just begun" as he predicted how France would now pounce to demand the Rhineland, reparations, and much else as well. But Weber's thoughts were also on another subject, and here he had to predict the outcome of a new ideology that took only ten days to shake the world.[51]

TEN

The German Revolution of 1918 and the Doctrine of Socialism

THE GENEALOGY OF FREEDOM

One gulf of misunderstanding between America and Germany during World War I, and specifically between Wilson and Weber, concerned the concept of freedom as it came to be embodied in democratic institutions. To the extent that freedom in America began its story in flight from the Old World, it preexisted in the environment of the New World before Europeans arrived. Freed from the necessity of overthrowing the power of feudal dynasties, American colonists enjoyed free land, open space, and unlimited possibility. To paraphrase Tocqueville, in America freedom had no birth trauma; it was born without the struggle of democracy against aristocracy. Germany, however, had yet to be transformed by a liberal revolution such as occurred in seventeenth-century England and eighteenth-century France, and hence the old order remained strong and the parliament weak.

Seeing his beloved country in the grip of history, Weber felt it all the more imperative to try to make Germany become what it could be by its own efforts. Weber tended to see history as genealogical: full of chance occurrences, potentialities and mutations, nonrecurring events and unconditional possibilities, ironic outcomes and fortuitous beginnings, all adding meaning and value to the way in which events originate and take shape. Thus Weber told readers of the *Frankfurter Zeitung* that the problem Germany faces is precisely the impending moment of its new political birth. Unlike in England, Holland, and America, Weber wrote, democracy in Germany would not be associated with a glorious revolution or an honorable peace but instead with defeat and humiliation. How, then, Weber asked, "can it become a treasured component of national self-consciousness?"[1]

Woodrow Wilson's idealism and aversion to force rendered him insensitive to the way in which democracy would be imposed upon Germany. Wilson had also changed his mind about Germany's responsibility for the war. In 1916 Wilson asserted that America was unconcerned with the "obscure fountains" from which the "causes" of the war had "burst forth."[2] But by 1918 he felt compelled to blame the war on Germany's government, the last remnant of autocracy whose elimination would pave the way for the transition to democracy and endow the war with ideological purpose. Weber also tended to hold government officials responsible, if not for starting the war, for stumbling into it, and he too desired to see Germany democratized. But Weber realized the devastating psychological implications of the war guilt accusation, and his reasoning about the question also has something of a Nietzschean slant.

Weber had all along made responsibility basic to his theory of ethics (and scholars still debate whether it was more important to him than intentionality). But Weber points out that the term implies not only admitting mistakes of the past but turning one's efforts toward the future. Just as Nietzsche held that the will cannot will backwards, Weber held that conscience should not allow itself to "wallow" in guilt for things that cannot be undone. In the white paper produced by the Heidelberg Association for a Policy of Justice, Weber stated that the guilt question was "worded backwards" and hence it was meaningless since the past by definiton is irrevocable. As an existentialist, Weber recognized that the past cannot be acted upon and hence freedom involves choices made in the present that affect the future. Weber charged Germany's accusers with fixating on past liabilities without taking account of future responsibilities. It is this prospective obligation, Weber concluded with a touch of his wicked brilliance, that weighs upon not the "losers" but the "victors."[3]

Weber was consistent. His idea of "responsibility before history," first announced in his Freiburg inaugural in 1895, meant that mind and conscience are answerable to events as they unfold. Thus years earlier, as we have seen, Weber chided his countrymen for making a fetish out of Germany as *der Vaterland* when the real Germany belongs to its "children," to the generations that are to come. Weber's stance comported with his belief in the responsibility for itself of the individual mind conscious of its own activity. History must be lived as well as thought, acted upon as well as pondered. "O my brothers, your nobility should not look backwards but ahead!" wrote Nietzsche. "Exiles shall you be from all father and forefather lands! Your *children's land* shall you love: this love shall be your new nobility."[4]

This focus on the foreground, on what is coming next, dramatizes Weber's conviction that a nation creates itself in freedom as it turns its face to the future. This forward orientation was by no means peculiar to Germany's cultural and philosophical orientation. Woodrow Wilson and V. I. Lenin alike believed that history was moving in predictable directions and that the future would be responsive to the strivings that each nation brought to it. Wilson saw the world bathed in a sea of goodwill; Lenin saw it about to burst out in a tide of class revolution. Weber, who recalled that the war began with a completely unforeseen assassination, and who saw history as contingent and carrying on its back the dead weight of the past, looked on the rush of events less with bright confidence than with brooding curiosity.

Hugo Preuss, the minister of the interior who had invited Weber to join a conference planning the new Weimar Constitution, believed he could sum up the situation facing Germany in November 1918. Drawing upon the French newspaper *L'Humanité*, Preuss asserted that Germany faced an inescapable alternative: "Either Wilson or Lenin. Either the democracy born of the French Revolution, strengthened by a whole century of struggle, further developed by the great republic of the United States; or the primitive, incoherent, brutal forms of Russian fanaticism. We must choose."[5]

With the German Revolution of 1918, Weber also saw his country faced with the alternative of liberalism or communism. "Here the most modern development begins," Weber wrote of the uprisings in Munich and Berlin and the move to capture state power, "and we see with our own eyes the attempt to inaugurate the expropriation of this expropriator of political means, and therewith of political power." The revolutionaries, whether "through usurpation or election," attain control of power and then "deduce their legitimacy—no matter with what right— from the will of the governed."[6] If Germany was in a revolutionary situation in 1918, and all revolutions claim to be popular and act in the name of the people, was the real choice between the French or the Russian revolutions?

Unlike Preuss and some other German scholars, Weber could hardly look to the French Revolution as the alternative to the Russian. Out of 1789 he saw the development of a Bonapartist statist tendency that led to a growing bureaucracy in a Catholic country where the Church feared revolution and fought liberalism. Weber's sympathies were Anglo-American—he was especially drawn to New England Puritanism where the Protestant sects were on the side of the revolution—and if he remained skeptical regarding Wilson's sanguine faith in democracy, he was far more skeptical of Lenin's desperate faith in revolution.

Historians of the recent era have also tended to regard World War I as offering to the western world the choice of Wilson versus Lenin. Depicting the two figures as prophets of the future, historians have emphasized the "utopian" visions of each as they looked upon either war or revolution to be the event that would end all wars. Comparisons are made between Lenin's "Petrograd Formula" for peace and Wilson's 14 Points to emphasize that both leaders appealed directly to the people of all countries as they called for a peace without victory or recriminations and also a "new diplomacy" of international openness, freedom, and self-determination.[7]

Weber had no such illusions about the promises of a new diplomacy or a new politics coming out of the Russian Revolution. A month after the bolsheviks seized power he observed, in a letter to a colleague, that although Germany's role in the world is temporarily over, the country has averted what would have been much worse—"the Russian knout." This glory, wrote Weber, sustains Germany as America, whose rise to world power was as inevitable as that of Rome after the Punic wars, "hopefully will remain" positioned to counter the Russian threat.[8]

Elsewhere Weber told an audience that Leon Trotsky, the leader of the Red Army, was misleading the German people with his false promises. Unsatisfied with trying out the socialist experiment "in his own house" to see if it could work there, "Herr Trotsky" wanted to reach for the world. "With the typical vanity of a Russian litterateur, he wanted more, and he hoped, by means of a war of words and the misuse of such words as 'peace' and 'self-determination,' to unleash civil war in Germany."[9]

"DER SOZIALISMUS"

The German revolution of 1918, although it would turn out to be abortive, was viable enough to throw Weber into depression. When the first uprising occurred in Kiel, where sailors on ships docked in the harbor mutinied, Weber made a speech in Munich. He spoke against the revolution and against German workers and intellectuals turning to Russia for inspiration. Jeers and heckling came from the communists while others in the audience remained silent. "These demagogic doings struck him as 'ugly,' a pernicious portent," wrote Marianne.[10]

The tremor of revolution rocked several cities. In Munich hundreds of workers defended railway stations and squares against a vast army of soldiers and police. Barbed wire and barricades sprouted as machine guns raked the streets. Neighbors turned on one another with the shout, "You bolshevik bastard!" Nobody was safe from informers. Arrested insurrectionaries were spat upon as "traitors." In a matter of weeks members of the Red Guard knew that they had lost their ill-conceived bid for power. But to surrender could possibly mean facing a firing squad. Madness continued to rage on the streets.

The turmoil occurred while Germany had yet to accept the Allied peace. Heading Munich politics was Kurt Eisner, the socialist prime minister of Bavaria. Eisner had helped publish documents on Germany's "war guilt," believing with the pacifists that such "confessions" would bring more lenient peace terms. Eisner also decided to replace Bavaria's "parliamentary swamp" with a Soviet government (*Rätergierung*). In spring of the fateful year 1918, he was assassinated; Munich immediately polarized into hostile camps. Socialists believed the communist threat could be checked by embarking upon the "full socialization" of Bavaria. Fears of a dictatorship of the Red Army spread through the city. That some of the revolutionaries were foreign Jewish leaders outraged many townspeople and students. The city grew tense with xenophobia, anti-Semitism, and pan-German nationalism.[11]

Although Weber had hoped that a revival of nationalism might create sufficient irredentist anger to cause France to ease up on peace terms, the crazy spectacle in Munich was not what he had in mind. The revolutionary thrusts of the Left played into the hands of the French. More seriously, the counterrevolutionary activity that now preoccupied the army meant it would be unavailable as a factor in the peace negotiations— Germany's last card, in Weber's mind. Weber also denounced workers' councils seizing power in the name of soviets. Fearing chaos and anarchy, he saw Munich becoming "a bloody carnival that does not deserve the honorable name revolution." The arrest and murder of the communists Karl Leibknecht and Rosa Luxemburg brought from Weber a characteristic judgment. He had earlier declared that Leibknecht belonged in a "madhouse" and Luxemburg in a "zoo" for allowing the revolution to get out of hand under the fanatical Spartakus vanguard. But Weber condemned the murders and added a reminder to readers of the *Heidelberger Zeitung*: "Leibknecht, who was no doubt an honorable man, *summoned the battle into the street*. The street killed him."[12]

In January 1920, Count Georg Graf Arco, Eisner's assassin, was released from jail. When students in Munich applauded the release, just as they had cheered when they heard about the assassination, and when they harrassed students with opposing views, Weber appealed to the rector to exercise his authority over the campus disruptions. Aware that the administration had done nothing, Weber took it upon himself to address the issue in the opening remarks in his lecture:

Contrary to my usual practice in political matters, I feel impelled to make a remark about what happened here last Saturday. And you have the right to demand that I show my true colors in actual *cases* as well. You have extolled Count Arco because—and this is my conviction, too—his conduct in court was chivalrous and manly in every way. His action was born of the conviction that Kurt Eisner brought disgrace after disgrace upon Germany. I share this opinion.

Yet it was a bad thing to pardon him so long as the law is in force, and if *I* had been the minister I would have had him shot. Your demonstration would not have prevented me; on the contrary! But the ministry yielded to you. Arco's tombstone would also have exorcised Kurt Eisner's ghost, which is still haunting us; now he will live on in people's hearts as a martyr, because Arco is alive. That is to the detriment of the country. And what will your demonstrations turn Arco into? Make no mistake about it: a coffeehouse celebrity! I would have wished something better for him! On Saturday accusations were made here, accusations that have not been withdrawn to this day. Anyone who fails to do so is a *Hundsfott* [son of a bitch]!

And another thing: It has been mentioned that the *Reichswehr* was ready to stage a putsch in association with the students. Gentlemen, I am not impressed with conspirators whose vanity is so great that they have to blab [*ausplaudern*] such things in public. There is no need to say anything about the plan as such.

But let me tell you this. To restore Germany to her old glory, I would surely ally myself with any power on earth, even with the devil incarnate, but not with the force of stupidity. So long as madmen carry on in politics from the right to the left, I shall stay away from it.[13]

Weber shares the students' desires to see Germany rise from the shame of defeat but he regards their politics as sick with paranoia. Eisner and Arco, he went on, are the symbolic objects of attitudes that are perilous to Germany's political sanity. But amid all the bitter rancor and dissension, the voice of reason must be heard, and some students and public officials believed that Weber should step forward, drop his denunciations of both sides, and assume a leadership role. "Among all politically active people I really saw no one whom I would trust, as I trust you," wrote a member of the Freideutsche Jugend (Free German Youth). We need, he went on, "a great educator" to explain to the nation what its needs are and how to obtain them. "People say primarily that you are not moving with the times," wrote the youth, adding that he disagrees with that view. "I, therefore, had the impression," he continued after separating his views from those of others and complimenting the "enormous vitality" of Weber's presentations,

> that, without talking about it, you were content to let the things that have changed change and that basically you may have cared most about trying to define clearly and incisively the attitude of a serious, chivalrous, and absolutely decent person in this revaluation of all values, which is threatening to become a devaluation of all values. . . .
>
> We badly need you as a leader—not to settle the question whether one should turn the other cheek or not tolerate any injustice, but to articulate the glaring contradiction inherent in a quantitative or qualitative socialism. It is an urgent task and every minute counts. It is now a question of whether we shall surrender to crowds and numbers or whether we shall make a quick attempt to channel the unleashed energies into paths where they will create valuable work and bring beauty and movement into our lives.[14]

Weber responded to such appeals to assume the role of a nation's educator and give the flux of events some clarification and direction. In June 1918 he was invited to speak by the Austrian Feindespropaganda Abwehrstelle (Department for Defense Against Enemy Propaganda)—an organization that reflected the widespread fear in central Europe of the spread of bolshevism after the October Revolution of 1917. At the University of Vienna Weber spoke to three hundred Austrian military officers. Weber's address, "Der Sozialismus" is remarkable for its evenhandedness at a time when many western intellectuals substituted passion for perspective. America had no Weber to temper the exuberance of the Greenwich Village intellectuals, who remained captivated by the October Revolution in poetry as well as politics. Many members of Weber's old "Heidelberg Circle" also became caught up in the mystique of Lenin's conquest of power. Weber's last letter to Lukács, it will be recalled, warned that Soviet "experiments" would discredit socialism for the entire twentieth century.[15] In the thirties radical intellectuals, reacting to Stalinism, claimed to be the first percipient anticommunists; after 1989, with the fall of the Berlin Wall, it seemed that every writer was saying "I told you so." But Weber's address, "Socialism," presented as early as 1918, less than a year after the bolsheviks stormed into history, analyzed what Russian communism was before it tragically became the monstrous reality it would be.

Weber begins his address by gallantly apologizing to the officers of Austria's Royal and Imperial Army for having no knowledge of military matters regarding organizational structures and duties and commands. He lets them know that whenever possible he travels third-class on trains and he is happy to see that, among men traveling to or from the front, there was "suspicion" of all attempts to subject them to the propaganda of party politics. But Weber noted that while soldiers acknowledged the military expertise of the officer corps, respect for authority does not carry over when men see themselves after the war "standing behind a machine or a plow." Recognizing that most foot soldiers are either farmers or union workers, Weber speaks of the tendency of the opponents of the Socialist Democratic Party to tell workers that they are being exploited by intellectuals and bosses who live off their wages. But workers reply, Weber notes wryly, "certainly they live off my pennies," which only means that bosses and intellectuals are dependent upon workers and must represent their interests. The German trade unions, Weber reassures the officers, are occasionally foolish but for the most part sensible and responsible:

> One may think what one likes about strikes. They are usually a fight for interests, for wages. Yet very often not just for wages, but also for ideal [ideele] things, for honor, as the worker happens to understand it (and each man claims to know for himself what it means). The feeling of honor, of comradeship among workers and allies in a factory or in a branch of industry binds them in solidarity, and that is, after all, a feeling upon which the solidarity of military groups rests, although it takes a different direction there.[16]

Weber seeks to have his audience see the laboring class as "allies" of even the officer corps, and hence he combines two terms—Genosse for worker comrade and Kamerad for soldier comrade—to suggest that the same spirit of comradeship (Kameradschaft der Genossen) moves both workers and fighters.[17] Here Weber characteristically both helps the Left before an audience of its potential enemies and undermines it in the larger context of Marxist theory. By indicating that union strikes are not only something society must live with but are based on legitimate aims, Weber implies that there should be no need for the military to turn its guns on workers. At the same time Weber is suggesting that the workers' struggle is, even when seemingly extremist in its tactics, moderate in its objectives, and as such can be accommodated through reform instead of revolution. In depicting the conservative character of the working class, Weber deprives the revolutionary Left of its most desperate illusion—the myth of the proletariat.

Weber referred to his opening comments as his "subjective impressions." He then turns to the topic of the evening, socialism, and to the nature of socialist parties, emphasizing that all such parties are democratic parties. "What, then, is democracy today?" Most discussions of democracy focus on equality, but Weber wants the audience to take a closer look. In the Swiss cantons people turn out to vote on issues large and small, but it is curious the extent to which offices continue to be held by the same men often with similar family connections. In America it is not so much family as money ("Quadrennial campaign costs in the U.S. already amount to about as much as a colonial war," Weber observed in the manuscript that became *Economy and Society*).[18] The size of government bureaucracy also deflects direct democracy and leaves voters subjected to a "professional officialdom," while parties must reward supporters with jobs and posts. The scramble for office is so accepted that "everyone had a turn putting his hands in the pork barrel."

It has been pointed out in an earlier chapter that Weber had been wrong in predicting that America would emerge from the war as a society where bureaucracy would control political parties, stifle leadership ("castration of charisma"), and produce a rule of domination by means of administration. Such a dire prognosis reflected Weber's conviction that democracy invites people not only to participate in politics but to place demands on the state which, in a large country, can only be met by expanding bureaucratic agencies. But why would conditions in America have any bearing upon the situation in Russia? They do so to the extent that Weber saw no "American exceptionalism" and instead foresaw democracy destined to bureaucratic domination even under socialism. "This inescapable universal bureaucratization is precisely what lies behind one of the most frequently quoted socialist slogans, the slogan of the 'separation of the worker from the means of work.' What does it mean?"

In answering that question Weber draws upon his vast historical knowledge to show that a medieval ideal cannot survive a modern reality. In the middle ages the worker owned the tools of his craft, just as the knight owned his horse and armor and scholars their own books. The modernization of life means that not only is the worker separated from his means of production but the soldier from the means of fighting and the scholar from the means of learning. When ownership loses its meaning of possession even capitalists lose their means of control to managers of the means of administration. "Everywhere we find the same thing: the means of operation within the factory, the state administration, the army and university departments are concentrated by means of a bureaucratically structured human apparatus in the hands of a person who has command over [*beherrscht*] this human apparatus." Since this development has little to do with capitalism, in what sense can socialism offer a solution to it? "As long as there are mines, furnaces, railways, factories and machines, they will never be the property of an individual or of several individual workers in the sense in which the materials of a craft in the Middle Ages were the property of one guild master or of a local trade cooperative or guild. This is out of the question because of the nature of present-day technology."

In a single disturbing description, Weber demonstrates how the means of existence and self-preservation has slipped silently away from human will to be lodged in the apparatus of institutions. The irony is that it was industry and industrialization, the fruit of reason and science, that brought about this condition of human alienation.

Socialism was born when the old free laborers passed away from history, with their heirs now facing the harsh discipline of factory work, treated as commodities whose wages continue to sink due to competition among capitalist producers. Socialist intellectuals today, Weber noted, refuse to criticize entrepreneurs but instead call for transforming the "order of production." A "communal economy" would eliminate the profit system and put decision making in the hands of officials or an association of the people (*Volksverband*). This possibility seems to Weber near in Germany's present war economy, which involves "joint management" between business and the state. Some socialists, Weber observes, already believe Germany is moving toward "genuine" socialism because they assume that entrepreneurs are subordinate to supervision by public officials. Perhaps. But after the war? In a peacetime economy, Weber warns, "this kind of state control, that is, compulsory cartelisation of the entrepreneurs in each branch of industry and the participation of the state in their cartels with a share in the profits in exchange for the concession of extensive rights of control, would in fact not mean the control of industry by the state but the control of the state by industry."

What is worse, Weber warns of a system where the state is allowed tax revenue from business in exchange for relinquishing some controls, is the "unpleasant" fate of labor. Representatives of the workers sitting in parliament would try to assure that public agencies maintain maximum wages and minimum prices, only to discover that the state, whose financial condition depends upon business profit, would "naturally have an interest in high prices and low wages." Again, in one stroke, Weber went to the heart of the Marxian analysis of the modern condition and showed it to be a compelling description without a convincing solution. What Marx himself had called in *Das Kapital* "the furies of interest" will remain just as furious no matter how an economy is restructured.[19] A change in the means of production scarcely changes the motives of action. Nor is production as important as consumption.

When it was asked what "needs" are to be satisfied in modern life, socialists are under the illusion that the worker feels deeply the need to overcome the alienation of coercive labor in order to find fulfillment in free, productive activity. The rise of consumer associations, Weber observes, possibly suggests that the delights of consumption drive people more than the drudgery of work. This prospect hardly pleased Weber, the discoverer of the Protestant work ethic. But Weber makes two observations that are almost Veblenesque in their implications. Not only are consumer desires arbitrary and incapable of sustaining a focus that might be politically organized, they are also irrational, and a reflection of status behavior that complicates a class analysis. Consider eating habits. "Even the present situation in Germany," Weber wrote of the wartime food shortages, "has not been able to persuade the housewife from the mass of population . . . to accept war canteen meals, which everyone found excellently prepared and palatable, instead of their own amateurish individual cooking, although the canteen meals were far cheaper." Status distinctions between classes are kept up, however irrational these are economically. Focusing critical analysis solely on the "point of production," as do socialists, misses the point of consumption.

KARL MARX AND THE BOLSHEVIK REVOLUTION

When one thinks of the subject of communism, one's mind turns to Soviet Russia and, more recently, China and Cuba, all underdeveloped countries when their respective revolutions took place, and still today further behind the rest of the liberal capitalist west. We tend to forget that the doctrine on which communist regimes are based came from a German philosopher who died when Weber was a beginning college student. No other thinker has inspired more mass movements and revolutions than Karl Marx (1818–83). The philosophy of Marxism looked ahead to the "end" of history; more precisely, to the end of the long travail of "pre-history," those stages of past epochs before consciousness arises beyond its brute conditions to make it possible for history to fulfill its goal—"the ascent of man from the kingdom of necessity to the kingdom of freedom." Marx expected that goal to be first reached in England and Germany, then the most advanced industrial nations in the world. But Lenin seized power in Russia, a backward country whose history was characterized more by stagnation than by progressive stages. Nevertheless, his hopes rested with Germany, where he was counting upon a successful communist uprising to spark the beginnings of world revolution. Unless this happened, the October Revolution would have no theoretical legitimacy, communism would find itself in a land of a resentful peasantry rather than a rising proletariat, and history would move backward from the promised kingdom of freedom and return to the groaning curse of necessity.

Marx's coauthor of the *Communist Manifesto* was Friedrich Engels, another German whose ancestors, like those of Weber, were in the world of business in Manchester, England, as well as Bielefeld, Germany. Weber regarded the *Communist Manifesto* as the "document which lays the foundations" of socialism. One may reject "its crucial theses," but it remains a "scholarly achievement of the highest order," a "prophetic" treatise that presages the disappearance of older artisan classes and agricultural existence. But would new forms of capitalism also be superseded according to an inevitable "law of nature"? Why are Marx and Engels convinced that capitalism is doomed to destruction? In his lecture to the Austrian military officers, Weber scrutinizes the three reasons offered for capitalism's collapse, which would come to be the trinity of truths for future generations of European and American radicals.

First is the theory of immiseration, the tendency of a profit-minded bourgeoisie to decrease relentlessly the wages of workers due to pressures of competition. Weber notes that the pauperization argument has been rejected by socialists like Karl Kautsky. Without mentioning the role of trade unions, he then reminds the audience that the thesis, though shorn of its "pathos-laden character," is still upheld in different formulations.

The second theory highlights capitalist contraction, the tendency of stronger entrepreneurs to drive their weaker competitors out of business.

In modified form this thesis still prevails today, Weber notes, but he makes a passing observation that would, many years later, take on considerable significance as the "new class analysis." Weber observed that the disappearance of an older bourgeoisie of shopkeepers is accompanied in a new economy by the rise of managers, technicians, and desk-based employees whose interests remain far removed from those of the working class.

The third theory focuses on business cycles and depressions, which result from overproduction and underconsumption due to falling wages. Weber notes that in recent times depressions have been averted by cartels regulating credit supply to reduce speculation and by state management and surveillance of private enterprise. In the present and future world neither workers nor business will rule; specially trained clerks and public servants will play that role. Bringing rational control to capitalism will advance "the dictatorship of the official."

The crisis theory of "classic socialism," the notion that business depressions progressively worsen and heighten class tensions, "has been abandoned today," Weber remarks. Unenlightened capitalism, "the anarchy of production," has been stablized by cartels and by the German Reichsbank. "Thus the hopes, full of high pathos, which the *Communist Manifesto* once placed in the collapse of bourgeois society have been replaced by very much more sober expectations." The view today, Weber tells his listeners, is that socialism will not burst upon history out of a crisis situation but slowly evolve as the economy becomes increasingly "socialized" to the extent individual entrepreneurs are replaced by "share companies" and business comes under the jurisdiction of the state. Those who still dream of socialism also point to advanced technology and the increasing standardization or uniformity of production, developments that will overcome class differences between types of work and render society more homogeneous. In responding to this expectation, Weber displays his sociological understanding of status at its best. The more society become standardized in production and organization, the more classes desire to remain distinct and separate in their styles of life. That entrepreneurs have been replaced by massive staffing of officials is conceded by Weber, who then suggests that socialists see only the tendency of a movement without probing its deeper meaning. The systematic standardization of the economy is

very true, but again only with the same reservation, namely, that this standardization too enhances the importance of one stratum, that of the officials, who have to be *educated* in quite a different way, and who therefore (it must be added) have the character of a different *estate*. It is

no coincidence that we see commercial high schools, trade and technical colleges springing up like mushrooms everywhere. At least in Germany, this is due in part to the desire to join a student "coiours" fraternity at these colleges, to get scars on one's face, to become capable of
"giving satisfaction" in a duel and therefore of being an officer in the
Reserve, and later on in the office to have a better chance of the hand
of the boss's daughter—in other words, the desire to be assimilated into
the strata of so-called "society." Nothing is further from the minds of
this class than solidarity with the proletariat; indeed, their aim is rather
to differentiate themselves increasingly from the proletariat. In varying
degrees, but noticeably, the same is true of many of the sub-strata
among these office workers. They all strive at least for similar qualities
of this *estate*, be it for themselves or for their children. One cannot say
that an *unambiguous* trend towards proletarianisation exists today.

Insofar as Marx had made it the proletariat's "mission" to carry history all
the way to its end, and the proletariat is the last driving force of history's
dialectic; and, what is more, both the proletariat and the dialectic are scientific propositions and not, as today's postmodernists would have it,
rhetorical metaphors, Weber's observations are devastating. They are also
so significant that Marxists have deliberately ignored them, even those
who admired Weber.

Two years after Weber's death his old friend Lukács wrote *History and
Class Consciousness* (1922), topics of which the author had been working
on since 1919. With the bravado of a bolshevik announcing the
inevitable march of history, Lukács sought to prove that the theory of the
proletariat found its practical embodiment and political fulfillment in
Lenin's party dictatorship. Lukács even drew upon Weber's "*Der Sozialismus*" for a description of the transformation of feudal craft labor to modern industrial work. A recent scholar has described Lukács as having
"brought together in a synthesis" Marx's dialectical theories with Weber's
analysis of western rationalism, categories of "abstract work" with categories of "formal rationality."[20] The fusion of categories resulted in a mis-
alliance. Lukács's synthesis rested on little more than the desperate self-
deceptions of the dialectical imagination.

As well as celebrating Lenin and the Bolshevik Revolution by elevating events to prove that *praxis* is the test of truth, Lukács's book also represented an assault on Weber's antinomic sensibilities. The Marxist philosophy of history, Lukács was convinced, would overcome all the
methodological quandaries that had been thrashed out in Heidelberg in
the years before the war: the "dark and empty chasm" between theory
and practice, the "hiatus irrationalis" between knowledge and reality, the

neo-Kantian divorce between scientific reasoning and metaphysics, fact and value, method and meaning. But the "methodological intractability" that supposedly blinded Weber and his circle did not prevent Lukács from using Weber's ideas of rationalization and specialization to discuss "reification" (*Versachlichung*), the objectification of human relations when seen as things to be manipulated and objects subjected to calculation and prediction. The theory of reification offered a variation on Marx's idea of alienation, which depicted workers divorced from the mode of production and denied the fruits of their labor, so mesmerized by "commodity fetishism" that products take on an independent existence standing over and against the very workers who had created such products. This state of alienation left workers bereft of a true consciousness of their condition, which would now be supplied by the Bolshevik Party supposedly embodying the "proletariat" and led by Lenin.

Lukács relished quoting Marx to cover up any suggestion that Lenin had broken with Marx's faith in democracy lodged in the masses. When the proletariat, Lukács wrote, "proclaims the dissolution of the existing social order, it does no more than disclose the secret of its own existence, for it is the effective dissolution of that order." Lukács convinced himself that Lenin's Russia, a country where the rural peasantry far outnumbered the industrial worker, presented the terrain on which history fulfilled its destiny as the proletariat leaps beyond the bourgeois stage of history and sets out to transform society in the name of the final synthesis that negates its own existence. "The proletariat only projects class struggle by annihilating itself and transcending itself, by creating the classless society through the successful conclusions of its own struggle."[21]

Everything that Weber warned Lukács against went ignored in *History and Class Consciousness*. The insistence that the proletariat itself "proclaims" this and that represented the conceit of what Weber called the "literati"; it was Lenin, and other decidedly non-working-class, educated elites, who were doing all the proclaiming. Nor could Lukács so confidently assume that he was "synthesizing" Marx's dialectical theories with Weber's theory of rationalization, which described phenomena moving unilaterally, not dialectically, absorbing all contradictions rather than intensifying them. While Lukács, like many American intellectuals, allowed himself to be seduced by Lenin's conquest of power, Weber could have told him that the apparatus the bolsheviks used in the struggle for power becomes the very means of preserving power.

To the extent that Lukács drew on Weber, the scandal is that he remained silent on the most telling feature of Weber's address on socialism—Marx's vision that economic emancipation can only be achieved by the workingmen themselves remained, for Weber, a vision on stilts, and thus Lenin's party organization would have to be described for what it was, a dictatorship *over* the proletariat. Where Lukács thought he saw the makings of a "classless society," Weber always saw the persistence of classes, factions, and agencies or their reemergence in other forms that continue to express the ineluctability of power and domination. Insofar as Weber showed why it cannot be demonstrated "that an *unambiguous* trend toward proletarianisation exists today," one can only conclude that Lukács's embracing of Lenin's dictatorship was, for all the philosophical claptrap of *History and Class Consciousness*, more hubris than history.

Although Weber has often been depicted as a conservative, and sometimes even as a "reactionary" and forerunner of fascism, it was precisely because he was concerned about the fate of the working class that he opposed communism. "He admired the proletarian movement so long as it possessed the strength to feel conscious of itself as a cultural movement," observed Albert Salomon.[22] Marx, Weber's countryman, would have agreed. "As philosophy finds its *material* weapons in the proletariat, the proletariat finds its intellectual weapons in philosophy. And once the lightning of thought has deeply struck this unsophisticated soil of the people, the *Germans* will emancipate themselves to become *men*."[23] But Lenin's dictatorial party hardly allowed the proletariat to feel conscious of itself and speak for its own interests and ideals. Weber's earlier studies of farm and factory work in an authoritarian Prussian state made him aware that labor needed viable representation. Without the extension of suffrage to the working class, bankers and business would become "the unconscious masters of the state," he warned. With workers having access to the ballot they could challenge the threatening aspects of "power exercised in the interests of profit."[24] Bereft of political liberty, workers will be oppressed by the communist party as much as by the Prussian state. Even more than Lenin and Lukács, Weber desired to see workers empowered with legitimate means of defending themselves.[25]

Yet here our story encounters a puzzle. Having discerned in Russia the potential for party domination and bureaucratic despotism, why did Weber not foresee that the October Revolution would follow his own sociological scenario and transform itself from a movement into an institution and eventually into the "iron cage" that haunted his imagination? In the United States the *New York Times* had predicted the collapse of communist Russia almost every other day in ninety-one editorials. Weber was not confident about foreseeing the future, but several considerations led him to believe that Soviet communism would soon come to an end.

In the first place, Russia lacked a viable middle class and a Protestant tradition that instilled a work ethic into the formative mentality of a culture. Without a commercially oriented bourgeoisie, communist Russia would not only be unable to obtain credits from the west but it would have no tradition to fall back on within its own border. Weber had insisted that "Puritanism enabled its adherents to create free institutions and still become a world power."[26] Individualism and freedom of conscience are not the only fruits of Puritanism. As Marx himself recognized, a capitalism inspirited by religious idealism had once produced the material wealth of nations. Weber doubted that new bureaucrats would replace older, pioneer entrepreneurs and perform the same function. "It was with good reason," he wrote, "that the *Communist Manifesto* emphasized the *economically revolutionary* character of the work of the bourgeois capitalist entrepreneurs. No trade union, much less state-socialist officials, can perform this role for us in their place."[27]

Soviet communism could neither repeat history in keeping with western traditions nor create history anew, leaving behind Russian traditions. To Weber freedom was born of a fortuitous combination of "constellations," and historically it became not a momentary happening but an enduring legacy. Freedom could break through the crust of tradition by force of a charismatic personality, but charisma arises in opposition to organization and its deadening impositions. The idea that an organized revolution could come into existence spontaneously and unexpectedly, that it could continue to move to the Left without a Thermidor or a bourgeois coup d'état, and that the military dictatorship of the Red Army could replace the administrative state—all such developments defied Weber's conceptual framework. Apparently Weber knew nothing of Trotsky's "law of combined development," the bolshevik's conviction that Russia could, indeed must, skip the liberal stage of history and move directly into complete communism. Nor did Weber seem to grasp that with Lenin socialism breaks with spontaneity as the revolutionary "vanguard" imposes itself from without, a deed of the party, and by no means the work of the proletariat. Weber also seemed unaware of Lenin's genius in seeing the necessity of withdrawing from the war, winning over the peasantry with land expropriations of the gentry class, and, through propaganda, presenting himself as a charismatic hero—as indeed he was in John Reed's *Ten Days that Shook the World*.

Yet if Soviet communism outlasted Weber's expectations, it endured as a failed monument to the fallacies of Marxism. Although the young Marx had delved into classical political thought in his early years, he later dismissed the western concept of political liberty as an offshoot of capitalism. In *On the Jewish Question* the "icy water" of capitalist circulation chills liberty as well as property. Without liberty, Marxism rested on nothing more than the mystique of history as a dialectical process, a philosophy of history without a solid philosophical foundation.

THE PROLETARIAT AND THE PURITAN

Almost all commentators on Weber assume that his critique of communism centered on his idea of bureaucracy, and thus that he foresaw the coming of "hyperbureaucratic planning" and the domination of party *apparatchiks*. One eminent American historian of Soviet communism dismissed Weber's perspective as "at best a half-insight."[28] But when he assessed communist Russia Weber fixated less on bureaucracy than on ideology. True, bureaucracy took up much of his discussion of Russia in particular and the modern world in general. But the tyranny of bureaucracy would become the ultimate consequence of a social formation that tried to reach the "kingdom of freedom" without a foundation in philosophical truth and moral value. And here we run up against another seeming puzzle in Weber's vast breadth of thought and reflection.

As a modernist, Weber believed that truth was epistemologically unknowable; as an ethical theorist, he believed values are subjectively chosen rather than objectively discovered. Such stances made it appear that Weber was a relativist, and long after his death a young German scholar, who would become influential in America after World War II, accused him of committing another intellectual crime. Having emphasized the uniqueness of historical phenomena and the contingency of events, and hence appearing to deny absolute truth and unconditional values, Weber was charged with being a "historicist." The charge was made by Leo Strauss in *Natural Right and History* (1953). Yet buried in Weber's *Economy and Society* (posthumously published, it will be recalled, in fragments in Germany in the early twenties) is a discussion of "natural law" and its vital importance in the course of western history; and even though Weber used the term "law" instead of "right," he was willing to grant the value of a concept that took its validity from nature rather than historical convention.[29]

Weber emphasized that the concept of natural law arose in the beginnings of modern times and particularly during revolutionary epochs, and he noted that it still exists in America. Having some of its origins in secular Stoic ideas, it was taken over by Christianity. What is natural law? A set of norms, Weber states, that are valid independently of and even superior to existing positive law. Its legitimacy derives not from its origins, which would (to anticipate the later Straussian critique) render it susceptible to a critical historicist analysis; instead its norms emanate "from their immanent and teleological qualities." It had a "birthright" in the Magna Carta and it became most pronounced in eighteenth-century Protestant sects. In natural law reason was regarded as identical with the "nature of things" as part of the laws of nature. Did natural law enter Russian history?

"The decisive turn toward substantive natural law is connected primarily with socialist theories of the exclusive legitimacy of the acquisition of wealth by one's own labor." Without citing Locke, Weber emphasizes that labor is the means by which the value of property is created and hence work is the ground of acquisition as well as the biological means of self-preservation. But in a section on "Class Relations and Natural Law Ideology," Weber suggests there exist three "socialist" rights that are mutually incompatible, especially in the rural society that is Russia.

In a peasant society natural law can mean the right to share in the land to the extent of one's own labor power (*tredovaya norma*); or a right to own land as part of the traditional standard of living (*potrebityelnaya norma*); or the right to the full product of one's labor. Thus it can mean either the right to engage in work, the right to a minimum standard of living, or the right to reap the fruits of one's labor. The problem is that the first two are possible under handicraft conditions, while the third, the socialist version that also derives from historical traditions, is impossible in a modern economy since labor no longer determines value in the act of production. The modern economy is market driven, and value responds mainly to the vagaries of consumer demand. "Where the return is determined by the sale of the product in a freely competitive market," wrote Weber of the modern supply-and-demand economy, "the content of the right of the individual to the full value of his product inevitably loses its meaning." Referring to the Revolution of 1905, Weber observes:

> As far as one can judge today, the Russian Revolution of the last decade will in all probability have been the last of the natural law–oriented agrarian revolutions. It has been bled to death by its own intrinsic contradictions, including those between its ideological postulates.

Twelve years after 1905, the bolsheviks come to power with a labor theory of value that could only work in a medieval period of handicraft labor. In the modern economy, value emerges from either the free competition of exchange transactions or from the state as it imposes its own criterion of allocation and reward. In the first instance value is determined by the impersonal chance of the market, in the second by the willed caprice of the commissar. With the second alternative we can only have bureaucracy and the "fixed wages" and "just price" system of the middle ages. With a command economy, Russia marches forward only to end backwards.

To suggest that Weber's critique of developments in Russia is "at best a half-insight" is at best only half right. Weber foresaw bureaucracy as inevitable under communism because Marxism had no foundation in a modern value theory relevant to a modern age, quite a spectacular failure for a philosophy that insists that ideas must change in response to changing conditions. Weber sympathized with the socialist critique of capitalism to the extent that modern business responds to market demands and thus caters to what people think they want as opposed to what they may actually need. In this respect capitalism reflects modernity in that the formal rationality of production excludes any moral consideration regarding the distribution of goods. But as a philosopher Marx himself excluded any moral concern for justice and ethics, and thus those who seized power in his name, and, in addition, invoked the idea of a "science of revolution," simply refused to face the fact that science cannot answer to ethical issues. Thus Weber alone among western scholars saw what Soviet Russia would become before its "ideological postulates" were put into practice. Long before the western world became aware of Stalin and the Gulag, Weber exposed communism as a theoretical mess.

Some scholars see elements of compatibility between Marx and Weber. Certainly Weber admired Marx's sense of history as a relentless movement that transforms the old into the new, and Marx would have admired Weber's passion for freedom and his disdain for power and domination disguised as authority. Karl Löwith has demonstrated brilliantly the similarities of Marx's preoccupation with alienation and Weber with rationalization.[30] But there remains an issue that renders Weber a more penetrating thinker by virtue of asking a question Marx refused to ask, or perhaps assumed it need not be asked because it need not be answered. Why does the worker work?

Seeing man as a "species being" inhabiting the "kingdom of necessity," Marx assumed that conditions of scarcity drove historical humanity to labor on earth in order to survive, and just when people were beginning to enjoy productive activity capitalism seemingly comes out of nowhere to appropriate "surplus value," with the workers now finding themselves alienated from their own products:

If the product of labor is alien to me, confronts me as an alien power, to whom does it belong?

If my own activity does not belong to me, if it is an alien and forced activity, to whom then does it belong?

To a being *other* than myself.

Who is this being?

Gods?

Marx recognizes that throughout history workers devoted their labor to the service of various deities. "But," he adds, "gods alone were never workmasters. The same is true of *nature*. And what a contradiction it would be if the more man subjugates nature through his work and the more the miracles of gods are rendered superfluous by the marvels of industry, man should renounce his joy in producing and the enjoyment of his product for love of these powers."[31]

What a contradiction indeed! Weber's interpretation of human alienation leaves us pondering a different premise and a different conclusion. God may have been no workmaster but He was a wrathmaster, and sin-struck man worked and saved to achieve the salvation of the soul, denying immediate gratification and thereby accumulating capital, after which indeed the "miracles of gods are rendered superfluous." Henceforth the contradiction of contradictions: work loses its spiritual meaning to science and technology, the very product of human labor; and the primal motive of labor—not the "joy of producing" but the fear of dying and the terror of eternal damnation—loses its angst when God is dead, exposed as the very product of human reason.

That the Soviet Union turned out to be a worker's state in which there was no motive to work would hardly have surprised Weber had he lived a few years longer. While Marx looked forward to the proletariat, Weber looked back to the Puritan. These differing orientations suggest profoundly different implications.

Marx assumed that labor creates value without telling us how a mode of existence born of necessity will continue to sustain its dignity and worth in the advanced stages of history. There was, as Hannah Arendt and Thorstein Veblen pointed out, a "tautology" and an "oracular obscurity" in Marx's attempt to carry English natural right theory over into a Hegelian teleology in order to envision labor producing the "erection of an objective world of things" that defies annihilation by waste, rot, and consumption.[32] The world of things and goods may be seen as an output of the unfolding life of humankind but modernity, with its marketplace, machines, and own system of distribution, makes a mockery of labor as a value-producing activity. As to Weber, he endowed the early work ethic with the dignity of a spiritual passion, only to observe that in present history "the idea of duty in one's calling prowls about our lives like the ghost of dead religious beliefs."[33] Somehow Marx could continue to believe in the possibility of human freedom without a theory of human motivation. Weber, living in a world where religion continued on as deadening ritual and work was more a compulsion than a conviction, saw no "end" to history, whose tendencies to generate conditions of alienation and reification could very well be an inevitable feature of the modern commodity-producing society.

It was not only the specter of bureaucracy that Weber saw emerging in Soviet Russia. Equally troubling was the spectacle of a political revolution without a coherent philosophical foundation. Marx himself never convincingly explained how labor, the activity that produces alienation, can also be the activity that overcomes it. Nor could other socialists explain how natural right necessarily privileges labor over capital. A natural right had once been regarded as an attribute of a person on the basis of which one is entitled to have or to do something. The producing of things derived from laboring on the materials of earth presupposes that workers' labor is theirs to own and the fruits of their labor are theirs to possess. Weber saw, as did Abraham Lincoln, that a value system founded upon labor is more likely to lead to capitalism than to socialism. Small wonder that after the bolsheviks came to power they made it clear that work confers no rights. In July 1918 the new bolshevik government, in Article 3 of its pseudo-constitutional charter, declared: "As a means of destroying the parasitic classes of society, work is made obligatory for all."[34]

It will be recalled that Weber observed of the fate of the Protestant ethic: "The Puritan wanted to work in a calling; we are forced to do so." Herewith the irony. While Marx assumed he was looking forward to the rise of a class-conscious proletariat, he was really looking backward, and trying to pull ahead, an ideal of work that had been born centuries earlier. In earlier times the act of labor could be seen and felt as the crown of creation, with workers tilling their own holdings with their own hands and seeing the results blossom before their eyes. Marx's attributing Promethean powers to labor as well as capital derived from the power of both to transform and melt away everything fixed and seemingly substantial. Yet while the forms of work and business may change, the value Marx attributes to labor remains constant, so much so that he appears to be an essentialist, assuming that "labor power" resides in the unchanging conceptual essence from which it emanates. When Weber describes the "high pathos" of the *Communist Manifesto* as a "prophecy," he comes close to treating Marxism as a religion which is unaware of itself. The presumed superiority of labor over capitalism, whether based on the mystique of dialectical logic or the illusions of definitional reasoning, clearly has no basis in empirical history. Nor does the labor theory of value. How can value continue to inhere in objects that are produced by labor when value is ascribed to things by the desire for them? With the waning of Calvinism, it is difficult to see anything standing in the way of a modern culture of consumption, which Weber disdained as little more than an economy of "sport."

Capitalism is the enemy of labor not necessarily because it is exploitative. Weber could readily grant the socialists that they have a genuine class enemy. The problem is that capitalism is progressive and betrays labor not only by exploiting it but by leaving it behind. Here and there in his vast and often meandering oeuvre, Weber describes the once-rich meaning of work that has been lost. But an Italian contemporary and admirer of Weber has put this description together in a passage that deserves to be quoted in full:

> Aristotle said ironically that men would be freed from the slavery of daily toil only when the plectrum played the lyre unaided by human hands and when shuttles wove cloth of themselves. . . . Those very times have come. Shuttles do weave of themselves, but man has become their servant, bound to the loom far more closely than the slaves of antiquity weaving from dawn till dark. . . . Karl Marx had a profound intuition of the truth that the essence of capitalist civilization lies in the transcendence of the brain over the arm, of the intelligence over the hand, of executive activity over actual labor. The more completely capitalistic civilization realizes in fact this essential principle of its being, the deeper the gulf between the man who directs work and the man who actually does it. The executive almost evolves into a creature on another plane of life, in a superior world ruled by higher laws. Between the apprentice and the master of medieval corporations, and between the working man and his employer in early manufacturing, the difference was small and easily overcome. . . . Today the great captain of industry, directing from his office the far-flung net of his affairs as a king directs a nation, lives at an interplanetary distance from one of his working men, slave of the machine he operates, [subject to] the monotonous repetition of the same gestures and movements. [The industrialist] can heartily and sincerely sing the hymn to labor as a source of joy; [the worker], a mere helpless cog or wheel or lever, would think it the bitterest mockery of life to which he is condemned. . . . At the end of the

road followed by the civilization of labor there may thus be, by a
supreme irony of history, a total denial of work as having any spiritual
value whatever.[35]

How could work ever again have the meaning and value it once had
for the worker in preindustrial times when labor was more fulfilling than
alienating? Shortly before he died, Weber returned to his manuscript on
the Protestant ethic and added a section, the fragments of which convey
the same message contained in the statement above. The irony is that
Weber saw socialism failing just when Marx assumed it would succeed
since history was behind it and history was ultimately benign and emancipatory. The time period separating Marx and Weber is hardly sufficient
to explain why one thinker believed in the continued potential of what
another thinker saw as a lost hope. Weber valued labor all the more
because its ascetic, spiritual dimension had been obliterated by history,
the very demiurge that Marx looked to as the promise of the future. The
entire edifice of communism rested on the wishful assumption that what
history had rendered irrelevant would rise again from the dead because
in history itself class consciousness was by definition ascendant and always
immanent even if not immediately imminent. Although aware of the
devastating effects of industrialization and modernization for labor, Marx
continued to see change and transformation as redemptive; history pro-
gresses toward its end with the development of productive forces; hence
workers were to work their way out of the very condition they had
worked themselves into. "This new formulation of the problem," Marx
wrote in reference to labor being both alienating and redeeming, "already
contains its solution." All development is through contradiction, and thus
"the overcoming (*Aufhebung*) of self-alienation follows the same course as
self-alienation."[36]

Whether or not Marx had unduly deified the creative strength of the
proletariat, as the Frankfurt "critical theorists" would later claim, was not
the issue that rendered Weber impatient with socialist prophecy. He foresaw that Russia as a self-proclaimed worker's state would not work as it
would claim to work because work no longer had a basis in anything
spiritual or even meaningful. In his reflections on Russia, it should be
noted, Weber was equally critical of Tolstoy and the American he often
drew upon, Henry George. It was not only fervent Marxists who refused
to see that the industrial machine and the market economy play havoc
with the precious values of the past. Tolstoy and George projected their
hopes against history when they assumed that value springs from com-
munally shared land and simple subsistence labor. Weber did not go as far

as Marx and ridicule farm communes as part of the "idiocy of rural life," but he knew from his earlier study of agricultural laborers that progress takes its toll of farmers as well as workers.[37]

With Weber there would be no "end" to history, no *Aufhebung*, no overcoming its contradictions by annulling them in the act of carrying them up into higher and higher syntheses. Living with the human condition, the impulses of freedom and liberation would forever be struggling against the long reach of domination. With Marx all struggle ends with the abolition of property. With Weber humankind must continue to struggle with itself in the realm of politics, where nothing sets limits to the will to power other than a consciousness of the dominating will. Whatever the outcome of the conflict between labor and capital, with politics power is never in abeyance, and with power there is no escape from responsibility just as with history there is no escape from tragedy.

ELEVEN

"The Centre Cannot Hold"

THE PROFESSION AND VOCATION OF POLITICS

Intellectual history, the study of past ideas and philosophies, is currently in ill repute. It is no secret that certain French schools of thought known as poststructuralism and deconstruction are derived from the German thinkers Martin Heidegger and Friedrich Nietzsche. But is it legitimate to indict the "German disease" for contributing to "the closing of the American mind"?[1] In addition to the animus of American neoconservatism, French intellectuals who were once not only Marxists but revolutionary Maoists have recently, as embittered ex-radicals, blamed their wayward youths on the "scandal" of German philosophy. Hence Fichte, Hegel, and Marx are held accountable for claiming to have uncovered the hidden logic of humanity's historical development and to have demonstrated that the individual, and freedom and responsibility, stand helpless in the face of inexorable historical laws.

Thus "the master thinkers" have supposedly lain the conceptual foundation of modern totalitarianism.[2]

In all such attempts to blame the treacheries of politics on the theories of intellectuals, almost no one bothers to study Max Weber on this particular subject. With Weber political and social philosophy, rather than coming to an end in nihilism, continue to radiate a special luminosity all the more rare in times of darkness, and nowhere was this light and learning more radiant than in his penultimate text, "Politics as a Vocation."

In Munich in 1919, the place and time Weber presented his now-famous address, Germany had not only lost a war but seemed to have lost its head as well. The "German Revolution" which had broken out in the previous winter resulted in the declaration of the "Soviet Republic of Bavaria," in Weber's mind a street politics of barricades and machine guns that would be snuffed out by the superior power of the state. Yet the kind of aristocratic liberalism Weber stood for came to be attacked from all sides. Had he heard the lines, Weber would have immediately grasped the Irish poet W. B. Yeats's "The Second Coming," written in recollection of Dublin's "time of troubles":

> Turning and turning in the widening gyre
> The falcon cannot hear the falconer;
> Things fall apart; the centre cannot hold;
> Mere anarchy is loosed upon the world,
> The blood-dimmed tide is loosed, and everywhere
> The ceremony of innocence is drowned;
> The best lack all conviction, while the worst
> Are full of passionate intensity.[3]

Politically Germany was Ireland drunk with madness at one extreme and meekness at the other. On one side the communists, believing that the moment of revolution had arrived, convinced themselves that the "contradictions of capitalism" would be magnified by calling for a mass strike and even insurrectionary violence. On the other side the pacifists, renouncing force and violence, convinced themselves that war and revolution could be replaced by love and humility. All extremes, the syndicalists as well as Spartacists, were futilely denying what Weber would call in his address the "unmistakable reality of politics." The "children of light" (to use Niebuhr's categories) assumed domination could be eliminated by moral persuasion, while the "children of darkness" were even more irresponsible in assuming that using power as a means would bring about the end of power itself. The realities of politics confounded others besides the Germans. Woodrow Wilson went from light to darkness during the war, becoming something of Nietzsche's priest and warrior, and thus a president who wanted to be loved ended up being loathed. In the demonic disorders raging through Germany in winter 1918–19, the best did indeed become confused while the worst became emboldened.

Weber's address on politics, as well as the companion address on science, had been prompted by an essay on "Vocation and Youth" written by Alexander Schwab, a student of Alfred Weber. The jaded young Schwab took a dim view of entering into a profession, seeing work as a "false idol" of the western-European and American world which can only give rise to "alienation" and betray the ancient Greek ideal by "endangering the soul." Schwab's romantic anticapitalism scarcely reflected the views of all the students but it did convey the concern many had about the choice of a career.[4]

The lecture series had been organized by the Freistudentische Bund, "The Association of Free Students" in Bavaria. A leftist-liberal group, the Bund stood poised between radical impatience for political change and loyalty to patriotism. Weber had to face what one described as "poetically revolutionary-minded students" and pacifists opposed to the "mindless" tradition of German *Realpolitik*.[5]

Tension was thick in Munich when Weber delivered his lecture. Rumors spread that followers of Kurt Eisner wanted to force open the meeting, and Ernst Toller, the anarchist who did not fear death, was liable to do anything. Marianne, who was serving in the Baden Parliament at the time, later received a letter. "I myself was among the audience and recall vividly the superior disregard with which Max Weber spoke of the workers' and soldiers' councils" and how he "mentioned casually the threat of machine guns from such councils against the hearings in the Baden Parliament, in which you have participated as a delegate."[6] If Weber showed no sign of nervousness, he anticipated the lecture with some doubts about how he would rise to the occasion. He wrote to Else Jaffé stating he still did not know what the date would be for the talk and worrying that it will "go badly" unless he can concentrate only on the specific topic assigned.[7]

The lecture was given at the University of Munich's Steinicke Art Hall, at 7:30 p.m., on January 28, 1919. At the outset few people in the audience would be aware that they were about to hear so meditative a treatise in political philosophy. One person remembered the opening:

It was a winter evening in a dank and meager hall which barely holds a hundred people. An old woman with a slightly bent posture goes with a cane along the aisles and takes a place up front: Ricarda Huch. Max Weber, impressively built yet gaunt, steps forth. The powerful head turned completely to the students, he speaks freely with a sonorous yet subdued voice, drawing on only notes, his violent head movements ruffling his hair and beard. He ties up his listeners through a compelling train of thought, apt examples, historically grounded ideas. In the strict demand on the politicians—passion, responsibility, good judgment; not ethics of character but ethics of responsibility—he gives, I feel, a creed.[8]

Ricarda Huch, the poetess who walked with a cane to take a front seat, also remembered the event. "I suddenly had this feeling again that Max Weber was like an actor. This was a spontaneous feeling—I was prepared for something else—that struck me when I had heard him lecture. I think it is because the fountain of instincts, instead of flowing through him, are channeled by his intellect and consciousness."[9]

Weber's lecture brought to fruition thoughts and tensions that went back to his Freiburg inaugural of 1895. The difference was that in 1919 the Germany that he once saw as so bold and brave had suffered defeat and, as the Paris peace negotiations dragged on and many of the 14 Points were discarded, a sense of betrayal and humiliation as well. Germany was also in the throes of sporadic revolutionary uprisings, and while the "bolshevik menace" appeared to be spreading, France and the United States had sent troops to Russia—the former for counterrevolutionary reasons, the latter for reasons complex but more democratic. Among American intellectuals intervention, like the war itself, was seen as a desperate effort to prop up the decadent, tottering old order, "a botched civilization . . . / an old bitch gone in the teeth," wrote the poet Ezra Pound. "1919," declared the novelist John Dos Passos, "is the springtime of revolution!"[10] Weber had no such illusions. If liberals and the Left felt that history was on the move, and that it was moving from the bottom up, Weber's address, which dealt with power even more than politics, leadership, and ethics, demonstrated why power mocks a war made in the name of democracy and a revolution made in the name of the people.

"The lecture which I am to give at your request," Weber begins, "will necessarily disappoint you." He went on: those who think that an analysis of the vocation of politics should instruct others on what stands to take miss the point. The sociologist is concerned with how politics functions as a phenomenon of organized relations, how the state exercises its authority, how rulers assert themselves, how parliaments vie with monarchs and presidents to maximize their influence, how politicians need the press to communicate favorably their positions and the press needs advertisement for income, how modern democracies expand the profession of advocates as litigation becomes subject to legal rationalization, how American electoral politics, where the president is elected independently of Congress, leads to a two-party system, political machines, patronage, and the spoils system. For much of the first part of his talk Weber drove home the point that the study of politics is the study of the movements and manifestations of power and the manner in which society submits to it. Well before Weber discussed his three types of legitimacy (traditional, legal-rational, charismatic) to show how and why authority comes to be accepted, he deliberately sought to shock the audience by quoting the hero of the Red Army. " 'Every state is founded on force,' said Trotsky at Brest-Litovsk." Weber could have quoted the hero of the American Revolution as well. "Government," said George Washington, "is not reason, it is not eloquence—it is force."[11]

Weber's thoughts are not so alien to the American mind as to preclude sensing parallels between "Politics as a Vocation" and the *Federalist*. In neither document do its authors draw upon the Enlightenment's concept of "reason" or the classical idea of "virtue" for guidance, and each reminds their respective countrymen of what Weber called the "average deficiencies of people" and what Madison called "the defect of better motives." Skeptical of democracy, the authors believed that the political leader must establish "distance" from the people so as to have "perspective" (Weber) and to "refine and enlarge" visions of the national interest (Madison). The American and German thinkers also insisted that politics cannot be separated from power, which might be defined as the ability of the will to command its objects and of the mind to enjoy the status power brings. "What is power, but the ability to do something," instructed Hamilton. "He who is active in politics," wrote Weber, "strives for power either as a means in serving other aims, idealistic or egoistic, or as 'power for power's sake,' that is, in order to enjoy the prestige-feeling power gives."[12] These comparisons can be drawn only to better highlight the more telling contrast: Weber bypasses the whole question of government by the conscious consent of the governed and then takes on two issues that go unaddressed in the *Federalist*: the theory of political leadership and the theory of ethical duty. But before turning to those topics he needed to address something America never experienced: defeat and foreign occupation.

In 1919, with Germany having just lost a war and facing a revolutionary situation, Weber had good reason to define government less by consent and voluntary contract than by coercion and irresistible force. Early on in the lecture he asked his audience to consider not so much how aspects of politics are formally defined as how they are ultimately settled. "At the present moment," he stated in reference to the revoutionary barricades in the streets of Munich, "the relation between the state and violence is a particularly intimate one." So much is the means (*Mittel*) of violence peculiar to the state that Weber feels "we have to say that a state is that human community which (successfully) lays claim to the monopoly of legitimate violence within a territory." If other associations or individuals are taking to violence it is because the state allows it to happen; for the "state is held to be the sole source of the 'right' to use violence."

After offering such brute descriptions, Weber refrains from suggesting how the present state should act. It will be recalled that Weber warned Woodrow Wilson against forcing Germany to accept an armistice before peace conditions had been negotiated; hence he regarded the sovereignty of the state as its capacity to wage violent war. But Weber is also addressing students, some followers of Eisner or Toller, and he seeks to tame their millennial dreams by making them aware of the consequences of their expectations if carried out. To that end Weber elaborates two points: the character of the modern state will remain a structure of commands regardless who runs it; and politics itself is as much a practical enterprise (*Betrieb*) of interest as a calling, a vocation (*Beruf*) of ideals.

The challenge facing Weber was to rescue politics from the corrosions of modernity, and here he faced somewhat the same issue that Marx was reluctant to face in regards to labor. Can the fate of political man escape the fate of working man? Marx assumed that his way of seeing historical development would assure the survival and ultimate triumph of the worker once again reunified with his tools and his total being. In classical thought it was similarly assumed that a specific activity, in this instance politics rather than labor, nourishes human growth, moral excellence, and civic virtue. Yet such qualities presupposed autonomy, independence, self-reflectedness, critical judgment, and other human attributes lost to the modern human condition haunting a bureaucratic society of interdependence and mind-numbing routinization. Earlier Weber had demonstrated how political liberty developed from the religious struggle for independence and freedom of conscience, but the historical consequences of Calvinism became a Yankee capitalism that could no longer sustain either the work ethic or the moral character necessary to political duty and civic responsibility. Under Calvinism man's mind was oriented toward God as the soul suffered anxiety over the riddle of salvation and damnation, and the mind looked upward to ponder the soul's fate. With capitalism the human gaze turned downward, toward crops and commodities. In the *Protestant Ethic* Weber cited Kant and Goethe for insights on character and the demands of duty to illuminate the qualities of a religious conscience. But the Calvinist sense of inwardness could not withstand the transition to capitalism and modernity. How, then, could politics be a "calling"? Or, to turn into a question Weber's remark about a "beautiful passage" in Machiavelli, how to enable modern citizens to deem the greatness of their political community higher than the salvation of their souls?

DEMOCRACY AND LEADERSHIP

In traditional political thought, and especially in Montesquieu's writings, it was assumed that while despotism rested on the reality of fear and democracy on the promise of virtue, aristocracy counted upon honor and pride in reputation. Weber's appeal to "honor," "nobility," and "dignity" indicates his affinity with the aristocratic tradition of politics. His reservations about democracy, it should be noted, scarcely bespoke an arrogant elitism but rather a cool-headed realism. Like Tocqueville, Weber recognized that it would not be a self-denying "virtue" that would animate modern democracy but rather a "virtuous materialism" where the pursuit of wealth took precedence over all other aspects of life. Weber, living later, saw further the implications of modernity and saw that industrial society, instead of "holding back" from what Tocqueville feared would be an all-devouring "pernicious materialism," had succumbed, and thus Montesquieu was wrong to look to virtue, for classical political thought is, like wage labor, one of the first casualties of capitalism.[13]

In showing the ways modern politics had come to take on the characteristics of business enterprise, Weber was exposing not only the unreliability of older republican ideals but also the unfeasibility of newer socialist dreams. Among European democratic socialists it had been an article of faith that democratic socialism would pose an answer to capitalism, that the mass majority of voters would use political means to bring under popular control the small minority of the wealthy by appropriating their means of production. But Weber asked students of politics to observe directly how party machines actually functioned.

Turning to American history, he traced the development of politics from Washington's era of squire aristocracy administered by "gentlemen" to the Jacksonian period, which was anything but gentle, with the rise of coarse professional politicians and cabinets; then to the post–Civil War period and the advent of bosses and machines, the selling of candidates, and other activities that made Wall Street and State Street one and the same. "Who is the boss?" asked Weber. "He is a political capitalist entrepreneur who on his own account and at his own risk provides voters." Neither fear, virtue, nor honor animated politics; now it was interest, money, and power (or the "social honor" that "material reward" brings). And the Americanization of Europe is not far behind, believed Weber, who could hardly forget the role that historical Protestantism played in the coming of modernity, which meant that in America Germany would find a glimpse of its own future. The rule of party cliques without a vocation for politics has emerged in Germany as well as America, Weber noted, emphasizing that everywhere people tend more and more to live "off" rather than "for" politics. Even more seriously, the only value that survives in a democracy under the domain of a profit-minded capitalist culture is interest, expressed either in the pursuit of wealth or the advancement of a career. Weber's jeremiad about "the disenchantment of the world," invoked in his companion addresss on science, describes the modern predicament as the devaluation of values. "Precisely the ultimate and most sublime values have retreated from public life." To the extent that politics, like science and capitalism, is involved in power and control, politics itself can only bring about a systematically managed society whose relentless rationalization drives out the redeeming realm of value and makes genuine ethical action increasingly difficult to undertake. How, then, can politics be an honorable vocation in a life of alienation?

It cannot be, at least not democratic politics. Weber's "Politics as a Vocation" is really about leadership, about the exceptional person who rules by clarifying and bringing to expression issues that modern democracy is incapable of articulating. The leader is a figure of conviction, insight, vitality, asceticism, devotion, sacrifice, preferring struggle to subordination, moved by values that are intrinsically worthy and not simply instrumentally useful. Politics, in contrast, is all pragmatic, an attempt at expedients, strategic coalitions, adaptations and readjustments, all of which aim toward mundane ends on the assumption that only the practicable could be the successful. Politics, rather than expressing democracy, actually mirrors its pluralistic, multifactional character. Democracy rests neither on a consensus nor on the coherent will of its citizens, which, Weber earlier told Michels, is a "fiction." A consensus that may happen to exist comes from social mores and institutions that precede democratic politics. The mobilization of mass politics is the problem rather than the solution; only leadership can answer the three nemeses of democratic politics: mediocrity, bureaucracy, mendacity.

Having earlier criticized the Kaiser and his cohorts for blundering into

World War I, Weber had no difficulty convincing himself that the problem of Germany was the problem of leaderlessness. It has been pointed out that earlier in his career Weber saw little possibility that a class, whether Junkers, workers, or the bourgeoisie, would be capable of assuming a leadership role. Thus later Weber generally had in mind an individual, for while the masses remain passive and while groups and committees prefer to talk rather than to act, the individual takes the initiative and shows the way. In his war writings Weber valued parliamentary government as the training ground for leaders, and he discussed the importance of democracy having plebiscitary leadership. In "Politics as a Vocation" he is less interested in the mechanisms and procedures of political leadership than in the specific qualities possessed by the leader.

Similarly, he seems unconcerned where leaders come from. Although Weber's values are aristocratic, he scarcely looks to the German gentry class or any specific social strata. Like Hamilton, he expects a genuine leader not to represent his class but to transcend it; like Emerson, he sees no opposition between the individual genius and the democratic masses. A leader can be a singular phenomenon, for while politics makes demands upon others, leadership makes demands upon itself, and the values that emerge from leadership are chosen in an act of freedom, the only basis of responsibility. A leader can aspire to greatness not by surpassing his people but by representing them better than the compromises and distortions of democratic politics. Nobility is far from an inherited attribute of the aristocratic class; on the contrary, it chooses to be itself against the drift of democracy and the slumber of society.

A genuine leader, Weber explains, drawing upon his three types of authority, is neither rule-bound nor stuck in the grooves of past traditions. Instead he is charismatic in commanding devotion on the part of followers and credible by his commitment to his cause (*Sache*). He yearns, Weber states (quoting Nietzsche anonymously), not for mere "happiness" but higher things—he "aspires after his work." There is no touch of the sordid or cynical in him. "The leader is personally regarded as someone who is inwardly 'called' to the task of leading men, and . . . the led submit to him, not because of custom or statute, but because they believe in him."

What are the springs of action that would motivate the politician as honorable statesman? One "inner joy" of politics, Weber admits, is that it "confers a feeling of power" which places a leading politician above others. But when one asks how such power is justified, ethical questions arise, and Weber specifies three qualities as "decisive for the politician: passion, a feeling of responsibility, and a sense of proportion. Passion in the sense of *concern for the thing itself* [*Sachlichkeit*], the passionate commitment to a 'cause' [*Sache*], to the god or the demon who commands the cause." Passion for Weber is neither "sterile excitement" nor "romantic" eruption but a kind of concentrated intensity on the issue at hand. Proportion requires perspective, a kind of stepping back in order to make responsible judgments, "the ability to maintain one's inner composure and calm while being receptive to realities, in other words *distance* from things and people." One responsibility is to regard politics as an exercise in power without allowing power to become an end in itself. Weber warned against *Machtpolitikers* whose struggle for power becomes "purely personal self-intoxication" so that commitment to an end disappears and every action is "a worship of power *per se*." But the relationship between devotion to a cause and responsibility for an act is an issue that takes politics beyond power to the realm of the ethical, and here Weber introduces the student of politics to the ambiguity of ethics, the treachery of hubris, the cunning of the ironic, and the rebirth of the tragic.

VALUES AND THE REBIRTH OF TRAGEDY

Weber's emphasis on leadership was not meant to address the few to the neglect of the many, as though Germany's future lay in the rule of an unrivaled chancellor or an oligarchy rather than the democracy that the Weimar Republic would become. Weber's address also aimed at the political education of a nation, and when he told the audience that a state cannot be defined by its ends but instead only by its means, he was laying the foundations for his thesis that all politics involves power, force, coercion, control, domination, constraint, even violence. Would not conceiving politics as the struggle for power lead to the Machiavellian conclusion that winning is everything and might right? Significantly, when the American philosopher John Dewey dealt with the same issue a year before Weber's address, he assumed he could resolve the quandary of America's entry into the war by defining the use of force as the rational organization of "efficiency." As did Weber, Dewey also had to face pacifists who opposed the call to arms, and his response appears to be Weberian. "It is the sacrosanct character thus attributed to the State's use of force which gives pungency to the Tolstoian charge that the State is the archcriminal, the person who has recourse to violence on the largest scale. I see no way out except to say that all depends upon the efficient adaptation of means to ends. The serious charge against the State is not that it uses force—nothing was ever accomplished without using force—but that it does not use force wisely or effectively."[14]

From Weber's point of view, however, the pragmatist's notion of politics only accelerates the rationalization of the world where all human action is instrumental and can be assessed by judging whether it is an "efficient adaptation of means to ends." Science, Weber would remind American thinkers, can instruct us how to choose the means to reach an end but as a technique of adjustment and control science can say nothing about why we ought to choose one end over another. Since science is silent on moral preferences, Weber believed only an individual can create values by choosing ends. To the extent that each individual creates his own ethical orientation, and does so to render a "disenchanted" world meaningful, and, what is more, must do so without guidance from science, ethical decisions are bound to be in conflict with one another.

It is precisely because politics has no objective standards to rely upon in the choice of ends that Weber treats politics more as a religion (a "calling") than a science. If politics simply dealt with power, Weber would be comfortable with Machiavelli; if it simply served as democracy's instrument, he would be comfortable with Dewey. But politics involves values as much as power, the subjective choice of ends driven by inner beliefs and needs to endow the world with meaning and significance. Moreover, to choose a value is to create it and not necessarily to find it, and one does so as a reflection of one's character and personality. Politics, then, concerns not only power but "ultimate and sublime values" that modernity has killed, and only the individual can create them anew or give them, in Nietzsche's expression, a "rebirth." Insofar as politics entails personal choices and desires on the part of different individuals, they cannot be objectively evaluated or rationally reconciled. Thus Weber introduces the subject of politics to something new in liberal political philosophy: "the ethical irrationality of the world."

Weber's philosophy of politics offers a philosophy of freedom at variance with almost all secular schools of thought. Freedom is founded in neither reason's capacity to know the laws of nature (rationalism), to obey universalizable imperatives of behavior (idealism), to be bound by society's "General Will" (liberalism, positive), to think and act without interference from authority (liberalism, negative), to apply reflective thought to the solution of problems (pragmatism), to subdue the "passions and interests" that give rise to capitalism (republicanism), to see reality as a lawful succession of observable phenomena (positivism), to listen for the whispers of the "Oversoul" (Transcendentalism), to rhapsodize nature and dwell on the extinct (romanticism), to see conscience as the mechanistic self-control of neurotic emotions (Freudianism), nor, finally, to discern the necessary processes of historical development, history's "dialectic," so as to march from the kingdom of necessity to the kingdom of freedom (socialism). Weber's philosophy of politics, freedom, and history itself seems religious in its emphasis on will in the face of fateful conditions and on character in the face of irrational circumstances.

That "Politics as a Vocation" stands closer to religion than to science may be seen when Weber explains what it is that stands in the way of the politician being a prudent, responsible person able to conduct himself objectively and scientifically. It is the old Calvinist sin of pride, a vanity and hubris that haunts religious thought far more than early classical thought:

> Vanity is a very widespread quality, and perhaps no one is completely free of it. In academic and scholarly circles it is a kind of occupational disease. In the case of the scholar, however, unattractive though this quality may be, it is relatively harmless in the sense that it does not, as a rule, interfere with the pursuit of knowledge. Things are quite different in the case of the politician. The ambition for *power* is an inevitable means (*Mittel*) with which he works. "The instinct for power," as it is commonly called, is thus indeed one of his normal qualities. The sin against the holy spirit of his profession begins where this striving for power becomes detached from the task in hand (*unsachlich*) and becomes a matter of purely personal self-intoxication instead of being placed entirely at the service of the "cause." For there are ultimately just two deadly sins in the area of politics: a lack of objectivity and—often, although not always, identical with it—a lack of responsibility. Vanity, the need to thrust one's person as far as possible into the foreground, is what leads the politician most strongly into the temptation of committing one or other (or both) of these sins, particularly as the demagogue is forced to count on making an "impact," and for this reason is always in danger both of becoming a play-actor and of taking the responsibility for his actions too lightly and being concerned only with the "impression" he is making. His lack of objectivity tempts him to strive for the glittering appearance of power rather than its reality, while his irresponsibility tempts him to enjoy power for its own sake, without any substantive purpose. For although, or rather precisely *because*, power is the inevitable means of all politics, and the ambition for power therefore one of its driving forces, there is no more pernicious distortion of political energy than when the parvenu boasts of his power and vainly mirrors himself in the feeling of power—or indeed any and every worship of power for its own sake. The mere "power politician," a type whom an energetically promoted cult is seeking to glorify here in Germany as elsewhere, may give the impression of strength, but in fact his actions merely lead into emptiness and absurdity. On this point the crit-

ics of "power politics" are quite correct. The sudden inner collapse of typical representatives of this outlook (*Gesinnung*) has shown us just how much inner weakness and ineffectuality are concealed behind this grandiose but empty pose. It stems from a most wretched and superficial lack of concern for the *meaning* of human action, a blasé attitude that knows nothing of the tragedy in which all action, but quite particularly political action, is in truth enmeshed.

To Weber modern politics required something close to a "rebirth" of tragedy, and tragedy as the imitation of noble actions cannot be expected to emerge from democracy, where we simply endure the ordinary while awaiting the remarkable. Weber's idea of tragedy is far from the playwright's strategy of depicting a dramatic rise and a calamitous fall, although it does involve trials of leadership, misunderstanding of intentions, and ironies of action. More specifically, Weber's sense of tragedy consists of two components. First, penetrating the illusions and rationalizations in the lives of people, who allow themselves to move toward power in the name of freedom; or, a different self-deception, to lose a deep emotion, like love, and, rather than suffering its loss, to legitimate it by using reason as psychological rationalization. Second, an understanding that there is no true meaning to the world other than the interpretations and values we bring to it, and we choose our values "through a glass darkly," without objective knowledge and to the exclusion of other values and commitments. Tragedy involves the conflict of irreconcilable choices, but knowledge of a tragic situation can also be educational in that it discloses the controlling impulses of our thoughts that preclude the mind's encounter with itself. Note the way Weber begins with the personal and moves on to the political to show that righteousness prevails in love as much as in war:

> Ethics can appear in a morally quite calamitous role. Let us look at some examples. You will rarely find a man whose love has turned from one woman to another who does not feel the need to legitimate this fact to himself by saying, "She did not deserve my love," or, "She disappointed me," or by offering some other such "reasons." This is a profoundly unchivalrous attitude, for, in addition to the simple fate of his ceasing to love her, which the woman must endure, it invents for itself a "legitimacy" that allows the man to lay claim to a "right" while attempting to burden her not only with misfortune but also with being in the wrong. The successful rival in love behaves in exactly the same way: the other man must be of lesser worth, otherwise he would not have been defeated. The same thing happens after any victorious war, when the

victor will of course assert, with ignoble self-righteousness, "I won because I was in the right." Or when the horrors of war cause a man to suffer a psychological breakdown, instead of simply saying, "It was all just too much for me," he now feels the need to justify his war-weariness by substituting the feeling, "I couldn't bear the experience because I was obliged to fight for a morally bad cause." The same applies to those defeated in war. Instead of searching, like an old woman, for the "guilty party" after the war (when it was in fact the structure of society that produced the war), anyone with a manly, unsentimental bearing would say to the enemy, "We lost the war—you won it. The matter is now settled. Now let us discuss what conclusions are to be drawn in the light of the *substantive* (*sachlichen*) interests involved and—this is the main thing—in the light of the responsibility for the *future* which the victor in particular must bear." Anything else lacks dignity and will have dire consequences. A nation will forgive damage to its interests, but not injury to its honour, and certainly not when this is done in a spirit of priggish self-righteousness. Every new document which may emerge decades afterwards will stir up the undignified squabble, all the hatred and anger, once again, whereas the war ought at least to be buried *morally* when it comes to an end. That is only possible through a sober, matter-of-fact approach (*Sachlichkeit*) and chivalry, and, above all, it is only possible where there is *dignity*.

Weber was approaching his argument, discussed earlier, that holding a country guilty for the past was reasoning backward since true responsibility takes place "before history," not afterwards. Such a "falsification" of the issue, he continues, merely allows the victor to enjoy its position of domination and expropriation with a clear conscience, "of exploiting 'ethics' as a means of 'being in the right.'" What, then, is the relationship of ethics to politics? With Weber posing this question, he proceeds to distinguish two different ethical orientations in order to dramatize their inherent incompatibility and inevitable inescapability. To paraphrase Milton and Nietzsche, Weber set out to justify the ways of politics to the politician by showing politics to be painful, and, as well, suggesting that in its human angst of choice lies its potential for greatness.

Weber cited the bolsheviks and Spartacists as examples of activists who are blind to the incompatibility between politics and ethics. Both resort to force and violence with a clear conscience since they are certain their intentions are idealistic and hence they need not heed the consequences of their actions. The result is that they are no different from any other power wielders in being the instruments of oppression. The pacifists, for their part, renounce force and violence but also rely on their intentions to absolve themselves of responsibility for the outcome of their stance. The Sermon on the Mount, deriving from the unconditional, absolute ethics of the Gospel, applies the injunctions "to turn the other cheek" and to "resist not evil with force." The pacifists, said Weber, in opposing the present war, have made it advantageous for the victor to exploit public confusions, with the result that *"peace, not war, will be discredited."* Similarly, those who felt their commitment to truth compelled them to publish secret state documents failed to consider the consequences of seeing such materials distorted and manipulated. Those who abide by an absolute ethics have no concern for consequences; they follow only an "ethic of principled convictions" (*Gesinnung*).

The "ethic of responsibility" (*Verantwortlichkeitsethik*) meant that "one must answer for the (foreseeable) *consequences* of one's actions." Weber could cite plenty of examples of its violation during wartime. Syndicalists who undertake political action that brings about reaction against their class are acting irresponsibly, as are socialists who think prolonging the war will bring on revolution. Those who adhere to absolute convictions hopelessly founder in squaring the means they advocate to reach the ends they desire. Such a figure is less a sober politician than a "chiliastic prophet"; he wants to sanctify politics instead of studying it. "The man who espouses an ethic of conviction cannot bear the ethical irrationality of the world. He is a cosmic-ethical 'rationalist.' Those of you who know their Dostoeyevsky will recall the scene with the Grand Inquisitor, where the problem is dissected very acutely. It is not possible to unite the ethic of conviction with the ethic of responsibility, nor can one issue an ethical decree determining which end shall sanctify *which* means, if indeed any concession at all is to be made to this principle."

Weber's address continues with references to Jesus of Nazareth and Francis of Assisi, to the Red Guard, to the Holy See and Machiavelli, to Luther, Calvinism, and the Quakers. Not only should politics be kept separate from ethics, he claims, it should never be confused with religion and the needs of the spirit. "Anyone seeking to save his own soul and the soul of others does not take the path of politics in order to reach his goal, for politics has quite different tasks, namely those which can only be achieved by force." The inescapable reality of applied coercion in politics means that the politician contracts with "diabolical powers" whether he is aware of it or not.

Where does Weber take a stand on the two ethics? He seems torn between choosing one over the other, and although early in the essay he describes the two as irreconcilable, he concludes with admiration for the person who can look reality in the face, be aware that anticipating consequences is hazardous, and still act on the demands of conscience. As indicated earlier, in the discussion of Woodrow Wilson, Weber could be comfortable neither with a consequentialist ethic that considered only power and its adaptations nor with an intentionalist ethic that considered only morality and its conceits. The sight of a person knowing the consequences and still taking a stand led Weber to exclaim: "That is something genuinely human and profoundly moving. For it must be possible for each of us to find ourselves in such a similar situation at some point if we are not inwardly dead. In this respect, the ethics of conviction and the ethics of responsibility are not absolute opposites. They are complimentary to one another, and only in combination do they produce the true human being who is *capable* of having a 'vocation for politics.'"

"And now, ladies and gentlemen, let us return to these questions *ten years* from now." By that time, Weber fears, an age of reaction will have set in, and as he speaks of the burdens facing Germany, he suddenly stops and quotes from Shakespeare's Sonnet 102, citing a springtime when "our love was new" and one could greet life looking forward to the "growth of riper days." Leaving the poem, Weber turns sad. "But that is not how things are," he states, referring to the coming days of the Weimar and possible foreign occupation. "What lies immediately ahead of us is not the flowering of summer but a polar night of icy darkness and hardness, no matter which group wins the outward victory now." He then describes the political scene in postwar Germany as the speech moves to its climax, a peroration of hope and heroism in a time of defeat and despair:

> Politics means slow, strong drilling through hard boards, with a combination of passion and a sense of judgment. It is of course entirely correct, and a fact confirmed by all historical experience, that what is possible would never have been achieved if, in this world, people had not repeatedly reached for the impossible. But the person who can do this must be a leader; not only that, he must, in a very simple sense of the word, be a hero. And even those who are neither of these things must, even now, put on the armour of that steadfastness of heart which can withstand even the defeat of all hopes, for otherwise they will not even be capable of achieving what is possible today. Only someone who is certain that he will not be broken when the world, seen from his point of view, is too stupid or too base for what he wants to offer it, and who is certain that he will be able to say "Nevertheless" in spite of everything—only someone like this has a "vocation" for politics.

Weber's historic address fructified brilliantly issues he had been dealing with since his earlier writings on methodology. Ever since Aristotle philosophers have taught that the political involvement of citizens in public affairs nurtures character and moral excellence. But Weber sought to tell the students in the audience about the limitations of politics as a career. If approached as a quest for some kind of transcendence, Weber pointed out, politics would call for self-denial rather than reconciliation with life; if approached scientifically, it could only mean the restrictions of a specific specialization. In no case can politics have "a Faustian universality."[15]

Moreover, philosophers are devoted to truth, and that intellectual pursuit is, like ethics, more a victim of politics than its virtue. Around the time Weber gave his address he had told Else Jaffé that politics was the great passion and "love" of his life. But he also remarked elsewhere, it will be recalled, that while a politician must make compromises, a scholar cannot allow them to be "covered up." The scholar's devotion to truth is at odds with a vocation that must engage itself in the world of power, and the conflict of ethics and politics has no resolution. Thus without rejecting altogether the old classical respect for politics, Weber sought to demonstrate a hitherto undisclosed conflict between what the philosophy of politics had promised and what the politics of power presents before one's very face. No longer can the statesman expect his intellectual horizons and ethical senses to be enlarged by philosophy. Politics has no foundation in anything transcendent and no promise in anything redemptive.

Weber succeeded in his goal of dramatizing the alienation of power from a mind that was meant to control it, and he succeeded in bringing to the surface long-unknown tensions and antinomies. But "Politics as a Vocation" failed to demonstrate how to act responsibly in a world that may not respond to the political mind.

Weber's distinction between conviction and responsibility echoes earlier categories in his theory of human action. Here *Wertrational* stood for some action undertaken with a conscious belief in its value for its own sake, while *Zweckrational* signified an action that is purposeful, instrumental to an end, and undertaken with the prospect of success in mind. In his later wartime "Vocation" address, Weber had no trouble pointing to examples of irresponsible behavior on the part of political figures acting upon their own subjective values, but he was conspicuously silent about figures whose actions would be instrumental and presumably successful and hence responsible. In several of his wartime articles he described Woodrow Wilson as "sincere" in his intent and conviction to bring peace to Europe, even if the means he chose would fail to bring a just settlement for Germany. But how could Weber demonstrate the adequacy of the opposite ethic of responsibility, when here a leader must choose a course of action and be answerable for its outcome, and do so in a world where history does not repeat itself, follows no rational pattern, yields no causal sequences that are uniform and possibly predictable, and, what is even more Weberian, takes unexpected, ironic turns? Weber himself, one recalls, rejoiced at the outbreak of the war in 1914, obviously believing it would lead somewhere hopeful, some outcome beneficial to Germany. As the poet tells us, the "corridors" of history can lead anywhere.

DEATH IN MUNICH

Munich in winter 1919–20 was as cold and grim as postwar Germany itself. The Webers lived first with friends and then moved into their own modest quarters, which contrasted sadly with the spaciousness of their house in Heidelberg. On morning walks Max and Marianne saw barren trees and frozen dead leaves everywhere. In the spring, when the creeks began to run again and the foliage sprouted once more, the Webers came upon a pleasant surprise near a lake outside of the city. "The discovery of little Bierderstein Castle which stood there dreamily, just as it had at the time of Goethe, gave the Webers a great pleasure," remembered Marianne. "What a boon it was not to be confined to the cold stone prisons of the city streets!"[16]

Working in a small den, Weber continued his research and writing on several topics almost simultaneously. He was also teaching at the University of Vienna as well as presenting lectures at the University of Munich. His classes were "so terribly overcrowded that I had to shout," he told Marianne. He began to wonder why the demands of work itself should now leave him exhausted—"very odd that this kind of *physical* activity should be such a strain on me."[17] Other people wondered why he drove himself so hard. "One day," Marianne recalled, "when Weber was asked what his scholarship meant to him, he replied: 'I want to see how much I can stand.' What did he mean by that? Perhaps he regarded it as his task to endure the *antinomies* of existence and, further, to exert to the utmost his freedom from illusions and yet to keep his ideals inviolate and preserve his ability to devote himself to them."[18]

One reason he may have thrown himself so intensely back into his scholarship is that he had been rejected by the world of politics, and politics had been, he once confided to Mina Tobler, his "secret love." Although Weber had been led to believe that his views would be seri-

ously listened to at the Versailles conference, he was left in the dark as to
the actual role he would assume. He agreed to go to Versailles after
Prince Max von Baden enthusiastically recommended him as a partici-
pant and, given his oratorical abilities, as one who would be best qualified to present the decisions reached at Paris to the German people. But
Weber refused to accept the implications of Germany's defeat and the
end of a powerful nation-state. On the issue of war guilt and economic
reparations Weber also took a stance that made him an outsider in the
circle of advisors at Versailles. He regarded the economic terms of peace
as so onerous that even a limited implementation of them would be irresponsible (a position similarly taken by John Maynard Keynes in *The
Economic Consequences of Peace*, 1920). Such terms, he wrote to Marianne,
comprise a slippery slope to disaster. "The closer one looks at them, they
are so terrible and so cunning, that if even only half of them were
accepted all one would be able to see is a black hole without the faintest
light in the distance."[19]

It was not only Germany's former enemies who cast a spell of gloom
over Munich. In 1918 the philosopher Oswald Spengler published the
massive tome *Der Untergang des Abendlandes (The Decline of the West)*, an
olympian effort to trace the deterioration of the human mind from the
heights of classical reason to the depths of modern biological explanations, where man is little more than a morphological mutant no different
from animals and plants. The much-discussed book had some of the same
fateful doom as Weber's idea of rationalization, and students in Munich
arranged a meeting between Spengler and Weber in the conference
room at the City Hall. The room was jammed with Freideutsche Jugend
and communists and anarchists were also present. To a rapt audience
Spengler and Weber debated for a day and a half. Both scholars respected
one another but neither could agree to the other's point of view. As a
result of the impasse the students had no answer to their question: "But
what shall we do?"[20]

Later Marianne would challenge Spengler's thesis in *Die Frau*. Meanwhile, after the debate ended, students gathered around Weber and
walked with him to a small house where they lit a stove and poured out
their thoughts about the future. They spoke of starting communes, of
being free from compulsion and coercion, of living off the soil and cultivating the soul. Weber sat silently listening, perhaps remembering what
he had said in his Freiburg inaugural when he declared that a country
need not grow old as long as it retains the passions of its youth. "His kind
eyes," wrote Marianne who was with him in the room, "reflected his
complete readiness to empathize with the young people."[21]

In the winter of 1919 Weber's mother Helene died unexpectedly in Heidelberg. On a visit to Munich she had expressed a desire to live to see Germany's recovery. She lived out her last years engaging in the acts of kindness that characterized her life. Before her open coffin Weber delivered the eulogy, praising her love of life and compassion for others that enriched everyone around her.

In April 1920 the Webers received a brief message that came as a shattering blow. Weber's sister Lili had taken her life by gas poisoning. Lili had resembled her mother in physical features but lacked the humor and patience to see her through the vicissitudes of fortune. She left four fatherless children, her husband having died the previous year in the war. When the Webers hurried to Heidelberg they were excited about the possibility of adopting the orphans. According to Marianne, Weber was moved profoundly by the thought that they would at last have children. But friends advised against it, reminding Max of his age. Marianne also had second thoughts when it struck her that Max "was the blessing of her existence." The children were turned over to several relatives and Weber returned to Munich alone while Marianne went on a lecture tour.[22]

In Munich Weber worked on "The Sociology of Music" and on revising the Protestant ethic manuscript. It is possibly at this time that Weber adds some of the last haunting passages to the work, passages about the fading of the "rosy blush" of the Enlightenment, the "fate" that decreed that the once "light cloak" of concern for external goods has turned into an "iron cage," the world of "specialists without spirit." Something else also enters the manuscript when a reference is added to Wagner's opera *Die Walküre*; here Weber expresses a fascination with Siegmund's attitude toward the fear of death and the longing for love, possibly reflecting thoughts about his deceased mother and sister and the two remaining women in his life: Marianne and Else. Thus the revisions made to Weber's greatest book contained some of the same emotional turmoil of the original essays in 1904, when Weber had recently recovered from an illness most likely brought on by thoughts of his father's death.[23]

In late May 1920, Weber fell ill. He had fevers and chills and would recover briefly only to relapse, sometimes into delirium. A doctor diagnosed his ailment as pneumonia, possibly a result of the influenza epidemic that had raged throughout western Europe after the war. When he managed to speak, he seemed to accept his approaching death with calm. He made a reference to Cato, and the next to last utterance was: *Das Wahre ist die Wahrheit* (The true is the truth).

Weber's thoughts about love in the face of death are perhaps the final signs of his passionate, romantic nature. Caught between the heart and the head, between being emancipated into the erotic and adhering to conventional respect and responsibility, Weber felt the presence of conflict and turmoil in his last hours as he felt it throughout his life. With Marianne and Else hovering outside the door, Weber lay dying without making up his mind about who to take with him into the unknown. As one scholar put it, "Max Weber did not decide. He died . . . in the presence of Marianne Weber and Else Jaffé without resolving the conflict."[24]

Perhaps Weber chose not to resolve the conflict, whose very presence gives life its tragic nobility. He saw it as his task, Marianne reminds us, "to endure the *antinomies* of existence." The divine Marianne deserves the last words:[25]

On Monday, June 14, the world outside became quite still; only a thrush sang incessantly its song of yearning. Time stopped. Toward evening Weber breathed his last. As he lay dying, there was a thunderstorm and lightning flashed over his paling head. He became the picture of a departed knight. His face bespoke gentleness and exalted renunciation. He had moved to some distant, inaccessible place. The earth had changed.

Epilogue

WEBER'S LEGACY AND NAZI GERMANY

After the death of Max Weber testimonials came from all over Germany. Conferences held in his honor and symposia in various publications eulogized the man and his work. Although the Heidelberg circle believed that Weber's thought quickly fell into neglect, interest in him continued during the Weimar period of the twenties. But direct knowledge of his vast body of work remained limited due to the fragmented nature of his writings, buried in specialized scholarly journals. In the United States he remained almost unknown until Talcott Parsons translated into English *The Protestant Ethic and the Spirit of Capitalism* in 1930 and Albert Salomon wrote a series of illuminating articles on Weber in 1933.[1] Even then his reputation remained marginal through the thirties, when the western world appeared to be polarizing into two camps. According to many intellectuals of the era, especially those fearful of Nazi Germany and fixated on Soviet Russia, liberalism was on its way to the graveyard. The quality of aristocratic liberalism Weber stood for, which valued individual autonomy and moral responsibility, seemed a quaint relic in a modern age of collectivism.

With the rise of the Third Reich Weber's legacy became an embarrassment to both the Left and the Right. Radical socialists in Germany had never been comfortable with Weber's reservations about Marxism, especially the labor theory of value, the doctrine of historical materialism, and a philosophy of historical stages determined by laws; nor could they forget his harsh judgments of the Bolshevik Revolution and his dismissal of the revolutionary potential of the proletariat. But few Marxists themselves anticipated the rise of Nazism as anything more than a transitory phenomenon, and when Hitler crushed the labor unions the promise of the proletariat turned from fantasy to tragedy.

Similarly, in the United States the radicalization of intellectual life in the thirties precluded writers from heeding Weber's wisdom. An exception was the Marxist philosopher Sidney Hook, who, writing a respectful review of Weber's *Protestant Ethic* in the liberal *Nation*, took seriously the relationship of religion to economy, the "superstructure" of ideology to the base of the mode of production.[2] The name Weber occasionally came up in the late thirties when American Trotskyists debated the nature of the Soviet Union and the expression "bureaucratic collectivism" entered the lexicon of the Left. But in 1940 the eminent literary critic Edmund Wilson's *To the Finland Station* appeared, and American readers were informed that Lenin's arrival in St. Petersburg symbolized the dramatic fulfillment of Marx's theory, which was now being put into practice. Twenty years earlier Weber warned the Hungarian communist Georg Lukács that bolshevism was betraying Marxism and what was happening in Russia risked disgracing the very meaning of socialism. The writings of Weber would be prohibited in Soviet Russia and had only a secret circulation until communism collapsed in 1989–90, leaving bureaucracy exposed to its greatest antagonist.[3]

Yet historically when Weber's name came up in America it had less to do with Soviet Russia than with Nazi Germany. In February 1945, as World War II was drawing to an end and words about the concentration camps were being whispered with a shudder, a controversy erupted in *Politics*, an urbane journal published by the anarchist Dwight Macdonald. The art critic Meyer Schapiro had written "A Note on Max Weber's Politics," which blamed Weber's alleged absorption in power politics for paving the way for Hitler and the Third Reich. The sociologist Hans Gerth responded to Schapiro's argument and emphasized Weber's courage in standing up against the Kaiser and defending Ernst Toller, and he reminded readers that Weber's brother Alfred, a critic of the Third

Reich, was condemned by the Nazis as a "November Criminal" for supporting the Spartacist revolution of 1918. Schapiro, it should be noted, had tremendous respect for Weber as a scholar and humanist but he insisted that Weber operated from a double standard that resulted in the obliteration of all standards save that of power. Weber, according to Schapiro, depicted the masses as acting from irrational emotions and interests and, in contrast, he attributed the highest ethical qualities to individual leaders, while at the same time elevating the power of nation-states to an ultimate criterion beyond criticism. Schapiro wrote as a Marxist outraged that Weber had made no protest over the assassination of Karl Leibknecht and had no heartfelt sympathy for the masses. Weber symbolized the "banality of nineteenth-century liberalism" and its nationalistic conceits and imperialist temptations. "We can easily understand how, with his fear of the left and his respect for the strong leader with 'charismatic' qualities, capable of inspiring an irrational devotion, he came to speak in a way that anticipates the Nazis."[4]

Controversy over Weber's alleged anticipation of Nazism erupted later in Germany. After World War II the subject came up implicitly in any discussion of Weber's insufficient dedication to democracy; his distrust of socialism as an alternative to capitalism; and his desire, voiced early in his career, before the turn of the century, to see Germany become a world power. Supposedly such stances suggested a direct affinity with the mentality of Nazism. Particularly vulnerable was Weber's World War I position advocating a plebiscitarian-democratic type of authority and its relation to Article 48 of the Weimar Constitution, whereby the *Reichpräsident* may undertake necessary measures, such as suspending certain rights, in periods of emergency. The jurist Carl Schmitt would develop a new philosophy of sovereignty from such materials in order to insist that power slumbers in normal times and only makes its presence felt in urgent, "exceptional" situations when a leader acts on his own after defining the situation as such. It did not help matters when an old member of the Heidelberg circle, Georg Lukács, spread the rumor that Schmitt was a "legitimate pupil" of Weber.[5]

Those who defended Weber, in contrast, pointed to his stance against anti-Semitism, his defense of academic freedom, his criticism of German leaders during World War I, his admiration for the liberal cultures of Great Britain and the United States, his hatred of racism, and his love for the underdog and others deprived of leading a freely determined life. Those who knew intimately Weber's personality, especially the philosopher Karl Jaspers, found it difficult imagining Germany's greatest social philosopher bowing before the Brown Shirts. So too the historian Wolfgang J. Mommsen, who made a valuable distinction between the danger of some of Weber's institutional positions and the courage and integrity of the man himself. Weber's charismatic-plebiscitarian formulations may have misled German people into acclaiming the "leadership position of Adolf Hitler," but Weber would have been opposed to a gutter politics that appealed to "the low instincts of the masses and nationalistic emotions." The "ethic of responsibility" that Weber steadfastly upheld "would have been diametrically opposed to the delusions of grandeur and the brutal narrow-mindedness of fascist domination."[6] Ironically, Weber's institutional analysis emphasizing the necessity of strong leadership gave the German people no clear basis on which to oppose Hitler, while his ethical imperatives emphasizing the necessity of resisting domination gave the same people the clearest basis to oppose a dictator. In an earlier address Weber asked how a nation of people might sustain their older liberties under the new forces producing the rule of "high capitalism," and his answer could well apply to the prospect of a people facing conditions leading to fascism. The survival of such liberties "are in fact only possible if they are supported by the permanent, determined *will* of a nation not to be governed like a flock of sheep."[7]

The debate about Weber and the Third Reich reached a crescendo at a conference, held in Heidelberg in 1964, celebrating the hundredth anniversary of his birth. The "Storm over Weber" involved several volatile issues. One was that Weber's preoccupation with power offered no guidance as to how to limit the possibilities of its misuse, and such alleged power-worship indicated that Weber himself harbored "dictatorial" tendencies. Another frequently recurring issue involved the dangers of Weber's value-neutrality when applied to politics. One cannot, it was claimed, derive from Weber any clear guidance as to which form of government is best and which is not legitimate on the basis of violating some principle. Neither can one arrive at a standard to decide the relative values of a culture against another culture; nor can one discover any sense of ethical obligation to a state that commands obedience and defines itself as having a monopoly on the use of force and violence. Raymond Aron, an admirer of Weber, admitted it was difficult to tell whether Weber was advocating power politics and acting as, in the description of J. P. Mayer, "the Machiavelli of the Age of Steel," or whether he was censuring it and, as a moralist in an immoral universe, adhering to only those values he himself would obey: "truth and nobility."[8]

The conference that took place in Germany in 1964 had repercussions in an America undergoing the turmoils of the radical sixties. In the eyes of many students and scholars the Vietnam War put liberalism on trial, and the Left took delight in seeing Weber held up to scrutiny by the philosopher Herbert Marcuse. A member of the Frankfurt School who originated the notion of "critical theory"—and who became exiles, fleeing Germany for the United States—Marcuse became one of the most influential academics of the sixties generation. Marcuse charged Weber with collapsing the distinctions among various aspects of reason and rationality to the point that all reality is seen as domination by means of the rational organization of society. Earlier Marcuse had written *Reason and Revolution* to insist that Hegel's idea of "Reason" as spirit struggling to realize itself still remains valid. It was not reason but "bad reasoning" that led to Weber's distortions of the modern predicament. We should not, warned Marcuse, succumb to Weber's "tragic pessimism" about the inexorability of the rationalizing process. Where there is Hegel there is hope.[9]

After the radical sixties subsided Weber's reputation grew dramatically in the western world. A veritable "Weberian industry" of publishing took hold in various countries and his writings became standard reading on college campuses. Weber emerged as a scholarly sage, a writer wholly devoted to expressing the passions of his convictions even if they are negations, an intellect of "negative capability" (to use Yeats's phrase) whose penetrations enable us to cope with a world of doubt and darkness. Weber has come to be hailed as a precursor of Michel Foucault and poststructuralism for having first anatomized power and its institutions and the precarious fate of the individual in modern society. "As we enter the closing decades of the twentieth century," wrote two scholars in introducing a collection of impressive essays, "there is a growing recognition that Max Weber is our foremost social theorist of the condition of modernity."[10]

And what of Weber's alleged relationship to the catastrophe of the Third Reich? Meyer Schapiro told Americans that "the tragedy of Weber is the tragedy of German culture" since the ideals of both the man and his country had no way of being actualized short of social revolution. The critics at the Heidelberg conference leveled two charges at Weber: his absence of clear-cut value criteria left society without standards of judgment and thus the human mind could only wander in a metaphysical void; his hankering after charismatic leaders and fixation on power left Germany without democratic standards and its people thus susceptible to the temptations of dictatorship. Whether or not these descriptions are valid, does it follow that Weber's alleged tragic disposition is peculiar to Germany alone? Consider the American figures Herman Melville and Abraham Lincoln. The novelist depicted a universe dark with ambiguity, and the president was accused of acting as a dictator during the Civil War. When it comes to the problems of knowledge and the problems of politics, both came close to standing for a Weberian sensibility. Let us consider these, to use the phrase Weber adopted from Goethe, "elective affinities."

WEBER AND THE POSTMODERN CONDITION

Max Weber may be appreciated as the Herman Melville of social science, the first sociologist to grasp that the universe has no true meaning. Melville and Weber both felt in their bones, as did Nietzsche and later the poststructuralists, that knowledge rarely grasps its object as it really is. "We cannot," wrote Weber, "read off the meaning of the world from our investigation of it, however perfect; rather, we have to create this meaning ourselves." That the meaning of the world is constructed in the act of trying to know it did not cause Weber to despair. As did Melville, Weber calmly understood that the universe remains as white and empty as the whale until we bring to it our own needs, desires, concepts, and values. Values themselves originate in freedom; they are chosen rather than found. Weber's writings on ethics and politics and on "ethical neutrality" could be called a critique of judgment. Always sensitive to unresolved antinomies and tensions, he urged scholars to rise above the temptation to engage in moral evaluation, since ethical judgment may be little more than a function of the will that imposes it. As in Melville, Weber's universe is a metaphysical nightmare, with society a myriad of vaguely seen systems and structures that require interpretive meaning, and human behavior a mélange of motives that require rational understanding. Facts and data may be derived from empirical investigation, but meaning and understanding cannot be obtained through rational analysis alone:

> We know of no scientifically demonstrable ideals. To be sure, our labors are now rendered more difficult, since we must create our ideals from within our chests in the very age of subjectivist culture. But we must not and cannot promise a fool's paradise or an easy street, neither in the here and now nor in the beyond, neither in thought nor in action, and it is the stigma of our human dignity that the peace of our souls cannot be as great as the peace of the one who dreams of such a paradise.[11]

To paraphrase what Nathaniel Hawthorne said of Melville, Weber could neither believe nor disbelieve, and he was too honest to insist that reality is nothing more than the ideas we have about it. A mind that radiates a brooding brilliance, Weber presages our contemporary postmodernist world. What is the postmodernist condition? An "abyss-situation" where everything is seen as created rather than found, constructed out of a desire for mastery rather than wisdom; where belief in "eternal laws" is seen as existing in the mind's wish to glorify them; where, indeed, belief itself arises from the need for certainty rather than the wonder of curiosity. Today's scholars, finding themsleves stymied by the postmodern condition, have announced the "end" of philosophy as a quest for truth in something irreducibly "foundational," something not conditioned on its being constructed.

Would Weber agree with the end-of-philosophy stance? The existentialist philosopher Karl Jaspers provides a partial answer to the question. Jasper's description bears repeating: "Max Weber taught no philosophy; he was philosophy." Weber, Jaspers continues, was philosophy incarnate because he led a philosophical existence, the point of which was not to call for the discipline's "end" but instead to pose better questions, more refined hypotheses even without knowledge of what one is looking for; interrogations that compel inquiry to grope its way in the dark, so that the life of the mind fulfills itself in the pursuit of truth rather than in the need to possess it. Jaspers reminds us that Weber saw scientific knowledge as tentative and the scientist himself as knowing his work will be surpassed; hence Weber groped and floundered because he was less interested in fame and achievement than in striving after what "was humanly true, but actually impossible":

> In research he produced work that remained fragmented; not because he lacked strength, but for the sake of the truth, in keeping to the task. He felt himself floundering because of his boundless knowledge, because it is the purport of knowledge to flounder at the boundaries in order to set free the expanse for deeper truth in action and existence. He *sought* the point where floundering becomes that which is true. Incompleteness is the essence of science; in it, an extraordinary fragment is greater than any apparent completion.[12]

The description above would rankle conservatives, who criticized Weber for offering us a "search that could not advance to the completion of order."[13] Does the value of truth depend on such completion? Consider the controversial issue of relativism. The influential philosopher Leo Strauss misled (inadvertently, for he admired Weber) generations of conservative and neoconservative students and scholars by claiming that the

way Weber looked at history denied objective truth and value and rested
knowledge on historical experience rather than on nature and nature's
laws. But Weber, as we saw in discussing the labor theory of value, did
acknowledge the importance of "natural law" in history; and in the face
of relativism, skepticism, and nihilism, he held out for objectivity as a
moral responsibility, whatever its epistemological impediments. He called
on scholars to dedicate themselves to the pursuit of the object (*Sache*)
under investigation, and it is that unswerving pursuit that makes objectivity (*Sachlichkeit*) a professional commitment. Knowing becomes genuine knowledge only when it is compelled by its object.

Other current issues and controversies make Weber more relevant than
ever. In our contemporary academic setting, many scholars regard themselves as "materialists" through and through, seeing people interacting
with an environment that ends up acting upon them and defeating their
own conscious aims, and thus people described in many of today's historical, literary, and sociological writings are creatures to whom things
happen rather than agents who make things happen. In this gloomy exte-
riorization of existence, where things happen from without human
beings and usually with no explanation, we consequently have oppression
without an oppressor, events without causes, processes without purpose,
structures without agency. To Weber such descriptions, coming from
today's schools of poststructuralism and deconstruction, would see history always moving along only one track. In view of this monotonously
trendy academic "discourse," Weber's perspective is far richer and more
nuanced and ironic.

Weber showed the drama of human experience moving back and forth
between material interest impinging from without and human ideals
springing from within, between determinism and freedom, society and
consciousness; a historical process that operates with the suddenness of
what Weber referred to as a "switchman" throwing the rod to change the
tracks on which history moves. Hence the Puritans saw themselves as ide-
alists working upon matter to fulfill spiritual purposes, only to produce a
crass Yankee capitalism that issued in a Jacksonian democracy indifferent
to moral issues (slavery, for one). This "life without principle," as Henry
Thoreau called it, led in turn to the Transcendentalists' revolt against
materialism, with the Transcendentalists seeing themselves as poets who
would, as Margaret Fuller said, borrowing from Goethe, "live from within
outward." Yet Emersonian self-reliance could also, in the post–Civil War
industrial America, issue in a rugged individualism that reinforced the culture of capitalism. In his essay on "Wealth," Emerson observed of those
who chose to pursue it: "Power is what they want, not candy."[14]

Nietzsche, who admired Emerson, and Weber, who admired Nietzsche, both would have no trouble seeing capitalism as the will to power, even if in its original religious impetus the doctrine of predestination rendered the will powerless. Whether it is power or poetry that people want, whether materialism or ideals, candy or conviction, Weber suggests that history moves with the potential for each at any moment. "Not ideas, but material and ideal interests, directly govern men's conduct. Yet very frequently the world-images that have been created by 'ideas' have, like switchmen, determined the tracks along which action has been pushed by the dynamics of interests."[15] Ideas as mental images of the world have their own inner compelling force and such indeterminate consequences that they cannot be reduced to reflections of determinate conditions and structures. What was happening in history was for Weber, in contrast to the Marxists of his time and the post-structuralists of ours, happening not "behind the backs" of people but before their minds as they acted upon world-images. The Puritans, told that their fate had been preordained, subtly modified their own world-image to see their will as free in possessing the free choice to take up the life of work in place of the doctrine of grace. Ironically, America's first settlers who believed fervently in God went on to begin the work of capitalism in defiance of God! The tracks of history can be switched in the most irrational directions.

More than anything else it was Weber's sense of history that enabled him to grasp much of the disastrous meaning of the modern world and, as well, the dilemmas of those regions of the world that had missed the fortuitous combination of circumstances making the rise of freedom possible centuries earlier. Although Weber misjudged the Soviet Union, seeing the Bolshevik Revolution as a transitory episode, he predicted the wretched outcome of communism even before its doctrines were put into practice.

Weber had some affinities with the American framers of the Constitution, and his "Politics as a Vocation" could be examined together with the *Federalist* papers to appreciate the dilemmas leaders face in a democracy responsive primarily to the irrationalities of interest and power. But ironically, when Weber's Germany encounters America in the twentieth century, American political thought is guided by philosopher-statesmen who had no interest in the *Federalist* authors' understanding of power and freedom. President Woodrow Wilson, whose *Congressional Government* bore comparison to Weber's *Parliament and Government*, assumed he was taking America into a war to end all wars. The philosopher John Dewey also believed that the war could safely bring democracy to Europe in general and Germany in particular, unaware of Weber's warning that with European powers dictating the terms of peace, democracy would be associated with defeat and betrayal.

Dewey also believed that with the end of philosophy as metaphysical speculation it could continue as a scientific enterprise, unaware of Weber's point that science would be incapable of addressing issues of meaning and value. American thinkers like Dewey and Thorstein Veblen looked to science as inherently progressive; that science could lead to bureaucratic rationalization as well as the "disenchantment of the world" never troubled American pragmatists. In 1917 pragmatism and Wilsonianism came together in assuming that power and domination could be disarmed by ideas and persuasion and that the League of Nations would render war obsolete in the modern age. Weber remained closer to the *Federalist* authors, who also insisted that power, in international affairs as well as domestic politics, would always gravitate toward coalitions and factions, phenomena whose causes cannot be eliminated. Thus their effects must be controlled.

WEBER, LINCOLN, AND THE SPIRIT OF TRAGEDY

The impression that Weberianism remains alien to America may be accurate if we think of America as having only a progressive tradition, the liberal tradition of Jefferson, Wilson, and Dewey. But American liberalism has another tradition, one that begins with Calvinism and culminates in the twentieth century in the theology of Reinhold Niebuhr, and this Niebuhrian, Augustinian strain in American thought includes the tragic sensibility of Lincoln and Melville. A comparison of Weber and Lincoln may help America transcend its progressive historical categories in order to enjoy a richer perspective on itself. Of course, there are obvious differences between the statesman who left school in the fourth grade and later went on to wield power and the intellectual who spent his life mastering the riddles of power but who never held political office. Nevertheless, consider the compelling parallels between Lincoln's Lyceum Address (1838) and Weber's Inaugural Address at the University of Freiburg (1895).

In both documents people are called upon to become conscious of their responsibility before history and posterity and to take on the task of political education. Each speaker appealed to nationalism as a conscience rather than a conceit, a sense that their respective countries could achieve greatness without the pretensions of superiority. Above all, both Weber and Lincoln saw politics as tragic, a realm where human freedom and historical necessity are somehow connected, and where political action calls for the use of power with its agents doubting they have the knowledge to assure its proper use. Even if "cool, calculating reason" prevailed (Lincoln), "rationalization" of the rules of life (Weber) deprives politics of the one ingredient that can elevate it—"passion." As Lincoln put in words that Weber would readily understand, the "passion" for liberty made the American Revolution, and later "reason" is the faculty that must preside over the government that came out of it. Within a generation the "spirit of '76" became a system of administration. Significantly, in both Lincoln's America and Weber's Germany politics carried the same stigma of sterility to those who saw it confined to institutions and their impersonal procedures.

Had he read and pondered it, Lincoln would have found Henry David Thoreau's "Civil Disobedience" as delusive as Weber had found Leo Tolstoy's doctrine of passive nonresistance. "Power ceases in an act of repose," wrote Emerson, who, like Thoreau, called upon Americans to turn their backs on the state and civic life. The power of evil, Weber warned, cannot be opposed by a mystical search for deliverance, a "world-fleeing asceticism" (*weltfluchtige Askese*). To Lincoln and Weber power remains as constant as the forces of nature and as ineluctable as sin; hence they rejected William E. Channing's pacifism while at the same time begrudgingly respecting the person of pure conviction whose presence assured that the "flame" of moral principle would not die out in the world of practical politics. What taxed both Weber and Lincoln was the person who acted on conviction regardless of the consequences. "You must perform your duty faithfully, fearlessly, and promptly," the abolitionist William L. Garrison told his followers, "and leave the consequences to God."[16] Without mentioning Garrison, Weber cites that passage as the height of ethical irresponsibility.

Much of Weberian scholarship has been written within the context of German history and philosophy, occasionally with a glance at the development of American sociology. But to contextualize Weber, to interpret his work and ideas narrowly by establishing the specific conditions out of which they came, diminishes the profound universality of his own concerns and categories of analysis. Some of the conscious ethical tensions in his political thought may be best seen and heard not only in the halls of Heidelberg but on the deck of the *Indomitable*, the setting of Melville's *Billy Budd*. Here the dialectic between what Weber called *Gesinnung* (conviction of mind) and *Verantwortung* (responsibility in action) is battled out with all the pathos of Greek drama. The story asks us to choose between

the innocence of Budd and the duty of Captain Vere, a tragic choice since
we must recognize the authority of both positions. Like Weber and Lincoln, Melville also believed that while goodness is helpless in the face of
evil, a power politics of mere consequences that forever adapts for the
sake of survival and success lacks conscience and firm principle. Yet power
grows, expands, subdues silently, and corrupts absolutely. Melville's poem
"The Conflict of Convictions" anticipates Weber's short essay "*Zwischen
zwei Gesetzen*" (Between Two Laws). Each text deals with the dilemmas
of power that all large countries must face and the dialectic of opposites
that switch history from one track to another. Melville fears that the
Republic's originating ideals turn into their opposite and thus American
history came to be seized by forces alien to freedom as the capitol's new
dome turns into a menacing shadow:

> Power unannointed may come—
> Dominion (unsought by the free)
> And the Iron Dome,
> Stronger for stress and strain,
> Fling her huge shadow athwart the main;
> But the Founders' dream shall flee.[17]

Weber's philosophy of history, in some ways as much American as
German, suggests the Calvinist sense of certain fall and possible resurrection. It is tragic in that history begins with ideals only to become a succession of forces that succumb to the sway of power. In contrast to Marx,
Hegel, and Darwin, in Weber's scenario of history there is no inevitable
ascent from lower to higher since Puritanism already started with ideals,
as did the American Founders, leaving Melville and Lincoln fearing their
dream would flee from the contemporary imagination. But Weber's reference to the "switchman" suggests that history can suddenly reverse
itself; thus the *Entzuberhauftung* (demagicalization) of the world under
capitalist and scientific secular forces cannot continue for long, emptying
life of meaning and value without creating the conditions for counter-
tendencies arising from opposite emotions and forces.

  This dialectic resembles Nietzsche's juxtaposition of Apollonian and
Dionysian principles in order to dramatize history as an eternal battle
between reason that resides in the dullness of routine and freedom that
breaks out spontaneously, between the weariest mechanisms of life and
the wildest music of the soul. For Weber, as for Nietzsche, this tragic view
sees the struggle of antagonistic principles as inherent in life itself,
explaining why freedom is itself contradictory and, once realized, cannot

be sustained as it passes over to forms and functions and spirit surrenders to systems and structures. Rising up against domination and control, freedom requires power for its realization, and power then parcels itself out to the tasks of administration and specialization. Dionysian spirit inevitably yields to Apollonian limits and reason turns into rationalization. But humankind cannot bear for long the boredom of normal, regulated life and soon the will to live yearns for a charismatic breakout. Freedom is born again and enters life anew with a desire to create.

Weber saw this dialectical pattern operating historically in politics, religion, and economics. The free spontaneity of charismatic authority disrupts the lifeless routines of everyday existence, only to succumb to its own routinization and bureaucratization. Thus the early strenuous spirit of Protestantism, having broken away from meditative orthodoxy of Roman Catholicism, would itself eventually sink into a mundane way of life. Hence, too, the fate of the work ethic, which started out as a spiritual conviction only to become a social compulsion; and also that of a political regime, which starts in high ideals and ends with low squalid realities, what Weber saw as America's "party boss system." This eternal dialectic between conviction and convenience, freedom and form, spirit and structure, soul and system, movement and maintenance, and passion and proportion has no happy resolution in Weber's thought. Nor does it in Lincoln's thought in his Lyceum Address.

In that speech Lincoln told Americans that the controlling apparatus of the Constitution had to be revitalized by the emancipatory ethos of the Declaration. Just as Weber juxtaposed initiation to institutionalization to dramatize the perils of organized existence to the birth-springs of freedom, so did Lincoln believe that the perpetuation of American institutions required a return to the founding. No less than Weber, Lincoln is haunted by history without heroism. The problem, he told listeners gathered at Springfield, Illinois, in 1838, is that glory goes to those who make a revolution and win liberty for their people, not to the politicians who turn up later merely to run the machinery of government. Could America ever again have such a moment of charismatic illumination? Lincoln's thoughts on that question suggest that the thirst for political greatness is incompatible with the normal operations of democratic government, that, in Weberian terms, charisma is at war with bureaucracy. As though thinking in Nietzschean terms, Lincoln worries that a Dionysian gratification for distinction is the "ruling passion" of outstanding leaders:

> The question, then, is, can that gratification be found in supporting and maintaining an edifice that has been erected by others? Most certainly

it cannot. Many great and good men sufficiently qualified for any task they should undertake, may even be found, whose ambition would aspire to nothing beyond a seat in Congress, a gubernatorial or presidential chair; *but such belong not to the family of the lion, or the tribe of the eagle.* What! Think you these places would satisfy an Alexander, a Caesar, or a Napoleon. Never! Towering genius disdains a beaten path.[18]

Both Lincoln and Weber saw political institutions as a threat to the political ideals born of passion, and charismatic passion itself a threat to order until it becomes normalized. To draw such parallels is, of course, to slight the difference between Lincoln and Weber, not the least of which is the difference between a Christian and a Nietzschean view of tragedy.[19] But both thinkers saw history as the tragic conflict of opposing forces, and the Weberian view of intellectual history switching tracks runs through American history itself. Jonathan Edwards, the great theologian of Calvinism, also saw the emotional exaltation of religious belief threatened by reason. Sensing that the Enlightenment would make religion calculable and practical at the expense of true consciousness, the scrupulosity of doubt and trembling as well as joy and ecstasy, Edwards described the "deadness of the heart" that would later lead to what the Transcendentalists called the "corpse-cold" nature of institutionalized religion in America. Such oscillating chapters in American history presage Weber's depiction of the coming of the "polar-ice" world of modern life, the chilling "iron-cage" of mechanistic structures which, in its original formulation, translated as the fate of living in "a shell as hard as steel."[20]

In reminding us that our Puritan roots offer much of the explanation of America's successful historical development, Weber is advocating neither a return to religion nor a contentment with capitalism from which it sprung. The spiritual ideals of America's founding preceded the Revolution and the Constitution, establishing the basis of the priority of culture to society and making work the liberating activity of humanity. But for Weber, history happens only once and the past is irretrievably lost to the present. Looking to the future, Weber discerned the paradox of progress: humanity's tendency to undertake activities that result in its own confinement and subordination as modernization brings forth the processes of rationalization that enter history without a name. In addition to seeing ironic reversals of intention, his tragic vision of history also saw endless conflict between the desire to be self-determining and the will to organize, between spontaneity and system, between charisma and structure, or what Lincoln called the "passion" of "towering genius" and "cool, calculating reason." Weber's preoccupation with control and domination, rather than indicating a mind given to power-worship and harboring a secret admiration of dictatorship, reveals a misunderstood titan of a thinker who could both value the wild and the free and remain committed to reason and responsibility. With Max Weber liberalism prepared itself for modernity.

Abbreviations

Archiv	*Archiv für Sozialwissenschaft und Sozialpolitik.*
E&S	Max Weber, *Economy and Society: An Outline and Interpretive Sociology*, 2 vols., ed. Guenther Roth and Claus Wittich (Berkeley: University of Califonia Press, 1978).
FMW	*From Max Weber: Essays in Sociology*, ed. H. H. Gerth and C. W. Mills (New York: Oxford, 1946).
GPS	Max Weber, *Gesammelte Politische Schriften*, ed. Johannes Winckelmann (Tübingen: J. C. B. Mohr [Paul Siebeck], 1988).
LA	Georg Lukács Archives, Budapest.
MWAB	Marianne Weber, *Max Weber: A Biography,* trans. Harry Zohn; intr. Guenther Roth (1926; New Brunswick: Transactions, 1988).
MWG	*Max Weber Gesamtausgabe*, ed. Horst Baier, M. Rainer Lepsius, Wolfgang J. Mommsen, Wolfgang Schluchter, Johannes Winckelmann (Tübingen: J. C. B. Mohr [Paul Siebeck], 1990–).
MWSAP	*Max Weber: Soziologie, Universal Geschichtlich Analysen Politik*, ed. Johannes Winckelmann (Stuttgart: A. Kröner, 1973).
MWW	*Max Webers Wissenschaftslehre: Interpretation und Kritik*, ed. Gerhard Wagner and Heinz Zipprian (Frankfurt: Suhrkamp, 1994).

MWWP   *Max Weber: Werk und Person*, ed. Eduard Baumgarten (Tübingen: J. C. B. Mohr [Paul Siebeck], 1964).

PE   Max Weber, *The Protestant Ethic and the Spirit of Capitalism*, trans. Talcott Parsons (1930; New York: Routledge, 1992).

WA   Weber Archives: Bayerischen Akademie der Wissenschaften, Munich.

WPE   *Weber's Protestant Ethic: Origins, Evidence, Contexts*, ed. Hartmut Lehmann and Guenther Roth (New York: Cambridge University Press, 1993).

WPW   *Weber: Political Writings*, ed. Peter Lassmann and Donald Spears (New York: Cambridge University Press, 1994).

W&G   *Wirtschaft und Gesellschaft: Grundrisse Der Verstehenden Soziologie*, ed. Johannes Winckelmann (Tübingen: J. C. B. Mohr [Paul Siebeck], 1972).

WST   *Weber: Selections in Translation*, ed. W. G. Runciman; trans. Eric Matthews (New York: Cambridge University Press, 1978).

ZPW   Max Weber, *Zur Politik im Weltkrieg: Schriften und Reden, 1914–1918*, ed. Wolfgang J. Mommsen (Tübingen: J. C. B. Mohr [Paul Siebeck], 1988).

Notes

1. "The German intellect wants the French sprightliness, the fine practical understanding of the English, and the American adventure; but it has a certain probidity, which never rests in a superficial performance, but asks steadily, *To what end?* A German public asks for a controlling sincerity." Ralph Waldo Emerson, "Goethe; or the Writer," in *Representative Men* (New York: Hurst, n.d.), 204.
2. D. H. Lawrence, *Studies in Classic American Literature* (1923; New York: Viking, 1964), 9–21.
3. Wolfgang J. Mommsen, "The Antinomian Structure of Max Weber's Political Thought," *Current Perspectives in Social Theory*, 4 (1983), 289–311; and "Personal Conduct and Social Change: Towards a Reconstruction of Max Weber's Concept of History," in *Max Weber, Rationality and Modernity*, ed. Scott Lash and Sam Whimster (London: Allen & Unwin, 1987), 35–51. "The antinomic model of historical change," writes Mommsen, "is the theoretical quintessence of Max Weber's his-

torical sociology. But it still requires an interpretation that differentiates out its particularity" ("Peronsal," 47). Among the particularities that Mommsen examines are the cross tendencies of charisma and routinization, leadership and democracy, and competitive capitalism and state intervention. These antinomies also exist in the thoughts of Abraham Lincoln in his distinction between "towering genius" and the "beaten path" of routine politics. See the book's Epilogue. In her biography of Max Weber, Marianne also uses "antinomie" to characterize her husband's mind and temperament and indeed to suggest that he "regarded it as his task to endure the *antinomies* of existence" (*MWAB*, 678). For an evaluation of Weber's legacy, see Chapter 11 of Ilse Dronberger's *The Political Thought of Max Weber: In Quest of Statesmanship* (New York: Appleton-Century, 1971), which is titled "The Tragic Ambivalence."

It is no coincidence that in 1920, as Weber lay dying, Georg Lukács, Weber's old fellow scholar from the pre–World War I Heidelberg "circle," was now, as a convert to Marxism, working on a book that would address "The Antinomies of Bourgeois Thought." See Georg Lukács, *History and Class Consciousness: Studies in Marxist Dialectics*, trans. Rodney Livingston, 1922; Cambridge: MIT Press, 1971, 110–49. Lukács's misuse of Weber's ideas is discussed in Chapter 10. This theme of the unresolved tensions and paradoxes in human existence by no means exhausts the numerous different themes found in Weber's work, as indicated by the many excellent essays in *Max Weber, Rationality and Modernity*. Nor is it peculiar to Weber alone.

Antinomie as the incommensurability and incompatibility of moral preferences is a position that has been articulated in our time by Sir Isaiah Berlin, and it is perhaps no coincidence that both Weber and Berlin remained preoccupied with Leo Tolstoy's agonizing dualities. Tolstoy had been translated into German in the late nineteenth century and Weber read the novel *Resurrection* and refers in several places to *The Death of Ivan Ilyich*. "All his broodings," wrote Weber of Tolstoy, "revolved around the problem of whether or not death is a meaningful phenomenon." Science is meaningless, Weber emphasized, because it cannot answer Tolstoy's questions: "What shall we do and how shall we live?" Berlin, of Russian-Latvian descent, remains haunted by the same Weberian-Tolstoyan impasse. "Questions such as 'What is *the* goal of life?' or 'What is *the* meaning of history?' or 'What is *the* best way to live?' can receive no general answer" (quoted in Jonathan Lieberson and Sidney Morgenbesser, "The Questions of Isaiah Berlin" and "The Choices of Isaiah Berlin," *New York Review of Books*, March 6 and 20, 1980, 38–42, 31–36). Compare Weber's discussion of Tolstoy in "Science as a Vocation" to Berlin's similar empathy in *The Hedgehog and the Fox*. Both Weber and Berlin also distinguish value pluralism from value relativism, the impossibility of judging different cultures according to a single standard from the assertion that all cultures are equally valid, and hence that there can be no basis for criticism. Compare Weber's *The Method of the Social Sciences* to Berlin's *The Crooked Timber of Humanity*.

The most notable American counterpart to Berlin and Weber is Reinhold Niebuhr, the theologian who also saw history as contingent and inscrutable and life a tragic struggle between natural fact and human spirit. "The human culture is under the tension of finiteness and freedom, of the limited and unlimited." See Reinhold Niebuhr, *The Nature and Destiny of Man*, vol. 2, *Human Destiny* (New York: Scribner's, 1943), 214. Like Weber, Niebuhr also had his quarrels with pacifists, respected Friedrich Nietzsche, and drew on Calvinist religion for a sense of irony. On the difficulties of finding a key that cracks open the central meaning of Weber, see Friedrich H. Tenbruck, "The Problem of Thematic Unity in the Works of Max Weber," in *Reading Weber*, ed. Keith Tribe (New York: Routledge, 1989), 42–84. Perhaps the reason there is no key is that Weber had a penchant for pushing knowledge to its limits, for raising questions that are unanswerable. This portrait of Weber as the implacable philosophical interrogator is developed by Karl Jaspers in *On Max Weber*, ed. John Dreijmanis; trans. Robert J. Whelan (New York: Paragon House, 1989); Benjamin Nelson, who described Weber as a "faithful helmsman remaining at his post though the landmarks are all gone," believes that the "longer we meditate on Weber's life and work from this vantage point, the more we must come to see him as did his friend, Karl Jaspers, as a Sisyphean hero of an age of ultimate trials" (Benjamin Nelson, "Dialogs Across the Centuries," in *The Origins of Modern Consciousness*, ed. John Weiss [Detroit: Wayne State Press, 1965], 149–65). The antinomic tensions in Weber's thought may also explain why there is no clearly coherent Weberian legacy, why his epigoni enjoy a happy eclecticism. See Ralf Dahrendorf, *Liberale und andere: Portraits* (Stuttgart: Anstalt, 1994), 67–80. The theme of tragedy that I employ, which occurred to me when reading Weber's marginal comments on Georg Simmel's *Schopenhauer und Nietzsche*, is developed in the Introduction and is more Calvinist and Niebuhrian than Nietzschean.

4. "Politics as a Vocation," *FMW*, 128.

5. Hyden Edward Rollins, ed., *John Keats: Letters*, vol. 1 (Cambridge: Harvard University Press, 1966), 193.

6. Max Weber, *The Methodology of the Social Sciences*, ed. and trans. Edward A. Shils and Henry A. Finch (New York: Free Press, 1949), 57; "Science as a Vocation," *FMW*, 129–56.

7. William Blake, "Inscriptions to Laocoon," in *The Complete Works of William Blake*, ed. Jeffrey Keynes (London: Oxford University Press, 1966), 777.

8. *E&S*, 1132; Ralph Waldo Emerson, "Greatness," in *Letters and Social Aims* (Boston: Houghton Mifflin, 1904), 432.

9. For a brief episode in American history the writings of Reinhold Niebuhr made the post–World War II generation aware of such a sensibility. Niebuhr's *The Irony of American History* (New York: Scribner's, 1952) did for political thought what R. W. B. Lewis's *The American Adam: Innocence, Tragedy, and Tradition in the Nineteenth Century* (Chicago: University of Chicago Press, 1955) and Harry Levin's *The Power of Darkness: Hawthorne, Poe, Melville* (New York: Knopf, 1958) did for literary thought, and what Louis Hartz's *The Liberal Tradition in America* (New York: Harcourt, 1955) did for American historiography. All such works questioned the simple moral categories that supposedly rendered America exempt from the power realities of Europe. But Niebuhr and other writers of the period became associated with the cold war, and thus Niebuhrian realism suffered the same fate in America as did Weberian skepticism when Weber's insufficient devotion to democracy was cited as leading to Nazism and the Third Reich. For a discussion of this issue see the Epilogue.

10. "Politics as a Vocation," *FMW*, 77–128; the expression "no relish of salvation" is in *Hamlet* and Lincoln uses it to denounce the Kansas-Nebraska Act that would open up the west to slavery expansion; see *The Collected Works of Abraham Lincoln*, vol. 2, ed. Roy P. Basler (New Brunswick, N.J.: Rutgers University Press, 1953), 270.

11. Max Weber, *The Methodology of the Social Sciences*, ed. and trans. Edward A. Shils and Henry A. Finch (New York: Free Press, 1949), 158.

INTRODUCTION

1. Alexis de Tocqueville to Louis de Kergorlay, Oct. 18, 1847, in *Alexis de Tocqueville: Selected Letters on Politics and Society*, ed. Roger Boesche; trans. Roger Boesche and James Toupin (Berkeley: University of California Press, 1985), 192; Tocqueville, *Democracy in America*, ed. J. P. Mayer; trans. George Lawrence (Garden City, N.Y.: Anchor, 1969), 279, 432.

2. Charles G. Sellers, *The Market Revolution: Jacksonian America, 1815–1846* (New York: Oxford University Press, 1991).

3. Peter Lassman, "Democracy and Disenchantment: Weber and Tocqueville on the 'Road to Servitude,'" in *Knowledge and Passion: Essays in Honor of John Rex*, ed. Hermino Martins (London: I. B. Tauris, 1993), 99–118.

4. Max Weber, "'Churches and Sects' in North America: An Ecclesiastical Socio-Political Sketch," reprinted in *Sociological Theory* 85 (1985), 7–13; "On the Situation of Constitutional Democracy in Russia" (1905), reprinted in *WPW*, 29–74; "Politics as a Vocation," *FMW*, 77–128; Tocqueville, *Democracy*, 246–61, 690–95.

5. Tocqueville's critique of the "courtier spirit" in America resembles Weber's critique of the bureaucratic functionary. One can imagine Tocqueville smiling upon reading Weber's answer to his own question as to how democracy and freedom will survive the advance of deadening institutions. "They are in fact only possible if they are supported by the permanent, determined *will* of a nation not to be governed like a flock of sheep." Weber, "On the Situation," *WPW*, 69; Tocqueville, *Democracy*, 254–61.

6. Tocqueville, *Democracy*, 507–47.

7. Weber, "On the Situation," *WPW*, 29–74.

8. Conor Cruise O'Brien, "The Long Affair: Thomas Jefferson and the French Revolution, 1785–1800" (forthcoming).

9. Tocqueville, *Democracy*, 412–13.

10. See the valuable work by Joshua Mitchell, *The Fragility of Freedom: Tocqueville on Religion, Democracy, and the American Future* (Chicago: University of Chicago Press, 1995).

11. Weber, "Science as a Vocation," *FMW*, 128–56.

12. Weber, *PE*, 182; on the debate over the idea of work in Weber's era, where Weber is quoted as denying it enjoyed status in the New Testament, see Karl Löwith, *From Hegel to Nietzsche: The Revolution in Nineteenth-Century Thought*, trans. David E. Green (Garden City, N.Y.: Anchor, 1967), 260–85, 436. In a section titled "Conditions Underlying the Calculability of the Productivity of Labor" in *E&S*, Weber noted that "inclination to work . . . must be determined either by a strong self-interest in the outcome, or by direct or indirect compulsion." Work motivated by earnings is characteristic of the market economy. In premarket conditions characteristic of rural societies, "the likelihood that people will be willing to work on affectual grounds is greater in the case of specification of functions than in that of specialization of functions. This is true because the product of the individual's own work is more clearly evident" and the "quality of the product is important." Only in traditional society does labor command value and resist rationalization and specialization, and in such an environment "motivations based on *absolute values* are usually the result of religious orientations or of the high social esteem in which the particular form of work is held" (*E&S*, 150–51).

13. Weber, *PE*, 181–82; on Marx amd the drama of a dead past and live future, see Harold Rosenberg, *The Tradition of the New* (New York: McGraw-Hill, 1965), 154–77. In 1905 Weber observed of the labor theory of value that it was being "bled to death" in Russia; on Marx and Calvin, see Georges Bataille, *The Accursed Share: An Essay on General Economics*, vol. 1, *Consumption*, trans. Robert Hurley (New York: Zone Books, 1991), 115–42.

14. Tocqueville, *Democracy*, 538.

15. Nietzsche's description of Pascal is quoted in Harold Bloom, "Introduction," *Blaise Pascal*, ed. Harold Bloom (New York: 1989), 3; Tocqueville, *Democracy*, 691–92; on Tocqueville and the historical vision of tragedy, see Hayden White, *Metahistory: The Historical Imagination in Nineteenth-Century Europe* (Baltimore: Johns Hopkins University Press, 1973), 191–229.

16. Max Weber to Karl Bucher, Feb. 1, 1909, *MWG* 11/6, 46–50.

17. Tocqueville, like Emerson and many of the Transcendentalists, also saw Unitarianism as a watered-down version of Christianity. "But are you not afraid," Tocqueville asked the theologian William Ellery Channing (a sage in the eyes of Weber's mother and aunt), "that by your efforts to purify Christianity, you may end by making its very substance disappear?" *Alexis de Tocqueville: Journey to America*, ed. J. P. Mayer; trans. George Lawrence (New Haven: Yale University Press, 1960), 64.

18. Dorrit Freund, "Max Weber und Alexis de Tocqueville," *Archiv für Kulturgeschichte* 56 (1974), 457–64; Wilhelm Hennis, "Freiheit durch Assoziation: Zwischen Tocqueville und Weber: William Ellery Channing," *Frankfurter Allegemeine Zeitung*, Apr. 1, 1995, p. 5; on Tocqueville and Weber see also the valuable discussion in G. L. Ulmen, *Politischer Mehrwert: Eine Studie über Max Weber und Carl Schmitt* (Bundes Republik Deutschland: Acta Humaniora, 1991), 345–61.

19. Tocqueville, *Letters*, 294.

20. Franco Ferraroti, *Max Weber e il destino della ragione* (Roma-Bari: Laterza, 1974); Phillipe Raynaud, *Max Weber et les dilemmas de la raison Moderne* (Paris: Presses Universitaires de France, 1987).

21. Tocqueville, *Democracy*, 72.

CHAPTER 1

1. *MWAB*, 279–81.

2. *MWAB*, 282.

3. German views of the American Revolution are discussed in Klaus Epstein, *The Genesis of German Conservatism* (Princeton: Princeton University Press, 1966), 293–96; on the impact of the American Revolution in Europe, see Franco Venturi's two volume work, *The End of the Old Regime in Europe, 1776–1789* (Princeton: Princeton University Press, 1991).

4. Albert R. Schmitt, *Herder und Amerika* (The Hague: Moulton, 1962), 129–80; Georg F. Hegel, *The Philosophy of History* (New York: Dover, 1956), 86; reservations about American society are also noted in Fritz Stern, *The Politics of Cultural Despair: A Study in the Rise of German Ideology* (New York: Anchor ed., 1965), 170–71; on Weber specifically and his work in relation to America, see Gottfried Eisermann, "Max Weber und Amerika," *Cahiers Vilifredo Pareto Revue Européenne d'histoire des Sci-*

ences Sociales 4 (1964), 119–45; Edward Shils, "La recezione di Max Weber tra paesi anglosassoni," in *Max Weber e le Scienzi Sociali del suo Tempo* (Bologna, 1988), 517–39; Agnes Erdelyi, *Max Weber in Amerika* (Munich: Passagen, 1992); Wolfgang J. Mommsen, "Max Weber in Modern Social Thought," in the author's *The Political and Social Theory of Max Weber* (Chicago: University of Chicago Press, 1989), 169–96.

5. Karl Marx to Joseph Weydemeyer, Mar. 5, 1852, in *Marx and Engels: Basic Writings on Politics and Philosophy*, ed. Lewis S. Feuer (Garden City, N.Y.: Anchor, 1959), 456–57; Friedrich Engels, *The Conditions of the Working Class in England in 1844*; preface to the American edition reprinted in ibid., 489–97; Werner Sombardt, *Warum gibt es in den vereinigten Staaten keinern Sozialismus?* (Tübingen: J. C. B. Mohr [Paul Siebeck], 1906), 7–36.

6. Heinrich Heine, "Which Way Now?" in *Heinrich Heine: Poetry and Prose*, ed. Jost Hermand and Robert C. Holumb (New York: Continuum, 1982), 73; Friedrich Nietzsche, "Twilight of the Idols," in *The Portable Nietzsche*, ed. Walter Kaufmann (New York: Penguin, 1954), 522; Theodor Adorno, "Veblen's Attack on Culture," *Studies in Philosophy and Social Science* 9 (1941), 389–413.

7. Georg Gottfried Gervinus, *Introduction to the History of the Nineteenth Century*, section reprinted in *German Essays on History*, ed. Rolf Salzer (New York: Continuum, 1991), 91–102.

8. Lewis Mumford, "Spengler's 'The Decline of the West,'" *Books That Changed Our Minds*, ed. Malcolm Cowley (New York: Kelmscott, 1938), 217–38; see also Roger Scruton, "Spengler's Decline of the West," in *The Philosopher of Dover Beach* (New York: St. Martin's Press, 1990), 12–30.

9. *MWAB*, 282.

10. *MWAB*, 284.

11. Marianne Weber to "Liebe Mutter," Sept. 9, 1904 (a copy of this letter in possession of Professor Lawrence Scaff).

12. *MWAB*, 286–87.

13. Ibid., 286–89.

14. *MWAB*, 294; *Muskogee Phoenix* 4 (Sept. 28, 1904).

15. The *Daily Oklahoman*, Sept. 29, 1904; see also Hans Rollmann, "'Meet Me in St. Louis': Troeltsch and Weber in America," in *WPE*, 357–83.

16. *MWAB*, 295; W. E. B. Du Bois, "Die Negerfrage in der Vereinigten Staaten," *Archiv* 22 (1906), 31–79.

17. A brief account quoting Weber's relatives is in *American Sociological Association Footnotes* 7 (Aug. 1980); see also, Larry G. Keeter, "Max Weber's Visit to North Carolina," *Journal of the History of Sociology* 3 (1981), 108–14.

18. Max Weber, "Churches and Sects in North America: An Ecclesiastical Socio-Political Sketch" (trans. Colin Loader), *Sociological Theory* 3

(Spring 1985), 7–13; see also the valuable preceding analysis by Colin Loader and Jeffrey Alexander, "Max Weber on Churches and Sects in North America: An Alternative Path Toward Rationalization," ibid., 1–6.

19. Henry Adams to Elizabeth Cameron, May 15, 22, 1904, *The Letters of Henry Adams*, vol. 5, ed. J. C. Levenson (Cambridge: Harvard University Press, 1988), 586–89; Henry Adams, *The Education of Henry Adams* (New York: Library of America, 1983), 1146.

20. John Dewey, "The St. Louis Congress of Arts and Sciences," in *Essays on the New Empiricism 1903–1906*, vol. 3 of *John Dewey: The Middle Works*, ed. Jo Ann Boydston (Carbondale, Ill.: University of Southern Illinois Press, 1977), 145–52; James quoted in Ralph Barton Perry, *The Thought and Character of William James*, vol. 2 (Boston: Little, Brown, 1935), 700.

21. The *St. Louis Post Dispatch*, Sept. 21, 1904, 6; *World's Fair Bulletin* 5 (Oct. 1904), 24.

22. *MWAB*, 290.

23. George Santayana, "The Genteel Tradition in American Philosophy," in *Winds of Doctrine and Platonism and the Spiritual Life* (New York: Harper, 1957), 186–216.

24. Weber's original title, "Deutsche agraverhaltnisse Vergangenheit und Gegenwart" (German agrarian conditions past and present) was given a slightly different title in the publication of the *Congress of Arts and Sciences* and then later published as "Capitalism in Rural Society in Germany" in *FMW*, 363–85.

25. For a treatment of this controversial thesis by Weberian-influenced American scholars, see *Turner and the Sociology of the Frontier*, ed. Richard Hofstadter and Seymour Martin Lipset (New York: Basic Books, 1968); Max Weber, "Zur Lage der bürgerlichen Demokratik in Russland," *Archiv* 22 (1906), 234–53; a partial translation of this important document is in *WST*, 269–84.

26. Guenther Roth, "Weber the Would-Be Englishman: Anglophilia and Family History," *WPE*, 83–122.

27. Lord Acton, *Lectures on Modern History* (New York: Meridian, 1961), 24–25. It is most likely that Weber's appreciation of British dissent thinkers derived from his absorbing the work of Georg Jellinek; see Hartmut Lehman, "Ascetic Protestantism and Economic Rationalization: Max Weber Revisited After Two Generations," *Harvard Theological Review* 80 (1987), 307–20.

28. *MWAB*, 416.

29. Herbert Croly's *The Promise of American Life* (1909) and Lippmann's *A Preface to Politics* (1912) both contain Weberian overtones in seeing democracy, especially egalitarian democracy, leading to group politics forged by demands of special interest constellations, while politics itself is presided over by bosses, machines, and what Lippmann called "routi-

neers," a term that would have brought a smile of agreement to Weber's face.

30. *E&S*, 1130–32.
31. Max Weber, *The Methodology of the Social Sciences*, ed. and trans. Edward A. Shils and Henry A. Finch (New York: Free Press, 1949), 26.
32. Max Weber to Georg Jellinek, Sept. 24, 1904, *WA*; Max Weber, "Science as a Vocation," *FMR*, 149; *MWWP*, 581; *Heidelberger Zeitung*, Jan. 21, 1905, 1–2.
33. Max Weber to Heinrich Rickert, Apr. 2, 1905, quoted in Lawrence Scaff's paper, "Max Weber's America: Protestantism and Progressivism," 1–2.
34. Weber, "Churches and Sects," 7–13.
35. Ibid., 3–13.
36. Ibid., 4–12.
37. H. L. Mencken, "Puritanism as a Literary Force," in *Critics of Culture: Literature and Society in the Early Twentieth Century*, ed. Alan Trachtenberg (New York: Wiley, 1976), 47–56.
38. Randolph Bourne, "The Puritan's Will to Power," in *The Radical Will: Randolph Bourne: Selected Writings, 1911–1918*, ed. Olaf Hansen (New York: Urizen, 1977), 301–6.
39. Van Wyck Brooks, "The Wine of the Puritans," in *Van Wyck Brooks: The Early Years, a Selection from His Works*, ed. Claire Sprague (Boston: Northeastern Press, 1993), 6.
40. J. David Greenstone, *The Lincoln Persuasion: Remaking American Liberalism* (Princeton, N.J.: Princeton University Press, 1993), 89; Greenstone and many other scholars cite, as conclusive proof that Calvinism "legitimated" capitalism and made possible America's inevitable culture of possessive individualism, the work of Sacvan Bercovitch, especially his *The American Jeremiad* (Madison: University of Wisconsin Press, 1978); for a critique of this interpretation of Puritanism as an ideology of domination, see David C. Harlan, "A People Blinded from Birth: American History According to Sacvan Bercovitch," *Journal of American History* 78 (1991), 949–97.
41. *PE*, 252–61; Norman O. Brown, *Life Against Death: A Psychoanalytic Interpretation of History* (Middletown, Conn.: Wesleyan University Press, 1959); Herbert Marcuse, *Eros and Civilization: A Philosophical Inquiry into Freud* (Boston: Beacon, 1955).
42. Many of Weber's thoughts on character formation come from his essays on religion, especially eastern religion; the quotes of Weber on this subject come from a book to which I am indebted: Harvey Goldman, *Max Weber amd Thomas Mann: Calling and the Shaping of the Self* (Berkeley: University of California Press, 1988), 131–68.
43. George Santayana, *The Last Puritan: A Memoir in the Form of a Novel* (New York: Scribner's, 1936), 58–82.

44. Paul Honigsheim, *On Max Weber* (New York: Free Press, 1968), 1–30.

45. Meinecke's observations are in *MWWP*, 635–36.

46. Karl Jaspers, *On Max Weber*, ed. John Dreijmanis; trans. Robert A. Whelan (New York: Paragon, 1989), 103.

47. Joseph Schumpeter, "Max Weber's Werk," *Der Oesterreichische Volkswirt* (Wien), Aug. 7, 1920, 831–34; further Schumpeter descriptions of Weber are also in Alan Sica, *Weber, Irrationality, and Social Order* (Berkeley: University of California Press, 1988), 118; on Ernst Toller's descriptions of Weber's courage during World War I, see Dittmar Dahlmann, "Max Weber's Relation to Anarchism and Anarchists: The Case of Ernst Toller," in *Max Weber and His Contemporaries*, ed. Wolfgang J. Mommsen and Jürgen Osterhammel (London: Unwin Hyman, 1987), 367–81.

CHAPTER 2

1. *MWAB*, 31–33.

2. Max Weber to Helene Weber, July 18, 1884, *MWWP*, 29–31.

3. On Channing, see Andrew Delbanco, *William Ellery Channing: An Essay on the Liberal Spirit in America* (Cambridge, Mass.: Harvard University Press, 1981); on Germany lacking an ascetic tradition, see Max Weber to Adolph Harnack, Feb. 5, 1906, *MWG* 11/5, 32–33.

4. Max Weber to Fritz Baumgarten, Apr. 25, 1877; Sept. 9, 1871; Oct. 11, 1879. In *MWWP*, 12–13, 54–57.

5. Weber on girls quoted in J. P. Meyer, *Max Weber and German Politics* (New York: Arno Press, 1979), 16.

6. Ibid., 23.

7. Max Weber to Helene Weber, June 16, 1885, *MWWP*, 32–33.

8. Max Weber to Fritz Baumgarten, Apr. 25, 1887, *MWWP*, 54–57.

9. Quoted in Albert Salomon, "Max Weber's Methodology," *Social Research* 1 (May 1934), 141–68.

10. A fragment of Weber's report has been reprinted as "Development Tendencies in the Situation of East Elbian Rural Labourers," trans. Keith Tribe in *Reading Weber*, ed. Keith Tribe (London: Routledge, 1989), 158–87.

11. Quoted in Dirk Kasler, *Max Weber: An Introduction to His Life and Work* (Chicago: University of Chicago Press, 1988), 58; and in Anthony Giddens, *Politics and Sociology in the Thought of Max Weber* (London: Verso, 1970), 8–33.

12. Quoted in Kasler, *Weber*, 55–62.

13. Quoted in Salomon, "Max Weber's Methodology," 151.

14. The Freiburg address has been reprinted as "The National and Economic Policy," in *Reading Weber*, ed. Keith Tribe, 188–209; unless otherwise indicated the following quotes are from that document.

15. See, for example, Gordon Craig, "The Kaiser and the Kritik," *New York*

Review (Feb. 18, 1988), 17–20; and "Demonic Democracy," ibid. (Feb. 13, 1992), 39–43.

16. Max Weber to Emmy Baumgarten, Oct. 21, 1887, *MWWP*, 61–62.

17. *MWAB*, 102.

18. Ibid., 247–48.

19. Many years ago the American sociologists Hans Gerth and C. Wright Mills offered some speculations about the causes of Weber's breakdown. They described the psychic stresses as a "constitutional affliction" that we might call today a genetic trait. Gerth and Mills called it a "hereditarily burdened" mental disorder "which undoubtedly ran through his family," noting that two relatives committed suicide and one spent time in an insane asylum. But the authors emphasize more the context of Weber's personal relations, particularly the tensions with his father and, after the latter's death, the supposed burden of remorse. "Weber came out of this situation with an ineffaceable sense of guilt. One may certainly infer an inordinately strong Oedipus situation" (*FMW*, 28–29). Weber's own thoughts on Freud, discussed in Chapter 6, suggest that he could scarcely understand why a person's deepest thoughts need to be repressed, particularly thoughts on sex and the erotic. Any possible verification of the Oedipal interpretation must await the complete publication of Weber's correspondence. Meanwhile, the most provocative Freudian interpretation is Arthur Mitzman, *The Iron Cage: An Historical Interpretation of Max Weber* (New York: Grosset, 1969).

    Weber also seemed obsessed by the idea of a vocation, as did a number of contemporary American intellectuals who spent many years trying to decide where to devote their energies and talents. Weber rose so rapidly in the academic world that he could not help but think that many of his relatives had succeeded in their careers at a slower rate yet experienced more fulfillment. But for Weber professional achievement brought little sense of satisfaction and completion. Without indicating he is talking about himself, he alludes to this emotion in "Science as a Vocation."

    During World War I Weber consulted a psychiatrist about his illness, and he wrote down some thoughts based on his own self-diagnosis. Some time shortly after his death Marianne showed Karl Jaspers the document. Four decades later Jaspers was asked about it and could only recall that he had been struck by Weber's capacity to step back and distance himself from himself. "The objectivity and concrete clarity of the descriptions," Jaspers wrote, was "better than any psychiatrist of our time could have made." During the Nazi period Marianne consulted Jaspers about destroying the document and apparently did so (Jaspers to Karl Engisch, Dec. 14, 1962, *WA*).

    For the most recent analysis, which traces Weber's "depressed personality" to concerns he had about "role conformity" and the pressures of modernity based on his academic studies, see J. Frommer and S. Frommer, "Max Webers Krankheit: soziologische Aspetke der depressiven Struktur," *Fortschritte der Neurologie-Psychiatrie* 61 (1993), 161–71.

The historian Friedrich Meinecke remembers Weber not as "depressed" but as "passionate" and "robust" until the time of his breakdown. Yet these "terrible dark years, which he mostly spent vegetating in the South, proved to have a decided benefit. They forced him to pull his wits together, deepen his character and his will, [which] freed him from frittering away [his talents] on a whole multitude of projects, so that he, as he slowly regained his strength to undertake intellectual work, found an unparalleled [ability to] concentrate, which allowed him to begin and bring to completion the gigantic research project on the spirit of capitalism and the significance of religion for economic life. . . . A second and newer Weber arose, which one may distinguish from the old as one does the old, fearsome and weighty Rembrandt from the younger, cocky, brilliant one" (Meinecke's statement is in *MWWP*, 635–37).

Meinecke's observation that Weber's "terrible dark years" proved to be a blessing raises the question of the possible relationship between mental illness and creative genius. Psychiatrists have long been investigating the connection between "mood disorders" and artistic creativity. In an effort at "understanding Weber's creativity," Martin Albrow focuses on Weber's numerous evokings of Goethe's idea of the "demon" (Albrow, *Max Weber's Construction of Social Theory* [London: Macmillan, 1990], 63–72). The relationship of sickness to intellectual brilliance runs through much of the works of Thomas Mann, and he often depicts this combination as characteristic of a once proud aristocracy faced with modernity. In German culture older writers such as Gotthold Lessing and Johann Winckelmann pondered the meaning of Sophocles' *Philoctetes*, suggesting that classical fortitude may have been born of suffering. Studying the same subject, the American Edmund Wilson concluded that "genius and disease, like strength and disability, may be inextricably bound up together" (Edmund Wilson, *The Wound and the Bow* [New York: Oxford, 1947], 223–42).

20. Weber quoted in Albrow, *Max Weber's Construction*, 72.
21. Quoted in Ronald Steel, *Walter Lippmann and the Twentieth Century* (Boston: Atlantic Monthly Press, 1980), 85.

CHAPTER 3

1. *MWAB*, 515.
2. *E&S*, 954.
3. Max Weber, *The Sociology of Religion*, trans. Ephraim Fischoff (1922; Boston: Beacon, 1963), 231.

4. Max Weber to Karl Vossler, May 5, 1908, *MWG,* 11/5, 560–61; Max Weber, *The Methodology of the Social Sciences,* ed. and trans. Edward A. Shils and Henry A. Finch (New York: Free Press, 1949), 57.

5. *E&S,* 359.

6. Ibid., 1403.

7. The ambassador is quoted in Abraham Ascher, *The Revolution of 1905: Authority Restored* (Stanford: Stanford University Press, 1992), 9.

8. Max Weber, *Zur Russischen Revolution von 1905: Schriften und Reden, 1905–1912* (Tübingen: J. C. B. Mohr [Paul Siebeck], 1984). I have benefited from Wolfgang J. Mommsen's informative introduction to this work and from Richard Pipe's "Max Weber and Russia," *World Politics* 7 (Apr. 1955), 371–401.

9. Quoted in Pipes, "Weber and Russia," 375–93.

10. "Zur Lage der burgerlichen Democratik in Rusland," 273.

11. For this illuminating passage I am indebted to Guenther Roth's translation, "Epilogue: Weber's Vision of History," in Guenther Roth and Wolfgang Schluchter, *Max Weber's Vision of History: Ethics and Methods* (Berkeley: University of California Press, 1979), 201–2.

12. Thorstein Veblen, *Imperial Germany and the Industrial Revolution* (New York: Huebsche, 1914).

13. A number of astute essays have recently appeared on Weber and the problem of ethics and values in *MWW.*

14. Wolfgang J. Mommsen, "Einleitung," *Max Weber: Zur Russischen Revolution,* 22.

15. Friedrich Nietzsche, "Thus Spoke Zarathustra," in *The Portable Nietzsche,* ed. Walter Kaufmann (New York: Viking, 1954), 301.

16. Max Weber, "Die Drei Reinen Typen der Legitiment Herrschaft," *MWSAP,* 151–66.

17. Randolph Bourne, "The State," in *The Radical Will: Randolph Bourne, Selected Writings, 1911–1918,* ed. Olaf Hansen (New York: Urizen, 1977), 355–95.

18. Like Nietzsche, Weber had no use for Darwin's idea of adjustment and adaptation (*Anpassung*), an idea more appropriate to biology than to political or moral life. Weber, *Methodology of Social Sciences,* 23–25.

19. See, for example, Frank Parkin, *Max Weber* (New York: Routledge, 1982).

20. *E&S,* 202–54.

21. *Federalist,* no. 58.

22. *MWAB,* 414–15.

23. Ibid., 416–17.

24. Weber, "Zur Lage der burgerlichen Demokratik," 170; *E&S,* 1401–2.

25. *E&S,* 1401–2; some of the quotes are from Weber's 1918 address, "Der Sozialismus," discussed in Chapter 11.

26. Weber's writings on bureaucracy are in *FMW,* 196–244, and *E&S,* 956–1005.

27. *E&S*, 1132.
28. Bernard S. Silberman, *Cages of Reason: The Rise of the Rational State in France, Japan, and the United States* (Chicago: University of Chicago Press, 1993).
29. H. L. Mencken, "Roosevelt: An Autopsy," in *Prejudices: A Selection* (New York: Vintage, 1955), 47–68.
30. Max Weber, "The Development of Bureaucracy and Its Relation to Law," *WST*, 341–54.
31. On this point see Robert J. Holton and Bryan S. Turner, *Max Weber on Economy and Society* (New York: Routledge, 1989), 156–57.
32. Max Weber to Robert Michels, Nov. 6, 1907; Aug. 4, 1908; *MWG* 11/5, 423, 615–20.
33. *E&S*, 1402.
34. Mark Warren, "Max Weber's Liberalism for a Nietzschean World," *American Political Science Review* 82 (1988), 31–50.
35. Max Weber, "Der Sozialismus," *MWWP*, 243–70.
36. Max Weber to Robert Michels, Oct. 15, 1907, *MWG* 11/5, 407–8.
37. Weber, "Sozialismus," *ZPW*, 245; "Wahlrecht und Demokratic in Deutschland," *ZPW*, 184.
38. For the following discussion I am indebted to the many fine essays in *Max Weber and His Contemporaries*, ed. Wolfgang J. Mommsen and Jürgen Osterhammel (London: Unwin Hyman, 1987).
39. *MWAB*, 131–37.
40. Ibid., 133–37, 218–23.
41. Quoted in Martin Albrow, *Max Weber's Construction of Social Theory* (London: Macmillan, 1990), 83; see also Max Weber to Friedrich Naumann, Apr. 26, 1908, *MWG* 11/5, 546–58.
42. Quoted in Paul Honigsheim, *On Max Weber* (New York: Free Press, 1968), 3.
43. Max Weber to Robert Michels, Mar. 26, 1906, *MWG* 11/5, 56–58.
44. Ibid., 56–58; see also Max Weber to Robert Michels, Feb. 1, 1907 and Feb. 4, 1907, ibid., 238–46; and Wolfgang J. Mommsen, "Robert Michels and Max Weber: Moral Conviction versus the Politics of Responsibility," in *Max Weber and His Contemporaries*, 121–38.
45. Max Weber to Robert Michels, Aug. 4, 1908, *MWG* 11/5, 615–20.
46. Ibid., 615.
47. *MWAB*, 653.
48. Wolfgang J. Mommsen, *Max Weber and German Politics, 1890–1920* (Chicago: University of Chicago Press, 1984); David Beetham, *Max Weber and the Theory of Modern Politics* (Cambridge, England: Polity Press, 1987).
49. *PE*, 169.

CHAPTER 4

1. *MWAB*, 270.
2. Ibid., 258.
3. Ibid., 276–79.
4. Max Weber to Alfred Weber, Mar. 25, 1885, *MWWP*, 24–26.
5. It appears that Weber began thinking about the relationship of religion to economics when he began thinking about America, and that came long after he established himself as a scholar. A decade before his trip to the United States Weber undertook a study of the stock market as the monetary facilitation of modern industry. Although America had experienced a severe banking panic the previous year, Weber made no mention of Wall Street or of America's peculiar development of finance capitalism with its "captains of industry" invoking God to justify the accumulation of wealth. Max Weber, *Die Borse* (Göttingen: Vandenhoeck, 1894).
6. *PE*, 104.
7. Paul Honigsheim, *On Max Weber* (New York: Free Press, 1968), 81.
8. Max Weber to Karl Vossler, May 5, 1908, *MWG* 11/5, 556–663.
9. *PE*, 49–54.
10. Franklin, to be sure, was no self-denying ascetic; nonetheless he is not altogether far from the character that Weber saw as emerging in eighteenth-century America; see Albert H. Wurth, "The Franklin Persona: The Virtue of Practicality and the Practicality of Virtue," in *Virtue, Corruption, and Self Interest*, ed. Richard K. Matthews (Bethlehem: Lehigh University Press, 1994), 76–102; see also the astute comments on Franklin by Guenther Roth, "Introduction," *WPE*, 16–24.
11. *PE*, 47–181.
12. The early critics are compiled in the valuable anthology *Protestantism and Capitalism: The Weber Thesis and Its Critics*, ed. Robert W. Green (Boston: D. C. Heath, 1959); more recent criticisms and defenses may be examined in *WPE*; see also Colin Campbell, *The Romantic Ethic and the Spirit of Modern Consumerism* (New York: Blackwell, 1987); and Karl-Ludwig Ay, "Geography and Mentality: Some Aspects of Max Weber's Protestantism Thesis," *Numen* 41 (1994), 163–94; Frank Parkin, *Max Weber* (London: Horwood, 1982), 57–70; Gabriel Kolko, "Max Weber on America: Theory and Evidence," *History & Theory* 1 (1960), 243–60; two comprehensive studies in support of Weber are Gordon Marshall, *Presbyteries and Profits: Calvinism and the Development of Capitalism in Scotland, 1506–1707* (Oxford: Clarendon Press, 1980); and Stephen Innes, *Creating the Commonwealth: The Economic Culture of Puritan New England* (New York: Norton, 1995).
13. *MWAB*, 335.
14. *PE*, 91.

15. Michael Walzer, *The Revolution of the Saints: A Study of the Origins of Radical Politics* (Cambridge: Harvard University Press, 1965).

16. Malcolm H. Mackinnon, "The Longevity of the Thesis: A Critique of the Critics," in *WPE*, 236–37.

17. James H. Henretta, "The Protestant Ethic and the Reality of Capitalism in Colonial America," in *WPE*, 343.

18. Edmund Leites, *The Puritan Conscience and Modern Sexuality* (New Haven: Yale University Press, 1986).

19. Perry Miller, *Jonathan Edwards* (New York: Meridian, 1959), 80, 137.

20. John Simmons, *The Lockean Theory of Rights* (Princeton, N.J.: Princeton University Press, 1992), 95–120.

21. Perry Miller, *The New England Mind: From Colony to Province* (Boston: Beacon, 1961), 27–52.

22. Max Weber, *The Religion of China: Confucianism and Taoism,* trans. H. H. Gerth and Don Martindale (New York: Free Press, 1951), 228–29.

23. *MWAB*, 527–28.

24. Weber, *China*, 252.

25. Ibid., 235–36.

26. Max Weber, *The Religion of India: Hinduism and Buddhism*, trans. H. H. Gerth and Don Martindale (New York: Free Press, 1958); Max Weber, *Ancient Judaism,* trans. H. H. Gerth and Don Martindale (New York: Free Press, 1958).

27. *PE*, 283.

28. *MWAB*, 527; the words are a paraphrase by Marianne.

29. *PE*, 181–82. See also Max Weber, "Religious Rejections of the World and Their Direction," in *FMW*, 323–59.

30. Interpretation of Weber's concept of rationalization as a form of alienation was first developed by Karl Löwith in an early study that has recently been published in English with an excellent preface by Bryan S. Turner: Karl Löwith, *Max Weber and Karl Marx*, trans. Tom Bottomore and William Outwaite (New York: Routledge, 1993); other valuable analyses of Weber on rationalization may be found in Martin Albrow, *Max Weber's Construction of Social Theory* (London: Macmillan, 1990); Roger Brubaker, *The Limits of Rationality: An Essay on the Social and Moral Thought of Max Weber* (London: Macmillan, 1984); and Lawrence A. Scaff, *Fleeing the Iron Cage: Culture, Politics and Modernity in the Thought of Max Weber* (Berkeley: University of California Press, 1989).

31. *PE*, 172.

32. Ralph Waldo Emerson, "Experience," in *Ralph Waldo Emerson: Selected Prose and Poetry*, ed. Reginald Cook (New York: Rinehart, 1966), 247.

33. Karl Jaspers tried to impress this point upon Hannah Arendt. He compared Weber to Friedrich Nietzsche and Soren Kierkegaard to suggest in what respects the two latter philosophers retained a ground to stand on. Despite their negations and sense of nothingness, Jaspers observed,

Nietzsche still clung to his belief in eternal recurrence and Kierkegaard to a Christian faith made credible by virtue of faith in the absurd. Thus "the fact remains that both of them, despite their own doubting of themselves as a result of their honesty, found their firm ground on it. It was very different with Max Weber. He was truly serious about unlimited honesty. That is what made him the archetypical modern man who opens himself completely to absolute inner chaos, to the battle between warring powers, and who doesn't allow himself any secreting cheating but lives passionately, struggles with himself, and has no goal. He felt that all of science and learning taken together was totally incapable of providing fulfillment in life. He grasped that aspect of the Old Testament that is usually overlooked, namely, that we experience God not only as an ally, as a merciful lawgiver, but also as an evil presence, as a devil. Whoever thinks, as Max Weber did, not just theoretically, but also who lives the human existence may well reach amazing heights but only momentarily; everything is called into question." Karl Jaspers to Hannah Arendt, Apr. 29, 1956, in *Hannah Arendt and Karl Jaspers: Correspondence, 1926–1969* (New York: Harcourt, 1985), 636.

34. Max Weber, "Science as a Vocation," *FMW*, 135.

CHAPTER 5

1. Marianne Weber, "Academic Conviviality," *Minerva* 15 (Summer 1977), 214–16; Paul Honigsheim, "Der Max-Weber-Kreis in Heidelberg," *Kölner Vierteljahrshefte für Soziologie* 5 (1924), 270.
2. The physical, temperamental description of Weber is in J. Frommer and S. Frommer, "Max Webers Krankheit: soziologische Aspetke der depressiven Struktur," *Fortschritte der Neurologie-Psychiatrie* 61 (1993), 166; Schumpeter is quoted in Alan Sica, *Weber, Irrationality, and Social Order* (Berkeley: University of California Press, 1988), 118.
3. For the Heidelberg circle some relevant essays may be found in *Max Weber and His Contemporaries*, ed. Wolfgang J. Mommsen and Jürgen Osterhammel (London: Unwin Hyman, 1987).
4. Marianne Weber, "Academic Conviviality," 214–46.
5. Eva Karadi, "Ernst Block and Georg Lukács in Max Weber's Heidelberg," in *Weber and His Contemporaries*, 499–514.
6. Weber quoted in ibid., 500–10.
7. Block quoted in ibid., 503.
8. Max Weber to Georg Lukács [March ?], 1920, in *Georg Lukács: Selected Correspondence, 1902–1920*, ed. Judith Marcus and Zoltan Tar (New York: Columbia University Press, 1986), 281.
9. On Lukács's later criticisms of Weber, see his *Die Zerstorung der Vernuft*, vol. 3, *Irrationalismus und Soziologie* (Darmstadt: Luchterland, 1974), 54–69; and *Die Eigenart des Asthetischen*, vol. 2 (Berlin and Weimar,

1981), 758–59. Despite their ultimate political differences, Lukács had great respect for Weber, as indicated in the letter he wrote to Marianne upon the death of her husband:

> The thought terrifies me that the distance . . . erected between us in the last years cannot be removed anymore. I've always found the fact of separation, the spatial as well as the divergence of views stupid, senseless, and a mere empirical necessity. I knew that I could remove all that separates us with a few words, talking man to man . . . and now one can never speak those words anymore. It has always been among the few hopeful thoughts which nurtured my human existence that the day would come when I'll down and talk to Max Weber. The number of people whose judgment about the human condition in which we live—whether we do the right thing or not—is so small, that one almost gives up this *Gemeinschaft* and freezes into solitude. (Georg Lukács to Marianne Weber, n.d., *Lukács: Correspondence*, 283.)

10. Georg Lukács, *Notizheft*, no. 6, s. 33; *LA*.
11. Quoted in Guy Oakes's "Introduction," Max Weber, *Critique of Stammler*, trans. Guy Oakes (New York: Free Press, 1977), 11.
12. Rudolph A. Makkreel, *Dilthey: Philosopher of the Human Studies* (Princeton, N.J.: Princeton University Press, 1992), 134.
13. Guy Oakes, "Weber and the Southwest German School: The Genesis of the Concept of the Historical Individual," in *Weber and His Contemporaries*, 434–46.
14. *MWAB*, 204–6; Jaspers on Rickert is quoted in Guy Oakes's excellent study, *Weber and Rickert: Concept Formation in the Cultural Sciences* (Cambridge: MIT Press, 1988), 9–10.
15. Rickert quoted in Gerhard Masur, *Prophets of Yesterday: Studies in European Culture, 1890–1914* (New York: Harper, 1966), 173.
16. Guy Oakes, *Weber and Rickert*, 26–40; see also Guy Oakes, "Rickerts Wert/Wertung-Dichotomie und die Grenzen von Webers Wertbeziehungslehre," in *MWS*, 146–66.
17. Max Weber to Karl Vossler, May 5, 1908, *MWG* 11/5, 556–63.
18. Weber quoted in Toby E. Huff, *Max Weber and the Methodology of the Social Sciences* (New Brunswick, N.J.: Rutgers University Press, 1984), 43–57.
19. Max Weber, *Critique of Stammler*, ed. Guy Oakes (New York: Free Press, 1977), 109.
20. *E&S*, 24–25.
21. Weber quoted in Martin Albrow, *Max Weber's Construction of Social Theory* (London: Macmillan, 1990), 217.
22. Friedrich Meinecke, *Die Entstehung des Historismus* (Munchen: Oldenbourg, 1965), xxxi.

23. Max Weber, *The Methodology of the Social Sciences*, ed. and trans. Edward A. Shils and Henry A. Finch (New York: Free Press, 1949), 110–11; Leo Strauss, *Natural Right and History* (Chicago: University of Chicago Press, 1953), 35–80.

24. Weber, *Methodology of Social Sciences*, 51.

25. Paul Honigsheim, *On Max Weber* (New York: Free Press, 1968), 81.

26. Max Weber to Marianne Weber, Apr. 21, 1908, *MWG* 11/5, 535.

27. Edith Hanke, *Prophets des unmodern: Leo Tolstoi als Kulturkritiker im der deutschen Diskussian der Jahrhundertwande* (Tübingen: Niemeyer, 1993), 167–208.

28. Max Weber, "Prospects for Democracy in Tsarist Russia," in *WST*, 283.

29. Hanke, *Prophets*, 170–208.

30. Friedrich Nietzsche, "Notes," in *The Portable Nietzsche*, ed. Walter Kaufmann (New York: Viking, 1954), 457.

31. Ibid., 458.

32. Georg Simmel, *Schopenhauer and Nietzsche*, trans. Helmut Loiskandl, Deena Weinstein, and Michael Weinstein (Amherst: University of Massachusetts Press, 1986), 140–41. Weber's copy of Simmel's German edition of the book, in the *WA*, has numerous marginal notes revelatory of Weber's thoughts. Simmel wrote: "Nietzsche overlooks the Christian emphasis on the value of one's soul. Jesus is not concerned with those who will receive or those for whom life is sacrificed, but with the giver and the one who sacrifices his life. The parable of the rich young man who is supposed to give all of his possessions to the poor is not a lesson on how to give alms but a commentary on how giving is a means and support for the liberation and perfection of the soul. These distinctions are subtle and invisible to the practical eye, but they are absolutely decisive for the inner value experience of life." To which Weber responded: *Richtig*! (Right!).

33. Friedrich Nietzsche, *Beyond Good and Evil* (Chicago: Regenry, 1955), 200.

34. Weber, "Politics as a Vocation," 128.

CHAPTER 6

1. Eduard Baumgarten quotes Weber making this statement during World War I; see Baumgarten, "Einleitung," *MWSAP*, xxvi.

2. Max Weber to Mina Tobler, Jan. 3, 1920, *MWG* 1/17, 20.

3. Ernst Toller, *I Was a German: The Autobiography of a Revolutionary*, trans. Edward Crankshaw (New York: Paragon House, 1991), 96–100.

4. The following descriptions of Weber's attractions as a teacher are all quoted in *MWG* 1/17, 33–34, 58.

5. Henry Adams, *The Education of Henry Adams* (New York: Modern Library, 1931), 70–81.

6. Quoted in Wilhelm Hennis, " 'Die volle Nuchterneit des Urteils': Max Weber zwischen Carl Menger und Gustav von Schmoller. Zum hochschulpolitischen Hintergrund des Wertfreiheitpostulats," in *MWW*, 104–45.
7. Ibid., 135.
8. Gordon A. Craig, *The Germans* (New York: Meridian, 1983), 175; for an informative portrait of German university life, see Fritz Ringer, *The Decline of the German Mandarins: The German Academic Community, 1890–1933* (Hanover: University Press of New England, 1991).
9. Weber, "Science as a Vocation," *FMW*, 134.
10. *MWAB*, 499–503.
11. *MWWP*, 610.
12. Weber's views on Zionism, from a letter written in 1913, are quoted in Hans H. Gerth and Don Martindale, "Preface," Max Weber, *Ancient Judaism* (New York: Free Press, 1952), xv.
13. Thorstein Veblen, "The Intellectual Pre-Eminence of Jews in Modern Europe" (1919), in *Essays in Our Changing Order*, ed. Leon Ardzrooni (1934; New York: Augustus Kelley, 1964), 219–31.
14. Weber, *Ancient Judaism*, 417–24.
15. Max Weber to Richard Graf du Moulin-Eckart, May 4, 1907, *MWG* 11/5, 287–96.
16. *MWG* 11/5, 289, *n*.8.
17. *Heidelberger Zeitung*, Jan. 15, 1919.
18. Quoted in Karl-Ludwig Ay, "Max Weber und der Begriff der Rasse," *Aschkenas: Zeitschrift fur Geschichte und Kulture der Juden* 3 (1993), 189–218.
19. Professor F. J. Berber to Weber Archives, Mar. 31, 1963; *München Zeitung*, Jan. 22, 1920; *Deutsche Corpszeitung* (Frankfurt am Main, Mar. 5, 1920), 24–25.
20. *MWAB*, 673.
21. *E&S*, 1090.
22. "The Bernhard Affair" and other Weber writings on education benefit from Edward Shils's valuable editing, compilation, and annotation in "The Power of the State and the Dignity of the Academic Calling in Imperial Germany: The Writings of Max Weber on University Problems," *Minerva* 2 (1973), 571–632.
23. Ibid., 587.
24. Ibid., 576.
25. Jaspers, *On Max Weber*, 23–24.
26. Max Weber to Else Jaffé, Jan. 29, 1917, *MWG* 1/17, 15.
27. *MWWP*, 554–55.
28. Max Weber to Else Jaffé, Jan. 20, 1919, *MWG* 1/17, 17–18.
29. See, for example, Anthony T. Cascardi, *The Subject of Modernity* (New York: Cambridge, 1992); and Lawrence A. Scaff, *Fleeing the Iron Cage:*

Culture, Politics and Modernity in the Thought of Max Weber (Berkeley: University of California Press, 1989).

30. All the following quotes are from "Science as a Vocation," in *FMW*, 129–58.

31. Quoted in *MWG* 1/17, 61.

32. A section of Dewey's *A Common Faith* is reprinted in *Intelligence in the Modern World: John Dewey's Philosophy*, ed. Joseph Ratner (New York: Random House, 1939), 1016.

CHAPTER 7

1. Henry Adams, *The Education of Henry Adams* (New York: Modern Library, 1931), 353.

2. See Guenther Roth, "Max Weber's Generational Rebellion and Maturation," *Sociological Quarterly* 12 (1971), 441–61.

3. *MWAB*, 93.

4. Max Weber to Emmy Baumgarten, Easter Sunday, 1887, *MWWP* 46–50.

5. *MWAB*, 182.

6. Ibid., 177–79.

7. Max Weber to Marianne Weber, Apr. 21, 1908, *MWG* 11/5, 535.

8. Quoted in Joseph Epstein, *Divorced in America: Marriage in an Age of Possibility* (New York: Dutton, 1974), 41.

9. *MWAB*, 188.

10. Quoted in J. Frommer and S. Frommer, "Max Webers Krankheit: Soziologische Aspekte der depression Struktur," *Fortschritte der Neurologie Psychiatrie* 61 (1993), 165.

11. Tilman Allert, "Max und Marianne Weber: Det Gefährtenehe," in Hubert Treibes, *Heidelberg im Schnittpunkt Intellektueller Kreises: Zur Topographic der Geistigen Gesselligkeit eines Weltdorfes*, ed. Karol Sauerland and Humbert Treibes (Oplanden: Westdeutschen, 1995), 210–41.

12. *Karl Jaspers on Max Weber*, ed. John Dreijmanis (New York: Paragon, 1989), xx.

13. In the English-speaking world the affair was first brought to light in Martin Green's *The von Richthofen Sisters: The Triumphant and the Tragic Modes of Love* (New York: Basic Books, 1974).

14. Max Weber to Else Jaffé, Sept. 13, 1907, *MWG* 11/5, 393–403; see also Horst Jürgen Helle, "Max Weber über Otto Gross: Ein Brief an Else Jaffé von September 1907," *Zeitschrift für Politik* 41 (1994), 214–23.

15. Arthur Mitzman, *The Iron Cage: An Historical Interpretation of Max Weber* (New York: Grosset, 1969), 285.

16. Max Weber to Marianne Weber, Mar. 8, 1908; Marianne Weber to Max Weber, Mar. 10, 1908; Max Weber to Marianne Weber, Mar. 19, 1908, *MWG* 11/5, 443–45, 450–51, 461–64.

17. These letters have yet to appear in print but are mentioned and quoted from in the valuable "Einlestung" to *Max Weber: Wissenschaft als Beruf, 1917/1919; Politik als Beruf, 1919*, ed. Wolfgang J. Mommsen and Wolfgang Schleuchter (Tübingen: J. C. B. Mohr [Paul Siebeck], 1992), 17–18.

18. Max Weber to Marianne Weber, Mar. 13, 1908, *MWG* 11/5, 450–51.

19. *MWAB*, 388.

20. The Ascona letters from Max to Marianne are quoted in Sam Whimster, "Max Weber and Magic Mountain: Weber's Views of the Counter-Culture on the Eve of World War I" (pp. 7–8), paper deposited in the *WA*.

21. Ibid., 12.

22. Ibid., 12–13.

23. Ibid., 13–14.

24. For Weber's responses to Tolstoy's thoughts I am indebted to Edith Hanke's *Prophets des unmodern: Leo Tolstoi als Kulturcritiker im der deutschen Diskussian der Jahrhundertwande* (Tübingen: Niemeyer, 1993).

25. *E&S*, 601; *MWAB*, 486–91.

26. *FMW*, 44–45.

27. Ibid., 346.

28. Ibid., 347–48.

29. Ibid., 348.

30. Ibid, 347–48.

31. Roslyn W. Bologh, *Love or Greatness: Max Weber and Masculine Thinking—A Feminist Inquiry* (London: Unwin Hyman, 1990).

32. *FMW*, 349–50.

33. Georges Bataille, *Eroticism: Death and Sensuality* (1959; San Francisco: City Lights, 1986), 38–39.

34. Max Weber to Georg Lukács, Mar. 10, 1913, in *Georg Lukács: Selected Correspondence, 1910–1920*, ed. Judith Marcus and Zoltan Tar (New York: Columbia University Press, 1986), 222.

35. Max Weber to Marianne Weber, Mar. 29, 1908, *MWG* 11/5, 488.

36. *MWWP*, 39–40.

37. Max Weber to Marie Baum, Jan. 27, 1907, *MWG* 11/5, 225–28.

38. *MWAB*, 205.

39. Max Weber to Heinrich Rickert, Apr. 19, 1908, *MWG* 11/5, 529–31.

40. Marianne Weber, *Leben-Erinnerungen* (Bremen: Jobs Storm, 1948), 56.

41. An excellent discussion of Marianne's career is Guenther Roth's new introduction to her biography, "Marianne and Her Circle," *MWAB*, xv–xli.

42. Daniel Bell, *The Cultural Contradictions of Capitalism* (New York: Basic Books, 1976).

43. *MWAB*, 429–46.

44. Guenther Roth, "Durkheim and the Principles of 1789: The Issue of

Gender Equality," and Klaus Lichtblau, "Gender Theory in Simmel, Tonnies, and Weber," *Telos* 82 (Winter 1989–90), 91–110.

45. *E&S*, 372–73.
46. Ibid., 933.
47. Ibid., 936.
48. Frank Parkin, *Max Weber* (New York: Routledge, 1982), 100.
49. Robert J. Holton and Bryan S. Turner, *Max Weber on Economy and Society* (New York: Routledge, 1989), 148.

CHAPTER 8

1. Walter Lippmann, *U.S. Foreign Policy: Shield of the Republic* (Boston: Little, Brown, 1943), ix.
2. *MWAB*, 517–18.
3. Ibid., 519; on the reaction of some eminent scholars to the outbreak of the war, see Fritz Stern, "Historians and the Great War," *Yale Review* 82 (1994), 34–54.
4. *MWAB*, 521–22.
5. Ibid, 519–21.
6. Ibid.; for Weber's reflections on the discipline question, see "Erfahrungsberichte über Lazarettverwaltung" (Report on the experience of military hospital administration), in *ZPW*, 1–16.
7. *MWAB*, 522–23.
8. Ibid., 528.
9. Ibid., 529–30.
10. Ibid., 532–33.
11. Roger Chickering, "Dietrich Schafer and Max Weber," in *Max Weber and His Contemporaries*, 334–44.
12. Quoted in Mommsen, *Max Weber and German Politics*, 196.
13. Ibid., 203.
14. Ibid.
15. Max Weber, "Zwischen zwei Gesetzen," in *ZPW*, 39–41.
16. *WPW*, 78–79.
17. The "ass" reference is quoted in *MWWP*, 495; Max Weber, "Der Verscharfte U-Bootkrieg," *GPS*, 146.
18. The report from the *Heidelberger Neuesten Nachrichten* (Mar. 25, 1918) is in *ZPW*, 354–55; the address was also reported in the *Heidelberger Tageblatt* (Mar. 25, 1918) and the *Heidelberger Zeitung* (Mar. 26, 1918).
19. Randolph Bourne, "The Disillusionment," in *The Radical Will: Randolph Bourne, Selected Writings*, ed. Olaf Hansen (New York: Urizen, 1977), 402.
20. Thorstein Veblen, *Imperial Germany and the Industrial Revolution* (1915; Ann Arbor: University of Michigan Press, 1968).
21. John Dewey, *German Philosophy and Politics* (New York: Henry Holt, 1915).

22. George Santayana, *Egotism in German Philosophy* (New York: Scribner's, 1915).
23. Weber, "Ethical Neutrality," in *Methodology*, 1–47.
24. Ibid., 5.

CHAPTER 9

1. *MWAB*, 575; Troeltsch is quoted in Friedrich Wilhelm Graf, "Friendship Between Two Experts: Notes on Weber and Troeltsch," *Max Weber and His Contemporaries*, ed. Wolfgang J. Mommsen and Jürgen Osterhammel (London: Unwin Hyman, 1987), 219.
2. *MWAB*, 572.
3. Ibid., 569.
4. Ibid., 569–70.
5. Ibid., 603.
6. Max Weber, *Ancient Judaism*, trans. H. H. Gerth and Don Martindale (New York: Free Press, 1958), 314–17.
7. Ibid., 112.
8. Max Weber to Friedrich Gruhle, Dec. 2, 1917, quoted in "Einleitung," *Max Weber: Zur Neuordung Deutschlands: Schriften und Reden, 1918–1920*, ed. Wolfgang J. Mommsen and Wolfgang Schwentker (Tübingen: J. C. B. Mohr [Paul Siebeck], 1988), 1.
9. Ernst Toller, *I Was a German: The Autobiography of a Revolutionary*, trans. Edward Crankshaw (New York: Paragon House, 1991), 98.
10. *MWAB*, 598.
11. Dittmar Dahlmann, "Max Weber's Relation to Anarchism and Anarchists: The Case of Ernst Toller," *Max Weber and His Contemporaries*, 374.
12. Toller, *I Was a German*, 238.
13. *MWAB*, 619.
14. "Einleitung," *MWG* 1/17, 1.
15. Ibid., 2.
16. G. F. W. Hegel, *The Philosophy of Right*, trans. T. M. Knox (Oxford: Oxford University Press, 1942), 178.
17. Max Weber, "Parliament and Government in Germany," *WPW*, 161.
18. Ibid., 130–77.
19. Ibid., 220–29.
20. Max Weber, "Uns Stadt und Umgebung," *Heidelberger Zeitung*, Jan. 12, 1919; David Beetham, *Max Weber and the Theory of Modern Politics* (Cambridge, England: Polity Press, 1987), 205.
21. Beetham, *Max Weber*, 205–6; Kasler, *Max Weber*, 90–91; Mommsen, *Max Weber*, 323; see also Colin Loader and Jeffrey C. Alexander, "Max Weber on Churches and Sects in North America: An Alternative Path Toward Rationalization," *Sociological Theory* 3 (1985), 1–13.

22. Max Weber, "Deutschlands Kunftige Staatsform," 120–21, 468–69; *WPW,* 230.

23. Weber, "Parliament and Government," 209–12.

24. Weber quoted in Beetham, *Max Weber,* 114.

25. Weber quoted in ibid., 235.

26. Mommsen, *Max Weber,* 185.

27. Weber, "Politics as a Vocation," *FMW,* 127.

28. Weber, "Parliament and Government," 178–79.

29. Ibid., 177–78.

30. Ibid., 180–83.

31. Walter Lippmann, "Introduction," Woodrow Wilson, *Congressional Government* (1885; New York: Meridian, 1956), 7–17.

32. Woodrow Wilson, "Up From the Soil," in *The New Freedom: A Call for the Emancipation of the Generous Energies of a People,* ed. William E. Leuchtenburg (Englewood Cliffs, N.J.: Prentice Hall, 1961), 59–64.

33. Max Weber, "Waffenstillstand und Frieden," *GPS,* 447; originally in the *Frankfurter Zeitung,* Oct. 27, 1918.

34. Quoted in Jan Willem Schulte Nordholt, *Woodrow Wilson: A Life for World Peace,* trans. Herbert Rowen (Berkeley: University of California Press, 1991), 262.

35. Quoted in Mommsen, *Max Weber,* 201.

36. Max Weber, "The National State and Economic Policy," in *Reading Weber,* ed. Keith Tribe (New York: Routledge, 1989), 188–209.

37. Wilson quoted in Robert W. Tucker, "The Triumph of Wilsonianism?" *World Policy Journal* 10 (Winter 1993–94), 85; Weber in Guy Oakes's "Introductory Essay," *Max Weber, Critique of Stammler* (New York: Free Press, 1977), 14–15.

38. Weber, "Politics as a Vocation," 78.

39. Weber, "Deutschlands Aussere und Preussens Innere Politik," *GPS,* 182.

40. "Die Politische Lage Ende 1918" (the lecture notes of Ernst Frankle on Weber), *ZPW,* 356–58.

41. Weber, "Waffenstillstand und Frieden," 447.

42. Weber, "Deutschlands Politische Neuordnung," *MWG,* 1/15, 364.

43. Weber, "Das Neue Deutschland," *MWG* 1/15, 394–95.

44. Max Weber, "Zum Thema der 'Kriegsschuld,'" *GPS,* 493.

45. Max Weber, "Das neue Deutschland," 390–94.

46. Weber quoted in Mommsen, *Max Weber,* 259; on the "shadow of 'Obrigkeitsstaat'" hanging over Weber's thoughts toward the conclusion of the war, see Beetham, *Max Weber,* 170–77.

47. Weber, "'Kriegsschuld,'" 488–97.

48. *MWAB,* 603.

49. Weber, "'Kriegsschuld,'" 495.

50. Ibid., 495–97.

51. *MWAB,* 647–58.

CHAPTER 10

1. Max Weber, "Die Staatsform Deutschlands," *Frankfurter Zeitung*, Nov. 22, 1918.

2. Wilson is quoted in Jan Willem Schulte Nordholt, *Woodrow Wilson: A Life for World Peace*, trans. Herbert Rowen (Berkeley: Univesity of California Press, 1991), 188.

3. Weber is quoted in Eduard Baumgarten, "Einleitung," *MWSAP*, xxv.

4. Friedrich Nietzsche, "Thus Spoke Zarathustra," *The Portable Nietzsche*, ed. Walter Kaufmann (New York: Viking, 1954), 315–16.

5. Quoted in Gary Ulman, *Politischer Mehrwert: Ein Studie über Max Weber und Carl Schmitt* (Wenheim: Acta Humaniora, 1991), 368.

6. Weber, "Politics as a Vocation," 82.

7. Arno J. Mayer, *Wilson versus Lenin: Political Origins of the New Diplomacy, 1917–1918* (New Haven: Yale University Press, 1959); Christopher Lasch, *The American Liberals and the Russian Revolution* (New York: Columbia University Press, 1962).

8. Wolfgang J. Mommsen and Jürgen Osterhammel, eds., *Max Weber and His Contemporaries* (London: Unwin Hyman, 1987), 322–23.

9. Weber, "Socialism," *WPW*, 299–300.

10. *MWAB*, 628.

11. Ernst Toller, *I Was a German: The Autobiography of a Revolutionary*, trans. Edward Crankshaw (New York: Paragon House, 1991), 137–201.

12. *MWAB*, 630–43; Weber on Leibknecht quoted in Mommsen, *Max Weber*, 305.

13. *MWAB*, 673.

14. Quoted in *MWAB*, 628–29.

15. Max Weber to Georg Lukács, *Lukács: Selected Correspondence*, 281.

16. Weber, "Socialism," *WPW*, 272–303.

17. This distinction would have escaped me; I am grateful to translator Ronald Speirs for pointing it out in his footnotes to "Socialism" in *WPW*, 275; unless otherwise indicated, all quotations that follow are from this text.

18. *E&S*, 1129.

19. Karl Marx, *Capital: A Critical Analysis of Capitalist Production*, trans. Samuel Moore and Edward Aveling, vol. 1 (Moscow, n.d.), 21.

20. Andrew Arato, "Lukács' Theory of Reification," *Telos* 11 (1972), 25–66; Ulman, *Politischer Mehrwert*, 7–8.

21. Georg Lukács, *History and Class Consciousness: Studies in Marxist Dialectics* (1922; Cambridge: MIT Press, 1971), 3, 10–24, 80, 94–95, 110–97.

22. Salomon is quoted in Ilse Dronberger, *The Political Thought of Max Weber: In Quest of Statesmanship* (New York: Appleton-Century, 1971), 19.

23. Karl Marx, "Toward the Critique of Hegel's Philosophy of Law," in

Writings of the Young Marx on Philosophy and Society, ed. Lloyd D. Easton and Kurt H. Guddat (Garden City, N.Y.: Anchor, 1967), 263–64.

24. Weber on defending workers is quoted in David Beetham, *Max Weber and the Theory of Modern Politics* (Cambridge, England: Polity Press, 1987), 209.

25. Where Lenin and Lukács assumed that the proletariat required the leadership of a tightly organized party vanguard, Weber presages the ideals of "participatory democracy" when he describes what workers need as a force of culture as well as labor. In Leipzig in 1912, in an attempt to convince Social Democrats that bourgeois reformers were just as committed to the cause of labor, Weber proclaimed:

> There is no doubt a basic presumption for us in the area of the workers' question: We reject, partly in principle and partly as inadequate, the point of view of master rule or patriarchalism, the bonds of welfare institutions and those who would treat the worker as an object for bureaucratic regulation, and insurance legislation that merely creates dependency. We affirm the equal participation of the workers in the collective determination of working conditions, and to this end we also affirm strengthening of their organizations, which spearhead this effort; we see the comradeliness and class dignity that develops in this way as a positive cultural value—whether or not solidarity expresses itself merely in pressure by the organization on the individual, which is somewhat the case within every social grouping based on honor and comradeship. We look upon the growing fruitlessness of orderly strikes as an evil caused by the increasing superiority of employers' organizations, legal and police chicanery, and the systematic creation of subsidized employer protection troops among the workers. We resist, without compromise, the conditions of capital hegemony, with government cooperation, according to the Pittsburgh pattern, in the Saar region and the heavy industry in Westphalia and Silesia, because we want to live in a land of citizens, not of subjects. (Weber's speech quoted in Mommsen, *Max Weber*, 120.)

26. Weber, *PE*, 261.

27. Weber quoted in Beetham, *Max Weber*, 83.

28. Martin Malia, *The Soviet Tragedy: A History of Socialism in Russia, 1917–1994* (New York: Free Press, 1994), 6.

29. In the German edition of *E&S* the term Weber used was "Natural Right"; see *W&G*, 496–513; unless otherwise indicated, all quotes from *E&S*, 865–80.

30. Karl Löwith, *Max Weber and Karl Marx*, ed. Tom Borromore and William Outwaith; Preface by Bryan S. Turner (1932; London: Routledge, 1993).

31. Karl Marx, "Economic and Philosophic Manuscripts," in *Writings of Marx*, 296.

32. Hannah Arendt, *The Human Condition* (Garden City, N.Y.: Anchor, 1957), 71–153; Thorstein Veblen, "The Socialist Economics of Karl Marx and His Followers," in *The Place of Science in Modern Civilization and Other Essays* (New York: Huebsch, 1919), 387–456.

33. *PE*, 182.

34. Quoted in Adriano Tilgher, *Homo Faber: Work Through the Ages*, trans. Dorothy Canfield Fisher (1930; Chicago: Gateway, 1963), 115–16.

35. Ibid., 152–55.

36. Marx, "Economic and Philosophic Manuscripts," 301.

37. Weber, "Zur Lage der burgerlichen Democratie in Rusland," *Archiv* 27 (1906), 334.

CHAPTER 11

1. Allan Bloom, *The Closing of the American Mind* (New York: Simon and Schuster, 1987).

2. Andre Klucksman, *The Master Thinkers* (New York: Harper, 1980).

3. William Butler Yeats, "The Second Coming," in *Yeats: Selected Poetry* (London: Macmillan, 1963), 99–100.

4. Schwab is discussed in Schluchter, "Einleitung," *MWG* 1/17, 51–55.

5. The description is Baumgarten's, quoted in ibid., 122.

6. Frithjof Noack to Marianne Weber, Oct. 26, 1924, *MWG* 1/17, 122.

7. Max Weber to Else Jaffé, Jan. 19, 1919, *MWG* 1/17, 121.

8. Max Rehm's memoir of Weber, quoted in *MWG* 1/17, 122–23.

9. Ricarda Huch to Marie Baum, Oct. 2, 1928, *MWG* 1/17, 123.

10. Ezra Pound, "Hugh Selwyn Mauberly" (1920), in *Diptych: Rome-London* (New York: New Directions, 1994), 37–42; Dos Passos, quoted in John P. Diggins, *The Rise and Fall of the American Left* (New York: Norton, 1992), 111.

11. Washington quoted in H. L. Mencken, *Prejudices: A Selection* (New York: Vintage, 1958), 178.

12. *Federalist*, no. 33; unless indicated otherwise, all of Weber's quotes that follow are from "Politics as a Vocation," which Peter Lassmann and Ronald Spears have retitled "The Profession and Vocation of Politics," *WPW*, 309–69.

13. Alexis de Tocqueville, *Democracy in America*, trans. George Lawrence; ed. J. P. Mayer (New York: Anchor, 1969), 525–41.

14. John Dewey, "Force, Violence and Law," in *Intelligence in the Modern World: John Dewey's Philosophy*, ed. Joseph Ratner (New York: Modern Library, 1939), 486–98.

15. Quoted in "Einleitung," *MWG* 1/17, 41.

16. *MWAB*, 669.

17. Ibid., 664.

18. Ibid., 678.

19. Max Weber to Marianne Weber, May 19, 1919, quoted in Wolfgang J. Mommsen, "Einleitung," *Max Weber Zur Neuordnung Deutschlands: Schriften und Reden, 1919–1920* (Tübingen: J. C. B. Mohr [Paul Siebeck]), 32.
20. *MWAB*, 674.
21. Ibid., 674–75; Marianne Weber, "Untergang oder Angang?" *Die Frau*, 9 (June 1920), 263–67.
22. *MWAB*, 686–88.
23. David J. Chalcraft, "Weber, Wagner and Thoughts of Death," *Sociology* 27 (Aug. 1993), 433–49.
24. Quoted in ibid., 447.
25. *MWAB*, 698.

EPILOGUE

1. Albert Salomon, "Max Weber's Methodology," *Social Research* 1 (May 1934), 147–68; "Max Weber's Sociology," ibid., 2 (Feb. 1935), 60–73; "Max Weber's Political Ideas," ibid., 2 (Aug. 1935), 368–84.
2. Sidney Hook, "The Protestant Ethic and the Spirit of Capitalism," *Nation* 131 (Oct. 29, 1930), 476–77.
3. Jurij N. Darydov and Piama P. Gaidenko, *Rußland und der Westen: Heidelberger Max Weber* (Frankfurt am Main: Suhrkamp, 1995).
4. Meyer Schapiro, "A Note on Max Weber's Politics," *Politics* (Feb. 1945), 44–48; Hans Gerth, "Max Weber's Politics—a Rejoinder" (April 1945), 119–20.
5. George Schwab, *The Challenge of the Exception: An Introduction to the Political Ideas of Carl Schmitt Between 1921 and 1936* (Berlin, 1970); Georg Lukács, *Die Zerstörung der Vernunft*, vol. 2, *Irrationalismus und Imperialismus* (Darmstadt: Luchterhand, 1974), 39–109.
6. Mommsen is quoted in Ilse Dronberger, *The Political Thought of Max Weber: In Quest of Statesmanship* (New York: Appleton-Century, 1971), 321–22; for Weber's legacy in Germany I am indebted to Mommsen's "Max Weber in Modern Social Thought," in *The Political and Social Theory of Max Weber* (Chicago: University of Chicago Press, 1989), 169–96.
7. Weber, "On . . . Russia," *WPW*, 69.
8. Raymond Aron, "Max Weber and Power Politics," in *Max Weber and Sociology Today*, ed. Otto Stammer (New York: Harper, 1971), 83–100, 131–32.
9. Herbert Marcuse, "Industrialization and Capitalism," ibid., 133–51.
10. Sam Whimster and Scott Lash, "Introduction," *Max Weber, Rationality and Modernity*, ed. Scott Lash and Sam Whimster (London: Allen & Unwin, 1987), 1.
11. Weber quoted in Wolfgang J. Mommsen, "Toward a Reconstruction of

Max Weber's Concept of History," in *Weber, Rationality and Modernity*, 35–36; and in Scaff, *Escaping the Iron Cage*, 82.

12. *Karl Jaspers on Max Weber*, 103, 131.

13. Eric Voegelin, *The New Science of Politics* (Chicago: University of Chicago Press, 1952), 14.

14. Ralph Waldo Emerson, "Wealth," *The Complete Works of Ralph Waldo Emerson* (New York: Centenary Edition, AMS Press, 1979), xi, 91–95; on Goethe and the Transcendentalists, see Van Wyck Brooks, *The Flowering of New England* (New York: Dutton, 1936).

15. Weber, "Social Psychology of World Religions," *FMW*, 280.

16. Ralph Waldo Emerson, "Self-Reliance," in *Ralph Waldo Emerson: Selected Prose and Poetry*, ed. Reginald. L. Cook (New York: Rinehart, 1950), 84; Garrison quoted in David J. Greenstone, *The Lincoln Persuasion: Remaking American Liberalism* (Princeton, N.J.: Princeton University Press), 246.

17. Herman Melville, "Conflict of Convictions," in *Herman Melville*, ed. R. W. B. Lewis (New York: Dell, 1962), 316–18.

18. Abraham Lincoln, "Lyceum Address," in *Abraham Lincoln: Selected Speeches, Messages, and Letters*, ed. T. Harry Williams (New York: Holt Rinehart, 1964), 5–14.

19. It may be an exaggeration to suggest that Lincoln learned from the Bible what Weber learned from Nietzsche: original sin itself, humanity's first act of disobedience, actually made freedom possible by introducing conflict, the essence of drama. The Christian and Nietzschean ideas of tragedy are, of course, almost incompatible. The former looks, as did Lincoln, to humility and magnanimity as an answer to the sin of pride; the latter leads, as with Weber, to strength and defiance as an answer to the doctrine of guilt. Still, Weber could agree with Lincoln that evil is inextricably involved in even the most just uses of power and that the political leader must endure necessity and expect irony. Aside from a similar sensitivity to tragedy, Lincoln and Weber have some dissimilar outlooks. In looking back to the Declaration, Lincoln believed values could be derived historically; Weber believed they could only be chosen creatively. Lincoln asserted that right and wrong must be distinguishable, only to absolve Southerners of the sin of slavery on the grounds that they had inherited the institution; Weber saw right and wrong as culturally contingent, only to criticize Otto von Bismarck for not living up to standards that Bismarck himself would not accept: he complained that the chancellor conditioned the German people to see things his way. Lincoln had more faith in democracy, convinced that all the people could not be fooled all the time; Weber worried more about political leaders fooling themselves with their pomp and pretense. Although both thinkers had a Christian and classical grasp of the perils of pride and hubris, one hardly finds in Weber Lincoln's sentiments of

pity, magnanimity, compassion, and forgiveness. Yet if Lincoln's thoughts were not consonant with the harsher *Realpolitik* of Weber's outlook, it should be remembered that during the Civil War Lincoln was forced to use the very extra-constitutional powers that Weber would prescribe for the presidency of the new Weimar Republic. In this instance America became one of the first modern republics to combine both democratic principles and decisionist possibilities, with Lincoln the sovereign who makes unilateral decisions in emergency situations. Even the democratic statesman, Weber realized, is fated to use power undemocratically.

20. " . . . das Verhängnis ein stahlhartes Gehäuse werden." Weber, "Askutischer Protestantismus und Kapitalistischer Geist," in *MWSAP*, 379.

Index

Academe: anti-Semitism in, 136–41; and bureaucracy, 142, 145–46; dangers of political power for, 217; ethical neutrality in, 197–98; freedom within, 140–44; militancy in, 202–3; nationalism of, 196; nature of inquiry in, 29; professor's role, 132–36

Actions, human: discerning meaning in, 104, 118–20; measuring value of, 129–31; methods of understanding, 114–17; Weber's principles of, 121–23

Acton, Lord, 32

Adams, Henry, 26–28, 77, 154

Addams, Jane, 24

Affectual action, 121

African Americans. *See* Black Americans

Agrarian society: decline of, 29; dependency in, 61; and rise of capitalism, 30–31; as utopia, 246–47; Weber's analysis of, 50–54; and worker migration to cities, 59–60

Alienation: Calvinism as source of, 130; and corruption of politics, 255, 264; in Marxist theory, 113, 237; in rationalized work, 106; and rise of eroticism, 168–69; science as catalyst for, 147–48; source of, 232; surrender to society as, 77; Weber's interpretation, 243. *See also* Rationalization

Allies of World War I. *See* Entente, the

Althoff, Friedrich, 141

319